How People Learn II

Learners, Contexts, and Cultures

Committee on How People Learn II:
The Science and Practice of Learning

Board on Behavioral, Cognitive, and Sensory Sciences

Board on Science Education

Division of Behavioral and Social Sciences and Education

A Consensus Study Report of

The National Academies of
SCIENCES · ENGINEERING · MEDICINE

THE NATIONAL ACADEMIES PRESS
Washington, DC
www.nap.edu

THE NATIONAL ACADEMIES PRESS • 500 Fifth Street, NW • Washington, D.C. 20001

This activity was supported by grants and awards from the Alfred P. Sloan Foundation (Grant No. 2014-3-06), the American Educational Research Association (unnumbered award), the Bill & Melinda Gates Foundation (Grant No. OPP1110470), the Institute of Education Sciences of the U.S. Department of Education (Grant No. R305U150005), the Teagle Foundation (unnumbered award), the William and Flora Hewlett Foundation (Grant No. 2014-1118), with additional support from the National Academy of Sciences' W.K. Kellogg Foundation Fund and the National Academies of Sciences, Engineering, and Medicine Presidents' Circle Fund. Support for the work of the Board on Behavioral, Cognitive, and Sensory Sciences is provided primarily by a grant from the National Science Foundation (Award No. BCS-1729167). Any opinions, findings, conclusions, or recommendations expressed in this publication do not necessarily reflect the views of any organization or agency that provided support for the project.

International Standard Book Number-13:   978-0-309-45964-8
International Standard Book Number-10:   0-309-45964-8
Library of Congress Control Number: 2018957415
Digital Object Identifier: https://doi.org/10.17226/24783

Additional copies of this publication are available for sale from the National Academies Press, 500 Fifth Street, NW, Keck 360, Washington, DC 20001; (800) 624-6242 or (202) 334-3313; http://www.nap.edu.

Suggested citation: National Academies of Sciences, Engineering, and Medicine. (2018). *How People Learn II: Learners, Contexts, and Cultures*. Washington, DC: The National Academies Press. doi: https://doi.org/10.17226/24783.

The National Academies of
SCIENCES · ENGINEERING · MEDICINE

The **National Academy of Sciences** was established in 1863 by an Act of Congress, signed by President Lincoln, as a private, nongovernmental institution to advise the nation on issues related to science and technology. Members are elected by their peers for outstanding contributions to research. Dr. Marcia McNutt is president.

The **National Academy of Engineering** was established in 1964 under the charter of the National Academy of Sciences to bring the practices of engineering to advising the nation. Members are elected by their peers for extraordinary contributions to engineering. Dr. C. D. Mote, Jr., is president.

The **National Academy of Medicine** (formerly the Institute of Medicine) was established in 1970 under the charter of the National Academy of Sciences to advise the nation on medical and health issues. Members are elected by their peers for distinguished contributions to medicine and health. Dr. Victor J. Dzau is president.

The three Academies work together as the **National Academies of Sciences, Engineering, and Medicine** to provide independent, objective analysis and advice to the nation and conduct other activities to solve complex problems and inform public policy decisions. The National Academies also encourage education and research, recognize outstanding contributions to knowledge, and increase public understanding in matters of science, engineering, and medicine.

Learn more about the National Academies of Sciences, Engineering, and Medicine at **www.nationalacademies.org**.

The National Academies of
SCIENCES · ENGINEERING · MEDICINE

COMMITTEE ON HOW PEOPLE LEARN II: THE SCIENCE AND PRACTICE OF LEARNING

Acknowledgments

There are many reasons to be curious about the way people learn, and the past several decades have seen an explosion of research that has substantially expanded understanding of brain processes and what they mean for individual learning, schooling, and policy. In 2000, the report *How People Learn: Brain, Mind, Experience, and School: Expanded Edition* (National Research Council, 2000; hereafter referred to as *HPL I*) was published and its influence has been both wide and deep, but 20 years later the research landscape has evolved still further. *How People Learn II* provides a much-needed update.

This book does not presume to provide answers to specific educational dilemmas—recipes for teaching or the proverbial "what to do on Monday morning." Instead, the committee hopes that the book will be a tool that can enrich discussions about research and practice in education and learning for people of all ages. We have tried to present the existing scientific evidence in the most straightforward, accurate, and complete way that we can, and to synthesize and interpret the findings creatively. However, the practical applications that derive from the science will never be completely straightforward because the real world is highly complicated, with many moving parts and hidden complexities. The committee therefore asks you, the reader, to think critically about the findings we present in relation to your own work, and about how the findings reviewed here square with evidence and policies used to justify educational strategies, policies, and research questions in your professional context. Only through active debates and attempts to contextualize and adapt the findings beyond the narrow settings in which they often were studied will we create significantly new understanding and better policy and practice as they relate to learning.

This report is made possible by the generous sponsorship of the Alfred P. Sloan Foundation, the American Educational Research Association, the Bill & Melinda Gates Foundation, the Institute of Education Sciences of the U.S. Department of Education, the Teagle Foundation, and the William and Flora Hewlett Foundation, with additional support from the National Academy of Sciences' W.K. Kellogg Foundation Fund and the National Academies of Sciences, Engineering, and Medicine Presidents' Circle Fund. We especially acknowledge Ed Dieterle (formerly with the Bill & Melinda Gates Foundation) who provided vision and enthusiasm for making this report a reality. We are grateful for the substantive core support to the Board on Behavioral, Cognitive, and Sensory Sciences received from federal agencies, particularly the National Science Foundation's Social, Behavioral and Economic Sciences Directorate and the National Institute on Aging's Division of Behavioral and Social Research, which ensured necessary oversight on the project. We also appreciate the funds provided by the American Psychological Association.

Over the course of the study, committee members benefited from discussion and presentations by the many individuals who participated in our three fact-finding meetings. At the first committee meeting, Marc Chun (Hewlett Foundation), Felice Levine (American Educational Research Association), and Daniel Goroff (Sloan Foundation) each provided valuable background information on the goals of the study's sponsors. In addition, Marianella Casasola (Cornell University) provided an overview of the research on thought and language in the bilingual infant. Barbara Rogoff (University of California, Santa Cruz) shared reflections on understanding cultural differences that influence how, why, and where people learn; and Guinevere Eden (Georgetown University) provided a review of the most recent neuroimaging research on reading and reading disabilities. Finally, members of the *HPL I* authoring committee provided insights on how best to approach the study process in order to meld ideas from diverse disciplines to maximize the impact of the report for research and practice. The *HPL I* committee members included Barbara Means (SRI International), Jose Mestre (University of Illinois at Urbana–Champaign), Linda Nathan (Boston University), Penelope Peterson (Northwestern University), and Barbara Rogoff. The Webcast audience for this first meeting included individuals from the United States and several other countries: Brazil, Denmark, Germany, Greece, Iceland, the Netherlands, Portugal, Russia, and Taiwan.

At the second meeting, three committee members (Patricia Bauer, David Daniel, and Jeff Karpicke) briefed the committee and audience on the evidence regarding cognitive and developmental factors affecting learning in context. Robert Mislevy (Educational Testing Service) provided insights on how developments in psychology and technology challenge assessment in learning contexts, and Kevin Crowley (University of Pittsburgh) provided an overview of learning in informal settings. Finally, Elizabeth Albro (Institute of Education Sciences) shared the perspectives of the sponsor with the committee. The Webcast audience included individuals from Canada and the United States.

The third committee meeting included discussions from two different panels: (1) Panel on Learning in Adulthood and the Use of Technology for Learning in Adulthood and (2) Panel on Learning Disabilities, Universal Design for Learning, and Assistive Technology. The Learning in Adulthood panelists were Philip Ackerman (Georgia Institute of Technology), Walter Boot (Florida State University), and Ursula Staudinger (Columbia University). The Learning Disabilities and Universal Design for Learning panel included Donald Compton (Florida State University), Jack Fletcher (University of Houston), and David Rose (CAST). The Webcast audience for this meeting included individuals from Brazil, Canada, and the United States.

This Consensus Study Report was reviewed in draft form by individuals chosen for their diverse perspectives and technical expertise. The purpose of this independent review is to provide candid and critical comments that will assist the National Academies of Sciences, Engineering, and Medicine in making each published report as sound as possible and to ensure that it meets the institutional standards for quality, objectivity, evidence, and responsiveness to the study charge. The review comments and draft manuscript remain confidential to protect the integrity of the deliberative process.

We thank the following individuals for their review of this report: Daniel E. Atkins, Electrical Engineering and Computer Science, University of Michigan (emeritus); Philip Bell, Learning Sciences and Human Development, University of Washington; John Dunlosky, Department of Psychological Sciences, Kent State University; Kris Gutiérrez, Educational Policy and Language, Literacy and Culture, University of California, Berkeley; Kenji Hakuta, School of Education, Stanford University; Karen R. Harris, Mary Lou Fulton Teachers College, Arizona State University; David Klahr, Department of Psychology, Carnegie Mellon University; Kenneth R. Koedinger, Pittsburgh Science of Learning Center, Carnegie Mellon University; Gloria Ladson-Billings, Department of Curriculum and Instruction, University of Wisconsin–Madison; Lisa Linnenbrink-Garcia, Department of Counseling, Educational Psychology and Special Education, Michigan State University; Bruce McCandliss, Graduate School of Education, Stanford University; James W. Pellegrino, Learning Sciences Research Institute, College of Education, University of Illinois at Chicago; Diana C. Pullin, Lynch School of Education, Boston College; Barbara Rogoff, Department of Psychology, University of California, Santa Cruz; Lorrie A. Shepard, Laboratory of Educational Research, School of Education, University of Colorado Boulder; and Brian A. Wandell, Department of Psychology, Stanford University.

Although the reviewers listed above provided many constructive comments and suggestions, they were not asked to endorse the conclusions or recommendations of this report nor did they see the final draft before its release.

The review of this report was overseen by Michael I. Posner, Department of Psychology, University of Oregon (emeritus), and Greg J. Duncan, School of Education, University of California, Irvine. They were responsible for making certain that an independent examination of this report was carried out in accordance with the standards of the National Academies and that all review comments were carefully considered. Responsibility for the final content rests entirely with the authoring committee and the National Academies.

Thanks are also due to the project staff and staff of the Division of Behavioral and Social Sciences and Education (DBASSE). In particular, special thanks to Tina Winters, associate program officer, who was instrumental in organizing data-gathering opportunities for the committee, agenda development, facilitation of commissioned paper selection and contracting, and invaluable assistance in the writing and development of the committee's final report. Renée Wilson Gaines, senior program assistant, also provided critical support to the study process by managing the study's logistical and administrative needs, making sure meetings and workshops ran efficiently and smoothly, obtaining copyright permissions, and engaging in other essential report activities. Appreciation is also extended to Barbara Wanchisen, director of the Board on Behavioral, Cognitive, and Sensory Sciences, and Heidi Schweingruber, director of the Board on Science Education, for their leadership, guidance, oversight of, and support for the study. We are also indebted to the National Academies consultant Robert Katt for final editing of the manuscript. We are particularly grateful to Patricia Morison and Alexandra Beatty for their support and significant assistance with improving the flow of the report. We thank the Executive Office staff of DBASSE, especially Kirsten Sampson-Snyder, who managed the review process, Yvonne Wise, who oversaw the final publication process, and Lisa Alston for financial oversight. Finally, we would like to thank the Research Center at the National Academies for their valuable support in conducting literature and data reviews, generating impact summaries, and supporting general research.

Cora Bagley Marrett, *Chair*
Sujeeta Bhatt, *Study Director*
Committee on How People Learn II:
The Science and Practice of Learning

Contents

Tables, Figures, and Boxes

TABLES

FIGURES

BOXES

Summary

Decades of research and the development of new technologies and research methods laid the foundation for a remarkable blossoming of research on the processes and functions of learning in the 1980s and 1990s. In 2000, the National Research Council summarized key findings from this work in *How People Learn: Mind Brain, Experience, and School: Expanded Edition* (*HPL I*). This report brought together the work of two committees that had summarized insights on the nature of learning, such as how experts differ from novices, how learning transfers across settings, and how children and adult learners do and do not differ. It described principles for the design of effective learning environments and offered examples of effective teaching in history, mathematics, and science; an examination of the extent to which opportunities for teacher learning enhance effectiveness in facilitating learning; and a discussion of the promise of technology for supporting learning. *HPL I* was widely used by teacher educators and other postsecondary faculty in courses related to learning, and it has guided the practice of countless educators. This report expands on the foundation laid out in *HPL I*.

Researchers have continued to investigate the nature of learning and have generated new findings related to the neurological processes involved in learning, individual and cultural variability related to learning, and educational technologies. In addition to expanding scientific understanding of the mechanisms of learning and how the brain adapts throughout life, they have continued to make important discoveries about influences on learning, particularly sociocultural factors and the structure of learning environments. At the same time, technological developments have both offered new possibilities for fostering learning and created new learning challenges.

The Committee on How People Learn II: The Science and Practice of Learning, created by the National Academies of Sciences, Engineering, and Medicine, was asked to summarize new insights related to the ground covered in *HPL I* and expand the discussion to include learning that occurs beyond kindergarten through twelfth-grade education and throughout the life span, as well as the constellation of influences that affect individual learning. The committee was charged[1] with:

> reviewing and synthesizing research that has emerged across the various disciplines that focus on the study of learning from birth through adulthood in both formal and informal settings. Consideration will be given to the re-search and research approaches with greatest potential to influence practice and policy. The report should specify directions for strategic investments in research and development to promote the knowledge, training, and technolo-gies that are needed to support learning in today's world.

To address our charge, the committee examined research that expands significantly on what was included in *HPL I*. This required us to explore numerous fields of study and therefore to draw on research that varied in both methodology and standards of evidence. Research on learning spans disciplines, including those centered on physiological processes, psychologi-cal and psychosocial functioning, and broader views of cultural context. We reviewed laboratory-based neuropsychology and cognitive science, as well as work from cultural and social psychology, classroom-based education research, and qualitative studies of adult learning and the workplace.

THE COMPLEX INFLUENCES OF CULTURE

Learners function within complex developmental, cognitive, physical, social, and cultural systems. Research and theory from diverse fields have contributed to an evolving understanding that all learners grow and learn in culturally defined ways in culturally defined contexts. While humans share basic brain structures and processes, as well as fundamental experiences such as relationships with family, age-related stages, and many more, each of these phenomena are shaped by an individual's precise experiences. Learning does not happen in the same way for all people because cultural influences are influential from the beginning of life. These ideas about the intertwining of learning and culture have been reinforced by research on many facets of learning and development.

CONCLUSION 2-1: Each learner develops a unique array of knowledge and cognitive resources in the course of life that

---

[1] The full text of the committee's Statement of Task is included in Chapter 1.

are molded by the interplay of that learner's cultural, social, cognitive, and biological contexts. Understanding the developmental, cultural, contextual, and historical diversity of learners is central to understanding how people learn.

TYPES AND PROCESSES OF LEARNING

Learning is a remarkably dynamic process; from before birth and throughout life, learners adapt to experiences and their environment. Factors that are relevant to learning include influences from the microscopic level (e.g., lead levels in the learner's blood) up to the macro level (e.g., qualities of the learner's neighborhood, society, and culture). Even at the most basic individual level, brain development and cognition (and the connectivity between cortical areas) are influenced and organized by cultural, social, emotional, and physiological experiences that contribute to both age-related and individual variability in learning. Different situations, contexts, and pedagogical strategies promote different types of learning.

An individual's brain develops and is shaped by the set of experiences and influences unique to her—a process that occurs through the pruning of synapses and other neurological developments that take place through adolescence. The brain continues to adapt as the learner ages, through the continuous shaping and reshaping of neural connections in response to stimuli and demands. While the learner gains knowledge and skills as the brain develops throughout childhood and adolescence, the relationship between brain development and learning is not unidirectional: learning and brain development interact in a reciprocal manner. Learning changes the brain throughout the life span; at the same time, the brain develops throughout the life span in ways that influence learning and are in turn influenced by the learner's context and cultural influences.

Learning requires that the individual orchestrate many different cognitive processes including, for example, memory and attention. Memory—the capacity to store and retrieve knowledge and information—is an essential component of learning because it allows individuals to use past experiences to adapt and solve problems in the present. Memory is not a unitary capacity; it is a set of processes by which a learner reconstructs past experiences and forges new connections among them.

CONCLUSION 3-1: The individual learner constantly integrates many types of learning, both deliberately and unconsciously, in response to the challenges and circumstances he encounters. The way a learner integrates learning functions is shaped by his social and physical environment but also shapes his future learning.

CONCLUSION 3-2: The brain develops throughout life, following a trajectory that is broadly consistent for humans but is also individualized by every learner's environment and experiences. It gradually matures to become capable of a vast array of complex cognitive functions and is also malleable in adapting to challenges at a neurological level.

CONCLUSION 3-3: The relationship between brain development and learning is reciprocal: learning occurs through interdependent neural networks, and at the same time learning and development involves the continuous shaping and reshaping of neural connections in response to stimuli and demands. Development of the brain influences behavior and learning, and in turn, learning influences brain development and brain health.

CONCLUSION 4-1: Successful learning requires coordination of multiple cognitive processes that involve different networks in the brain. In order to coordinate these processes, an individual needs to be able to monitor and regulate his own learning. The ability to monitor and regulate learning changes over the life span and can be improved through interventions.

CONCLUSION 4-2: Memory is an important foundation for most types of learning. Memory involves reconstruction rather than retrieval of exact copies of encoded mental representations. The cues available in a learner's environment are critical for what she will be able to recall; they also play a role in the way the learner begins to integrate new information as knowledge.

KNOWLEDGE AND REASONING

Learners identify and establish relationships among pieces of information and develop increasingly complex structures for using and categorizing what they have learned. Accumulating bodies of knowledge and the capacity to reason about them are key cognitive assets throughout the life span. The strategies that have shown promise for promoting learning help learners to develop the mental models they need to retain knowledge so they can use it adaptively and flexibly in making inferences and solving new problems.

CONCLUSION 5-1: Prior knowledge can reduce the attentional demands associated with engaging in well-learned activities, and it can facilitate new learning. However, prior knowledge can also lead to bias by causing people to not attend to new information and to rely on existing schema to solve new problems. These biases can be overcome but only through conscious effort.

CONCLUSION 5-2: Learners routinely generate their own novel understanding of the information they are accumulating and productively extend their knowledge by making logical connections between pieces of information. This capacity to generate novel understanding allows learners to use their knowledge to generalize, categorize, and solve problems.

CONCLUSION 5-3: The learning strategies for which there is evidence of effectiveness include ways to help students retrieve information and encourage them to summarize and explain material they are learning, as well as ways to space and structure the presentation of material. Effective strategies to create organized and distinctive knowledge structures encourage learners to go beyond the explicit material by elaborating and to enrich their mental representation of information by calling up and applying it in various contexts.

CONCLUSION 5-4: The effectiveness of learning strategies is influenced by such contextual factors as the learner's existing skills and prior knowledge, the nature of the material, and the goals for learning. Applying these approaches effectively therefore requires careful thought about how their specific mechanisms could be beneficial for particular learners, settings, and learning objectives.

MOTIVATION TO LEARN

Conscious learning requires sustained effort. To learn intentionally, people must *want* to learn and must see the value in accomplishing what is being asked of them. Numerous factors and circumstances influence an individual's desire to learn and the decision to expend effort on learning. Engagement and intrinsic motivation develop and change over time; they are not properties of the individual or the environment alone, and they are strongly influenced by cultural and developmental processes.

CONCLUSION 6-1: Motivation to learn is influenced by the multiple goals that individuals construct for themselves as a result of their life and school experiences and the sociocultural context in which learning takes place. Motivation to learn is fostered for learners of all ages when they perceive the school or learning environment is a place where they "belong" and when the environment promotes their sense of agency and purpose.

CONCLUSION 6-2: Educators may support learners' motivation by attending to their engagement, persistence, and performance by:

- helping them to set desired learning goals and appropriately challenging goals for performance;
- creating learning experiences that they value;
- supporting their sense of control and autonomy;
- developing their sense of competency by helping them to recognize, monitor, and strategize about their learning progress; and
- creating an emotionally supportive and nonthreatening learning environment where learners feel safe and valued.

IMPLICATIONS FOR LEARNING IN SCHOOL

This report focused on learning that occurs throughout life and beyond formal educational settings, but it has profound implications for school. We highlight four topics related to schooling. First, understanding of the cultural nature of learning and development means that what takes place in every classroom—the learning environment, the influence of educators, and all students' experience of school—cannot be fully understood without attention to cultural influences. Second, there is a growing body of research that examines learning in academic content areas that can provide guidance to educators. Third, a part of what is accomplished when educators attend to the influences of culture on the classroom environment and the perspectives students bring to their learning is that learners are better supported in taking charge of their own learning. Many strategies for fostering specific types and functions of learning are primarily ways of supporting the learner in actively making progress and improvements for himself. Finally, assessing learning is a central part of education in school; effective assessment depends on understanding of how learning occurs.

CONCLUSION 7-1: Effective instruction depends on understanding of the complex interplay among learners' prior knowledge, experiences, motivations, interests, and language and cognitive skills; educators' own experiences and cultural influences; and the cultural, social, cognitive, and emotional characteristics of the learning environment.

CONCLUSION 7-2: A disparate body of research points to the importance of engaging the learner in directing his own learning by, for example, providing targeted feedback and support in developing metacognitive skills, challenges that are well matched to the learner's current capacities, and support in setting and pursuing meaningful goals.

CONCLUSION 7-3: A growing body of research supports adopting an asset model of education in which curricula and instructional techniques support all learners in connecting academic learning goals to the learning they do outside of school settings and through which learning experiences and opportunities from various settings are leveraged for each learner.

CONCLUSION 7-4: Purposefully teaching the language and practices specific to particular disciplines, such as science, history, and mathematics, is critical to helping students develop deep understanding in these subjects.

CONCLUSION 7-5: Assessment is a critical tool for advancing and monitoring students' learning in school. When grounded in well-defined models of learning, assessment information can be used to identify and subsequently narrow the gap between current and desired levels of students' learning and performance.

LEARNING TECHNOLOGY

There is strong empirical support for the effectiveness of learning technologies, but there is no one universally ideal learning technology. The effectiveness of technology depends on the characteristics of the learner, the types of learning being targeted, sociocultural context, and support from instructors in the use of the technologies.

CONCLUSION 8-1: The decision to use a technology for learning should be based on evidence indicating that the technology has a positive impact in learning situations that are similar with respect to:

- the types of learning and goals for learning;
- characteristics of the learners;
- the learning environment;
- features of the social and cultural context likely to affect learning; and
- the level of support in using the technology to be provided to learners and educators.

CONCLUSION 8-2: Effective use of technologies in formal education and training requires careful planning for implementation that addresses factors known to affect learning. These factors include alignment of the technology with learning goals, provision of professional development and other supports for instructors and learners, and equitable access to the technology. Ongoing assessment of student learning and evaluation of implementation are critical to ensuring that a particular use of technology is optimal and to identifying needed improvements.

LEARNING ACROSS THE LIFE SPAN

Individuals learn throughout their lives in every setting. What and how much they learn, particularly outside of compulsory education, is largely directed by their own choices and circumstances. Learners' capacities and resources shift over time. For example, both reasoning and knowledge increase up to early adulthood, when their paths begin to diverge. One's abilities to quickly generate, transform, and manipulate factual information begin to decline, while knowledge levels remain stable or increase. However, the brain adapts throughout life, recruiting and orchestrating its resources to compensate for declines and adapt to circumstances.

CONCLUSION 9-1: People continue to learn and grow throughout the life span, and their choices, motivation, and capacity for self-regulation, as well as their circumstances, influence how much and how well they learn and transfer their learning to new situations.

CONCLUSION 9-2: People learn continually through active engagement across many settings in their environments; learning that occurs outside of compulsory educational environments is a function of the learner's motivation, interests, and opportunities. Engagement with work (especially complex work that involves both intellectual and social demands), social engage-

ment, physical exercise, and adequate sleep are all associated
with lifelong learning and healthy aging.

RESEARCH AGENDA

The research the committee has explored for this report demonstrates
that learning involves lasting adaptations of multiple systems to the changing
external and internal environment. Learning is a dynamic, ongoing process
that is simultaneously biological and cultural. Attention to both individual
factors (such as developmental stage; physical, emotional, and mental health;
and interests and motivations), as well as factors external to the individual
(such as the environment in which the learner is situated, social and cultural
contexts, and opportunities available to learners) is necessary to develop a
complete picture of the nature of learning. We have focused on key ideas that
can be distilled from a diverse body of work to build on the picture of how
people learn as it stood in 2000. That picture has grown more sophisticated,
but there is still much more to learn.

We have identified specific research objectives in two primary areas, which
we hope will guide researchers and funders and spur work that integrates
levels of analysis, methods, and theoretical frameworks across the diverse
disciplines that make contributions to the study of how people learn.

> **Research Area 1:** Meeting the needs of all learners by connecting
> research on internal mechanisms of learning with the shaping forces
> of contextual variation, including culture, social context, instruction,
> and time of life.

Specifically, it is now possible to move beyond the idea of an "average"
learner to embrace and explain variation among individuals. It will be valuable
to have more interdisciplinary research that examines how individual variation and developmental and contextual factors, including social, emotional,
environmental, institutional, and experiential factors, influence the lifelong
learning process and learning outcomes. It would be valuable to have research
that addresses diverse study populations, interest in learning, the role of identity in learning, motivation to learn, self-regulated learning, the influence of
learning environments, learning across the life span, and learning disabilities.

> **Research Area 2:** The implications of the science of learning for the
> design of technology to support learning across the life span; the com-
> plex interactions between characteristics of the learner, the content
> to be learned, and the learning environment; how technology may be
> influencing the nature of what people need to learn and the psychology
> of learners; and potential drawbacks.

Among the topics on which further research is needed are whether a technology is well suited to the ecological learning niche in which it may be used, the effects of engagement in self-selected online activities on academic learning, and ways to improve the suite of learning technologies available.

1

Introduction

People learn every day, in many different settings and in many different ways. Sometimes learning happens intentionally and with great effort, as when a master craftsperson spends years learning a trade. Sometimes it seems to happen almost effortlessly, as when someone realizes he knows how to make his grandmother's tamales without ever being taught. Research conducted over the past few decades has expanded understanding of human cognition and of how individual and group experiences and differences shape how and what people learn. Much has been learned about how people acquire expertise, how individual learners can monitor the influences on their own understanding, and many other aspects of learning.

Nearly two decades ago, the report *How People Learn: Brain, Mind, Experience, and School: Expanded Edition* (National Research Council [2000]; hereafter referred to as *HPL I*) described groundbreaking research from disciplines including neuroscience; cognitive, developmental, and social psychology; anthropology; and education. It offered conclusions about learning that were based on these various lines of research and that would be most relevant to teachers, school officials, parents, and policy makers, as well as a research agenda to guide funders and scholars.

In this report, we offer an update to and expansion of *HPL I* that incorporates insights gained from research conducted over the past decade, considers learning in contexts other than school, and explores how learning changes across the life span. To set the stage, we offer a few observations on what it means to study how people learn.

"How" suggests that learning involves processes that unfold over time. People do not simply collect memories, knowledge, and skills in a linear, in-

cremental fashion—slowly and steadily stashing away bits of information in their heads like a video camera recording images and sounds. Rather, learning involves myriad processes that interact over time to influence the way people make sense of the world.

The processes are the activities and interactions in which individuals engage that help them make sense of their world and their place in it. Play, conversation, reading or being read to, and being alone are all processes. Emotions, goals, social relationships, prior experiences, and cognitive and biological predispositions all influence how individuals interpret situations and hence what they learn. The changing demands, features, and supports of the learning situation further influence people's interpretations and emotions, what they will decide to do, and consequently what they learn.

"People (or persons)" can be characterized in many ways: by age, gender identity, skin color, skills, past experiences, and physical and intellectual resources, for example. People have likes and dislikes; strengths and weaknesses; families, friendships, and identities; experiences and memories; and interests, goals, and dreams. All of these characteristics also influence learning.

"Learn" is an active verb; it is something people do, not something that happens to them. People are not passive recipients of learning, even if they are not always aware that the learning process is happening. Instead, through acting in the world, people encounter situations, problems, and ideas. By engaging with these situations, problems, and ideas, they have social, emotional, cognitive, and physical experiences, and they adapt. These experiences and adaptations shape a person's abilities, skills, and inclinations going forward, thereby influencing and organizing that individual's thoughts and actions into the future.

CHARGE TO THE COMMTTEE

The foundational research that was documented in *HPL I* holds true today, but after nearly two decades an examination of new research was needed. The National Academies of Sciences, Engineering, and Medicine formed a committee to expand on and update *HPL I* with recent research.[1] The new committee's 16 members brought diverse expertise in disciplines and fields related to the science and practice of learning, including cognitive science, learning theory, cognitive neuroscience, educational psychology, developmental psychology, workforce development, and educational technology (see Appendix D). The committee was asked to examine new research on learning and to identify the findings with the greatest potential to influence policy. The committee was directed in its formal charge (see Box 1-1) to examine the cultural nature of learning and the influence of context and to explore what

---

[1] The committee worked from the expanded edition of *HPL I,* published in 2000; see Appendix A.

BOX 1-1   Statement of Task

An ad hoc committee will conduct a study and prepare a report that will update and extend the National Research Council report, *How People Learn* (National Research Council, 2000), by reviewing and synthesizing research that has emerged across the various disciplines that focus on the study of learning from birth through adulthood in both formal and informal settings. Consideration will be given to the research and research approaches with greatest potential to influence practice and policy. The report should specify directions for strategic investments in research and development to promote the knowledge, training, and technologies that are needed to support learning in today's world.

To address its charge, the committee will review research on learning and learning contexts across the life span (specifically, infancy and early childhood, middle childhood, adolescence and young adulthood, middle adulthood and older adulthood). The committee also will consider advances in such rapidly growing fields as cognitive neuroscience and learning technologies, as well as discoveries, innovations, and inventions in education and education research; cognitive science; developmental cognitive neuroscience; cognition, learning, and memory; cognitive aging; the influence of culture on learning; language and linguistics to include supporting students learning English as a second language; social, emotional, and motivational aspects of learning; learning in academic domains; learning disabilities; assessment (e.g., of learning, achievement, and performance in academic, cognitive, social, and affective domains); and research methodology ranging from basic research to implementation and dissemination science.

Attention will be given to methodological advances and designs that permit the integration of knowledge from multiple fields (e.g., network modeling, multilevel modeling, simulation modeling) and that enable study of the complexities of learning across various contexts (e.g., the interplay of micro and macro level learning and how teacher-learner interactions within specific curricula and approaches to pedagogy result in learning in domains over time).

is known about learning across the life span, looking beyond the learning of children and adolescents and the educational setting of kindergarten through twelfth grade (K-12).

This report (referred to as *HPL II*) describes the committee's consensus conclusions and recommendations. It is intended not as a replacement for *HPL I* but as a companion volume that builds on the picture of how people learn, as laid out in that report, and adds new conclusions based on recent research.

Contributions of *HPL I*

Published in 2000, *HPL I* combined the principal messages from two 1999 reports (see Box 1-2). It summarized key findings from decades of research on (1) memory and the structure of knowledge, (2) problem solving and reasoning, (3) the early foundations of learning, (4) metacognitive processes and self-regulatory capabilities, and (5) how symbolic thinking emerges from the culture and community of the learner. It examined the ways experts differ from novices, how individuals transfer learning to new contexts, how children learn, and findings from neuroscience and cognitive science about brain functioning and development. It distilled from that work key insights about learning, including the following:

- Experts differ from novices in more than just their general abilities (i.e., memory or intelligence) and the use of general strategies. Experts have acquired extensive knowledge that affects what they notice and how they organize, represent, and interpret information in their environments, which in turn affects their abilities to remember, reason, and solve problems.
- Skills and knowledge must be extended beyond the narrow contexts in which they are initially learned in order for deeper learning to occur.
- The development of a sense of the application of knowledge—when the knowledge can be used—is an essential component of learning.
- Learning transfer—the capacity to apply learning in a new context—most likely occurs when the learner knows and understands the underlying general principles that can be applied to problems in different contexts.
- The construction of conceptual understanding of abstract ideas promotes learning.
- Learners are most successful at learning and will sustain their own learning if they are mindful of themselves as learners and thinkers (i.e., use a metacognitive approach to learning and instruction).

The authoring committee of *HPL I* also explored the implications of new insights about learning for education, focusing particularly on the design of

BOX 1-2 History of *HPL I*

HPL I summarized the work of two separate committees of the Commission on Behavioral and Social Sciences and Education of the National Research Council (NRC). The original volume, published in April 1999 with the title *How People Learn: Brain, Mind, Experience, and School* was the product of a 2-year study conducted by the Committee on Developments in the Science of Learning. This committee was asked to distill from research on human learning and cognitive development the insights most relevant to education in the elementary and secondary grades and to identify the developments most useful to teachers, school officials, parents, and policy makers (National Research Council, 1999b).

A second NRC committee, the Committee on Learning Research and Educational Practice, was formed to plan a workshop for practitioners, policy makers, and researchers to respond to *How People Learn: Brain, Mind, Experience, and School* and to consider ways to apply its messages to school practice. The results of the workshop were captured in *How People Learn: Bridging Research and Practice* published in June 1999 (National Research Council, 1999c). A subsequent report focused on how students learn in the disciplines of history, mathematics, and science (National Research Council, 2005). (Appendix A provides more detail about *HPL I* and associated reports and how they have been used.)

learning environments, teaching strategies, the education of teachers, and the use of technology to support learning. Among the committee's major points were several that are important for educators:

- Learning and development in childhood are influenced by the interactions between each child's early competencies and environmental supports and experiences, as well as by the individuals who care for them.
- Learning is promoted and regulated by both the biology and ecology of the child.
- Learning in itself changes the physical structure of the brain, and the changing structure in turn organizes and reorganizes how the brain functions. Thus, different parts of the brain may be ready to learn at different times.

HPL I has had wide influence, particularly as a text used in teacher preparation programs and other educational settings; nearly two decades after its publication, the report remains the third most popular report published by the National Academies. Since 2000, however, there have been significant developments in research on learning. Users of *HPL I* have noted the importance of topics that were not emphasized in that report and areas in which there have been notable developments since 2000, including the role of culture in learning, out-of-school learning, how learning changes from childhood through adulthood, and the learning skills needed for college and work.

Interpreting the Charge

The committee was not asked to answer a specific question but to provide an update on a wide and diverse body of work. We needed to consider learners' developmental needs and interests throughout the life span, from birth through old age. A more fundamental shift in focus from *HPL I* was indicated by the charge to address learning settings outside of school, often referred to as informal settings.

In addition, although the authors of *HPL I* recognized the importance of culture and context for learning, they concentrated on specific ways that cultural variation influences learning in school and ways educators can take that into account. Since *HPL I* was published, there has been a growing appreciation for the fundamental role that culture plays for every individual learner in every learning context, for every learning purpose. Navigating the different underlying assumptions and goals associated with the infinitely variable challenges and circumstances people encounter is a critical part of learning. Thus, we needed to explore how people learn as they move through all the varied settings and activities that make up human experience.

We discuss developments in understanding the cultural nature of learning in greater detail in Chapter 2, but the committee was mindful that learning occurs in a complex and dynamic ecosystem. Our investigation encompassed what is known about the individual learner both as a biological organism, with needs such as adequate sleep and nutrition, and as a social being. The very long list of factors that influence learning begins at the microscopic level (the level of lead in the learner's blood is just one of many such factors) and extends to the macro level (e.g., the impact of the qualities of the learner's neighborhood, society, and culture).

Gathering Evidence to Address the Charge

There was a wide range of research for the committee to consider. We sought to provide a flavor of the varied and creative research going on in diverse disciplines but without attaching too much weight to findings from individual studies. Our goal is to give the reader a sense of the principal findings and prevailing themes in recent research without oversimplifying sometimes extremely subtle and complex work.

Certainly it was not possible to explore every avenue relevant to the science and practice of learning. Moreover, other reports of the National Academies have already explored related topics from the vast literature on learning, including some that fall under our charge (see Appendix B for a partial list of relevant reports).[2]

Our goal was to report on research-based findings that would be of most use to audiences who have relied on *HPL I* and to all readers eager to know about strategies for applying the research to support and foster their own and others' learning. Two lenses for understanding learning guided our search for relevant research findings.

First, understanding learning as a developmental process requires many levels of analysis. This means that knowledge relevant for understanding learning comes from diverse disciplines that address neurological and biological processes, as well as social and cultural phenomena and contexts. Thus, we explored evidence about learning as a developmental process that undergoes changes over time across the life span. We sought to understand how learning occurs as people age, and we sought new insights into learning disabilities. We looked beyond the neuroscience literature to explore research on how cognitive processes such as executive function and reasoning change across the life span and how affective states such as emotion and motivation, social relationships, systems, and culture influence learning.

We drew on research from diverse fields in order to examine learning at different levels of analysis—from the molecular and cellular to the sociocultural—and thereby to demonstrate the complex systems involved in learning. We sought to accentuate the interdependencies among these levels and domains because we believe that learning is a complex process to be unraveled by analyses that span interdependent biological, cognitive, affective, interpersonal, and sociocultural conditions.

Second, our charge explicitly directed us to consider a wide variety of settings across the life span. People are engaged within formal learning environments such as school for only a small portion of their waking lives, and they learn in many other types of settings throughout their lives. Basic knowledge and skills (reading comprehension, literacy, mathematics, science, geography, oral and written communication, etc.) gained in formal educational settings remain important. But the importance of other kinds of learning, such as those often referred to as 21st century skills (e.g., flexibility and adaptability;

---

[2]For example, our charge mentions "supporting students learning English as a second language," but this topic is addressed in depth in a new National Academies report, *Promoting the Educational Success of Children and Youth Learning English: Promising Futures* (National Academies of Sciences, Engineering, and Medicine, 2017).

teamwork and collaboration; inventive thinking; digital literacy; and deep, motivated, and self-regulated learning), is now well established (Rader, 2002). The committee also recognized the importance of rich knowledge and competencies that people develop in the context of their families and communities outside of formal schooling.

The committee met six times in person for closed-session meetings and held three public information-gathering sessions. Our information-gathering process also included discussion sessions with researchers on the following topics:

- Thought and language in the bilingual infant
- Understanding cultural differences that influence how, why, and where most people learn
- The neuroscience of reading and reading disabilities
- Cognitive and developmental factors affecting learning in context
- Assessment challenges in learning contexts related to developments in psychology and technology
- Learning in informal settings
- Learning in adulthood and the use of technology for learning in adulthood
- Learning disabilities, universal design for learning, and assistive technology

Although the idea that learning occurs across the life span is not new, the increased focus on learning that takes place outside of and beyond K-12 education helped us shape our report, which is designed to provide information useful to multiple audiences: teacher-educators; persons preparing for an education profession; new teachers; and others connected to the world of education, including those who make policies that affect or direct education, as well as individuals.

TREATMENT OF EVIDENCE

Much of the research described in *HPL I* is still supported empirically; we have drawn on this body of evidence, but our task was to review new research. We therefore primarily confined our attention to material published after 2000, although in some cases we included older work that had not been addressed by *HPL I*. Addressing our charge required us to explore numerous fields of study and therefore to draw on research that varied in both methodology and standards of evidence. A few broad principles guided us in assessing the material we collected:

First, we placed greatest credence in evidence from those controlled studies that (1) included subjects who varied in key characterisitics, (2) drew on the methodologies of multiple disciplines, and (3) targeted multiple learning outcomes. However, there was not an extensive array of studies of this type for every important subject we hoped to address. Therefore, we also reviewed other types of studies, including case studies, exploratory research examining correlational relationships among variables, design and development research, small and large quasi experiments, small and large random-assignment experiments, studies that document promising practice (or "hot-house" studies), and research reports and online publications not presented in refereed publications. (See Moss and Haertle [2016] for discussion of the value of methodological pluralism in the conduct of research on teaching and learning.)

We recognize that these varied sources offer different sorts of evidence and note that blending findings from different perspectives and disciplines is not easily accomplished. Study designs, samples, and analytical techniques are not always comparable, and findings from laboratory-based studies often prove difficult to reconcile with those from classrooms, workplaces, or other settings. We characterize the nature of the available evidence we relied on for the main areas we explored within each chapter. We also gave greater credence to findings that are replicated and reported in meta-analyses and research syntheses than to empirical findings confined to a single study.

One problem that affects a variety of research on human behavior complicated our capacity to draw firm conclusions from some of the available research. As documented by Henrich and colleagues and by others (Henrich et al., 2010a; Nielsen et al., 2017), the social and behavioral sciences have relied very heavily on study subjects from cultures that are Western, educated, industrialized, rich, and democratic, or "WEIRD" (thus, this issue of potential sample bias is known as the WEIRD problem). These researchers also noted that a substantial proportion of research subjects are college students and thus are also disproportionately younger as a group than adults in general. This issue is a particular challenge with laboratory-based research. Field research in real-world settings can much more readily include diverse populations. Findings based only on research with WEIRD subjects cannot be assumed to characterize human beings in general because this population is not representative of the entire human population.

We note that this caveat must be considered with respect to many research studies, although in other cases the composition of the study population is less relevant (e.g., in neurobiological studies of brain structures). Identifying a way to resolve the WEIRD problem was beyond the scope of our charge, but we note particular areas where it is most pertinent as they arise. Appendix C provides a more detailed discussion of the WEIRD problem and related concerns regarding study populations in learning research.

We also note that over the past several decades, attention to the evidence underpinning education research has increased (Lodge, 2013; Slavin, 2008). For example, the U.S. Department of Education has stressed the importance of rigorous scientific evidence that includes findings from randomized, controlled trials (U.S. Department of Education, 2001) and offers practice guides and other resources through its What Works Clearinghouse Website.[3] Researchers have also pointed out that the research design and methodology used in laboratory-based cognitive psychology and neuroscience research often cannot be practically applied to classroom settings (Oliver and Conole, 2003; Smeyers and Depaepe, 2013). In other words, one of the major ongoing challenges for educational research is that findings from the studies examining fundamental learning processes require substantial translation and interpretation in order to be applicable to practice.

GUIDE TO THIS REPORT

The report begins with an overview of the landscape of current research on learning. In Chapter 2, we elaborate on the heightened interest in and more nuanced understanding of the cultural nature of learning. That chapter describes the committee's understanding that learning is situated and why learning must be understood not as a phenomenon that occurs in predictable ways within individuals' brains but rather as a function of dynamic processes that occur within a dynamic system that depends on people, time, and context.

In Chapter 3, we provide an overview of types of learning and of the key brain processes through which learning takes place. In Chapter 4, we describe two key cognitive processes that support learning: the means by which an individual orchestrates his learning and a key element of almost all learning, memory. Chapter 5 discusses the dynamic interplay between knowledge development and reasoning. Chapter 6 examines the roles of motivation, beliefs, goals, and values in learning outcomes.

In the last portion of the report, the committee turns to specific implications of the research we have reviewed for learners at different stages of life and educators. Chapter 7 revisits key findings presented throughout the report and elaborates on their implications for learning in school. Chapter 8 considers the potential for digital technology to support learning. Chapter 9 examines learning in adulthood and into old age, as well as learning disabilities that affect learners of all ages. We close in Chapter 10 with a brief synthesis of the primary themes in this complex body of work and offer an agenda for further research to support sound policy and practice.

---

[3] See https://ies.ed.gov/ncee/wwc/PracticeGuides [November 2017].

2

Context and Culture

An individual's development is affected by the environment in which she lives—including not only the family and other close relationships and circumstances but also the larger contexts in which families and communities are situated. This idea is not new, and debates about the relative contributions of "nature" and "nurture" to people's characteristics and abilities date at least to the 19th century. Since the 1970s, many scholars have explored ideas about culture and context and have also asked questions about the act of investigating such things. Understandings of race and ethnicity, cultural values, historical perspectives, modes of communication, and the importance attached to different kinds of knowledge and skill are just a few of the topics that have been examined and reexamined as researchers have sought to understand the complex dynamics between culture, context, and learning.

The authors of *HPL I*[1] acknowledged the importance of culture but confined their attention to specific ideas for educators. For example, that report noted the following:

- Experts have knowledge that is "conditionalized"; that is, they understand the contexts in which their knowledge can be useful and how to apply it.
- School failure may be partly explained by the mismatch between what students have learned in their home cultures and what is required of them in school.

---

[1] As noted in Chapter 1, this report uses the abbreviation "*HPL I*" for *How People Learn: Brain, Mind, Experience, and School: Expanded Edition* (National Research Council, 2000).

- Because learning is influenced in fundamental ways by the context in which it takes place, schools and classrooms should be learner and community centered.

What has become far clearer since *HPL I* was published is that every individual's learning is profoundly influenced by the particular context in which that person is situated. Researchers have been exploring how all learners grow and learn in culturally defined ways in culturally defined contexts. While humans share basic brain structures and processes, as well as fundamental experiences such as relationships with family, developmental stages, and much more, each of these phenomena is shaped by the individual's precise experiences. Learning does not happen in the same way for all people because cultural influences pervade development from the beginning of life.

We focus on the rich cultural, contextual, historical, and developmental diversity of learning itself and how understanding of this diversity offers ways to improve learning and create optimal learning environments. We recognize that learning is the product of a complex, interactive system of physical processes, which also interact with the complex systems and environments in which individuals live.

This chapter sets the stage by providing a brief overview of developments in thinking about culture and learning since *HPL I*. We examine how the word "culture" is used, explain why the committee has approached its work from a sociocultural perspective, and briefly describe some key ways that culture is an integral part of development and learning.

THE CULTURAL NATURE OF LEARNING

The committee has taken a sociocultural view of learning. Because our concern is with how *people* learn (not, say, with how computers learn), we viewed our charge as including the social, emotional, motivational, cognitive, developmental, biological, and temporal contexts in which learning occurs. This stance derives from our understanding of what culture is, a subject about which much has been written.

Defining Culture

In its broadest sense, culture is the learned behavior of a group of people that generally reflects the tradition of that people and is socially transmitted from generation to generation through social learning; it is also shaped to fit circumstances and goals (Dirette, 2014; Hofstede, 1997; see also Nasir et al., 2006).

Culture is reflected in the behavior and beliefs of a single individual, but it is also fundamentally social. Culture is a product of the way individuals learn to coordinate desirable and useful activities with others, and it is expressed in many ways, including through the actions, expectations, and beliefs of individual persons; physical elements such as artifacts, tools, and the design of physical spaces; norms for interacting with others, both verbally and nonverbally; and beliefs and ways of looking at the world that are shared with others.

Integrating different cultural practices is a key learning challenge, and culture is a matter not only of *what* people learn but also *how* they learn. Culture is also reflected in the historical time period and society in which someone lives. The dynamic nature of culture is evident in the fact that people who make up a cultural community maintain cultural practices acquired from previous generations, while also adapting practices over time to fit changing circumstances or even transforming them altogether (Cole and Packer, 2005; Lave and Wenger, 1991; Super and Harkness, 1986; Tomasello, 2016). In this way, a culture is a living system. People living now are the bearers of the culture they received from the prior generation, but they also become the generators and carriers of culture, as they have adapted it, into the future. Culture refers not only to the manifestations of membership in a group; it also refers to something much less static: a way of living that sustains a particular community (Nasir et al., 2006; Rogoff, 2016). People live in, reflect, and transform their culture (Gauvain, 2009). Yet within each cultural community, there is great diversity, as people take on different roles, employ different tools, and engage in varied practices.

All settings for learning, including schools, are socially constructed contexts shaped by culture. School is designed to provide young people with the experiences necessary to adapt to the demands of modern society by providing a broad array of cultural knowledge of specific topics (e.g., reading, mathematics, and science) but also knowledge of how people interact with one another. The social practices of school, such as coordinated activities and routines, reflect the culture of that school and the goals and values of the larger society in which the school is embedded. Individuals learn to navigate that culture and may do so in different ways that reflect their own unique experiences within their homes and communities. Within classrooms and in all learning contexts, the learner may embody and express the culture of his own family and group in many ways, for example by using particular speech patterns or gestures, or averting his gaze from the teacher out of respect.

An important point is that although questions of race and ethnicity frequently arise in the context of examinations of culture, these are distinct constructs. The terms "race" and "ethnicity" do not have generally agreed upon definitions. "Ethnicity" is often used to refer to a person's group and cultural identification, including nationality and ancestry (Sue and Dhinsda, 2006). While the concept of race has often been used in Western societies to create taxonomic categories based on common hereditary traits related to an individual's physical appearance (such as skin and eye color and hair texture), both concepts—ethnicity and race—carry complex implications that reflect culture, history, socioeconomics, political status, and connections to geographic origins of ancestors (Collins, 2004). Research on genetic differences among population groups has established that there are not scientifically meaningful genetic differences among groups commonly identified as belonging to different races (Smedley and Smedley, 2005). It has long been recognized by social scientists that race is a social construction and that criteria for inclusion in a racial category or definition of particular groups as racial ones have varied over time (see, e.g., Figueroa, 1991; Kemmelmeier and Chavez, 2014; López, 2006).

The Role of Culture in Learning and Development

Perspectives on what constitutes culture and how it relates to learning have changed over time. There are also differences in how the dynamic relation between culture and learning is conceptualized across fields of study. At least four disciplines—anthropology, education, linguistics, and psychology—have contributed to the evidence the committee discusses regarding the role of culture in learning, particularly learning that occurs during childhood and adolescence. We do not discuss the full range of culturally shaped differences in children's developmental environments in depth, as these have been well documented (see, e.g., Bornstein, 2010; Rogoff, 2003; Super and Harkness, 2010). Rather, we focus on examples that illustrate the ways early experiences in childhood can influence learning.

Perhaps two of the most important and longstanding insights gained from early work in these disciplines are that caregiver practices vary across cultures and that these variations influence learners. A large body of work published before *HPL I* (but not addressed there) established that socialization practices—caretakers' ways of interacting with children—shape how children learn, what they learn, how quickly they learn, and even what the developmental end point of that learning is (for everything from walking to how they interact socially). More recent work has explored how ideas of what is desirable to learn may vary across cultures. For example, a study that compared parental expectations in the United States and Vanuatu suggested that whereas U.S. parents tend to consider deviation from a model as showing creativity, parents in Vanuatu tend to equate precise imitation with intelligence (Clegg et al., 2017).

Another major contribution to understanding of the interplay between culture and learning arose out of efforts to establish developmental norms: benchmarks against which children could be compared to assess whether they were developing normally. Arnold Gesell—considered a pioneer for systematically mapping motor development using large samples of children—inspired many researchers to explore what children were able to physically do, in what order, and at what age, across a wide variety of cultural contexts (Gesell, 1934).

Subsequent work revealed surprising differences in rates of motor development across cultures in different countries, regardless of poverty status (Karasik et al., 2010). For example, studies with children from African countries showed infants holding their necks up and walking earlier than average European American children. Most important, this work showed that precocity was most likely to be noted in cultural groups in which parents expected their children to acquire the milestones at earlier ages or adopted child-rearing practices that facilitated accelerated growth, such as formalized massage and stretching of children's limbs during daily baths (for a summary of this work, see Karasik et al., 2010).

Similarly, work on social and moral development reveals that cultural groups differ in their conceptualization of the relationship between "self" and "others." Even early in life, community expectations regarding this relationship strongly influence how children go about learning, how they think about themselves, and the ways in which they socially engage (Keller et al., 2009).

There is a large body of work on culture and cognition that has examined how children and adults across different cultural groups and societal contexts (remote, urban, rural) perform on cognitive tasks (see Cole and Scribner, 1974, for an influential early example). This work was designed to assess whether developmental milestones on problem-solving tasks were universal or varied across cultures and to try to uncover processes that could account for any observed differences in the rate of development or in the highest level of development obtained (Cole, 1995; Rogoff and Chavajay, 1995). These and other studies strongly suggest that culture plays a role in basic cognitive processes that help learners understand and organize the world, such as memory and perception.

A classic example that illustrates culture's influence on basic developmental processes is the illusion susceptibility study by Segall and colleagues (1966). This work challenged the assumption that people everywhere, regardless of their backgrounds, see the world in the same way because they share the same perceptual system. It showed that people living in urban, industrialized environments are more susceptible to the Muller-Lyer illusion (the perception that a set of lines of the same length, but flanked by angles pointing inward (<) or outward (>) are actually different lengths) than people who live in physical environments in which straight lines and right angles are not often seen. Work on these kinds of cross-cultural differences demonstrates that the environment in which a person lives matters and that people construct their perceptions by drawing on their prior learning experiences, including cultural ones. More recent work has explored cultural differences in attention and other cognitive processes (e.g., Chua et al., 2005).

Culture also affects the cognitive processes that shape learning (Markus and Kitayama, 1991; Nisbett et al., 2001; see also Gelfand et al., 2011; Kitayama and Cohen, 2007; Kronenfeld et al., 2011; Medin and Bang, 2014).

Researchers have identified many examples of cultural differences in what are considered "basic" cognitive processes once assumed to be universal (Henrich et al., 2010a; see also Ojalehto and Medin, 2015b). This work illustrates the important point that by taking cultural processes into account, researchers can develop a more complete understanding of processes that underlie developmental change and of the course and end points of development (Henrich et al., 2010b).

Learning as Social Activity

Another body of work in psychology that explores the role of culture in shaping psychological processes has focused on learning as a dynamic system of social activity. Many of these researchers draw from a set of ideas about development advanced by Lev Vygotsky, Alexander Luria, and Aleksei Leontiev: the "troika" of pioneers in what is variously known as the sociocultural, social historical, or cultural-historical theory of development (Cole, 1998; Wertsch, 1991): the idea that social, cultural, and historical contexts define and shape a particular child and his experience (John-Steiner and Mann, 1996).

The underlying principle in this body of work is that cognitive growth happens because of social interactions in which children and their more advanced peers or adults work jointly to solve problems. Adults help children learn how to use their culture's psychological and technical tools (e.g., number and writing systems, calculators, computers). These types of tools have skills and ideas built into them, and learning how to use them is a critical aspect of cognitive development. Each child does not reinvent these tools; they are passed on across generations and adapted (Wertsch, 1991).

The use of this theory to understand the cultural nature of learning emerged among cross-cultural psychologists who began their work testing Piagetian cognitive tasks in different societies. Researchers who adopt the sociocultural-historical perspective in examining learning do so within the cultural context of *everyday life*. This body of research illustrates through rich and detailed examples how everyday cultural practices structure and shape the way children think, remember, and solve problems (see Gauvain and Monroe, 2012; Greenfield, 2004; Rogoff, 2003; Saxe, 2012a, 2012b). For example, Saxe's work among the Oksapmin people in Papua New Guinea documented a body-counting practice that shapes mathematical thinking and problem solving in that community. Rogoff's work demonstrates how, among the Mayan people, aspects of family life and community practice promote learning by keen observation.

These in-depth studies demonstrate that approaches to learning are embedded in the practices of communities and that as these communities change over time, cultural adaptation happens (Greenfield, 2009). This adaptation, in turn, transforms how people within these communities learn and solve problems

(Gauvain and Munroe, 2009; Greenfield, 2009). Many of these ethnographic research studies address learning in countries and cultural settings that may seem very distant from a U.S. context. However, the same principles can be applied in examining cultural practices and tools everywhere, including urban metropolitan areas. Consider, for example, how the emergence of cultural tools, such as calculators, the Internet, and Twitter, has transformed not only expectations about what people learn but also how they learn (these issues are discussed further in Chapter 6).

Not surprisingly, embrace of sociocultural theory led to one of the most important recent theoretical shifts in education research: the proposition that all learning is a social process shaped by and infused with a system of cultural meaning (Nasir and Hand, 2006; National Research Council, 2009; Tomasello, 2016). This work bridges the worlds of home and school. It examines how culturally defined expectations and the ways caregivers in a community engage with their children interact with *school learning*: the context and the content of what one learns in the structured setting of a school. Some of this work was described in *HPL I*; it addresses issues of congruence or match between expectations and practices children learn at home or in their cultural communities and the expectations embedded in the culture of school. Examples include variations between how language is used at home and how it is used in the classroom (Cazden, 1988), including expectations about whether a child should learn by observing or through directed individualized verbal instruction (Cajete, 1999; Correa-Chávez and Rogoff, 2009); how conceptions of time influence how children differentially adapt to expectations and the pace set in the classroom (Levine, 1997); whether instructional practices promote individual or collaborative learning (Swisher, 1990; Tyler et al., 2006); or even what skills—for example, "book" knowledge or socially responsible behavior—children need to demonstrate to be considered intelligent (Serpell and Boykin, 1994).

These studies documenting the cultural nature of learning have largely been *ethnographic*: systematic descriptions of the culture of a particular set of people at a particular point in time. And they often were conducted with small study samples. However, as with the early cross-cultural work on cognitive development, these studies yielded significant insights about learning that are relevant for understanding all people, from infancy to old age: Namely, that *everyone* brings to their opportunities to learn the experiences they have acquired through participation in cultural practices in their communities.

THE DYNAMIC INTERACTION OF CULTURE, BIOLOGY, AND CONTEXT

Learning is a dynamic process that requires coordination of multiple systems within the individual and occurs within a dynamic system encompassing the changing contexts and people that surround an individual throughout life. Recognizing this principle is essential to understanding the forces that help shape learning over the life span. Human development, from birth throughout life, takes place through processes of progressively more complex reciprocal interactions between the human individual (an active, biopsychological organism) and that individual's immediate physical and social environments. Through these dynamic interactions, culture influences even the biological aspects of learning.

In the 1970s, Urie Bronfenbrenner offered a formal model to illustrate the complex and diverse influences of context on the development of individuals (Bronfenbrenner, 1977, 1994; Bubolz and Sontag, 2009). His model is a set of concentric rings representing the different systems in which the individual develops, moving from family, school, peer groups, and workplaces outward to broader social and institutional settings, ideologies, value systems, laws, and customs. The model also depicts change and consistency in all of these elements over time, representing the cumulative experiences in an individual's lifetime.

Similarly, learning at the individual level involves lasting adaptations of multiple systems to the changing external and internal environment, including changes in the biology of the brain. The biology of the brain provides the physiological platform for learning and is shaped by the social and cultural influences outside of the individual. For example, there is evidence that individuals' brains are critically shaped by social relationships and that the information people learn through these relationships supports not only their knowledge about facts and procedures but also their emotions, motivations, and interests (Immordino-Yang et al., 2014; Nelson et al., 2007).

Culture coordinates the biological systems involved in learning and is the broader social context in which people engage in the experiences that enable them to adapt to the world and learn. Study of the role of cultural adaptation in learning, pioneered by Giyoo Hatano, has shown how cultural influences may both promote and hamper learning. For example, a cultural context may promote particular types of learning such as observation versus explanation (Gutiérrez and Rogoff, 2003). It might convey expectations about exploration and experimentation that foster or hinder adaptation and experimentation and influence the ways learners apply what has been learned in novel situations (see, e.g., Hatano and Inagaki, 1986; Hatano and Oura, 2003).

In the next two sections, we discuss two aspects of an individual's environment that have an impact on individual's learning and are shaped by culture. The first aspect is the social and emotional interactions an individual experiences. The second aspect comprises the factors related to an individual's physical well-being.

Social and Emotional Influences

Brain development and functioning, like the learning it supports, is socially contextualized. It happens in the context of experiences, social relationships, and cognitive opportunities as subjectively perceived and emotionally experienced by the learner. Cultural norms and goals shape how and what people think. This is true even when a person is working alone or independently.

The brain's processing of emotional and social stimuli and experiences has considerable influence on the development of brain networks (Goldin-Meadow, 2000; Hackman and Farah, 2009; Leppänen and Nelson, 2009; Nobel et al., 2015). Humans have evolved to be highly socially interdependent: From birth through old age, no one can manage life without relying on many other people (Rogoff, 2015; Tomasello, 2001). Individuals' brains are critically shaped by social relationships, and the information they learn through these relationships supports both their emotions and their knowledge about facts, procedures, motivation, and interests (Immordino-Yang et al., 2014; Nelson et al., 2007).

Studies of institutionally raised Romanian children provide a tragic demonstration of the effects of social deprivation on brain and cognitive function (e.g., Nelson et al., 2014). Though children reared in Romanian government institutions during the period studied had enough food, clothing, bedding, and other material supplies, they had a rotating staff of caregivers and little opportunity to develop a meaningful, stable relationship with a loving, committed adult. The result was that these children did not simply fail to adequately develop socially, emotionally, and cognitively; they also failed to develop biologically. These children were stunted in physical growth and in brain development: Both their brains and bodies were abnormally small.

Emotion plays a role in developing the neural substrate for learning by helping people attend to, evaluate, and react to stimuli, situations, and happenings. In the past, it was generally assumed that emotion interferes with critical thinking and that knowledge and emotion are separate (Gardner, 1985). However, extensive research now makes clear that the brain networks supporting emotion, learning, and memory are intricately and fundamentally intertwined (Panksepp and Biven, 2012), even for experts in technical domains such as mathematics (Zeki et al., 2014). Emotions are an essential and ubiquitous dimension of thought, and emotional processing steers behavior, thought, and learning (Damasio, 1994; Immordino-Yang and Damasio, 2007).

Quite literally, it is neurobiologically impossible to think deeply about or remember information about which one has had no emotion because the healthy brain does not waste energy processing information that does not matter to the individual (Immordino-Yang, 2015). Emotions help learners set goals during learning. They tell the individual experiencing them when to keep working and when to stop, when she is on the right path to solve a problem and when she needs to change course, and what she should remember and what is not important.

People are willing to work harder to learn the content and skills they are emotional about, and they are emotionally interested when the content and skills they are learning seem useful and connected to their motivations and future goals. Conversely, emotions like anxiety can undermine learning by causing worry, which depletes cognitive resources and activates brain regions associated with fear and escape rather than with academic thinking (Beilock, 2010; Schmader and Johns, 2003).

Physical Influences

The developing brain is sensitive to physical influences that also affect other aspects of health and development, including nutrition, exposure to environmental toxins, sleep, and exercise. These physical influences can vary dramatically across context and are often shaped by cultural practices.

Nutrition

Sufficient, high-quality nutrition is necessary for health, development, and learning for infants (who are affected by prenatal nutrition), children, and adults. In particular, adequate protein, calories, and other nutrients are needed for brain development and function. Because of the protracted course of brain development, nutrition is especially important through the years of adolescence. Deficiencies in protein, calories, and other essential nutrients have been linked to negative effects on cognitive functioning (e.g., inhibitory control and executive function) and emotional functioning (Bryan et al., 2004).

Iron deficiency, for example, is relatively common in the United States; 9 percent of U.S. children ages 1–3 during the period 1999–2002 were iron deficient (Baker and Greer, 2010), as were 2–3 percent of adult males and 9–22 percent of adult females (Gupta et al., 2016). Iron deficiency, which can lead to iron-deficiency anemia, impairs learning, memory, and cognition. Lower test scores in early education have been correlated with infantile iron-deficiency anemia. Further, severe iron-deficiency anemia in infancy has effects that last through adolescence, resulting in lower test scores in motor function, written expression, arithmetic achievement, spatial memory, and selective recall (National Research Council and Institute of Medicine, 2000). It is unclear whether iron deficiency without anemia leads to similar outcomes (Taras, 2005). Iron supplementation has been shown to reverse some of the effects of anemia, but the degree of improvement may vary with socioeconomic status (Lozoff, 2007, 2011; Lozoff et al., 2014).

Sleep

The cumulative long-term effects of sleep loss and sleep disorders have been associated not only with health problems (e.g., increased risk of diabetes, obesity, depression, heart attack, and stroke) but also with performance deficits in occupational, educational, and other settings (Institute of Medicine, 2006). As sleep deficiency accumulates, the cognitive functions associated with learning (e.g., attention, vigilance, memory, and complex decision making) deteriorate proportionately and substantially (Jackson et al., 2013). For instance, one study reported that 36 hours of sleep deprivation (one "all-nighter") resulted in a 40 percent loss in the ability to form new memories (Walker, 2006).

For adults, work schedules that impede sleep, such as shift work, will exacerbate the effect of sleep deprivation on memory formation (Mawdsley et al., 2014). For young children, sleep plays an important role in the consolidation of memories in infancy and early childhood (Henderson et al., 2012; Seehagen et al., 2015), and insufficient sleep dramatically decreases memory for previously acquired knowledge (Darby and Sloutsky, 2015). In adolescents, insufficient sleep can be related to attention problems both in and out of school, general cognitive functioning, emotional regulation, mood disorders, engaging in risky behaviors, and academic outcomes (Wahlstrom et al., 2014).

The amount of sleep considered biologically normal or optimal varies across the life span: the National Sleep Foundation recommends 14 to 17 hours for newborns and 7 to 8 hours for older adults (Blunden and Galland, 2014; Hirshkowitz et al., 2015). However, adults are averaging 1 to 2 hours less daily sleep than they did in the mid-20th century, and 39 percent currently get less than 7 hours of sleep, as compared with 15 percent in the mid-20th century (Institute of Medicine, 2011; National Sleep Foundation, 2008). Average sleep duration for infants, children, and adolescents has decreased by 30 to 60 minutes over the past 20 years, largely because of late bedtimes (Dollman et al., 2007; Iglowstein et al., 2003). Many young children also experience compromised sleep quality, and few outgrow the problem as adults (Centers for Disease Control and Prevention, 2009; Kataria et al., 1987; Lauderdale et al., 2006; National Sleep Foundation, 2006; Nevarez et al., 2010; Pollock, 1994; Spilsbury et al., 2004).

Exercise

The strong association between physical exercise and positive outcomes in physical health and disease prevention is well established (U.S. Department of Health and Human Services and Administration for Children and Families, 2010), but exercise can also be beneficial for learning and cognition.

Because exercise varies considerably in form, duration, and frequency, researchers focus separately on its acute and enduring effects on cognition, emotion, and behavior. Acute effects of exercise on learning are evident in tests given immediately following the physical activity, while enduring effects are cognitive changes that are evident over a period of numerous exercise sessions. These studies help to clarify when and how exercise is most beneficial to people's mental development and emotional well-being at different ages.

There are many neurochemical changes that follow intense exercise and may cause the brain to be primed for better skill attainment and greater learning immediately following a workout (Meeusen et al., 2001). Older studies of children who have just exercised have identified improvements in mathematical computation (Gabbard and Barton, 1979; McNaughten and Gabbard, 1993), psychomotor performance (Raviv and Low, 1990), and stimulus-matching performance (Caterino and Polak, 1999). More recent studies have found improvements in children's abilities to concentrate and complete complex tasks including reading comprehension, inhibition (impulse control), and attention (Hillman et al., 2009).

Improvements in cognition and academic performance, particularly integrative tasks that involve self-monitoring and executive function, as well as higher-order cognition, have also been associated with consistent exercise training in children (Keeley and Fox, 2009; Tomporowski and Ellis, 1984, 1985; Tomporowski et al., 2011). Beneficial relationships between physical exercise and cognition have been shown in the domains of perceptual skills, verbal tests, math tests, academic readiness and achievement (among children ages 4-18, Sibley and Etinier, 2003), and executive functioning tasks (Davis et al., 2011).

Some research has suggested that the degree to which exercise affects higher-level thinking skills may differ depending on the nature of the exercise and on developmental age (Best, 2010). Exercise that is more challenging—for example, involving attention and learning of new motor skills and patterns, more coordinated activity, and social interaction—may lead to stronger immediate cognitive benefits among adolescents (Budde et al., 2008; Pesce et al., 2009; Stroth et al., 2009).

There is also evidence of a relationship between exercise and cognitive performance in older adults. The positive effects of physical activity on cognitive ability are seen in both cognitively normal adults and those with beginning signs of cognitive impairment (Colcombe and Kramer, 2003; Etnier et al., 2006; Heyn et al., 2004). Although these effects have been seen across all domains, Hillman and colleagues (2008) found that particularly marked benefits are evident in executive control, defined as the cognitive ability for planning, organizing, and thinking flexibly.

Environmental Toxins

Exposure to environmental neurotoxins also can have significant impacts, particularly for developing fetuses and young children. For example, mothers exposed to higher levels of environmental neurotoxins (such as pesticides and lead) tend to bear children who have poorer developmental outcomes compared with the children of equally disadvantaged mothers who have lower degrees of exposure (Institute of Medicine and National Research Council, 2015). Young children are especially vulnerable for two reasons: They tend to absorb more of a toxin relative to their body weight because their metabolisms are faster than those of older people, and their rapidly developing brains are more sensitive to toxins (National Scientific Council on the Developing Child, 2006; Rauh and Margolis, 2016).

Although lead toxicity levels in American children have declined markedly since legislation prohibiting the use of leaded paint (1971) and leaded gasoline (1984), lead poisoning has returned to public attention through news reports of contaminated drinking water in Flint, Michigan, and elsewhere. Even very low blood-lead levels have been shown to reduce children's scores on reading, writing, and IQ tests. Indeed, according to current guidance from the Centers for Disease Control and Prevention, no blood-lead level is safe and the consequences of lead exposure are irreversible.[2] However, cognitive decline associated with lead exposure is estimated to account for a far smaller degree of variance in IQ levels (1–4%) than social and parenting factors and institutional resource quality, such as early child care and preschools (40% or more) (Koller et al., 2004, p. 987).

CONCLUSION

We have emphasized that each individual learner occupies a unique place in time and space and responds throughout life to a set of circumstances, influences, and experiences that shape both what and how he learns. We examine specific implications of this principle in the chapters that follow, and we return to its implications for education in Chapter 7. But an implication necessary to note from the start is that what were once called "cultural differences" may be better characterized as variation in learners' involvement in common practices of particular cultural communities (Gutiérrez and Rogoff, 2003).

> **CONCLUSION 2-1:** Each learner develops a unique array of knowledge and cognitive resources in the course of life that are molded by the interplay of that learner's cultural, social, cognitive, and biological contexts. Understanding the developmental, cultural, contextual, and historical diversity of learners is central to understanding how people learn.

---

[2] See http://www.cdc.gov/nceh/lead/acclpp/blood_lead_levels.htm [November 2017].

3

Types of Learning and the Developing Brain

Learning involves a complicated interplay of factors. Chapter 2 discussed the importance of focusing on the cultural factors that influence learning. The committee explained new ways of understanding what culture is and the complex ways it influences development and learning. In this chapter, we examine different types of learning in order to understand the variety of complex processes involved. We then discuss brain development through the life span and changes in the brain that both support learning and occur as a result.

In this discussion, we draw on research in education and in social, cultural, and cognitive neuroscience. We build on what was discussed in *HPL I*[1] and other reports that have contributed to a neurobiological account of how brains develop. These sources have explored how both experience and supportive environments can fundamentally alter developmental trajectories—both normative and maladaptive—across the life span.

TYPES OF LEARNING

It may seem obvious to say that there are many types of learning, but researchers have explored this multifaceted construct from a variety of angles. People learn many different kinds of things and use different learning strategies and brain processes in doing so. Consider three scenarios that highlight the wide range of activities and accomplishments that all can be called "learning."

---

[1] As noted in Chapter 1, this report uses the abbreviation "*HPL I*" for *How People Learn: Brain, Mind, Experience, and School: Expanded Edition* (National Research Council, 2000).

Three Learning Scenarios

In scenario 1, Kayla is learning about the Pythagorean theorem in her geometry class. Her immediate motivation is to do well on a math exam, but she may have other motivations, such as impressing her parents, teachers, and friends, or at least not losing face; maintaining the grade-point average needed for a competitive college application; appreciating that this material is a prerequisite for learning advanced topics in math and science; seeing the application of the Pythagorean theorem to her interests in computer graphics and game programming; and seeing beauty and timelessness in the elegant and definitive proofs of the theorem.

As she works, Kayla is likely to engage in several types and applications of learning. She will probably learn both key terms and *rules*: for she will learn that "hypotenuse" is the term for the longest side of a right triangle and how to find the length of any hypotenuse using a formula. She will *encode* the formula in words or a picture so that she can later *retrieve* the rule for a test. She may learn to create and transform a *spatial model* that provides an intuitively compelling justification for the theorem. She may learn to *link* the spatial model to algebraic notation, and she may learn *procedures to manipulate this symbolic notation* to provide a formal proof of the theorem. She will learn to *apply* the Pythagorean theorem to closely related problems like finding the distance between two coordinates on a computer screen. She may even learn how to *transfer* the bigger concept to other contexts such as analyzing a communication network (Metcalfe, 2013).[2]

In scenario 2, Martina is developing her abilities on the guitar. Her motivations are very different from Kayla's. She began playing the instrument so that she could accompany her own singing, but after some years of experience, she has become interested in learning more sophisticated skills, such as using new chord progressions and picking styles to better reproduce her favorite musicians' performances and craft her own compositions. She has engaged in *motor learning* to improve her finger work, *perceptual learning* to pick out chord progressions from recordings, and *observational learning* by watching others' live and recorded performances. Practice and regimentation figure prominently in her training. Her playing has improved considerably with individual lessons and her accompanying efforts to use both *verbal and example-based instruction* to improve.

The third scenario is Foldit,[3] a computer-based game in which players learn to find solutions to the notoriously difficult problem of protein folding. (Figure 3-1 is an illustration of what a Foldit learner-player sees.) Foldit is an

---

[2] According to Metcalfe's law, the usefulness of a communications network increases proportionally to the square of the number of connected users because each person can connect to each of the other users (Metcalfe, 2013).

[3] Information about Foldit can be found at https://fold.it/portal [November 2016].

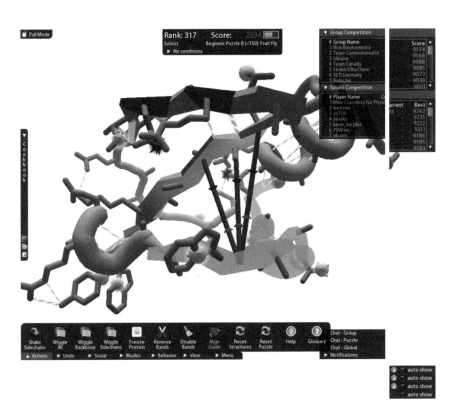

FIGURE 3-1 *User interface for the Foldit game.*
SOURCE: Adapted from Cooper et al. (2010).

example of a "serious game": one designed not only to entertain but also to educate or train users to solve real-world problems (Mayer, 2014). Foldit challenges its players to fold proteins into as low an energy state as possible, a difficult problem even for the most sophisticated artificial intelligence systems available (Cooper et al., 2010). Scientists can analyze the best solutions found by players to determine whether they can be applied to understanding or manipulating proteins in the real world. For example, in 2011, Foldit players, who include retirees and citizens of more than 13 countries, as well as science students, uncovered the crystal structure of a virus that causes AIDS in monkeys, producing a solution that had eluded professional scientists for 15 years (Khatib et al., 2011).

In 2012, using a version of the game that allows for the creation of new proteins, game players constructed an enzyme that can speed up a biosynthetic reaction used in a variety of drugs, including cholesterol medications, by 2,000 percent (Hersher, 2012). Khatib and colleagues (2011) studied the strategies that 57,000 Foldit players used to achieve these successes and found that a key to these players' results is that they *create new tools*, in this case computer software "recipes." They also *learn collaboratively* by forming teams, sharing specific solutions and general software recipes, distributing tasks among the team members, and regularly updating one another on their failures and successes.

These scenarios give a sense of the range of functions and processes involved in learning; they illustrate the complexity of learning to solve even fairly straightforward challenges. Contexts matter, as do the variety of factors that influence learners' motivations and approaches and the range of strategies and processes learners can recruit. We explore these issues further in this and later chapters.

We will return to these three scenarios to illustrate some of the basic universal types of learning researchers have investigated. We emphasize that these are not discrete functions that operate independently but are aspects of complex, interactive learning processes.

Basic Types of Learning

There are many types of learning, and as the scenarios illustrated, they often operate in concert. In this section, we describe several important types, chosen to acquaint the reader with the range, diversity, and dynamic nature of learning, rather than to provide a comprehensive taxonomy of learning types. We begin with forms of learning that may be considered "knowledge lean" such as the learning of habits and patterns and move toward more complex, "knowledge-rich" forms of learning such as inferential learning. The knowledge-rich types may be implicit, occurring outside the learners' conscious awareness and requiring limited verbal mediation. More explicit learning would include learning with models and learning executed with the learner's intention.

Research on types of learning is often conducted in laboratory settings where an effort is made to simplify the learning task and "strip away" nuances that reflect specific contexts. Often, participants in these studies are from cultures that are Western, educated, industrialized, rich, and democratic, which may limit the generalizability of findings to people who live in different cultural contexts (see Chapter 1 and Appendix C on the WEIRD problem). In the real world, learning situations almost always involve multiple learning processes and always are influenced by context and by the learner's own characteristics and preferences.

Habit Formation and Conditioning

Habits are behaviors and thought patterns that become engrained and feel fluent in particular contexts (Wood et al., 2002). Habits can be positive (e.g., making healthy snack choices or double-checking one's math homework), or they can be harmful (e.g., skipping meals and instead grabbing a candy bar from the vending machine, or giving up when one's math homework seems difficult). Both learning and unlearning of habits occur gradually and usually unconsciously, though one can become aware of one's habits and work to reinforce or change them mindfully. Habits tend to be self-reinforcing; because they achieve some short-term goal and are enacted relatively automatically, bad habits especially are notoriously hard to unlearn. Good habits, once established, can grow into rich patterns of behavior that help the learner succeed.

The gradual learning and unlearning of habits follows principles of *conditioning*, a nonconscious form of learning in which one automatically adjusts one's decisions and behaviors when particular and familiar contextual cues or triggers are present. These decisions and behaviors can be strengthened when they are closely followed by rewards; for example, when the candy bar tastes good and gives an energy rush (even if the rush is followed by an energy crash) or the homework-checking habit reveals a careless error. The rewards might be external, but they can also be generated by the learner, as when Martina, the guitar student, realizes that her playing has improved because she has made a habit of practicing every day before bed.

The probability and time horizon of rewards also matters. For example, Martina may not notice any difference in her playing right away after she starts practicing regularly, and she may be tempted to give up before she experiences the reward. Or, the diligent student checking her math homework may not perceive the reward for her extra effort if homework is graded for completion so careless errors do not count. It might be thought that habits will become strongest when the behavior is always rewarded—when Martina's progress is steady and the math student always earns praise—but predictable rewards actually reduce the durability of habits. That is, bad habits are often harder to extinguish when they are only intermittently rewarded, and the benefits of good habits may seem unclear when one takes the reward for granted. For example, if a child's tantrums are occasionally rewarded by a parent who "caves in," then the tantrum habit may resist extinction. The child learns that she might possibly be rewarded for a tantrum and so becomes more persistent. Similarly, though Martina may need to push herself to continue practicing nightly, on the night when she suddenly makes a breakthrough, the effort she put in will make the reward feel even sweeter.

People often think that they are in rational control of their behaviors and that they act the way they do because they have made a conscious decision. However, the prevalence of habit-driven acts shows that much of our behavior is not consciously chosen. Both negative habits such as obsessively checking one's cell phone for messages and positive habits such as morning exercises are frequently initiated without a conscious decision to engage in the activity: one begins before fully realizing a habit is being formed. This means that establishing a new, good habit might initially take effort and significant application of will power. As Martina works on her guitar playing, she develops good habits for holding the guitar with the neck pointed up rather than down, sitting with a straight back, and holding the pick loosely enough for it to have some play, habits that are critical for her growth in skill. Over time these behaviors need to become automatic, rather than deliberate, if she is to have sufficient mental resources left over to learn new pieces and techniques.

It is easy to be impatient with learners who have not yet instilled successful learning habits, such as listening attentively, creating outlines before writing, or periodically summarizing material that is read, and jump to the conclusion that they are not trying hard to learn. But these habits of learning take effort initially and only gain momentum over time. Once acquired, they can become second nature to the learner, freeing up attentional resources for other, more cognitively demanding aspects of a task.

There are many ways to establish a habit, such as classical conditioning.[4] Ivan Pavlov's research on classical conditioning is so well known that it appears in cartoons: Pavlov noticed that a dog automatically salivates when it is presented with food. Cleverly, he began playing a bell whenever he presented the dog with food. Soon he observed that the dog salivated when it heard the bell, even when no food was present. Classical conditioning such as this can be viewed as a form of adaptation to the environment, in the sense that salivation aids the digestion of food.

Although conditioning is an adaptive learning process, sometimes it can lead to undesirable consequences, as in some acquired taste aversions, or in the case of abused children who learn antisocial strategies for protecting themselves. For example, cancer patients who become nauseated from chemotherapy drugs may begin to feel nauseated even when thinking about the drugs or when eating a food they had previously eaten before a treatment (Bernstein et al., 1982).

Conditioned learning is so basic to survival and adaptation that it extends beyond just mental processing to also include adaptive patterns of processing in the body. For example, there is evidence that the immune system is subject to classical conditioning. Researchers have found that reactions of the immune system can be suppressed or enhanced as a learned response to a taste stimulus (Ader et al., 2001; Schedlowski et al., 2015). This work has given rise to the new interdisciplinary field known as psychoneuroimmunology, which explores possibilities for using conditioning of the immune system to fight disease. For our purposes, it highlights that learning is a fundamental

---

[4] One of the characteristics of habit learning is that it is gradual. However, classical conditioning is not always gradual. Even a single exposure to a taste that later results in a stomach ache may result in avoidance of that flavor (García et al., 1955). We nonetheless include classical conditioning in this section on habit formation because it is one of the major mechanisms through which habits are formed.

property of humans and of all animals. It is not only our minds that are shaped by experience; even our bodies are.

Observational Learning

People also learn by observing and modeling others' behavior, attitudes, or emotional expressions, with or without actually imitating the behavior or skill. Humans' talent, rare among animals, for observational learning has been called "no-trial learning" (Bandura, 1965) because it is even faster than the one-trial learning observed in animals that have a strong built-in tendency to form certain associations (e.g., between the taste of a food and a subsequent stomach ache). Learning by observation allows the learner to add new behaviors to his repertoire while minimizing the costs of trial-and-error learning, and it often can proceed without any explicit feedback.

Learning by observation is a sophisticated skill requiring advanced cognitive capacities for imitation, interpretation, and inference (Blackmore, 2000). It requires the learner to observe something that may not be immediately visible (such as an attitude or recipe), and figure out how to reproduce what she has observed. Martina likely learns about how to improve aspects of her guitar playing through watching and listening carefully as her teacher plays, even if neither she nor the teacher could describe in words every aspect of what she is learning.

The human penchant for learning by observation underscores the importance of the social milieu of the learner, a connection that has long been established. Studies by Bandura and colleagues beginning in the 1960s established the role of observational learning and social modeling in learning and motivation (Bandura, 1989; Bandura et al., 1961, 1963). The researchers found that for modeling to be a successful learning method, learners must not only pay attention to the critical components of the modeled behavior but also ignore irrelevant features of the behavior or skill; they must also be able to remember and replicate what they have observed. The Foldit players in our third learning scenario benefit from observational learning as they follow both general strategies and particular solutions they see their peers do. They organize teams, online forums, and recipe repositories specifically to promote their own observational learning.

Various factors may influence observational learning. For example, an individual's perception of his own potential role and goal with respect to the behavior being observed influences how well he reproduces the learning behavior (Lozano et al., 2006; Zacks et al., 2001). But, it has long been known that people readily take cues for how to behave from others, particularly from authority figures such as teachers or parents but also from peers (Schultz et al., 2007). Peer observation is a key source of information about *descriptive norms*: standards for conduct among socially related people, which are acquired by seeing how peers actually do behave. By contrast, *injunctive norms* describe how people *should* behave and are traditionally provided by higher authorities. Both descriptive and injunctive norms contribute to learning in social settings.

Descriptive norms are especially influential to learning (Cialdini, 2007). For example, people are more likely to litter when they observe a lot of other litter on the ground, even though they know that littering is against the official rules. Messages such as "Many people litter. Don't be one of them!" may have the paradoxical effect of increasing littering because it suggests a descriptive norm that littering is commonly tolerated (Cialdini et al., 1990). Teachers and parents frequently lament that students seem to pay more attention to what their peers do than to advice given by more authoritative voices. However, this tendency to favor descriptive norms has been harnessed by the "peer learning" approach, which encourages learners to interact with and teach each other (Crouch and Mazur, 2001; Slavin, 2016). Understanding of descriptive norms highlights the need to establish classroom cultures that promote high-quality peer learning, especially through descriptive norms (Hurley and Chater, 2005).

Empirical studies also illustrate cultural differences in observational learning. For example, working with pairs of American and Mayan children ages 5 to 11, Correa-Chávez and Rogoff (2009) showed one child how to construct a novel toy while the other child was nearby doing a similar activity independently, without explicit instruction. They then asked the second child to attempt the task in the structured teaching situation. The researchers found that the children who first worked independently had learned from observing the other children. They also noted that the children's observational learning differed, depending on their cultural community as well as their degree of exposure to Western schooling (in the case of the Guatemalans). In this study, the Mayan children were more likely to watch intently as the other child was given instruction, while the American children, and the Mayan children with more exposure to Western education, were more likely to focus exclusively on their own task rather than watching. The children who learned the most during the waiting period were from families with the most traditional Mayan practices.

Implicit Pattern Learning

Observational learning is not the only way a person can learn without receiving external feedback or rewards. *Implicit pattern learning*, also called *statistical learning*, involves the learning of regular patterns in a particular environment without actively intending to do so. This kind of learning requires extended exposure to a pattern sufficient for unconscious recognition of regularities in an otherwise irregular context, without conscious attention and reflection (Willingham et al., 1989). Statistical learning is observed in many species and across age groups in humans, and it is relatively unrelated to IQ; even infants can do it (Cleeremans, 1996). In a 1996 study, researchers exposed 8-month-old infants to a 2-minute, continuous, monotone stream of speech that was random except for a repeated pattern of several nonsense words made up of three syllables (e.g., "bi-da-ku") (Saffran et al., 1996). Even though there was no gap between the words, the infants showed a novelty preference after this exposure, listening longer to new nonsense words than the nonsense words they had already encountered.

Language learning is a good example of statistical learning because people spontaneously and without conscious effort use the regularities that language contains to produce their own utterances (Bybee and McClelland, 2005). Imagine hearing a new verb, "sniding," which means, "to try to humiliate somebody with a disparaging remark." To use the verb in the past tense you might say, "he snided his cousin," applying the regular "+ed" way of forming a past tense, or, "he snid his cousin," basing your verb form on other similar irregular verbs such as "hide→hid," "slide→slid" and "bite→bit." You might even say, "he snode his cousin," but you probably would not say "snood," "snade," or "snud" because without realizing it you have learned the rules for indicating past tense in English.

Learning patterns without feedback generally requires extended experience with an environment and is gradual. The regularities learned in this fashion may not be easily verbalized because they are not the result of explicit hypothesis formation and testing. Figure 3-2 shows how a learner can extract patterns from an environment without a teacher or parent providing feedback. In this environment, 80 circles varying in size and color are distributed in distinctive clusters. Even if none of the circles is categorized or given a label, it is possible to see that they fall into four clumps. Many real-world categories are clumpy in exactly this way. For example, the category *bird* encompasses several properties that are correlated with each other, such as nesting in trees, laying eggs, flying, singing, and eating insects. Other categories such as *snakes* and *fish* have different constellations of correlated properties (Rosch and Mervis, 1975). Learners often come to recognize which attributes define categories simply through observation over time; even very young children recognize, for example, that it would be a strange, improbable animal that borrows hissing and scales from snakes but feathers and chirping from birds.

Perceptual and Motor Learning

We have seen that some types of learning are unconscious and some require deliberate intention. Perceptual and motor learning are ways that an individual learns skills primarily through sensory experiences. This type of learning may take place without the learner being able to put into words how it occurred, but it may be deliberately pursued. Learning to hear the difference

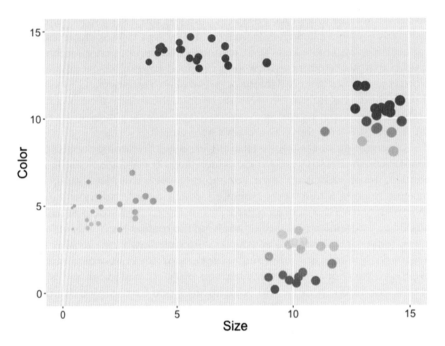

FIGURE 3-2 *Pattern recognition.*
NOTE: Imagine a world that contained these 80 circles that vary in their size and color. Individuals are able to assign clusters to the circles without receiving any feedback. For example, they may cluster the circles by their location in the graph, by color, by size, etc.

between major and minor chords, practicing a golf or tennis swing, improving one's skill at smoothly maneuvering a car, or learning (as a dermatologist) to distinguish between benign and malignant skin growths are all examples of this type of learning. Skills learned this way gradually increase over a protracted course of years, or decades, of practice. Different training regimes may accelerate skill training, but there is usually no simple shortcut that will yield skilled performance without long hours of practice; it is doing the activity, not being explicitly instructed, that brings the gains (Ericsson, 1996).

Motor learning, such as learning how to swim, ride a bicycle, or play a guitar chord without a buzzing sound, is often highly specific. That is, if a person who has learned to play guitar is asked to switch which hand strums and which hand fingers the chords, she will suddenly regress to a nearly novice level (Gilbert et al., 2001). This high degree of specificity has been associated with changes to brain areas that are activated rapidly after an object is shown and are specialized for perception. It is easy to forget how dramatically people's perceptions and actions can be changed by experience because once they have changed, the individual no longer has access to the earlier perception.

People learn from the world through their senses, but these same senses are changed by that learning. Both perceptual and motor learning can lead to surprisingly robust changes in the perceptual system. A striking demonstration of this is a phenomenon known as the McCollough Effect (McCollough, 1965), in which a very brief exposure to some objects can have a relatively long-lasting influence on the continued experience of other objects.

As an example, look at the pattern in Figure 3-3 and confirm that the vertical and horizontal striped quadrants appear black and white. Then, alternate between looking at the red and green stripe patterns in Figure 3-4 for 3 minutes, looking at each pattern for 2 to 3 seconds at a time. Now look back at the pattern of four quadrants in Figure 3-3. The quadrants with the vertical lines should appear red-tinged, and the quadrants with the horizontal lines should appear green-tinged. Celeste McCollough's explanation, which continues to receive empirical confirmation, is that there is adaptation in early stages of visual processing in the brain to combinations of orientation and

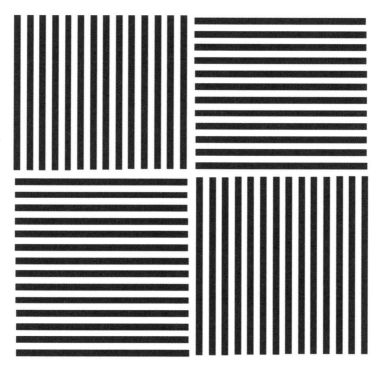

FIGURE 3-3 *The McCullough effect, part 1. See instructions in text for viewing these patterns before turning the page to view Figure 3-4.*
SOURCE: Adapted from McCullough (1965).

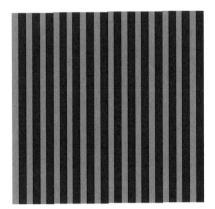 

FIGURE 3-4 *The McCullough effect, part 2. Before studying these images, see the instructions in the text for viewing Figure 3-3 first.*
SOURCE: Adapted from McCullough (1965).

color. This adaptation, which creates orientation-specific reference points to which subsequent colored bars are compared, is surprisingly robust. As little as 15 minutes of exposure to the red and green stripes can make people see color differences in the quadrants lasting for 3.5 months (Jones and Holding, 1975). If you followed the viewing instructions above, your experience of the world in just 3 minutes has had a durable and hard-to-suppress influence on how you see it.

Figures 3-5 and 3-6 show another example of how a very brief experience can rapidly alter future perceptions. Look at Figure 3-5 first, before you view Figure 3-6. If, like most people, you are not able to identify all four of the objects in the images shown in Figure 3-5, you may experience the frustrating but gripping phenomenon of not being able to form a coherent interpretation of your visual world. Now look at Figure 3-6. The images in this figure provide hints that will make the images in Figure 3-5 readily interpretable. If you now go back to view the images in Figure 3-5, you will most likely not be able to return to your naïve state of incomprehension. The striking difference between how the images in Figure 3-5 appeared to you before and after the clarifying experience of seeing Figure 3-6 provides a compelling, rapid analog for the greater, often gradually accumulated, power of experience to change what we see.

Perceptual-motor learning can also play a large role in the development of academic knowledge. Not only does it support abilities to see and discriminate letters for reading, it also supports what Goodwin (1994) called "professional vision." Goodwin described the ways in which training in archeology involves changes to how one perceptually organizes objects of inquiry, such as the texture and color of dirt found at an excavation site.

FIGURE 3-5 *Unaided pattern interpretation.*
NOTE: Can you identify the object hidden in the upper-left image and the animals in the three black and white images? Try for a few moments, and if you cannot, look at Figure 3-6 for hints. Once you see the Figure 3-6 images, then see the objects in the images here, you probably will never be able to "unsee" the objects, so savor the moment of incomprehension before looking at the hints.
SOURCES: The photographer for the upper-left image is unknown (see, for example, http:// www.slate.com/blogs/bad_astronomy/2016/05/18/sometimes_a_cigar_isn_t_just_a_ cigar.html), but one of the early sources for it is Arron Bevin's Facebook page: https://www. facebook.com/Bevvoo/posts/487921018070478). The remaining three images are committee-generated.

It is possible to organize instructional experiences that maximize people's abilities to leverage perceptual learning. Kellman and colleagues (2010) developed brief online modules to support perceptual learning in mathematics. Students using the modules make quick decisions for 120 problems. For instance, they have to decide which of three equations, all using similar num-

FIGURE 3-6 *Hints for pattern interpretation in previous figure.*
NOTE: Once you see the clear cigar, frog, zebra, and penguin in these images, you will easily see them in Figure 3-5. In fact, it may be impossible for you not to see them.
SOURCE: Images are from https://www.flickr.com/creativecommons and are available under a public domain creative commons license. The photographers are Gabriel González (frog), Laura Wolf (zebra), and nchans (penguin).

bers but differing in operators (e.g., 3X + 5 versus –3x + 5), goes with a given graph and which of three graphs goes with a given equation. After choosing an answer, students simply see the correct answer without explanation. The goal is to have the students see the structure, not explain it. The juxtapositions of the similar equations and similar graphs create contrasting cases as in wine tasting, exploring near contrasts helps people learn to perceive the distinctive features. Twelfth-grade students who completed the module nearly tripled their abilities to translate between graphs and equations, even though they had previously completed algebra.

The importance of perceptual learning for academic topics can easily be underestimated. One reason is that experts may not realize how much of their understanding stems from perceptual learning. As mentioned previously, once one has learned how to see something, it is hard to remember what it looked like when one was a novice. Experts may not realize that novices cannot see what they themselves see because it seems so self-apparent to their perception.

Learning of Facts

Humans have many reasons to learn facts and information, such as the elements of the periodic table or the factors that ushered in the industrial revolution, and they may do so intentionally or without realizing it. A single exposure to a striking fact, such as that human and koala bear fingerprints are highly similar, could be sufficient for a listener to remember and subsequently recall it, though he may forget when and where he learned it.

Although fact learning may seem mundane and highly restrictive in what it can mobilize a learner to do, it is a kind of learning at which humans excel, compared to other animals. It allows educators to impart information efficiently to learners by harnessing the power of language. The power and convenience of being able to simply say something to somebody and have it change their behavior is undeniable. A naturalist who tells a hiker about the likely consequences of eating the mushroom *Amanita phalloides* conveys information that would be impractical, if not deadly, for the hiker to learn from experience.

Although a fact might be learned in a single exposure or from being told, it is important to note that this apparent efficiency and directness can be misleading. Facts are rarely learned in a single instance, and accurate generalizations are rarely learned from a single example. It is generally only in cases where learners have substantial background knowledge already that one example or one instance of exposure can suffice (e.g., the hiker would need to already know a lot about poison and mushrooms to appreciate the information about *Amanita phalloides*). Moreover, a considerable body of research on memory shows that repeated opportunities to retrieve facts strengthen memory, particularly if they are spread over time, location, and learning contexts (Benjamin and Tullis, 2010; see Chapter 6).

Fact learning need not be rote: It is promoted when learners elaborate by connecting the information to be learned with other knowledge they already have (Craik and Tulving, 1975). One could simply try to memorize that Christopher Columbus was born in 1451, or one could connect this fact to others, such as that the Eastern Roman Empire (Byzantium) fell 2 years after Columbus was born (with the fall of Constantinople in 1453), a connection that adds meaning to both facts. Organizing items to be remembered into related groups makes them easier to retain (Bower et al., 1969), as does forming strong mental images of the information (Sadoski and Paivio, 2001). Taxi drivers have better memory for street names when they are part of a continuous route than if the street names are presented in random order (Kalakoski and Saariluoma, 2001). All of these results are unified by the notion that facts that are placed into a rich structure are easier to remember than isolated or disconnected ones.

Learning by Making Inferences

To make sense of their world, people often have to make inferences that while not certain to be correct, are necessary to move forward. The philosopher Charles Sanders Peirce used the term "abductive reasoning" to describe this type of inference. He described it as forming a possible explanation for a set of observations. As an example of this type of reasoning, John Couch Adams and Urbain Jean Joseph Leverrier inferred that a previously undetected planet of a particular mass must be located beyond Uranus, based on observations of Uranus' deviations from its predicted orbit. Following up on this prediction, Johann Gottfried Galle discovered Neptune in 1846.

Chemistry students inferring that substances are "acid" or "base" and hypothesizing possible electrostatic interactions between them is another example of abduction (Cooper et al., 2016). However, abduction is not only practiced by scientists. The dog owner who sees dog footprints on the dining room tablecloth, a spilled glass of wine, and an empty hotdog bun is using abduction when she assumes the worst. Even modern machine-learning systems have shown that abductive inference is important for making efficient learning possible. Such systems can inspect their world and infer in human-like ways which processes created the objects they see. When they use abductive reasoning, they can learn more from less data and better generalize what they have learned to new situations (see Figure 3-7; Lake et al., 2015, 2017; Tenenbaum et al., 2011).

Model building is an important special case of abductive inference that people use when seeking to understand complex phenomena. Educators and others often use models to teach and explain. A three-dimensional pictorial, diagrammatic, or animated model of the Earth, Moon, and Sun can help students grasp how night-day, tidal, and seasonal cycles are generated. Adults may often rely on established models such as the circle of fifths in music theory, but people also develop their own models in many circumstances, for example to try to understand the most economical way to manage their home heating system. Models are powerful tools for making inferences in novel situations, but almost all models can yield incorrect predictions in circumstances that do not fit, so it is important to consider the purposes for which they are used. For example, the Newtonian laws of physics are adequate for predicting the movement of planets in the solar system, but they fall short of accurately

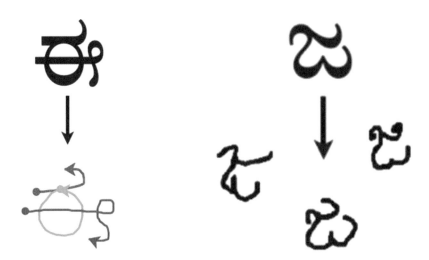

FIGURE 3-7 *Abductive reasoning in a machine-learning system.*
NOTE: When a new character (the well-drawn black character in the upper left) is shown to a machine-learning system, the system infers which handwriting strokes were involved in producing the character—the red, green, and blue strokes on the left. By inferring these strokes, the system is able to both produce new instances of a character (shown on the upper right) when shown only a single example and correctly categorize new instances of the character (imperfect instances shown in lower right).
SOURCE: Lake et al. (2015, Fig. 1).

predicting black holes (which are much more massive than anything Newton knew) or subatomic particles.

The primary advantage of model-based learning is that the learner who is equipped with an apt model can make good predictions about new situations that go well beyond the originally experienced situations. For example, if a learner has a model of water as being composed of molecules whose random movements increase with the water's temperature, then he might be able to predict that a drop of food coloring will diffuse faster in hot water than cold; a bit of experimentation will reveal that he is correct (Chi et al., 2012).

Overcoming model-based misconceptions is a major goal in formal education (Clement, 2000). Figure 3-8 illustrates how students may reconcile their visual experience of the Earth as flat with their teacher's instruction that the Earth is spherical, by concluding that Earth is shaped like a pancake (or disc): people do not fall off the round (flat) Earth because they live on the top portion of the pancake! A typical strategy for addressing this sort of misconception is to first understand what the students' model is (Osbourne

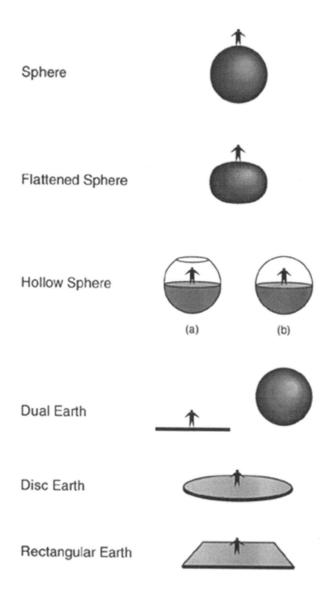

Sphere

Flattened Sphere

Hollow Sphere

(a)   (b)

Dual Earth

Disc Earth

Rectangular Earth

FIGURE 3-8 *Children's mental models of the Earth.*
NOTE: Elementary school-age children were asked a series of questions about the shape of the Earth. Their responses to these questions were inconsistent: Many children said that the Earth is round but also stated that it has an end or edge from which people could fall. In these responses, it seemed that the children used a mental model of the Earth other than the spherical Earth model. Five alternative mental models of the Earth were identified: the rectangular Earth, the disc Earth, the dual Earth, the hollow sphere, and the flattened sphere.
SOURCE: Vosniadou and Brewer (1992, Fig. 1, p. 549).

and Freyberg, 1985), then to present challenges to that model by raising analogies and special cases, and eventually to offer improved models (Brown and Clement, 1989; Chi, 2009).

Because the models that people use to help them reason and act are often implicit, children and adults rarely critique their own models. People may only discover that alternative models for a situation are even possible when they encounter one. For example, two common but incompatible models for home heat control are the "valve model" and the "feedback model" (Kempton, 1986). According to the valve model, the temperature at which the thermostat is set determines how hard the furnace works to produce heat. That is, higher temperature settings make the furnace run harder, much as further depressing a gas pedal on a car makes the engine rev up more and more. According to the feedback model, the thermostat sets the threshold below which the furnace turns on, but the furnace runs at a constant rate.

These different models drive very different home heating behaviors. If two people come home to a 55 °F home and would like it to be 65 °F, the valve theorist might set the thermostat to 75 °F because she wants the house to warm up quickly, whereas the feedback theorist would set it to exactly 65 °F, realizing that setting the thermostat higher than 65 °F will not make the house warm up to 65 °F any faster. Applying the common but inaccurate valve model wastes both energy and money.

In other cases, different models exist not because some people are wrong but because of culture differences. What is considered rude behavior in a business meeting, which direction to push or pull a saw, and conceptions of time reflect varying models that are neither correct nor incorrect. A study that illustrates this point examined views of the future among U.S. residents and members of the Aymara people of the Andes region (Núñez and Cooperrider, 2013). The researchers found that whereas the U.S. residents tended to conceive of the future as spatially in front of them, the Aymara participants conceived of it as spatially behind them (perhaps because it is invisible). Such differences can cause misunderstanding and miscommunications when a member of one culture comes to a new culture; these problems occur not because of weak cognitive capabilities but because of a cultural mismatch of models. Learners and instructors may not recognize the extent to which their models are not shared (Pronin et al., 2002).

Despite the potential for misunderstanding, it is difficult to imagine an area of advanced human creative or scholarly pursuit that does not involve models: the artist's model of complementary and analogous colors, the medical model of blood sugar–insulin regulation, the historian's use of Marxist accounts of class struggles, the double helix model of DNA, and the physicist's model of atomic and subatomic particles are just a few examples. The power of model-based learning in education has been showcased in the Next Generation Science Standards and Common Core Mathematics standards[5] because models make it easier for learners to describe, organize, explain, predict, and communicate to others what they are learning.

While experts in virtually all domains see the value of hypothesizing models because they are trying to organize a wealth of observations, sometimes early learners are not as convinced of the value of models because they may seem speculative, indirect, and invisible. This student resistance can be reduced by facilitating better learning of and with models through use of spatial representations, diagrams, animations, and interactive computer simulations (see Chapter 6).

Creating models for themselves, rather than simply using models suggested by others, can be a beneficial activity for learners (VanLehn et al., 2016). The value of constructing models for understanding and organizing material has been associated with specific learning approaches, including discovery learning, inquiry-based learning, problem-based learning, learning by invention, learning by doing, and constructivism. In each of these approaches learners are encouraged to either discover for themselves or explore with guidance the applicable rules, patterns, or principles underlying a phenomenon (Bruner, 1961). Foldit players demonstrate remarkable learning by creating models when they program (code) new computer algorithms to help in their efforts to fold proteins, sometimes learning how to program just so that they can create tools to help them play the game better (Khatib et al., 2011). Likewise, Schwartz and colleagues (2005) showed that if children are prompted by a teacher to use mathematics, they could use their mathematical knowledge to model the complex causal relationship between distance and weight to determine balance on a scale.

Inferential learning is likely most effective when the learner receives some guidance. For example, someone making yogurt for the first time might want to determine experimentally how the fat content of milk affects the firmness, acidity, and smoothness of the yogurt. In a pure case of discovery learning, this cook would develop the question, experimental methods, measures, and analyses. However, without some guidance, beginning learners may not know enough to ask good questions or identify critical variables, and they may become frustrated because of lack of progress (Mayer, 2004; Spencer, 1999). Research has shown that allowing learners to experiment on their own, with no guidance (unassisted discovery), does not improve learning outcomes (Alfieri et al., 2011).

Guided, or assisted, discovery learning is an approach in which the educator provides a level of guidance tailored so that the task is at a level of difficulty that fits the learner. (This approach builds on the notion of the

---

"zone of proximal development," or "sweet spot," proposed by Vygotsky in the 1930s. Ways to do this include providing just-in-time access to critical knowledge, worked-out examples, assistance with hypothesis generation, and advice as needed. This approach allows learners to take ownership of the construction of their own knowledge. Evidence suggests that learners who engage with these types of learning resources, rather than learning by rote, are more likely to retain the knowledge beyond the original context of instruction (Lee and Anderson, 2013).

Integrating Types of Learning

Most learning experiences involve multiple types of learning, not just one. For example, collaborative learning and problem solving in teams would engender learning by observation, feedback, facts, rules, and models, as well as possibly other types of learning. At the same time, research supports the principle that different situations and pedagogical strategies promote different types of learning. Before a teacher or learner can design an ideal learning situation, she has to decide what kind of learning she is trying to achieve. For example, one generalization that has emerged from decades of research is that promoting memory for specific facts requires different learning experiences than promoting knowledge that is transferable to new situation (Koedinger et al., 2013). Techniques focused on improving memory include spacing practice over time, rather than massing all practice at a single time; practicing retrieval of memorized information, rather than just studying the information again; and exposing learners to materials in different settings. By contrast, techniques focused on promoting transfer to new situations include comparing and contrasting multiple instances of concepts; having students reflect on why a phenomenon is or is not found; and spending time developing powerful models, rather than asking learners to simply repeat back what they are told. Chapter 5 discusses in more detail techniques for supporting different types of learning.

LEARNING AND THE BRAIN

One of the most striking advances in learning sciences in the past 15 years has been in understanding the protracted course of brain development, which begins in utero and continues well into adulthood. Several reports have examined the research on brain development and the implications for learning. *From Neurons to Neighborhoods: The Science of Early Childhood Development* (National Research Council and Institute of Medicine, 2000) drew attention to evidence that infants are born able and ready to learn, that early childhood experiences and relationships are critical to development, and that individual biology and social experiences are equally influential in determining developmental outcomes. *Transforming the Workforce for Children Birth Through Age 8: A Unifying Foundation* (Institute of Medicine and National Research Council, 2015) and a review of the literature by Leisman and colleagues (2015) identified key findings from recent research on early brain development as it affects lifelong learning. Among these findings are the following:

- Experience and genetics both contribute to observed variability in human development.
- The human brain develops from conception through the early 20s and beyond in an orderly progression. Vital and autonomic functions develop first, then cognitive, motor, sensory, and perceptual processes, with complex integrative processes and value-driven and long-term decision making developing last.
- Early adversity can have important short- and long-term effects on the brain's development and other essential functions.

Prenatal and Lifelong Brain Development and Maturation

The prenatal period is marked by an astounding rate of formation of new neurons, synapses, and myelinated axons—with the result that the brain has more of these structural elements than it needs. This development continues after birth: the brain increases fourfold in size during the preschool years and reaches approximately 90 percent of adult brain volume by age 6 (Lenroot and Giedd, 2006). Beginning in early childhood, this explosion in growth, which continues until adolescence, is the result of the dramatic increase in synaptic connections among neurons (gray matter) and in the myelination of nerve fibers (white matter) (Craik and Bialystok, 2006).

Although vigorous growth continues, the synapses and neurons are also pruned, a process that continues until after puberty. This pruning occurs in a specific way: the synapses that are continually used during this period are retained, while those that are not used are eliminated (see Low and Cheng, 2006, for more on synaptic pruning). The removal of unnecessary or unused synapses and neurons improves the "networking" capacity of the brain and the efficiency of the cortex (Chechik et al., 1999). Because this pruning is influenced by environmental factors, the developing child's experiences determine which synapses will be strengthened and which will not, laying a critical foundation for future development and learning (see Box 3-1). Just as strategic placement and pruning of plants yields a healthy garden, a balance between strengthening of some connections and pruning of others fosters healthy brain development: having more neurons left alive is not a better outcome.

BOX 3-1 Critical and Sensitive Periods in Development

Landmark vision studies by Wiesel and Hubel (1965) helped to define and differentiate the concepts of critical and sensitive periods for early cognitive development. These studies defined critical periods of development as times in which the brain requires certain environmental stimuli to organize its physical development. The best-known example of a critical period is that for development of vision: without the opportunity for sight during certain periods of infancy, the brain will forever be visually impaired. Sensitive periods are similar to critical periods but less fixed. For example, it is thought that both a loving relationship with a caretaker early in infancy and throughout toddlerhood and early exposure to language are essential for healthy brain development. Yet the boundaries are fuzzier for the developmental time periods in which exposure to strong relationships and good language are essential; the effects of deprivation and possibilities for catching up later are imprecise. There is also mounting evidence that adolescence is a second sensitive period for exposure to high-quality social relationships (Crone and Dahl, 2012).

Both critical and sensitive periods influence later development: an interruption (e.g., insufficient or inappropriate stimulation) during these times leads to difficulty (or even inability) to process in the affected domain later in life. The importance of these periods is further evidence for the vital importance of high-quality early childhood education, particularly for children who are at risk (Chaudry et al., 2017).

Sensitive periods can also be associated with negative outcomes. For example, research with animals (usually rats) has consistently shown that exposure to alcohol in adolescence greatly increases the risk for alcohol overconsumption in adulthood and that this effect is exacerbated under conditions of social isolation. In rats with genetic predispositions to mental disorders similar to schizophrenia in humans, both alcohol consumption and social isolation increase the risk of developing the disorder. Though these effects cannot be explored through causal experiments on humans for ethical reasons, the evidence points strongly to the same adolescent sensitivity in humans: those who begin drinking alcohol in adolescence are more likely to abuse substances later in life, and among people with predispositions to mental illness, social isolation and substance abuse in adolescence can be triggers (see Silveri, 2012).

Environmental stimulation and training can affect brain development throughout the life span (Andersen, 2003; Diamond et al., 1964; Leisman, 2011). The organization of cortical and subcortical signaling circuits, which are integrated into networks with similar functions, also occurs during this period. In other words, as the learner acquires new knowledge, regions of the cortex develop specialization of function. This is known as experience-dependent learning (see Andersen, 2003; Greenough et al., 1987; Leisman et al., 2014). These structures and associated circuits underlie the neural systems for complex cognitive and socioemotional functions such as learning and memory, self-regulatory control, and social relatedness, as discussed in a 2009 National Academies report (National Research Council and Institute of Medicine, 2009).

Beginning in the fourth decade of life, changes occur in both cortical thickness and connectivity that seem to be the start of the cognitive decline often observed in aging adults. These changes occur after a period during which the parts of the brain that support learning seem to be stable with respect to gross physiological features. The changes are illustrated in Figure 3-9, in which warm colors (red, orange, yellow) indicate greater cortical thickness. As the

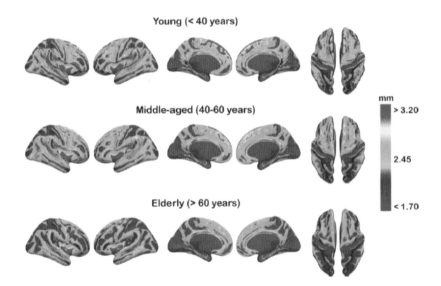

FIGURE 3-9 *Mean cortical thickness across the adult life span.*
NOTE: The figure shows the mean cortical thickness in the right and left hemispheres for three age groups (individual participant data pooled into respective age groups).
SOURCE: Fjell et al. (2009, Fig. 2).

figure shows, the brains of healthy middle-aged adults (40–60 years) have less cortical thickness compared to the brains of healthy individuals under 40 years of age, though it is not clear whether this is the result of decreases in brain tissue or, for example, lower hydration levels. These effects are found across the cortex, although they are larger in some areas (e.g., the prefrontal cortex) than others (e.g., anterior cingulate; see Fjell et al., 2009).

Brain Adaptation in Response to Learning

The brain operates as a complex interconnected system, rather than as a collection of discrete processors (Bassett et al., 2011; Medaglia et al., 2015). Different parts of the brain do not act in isolation but instead interact with one another, exchanging information through extraordinarily complex networks (Sporns, 2011). There is no learned skill that uses only one part of the brain, and there is no one part of the brain with a singular function. Instead, the brain systems that support learning and academic skills are the same brain systems that are integral to personhood—that is, to social, cognitive, emotional, and cultural functioning and even to health and physiological survival (Farah, 2010; Immordino-Yang and Gotlieb, 2017).

Moreover, learners dynamically and actively construct their own brain's networks as they navigate through social, cognitive, and physical contexts. It has been assumed that brain development always leads the way in cognitive development and learning, but in fact the brain both shapes and is shaped by experience, including opportunities the individual has for cognitive development and social interaction. The reciprocal interactions in learning between the dynamically changing brain and culturally situated experience form a fascinating developmental dance, the nuances of which are not yet fully understood. A person's brain will develop differently depending on her experiences, interpretations, needs, culture, and thought patterns (Hackman and Farah, 2009; Immordino-Yang and Fischer, 2010; Kitayama and Park, 2010). In addition, features internal to the brain's development and structure will constrain the way a person engages with the world.

The brain has remarkable capacity to adapt to phenomena that are new, such as cultural innovations or new challenges. Researchers continue to develop new insights in this area, but one particularly intriguing finding is that adaptation can take place in a time frame far shorter than has been traditionally associated with evolution. Written language and written, symbolic mathematics are two classes of skill with which the human species has not collectively had long experience. Numerous archeological artifacts for both written language and mathematics date back to the Sumerians of Mesopotamia, but it is likely that neither has existed for more than 6,000 years. Despite this relatively short history, specific neural regions are implicated in reading and mathematical reasoning (Amalric and Dehaene, 2016; Dehaene and Cohen, 2011). How might this occur?

Sharing and Recycling of Neural Tissue

First, people solve new cognitive tasks by reusing brain regions and circuits that likely originally evolved for other purposes (Anderson, 2015a; Bates, 1979). Research has shown that just as multiple types of learning blend in practice, circuits in the brain also combine in diverse ways in different types of learning. One might expect that different types of learning depend on different neural mechanisms, but seemingly very different types of learning behavior share brain circuitry. For example, the hippocampus is heavily involved in fact and rule learning as well as spatial navigation, but it is also centrally important for statistical learning (see section above on "Implicit Pattern Learning"; also see Schapiro and Turk-Browne, 2015). This finding may seem surprising, but it is consistent with the fact that the hippocampus is involved whenever learning requires that different events or features be bound together into a single representation (see Chapter 4). This possibility for combining and recombining circuits is key to adaptation.

Research on the way blind people use the visual cortex, which normally processes visual inputs, offers a striking illustration of this circuit adaptability. In one study, for example, blind research subjects were able to recruit a particular subregion of the visual cortex—a portion associated with constructing spatial representations and relations for hearing and touch—when they were performing spatial tasks like reporting where in space they heard a sound (Renier et al., 2010). Other research has shown that activity in the spatial reasoning part of the visual cortex increased with blind study subjects' accuracy in solving auditory and tactile spatial tasks. Likewise, when sighted adults are taught to read braille, the brain regions that normally process visual, not tactile, information undergo the most significant reorganization (Siuda-Krzywicka et al., 2016). This research suggests that spatial reasoning, whether it is visual, auditory, or tactile, shares basic attributes, so parts of the brain that are normally responsible for visual tasks can be effectively reused for nonvisual spatial tasks if they are not being used for vision. Brain organization through learning is therefore more about the *character or logic* of thought than it is about the modality, such as visual or tactile (Bates, 1979; Immordino-Yang and Damasio, 2007).

"Tuning" to New Requirements

Second, the brain is sufficiently adaptive that its parts become "tuned," over an individual's life span, in response to needs and experiences. Neuroscientists use the term "tuning" to describe their observation that neural responses are strongest when the stimulation is at an ideal level, as the tones produced by the strings of a musical instrument correspond to their tautness and the position and angle at which they are struck. Neurons become tuned over time to respond in particular ways, based on the kinds of stimuli that have arrived and on how the learner has engaged with these stimuli to build experiences and skills.

Neural tuning, which occurs in response to experience, is part of the reason that individual learners' brains are organized differently. For example, the brains of people who can read show greater specialization for words than those of illiterate individuals, and learning to read as an adult engages a broader set of brain regions than does learning when young (Dehaene et al., 2010). In another striking example, Elbert and colleagues (1995) measured brain activity in the sensory cortex of violinists as their fingers were lightly touched and found greater activity in the sensory cortex for the left hand than the right hand. This is logical because a violinist needs to control each of the fingers on his left hand individually, whereas the job of the right hand, bowing, does not require manipulation of the individual fingers.

Varying Time Frames for Adaptation

The explanation of how brains come to effectively accommodate new cultural requirements intertwines three temporal scales of adaptation: (1) the slow evolution of bodies, including brains, in response to challenges to survive and reproduce; (2) the creation over human evolution of cultural innovations like stone tools, pencils, calculators, and online tutoring systems; and (3) the adaptation of an individual's brain over a lifetime to meet the demands of one's culture and one's particular role within that culture.

The slow evolution of the human brain in comparison with the faster pace of cultural changes suggests that humans' distant evolutionary past may provide hints as to what can be learned with efficiency. Humans seem to be born with certain biases,[6] such as for learning human faces and voices (Cohen-Kadosh and Johnson, 2007) or attending to objects that have long evolutionary histories of being dangerous, such as snakes and spiders. (Newer objects such as guns and electrical outlets, whose risks are culturally specific, do not elicit comparable reactions) (LoBue, 2014; Öhman and Mineka, 2001; Thrasher and LoBue, 2016). Because of these evolutionary biases, situating material to be learned in relation to the kinds of objects and contexts to which our brains have evolved to attend, such as food, reproduction, and social interactions, may improve learning outcomes.

The ability of cultural innovations to change to better fit human capabili-

---

[6] Bias in the context of learning refers to a learner's capacity to take into account knowledge she has already acquired in processing new information; see Chapter 5.

ties suggests another leverage point for learning: adapting technologies to better fit how people naturally learn. For example, technologies for immersing individuals in three-dimensional interactive worlds leverage people's naturally strong memories for objects encountered during first-person navigation, such as finding one's way to one's office (Barab et al., 2005; Dunleavy and Dede, 2013). Likewise, some computer-based dialogue tutoring systems are designed to recreate the kinds of interaction that a human student and teacher would naturally have, leveraging humans' proclivity to seek desired information from perceived experts (Graesser et al., 2014; Tomasello, 2008).

The final leverage point for change is the individual's ability to change in response to a cultural context. This ability underlies the sometimes striking differences that can be observed in learning trajectories across different cultures. For example, whereas 11-month-old Efe children living in the Ituri rainforest of the Democratic Republic of Congo can safely use a machete, middle-class 8-year-old children in America are rarely trusted with sharp knives (Rogoff, 2003). Learning trajectories are often massively influenced by the expectations and training practices within a community. Individuals are not infinitely adaptive, but the extent to which they can rise to cultural expectations when provided with opportunities and support is impressive.

Evidence of Learning-Related Changes in the Brain Throughout the Life Span

The finding that dramatic brain reorganization takes place throughout early childhood and adolescence clearly has implications for education, but linking developmental neuroscience and human behavior research directly to instructional practice and to education policy is complex (Leisman et al., 2015). Nevertheless, educators may be able to use some developmental neuroscience findings to improve instructional practice. For example, research suggests that middle and secondary school students may benefit from instruction that takes advantage of abilities (such as multitasking and planning, self-awareness, and social cognitive skills) that are controlled by the parts of the brain that undergo the most change during adolescence (Blakemore, 2010).

The sequence of cortical maturation in childhood seems to parallel developmental milestones and is reflected in behavior, with motor and sensory systems maturing earliest (Keunen et al., 2017; Lyall et al., 2016; Stiles and Jernigan, 2010). After a pre-pubertal period of cortical thickening (i.e., an increase in the number of neurons and thus the density of gray matter), there is a post-pubertal period of cortical thinning. In general, these processes are the physiological ways in which children's and adults' relationships and opportunities—including learning opportunities—and habits of mind directly shape the anatomy and connectivity of the brain. Current developmental neuroscience is largely focused on understanding how networks of communication and regulation are formed and maintained and how they subtly change with age and experience. In humans, for example, cultural experiences with particular kinds of social values and interactions shape the networks of key regions of the brain involved in social emotional and cognitive processing (see, e.g., Kitayama et al., 2017). Social engagement and cognitive activity help even elderly adults maintain a healthy brain and mind (see Chapter 8).

These facts about how the brain develops throughout life have important implications. First, the processes of brain development persist beyond the first 3 years of age and well into the second decade of life and beyond—that is, throughout the period of formal schooling for most Americans. At the same time, extensive research has revealed that the brain continues to undergo structural changes as a function of learning and experience (e.g., Draganski et al., 2004), and these changes continue into old age (e.g., Lövdén et al., 2010). This research emphasizes that a core mechanism of learning—the brain's ability to modify its connections on the basis of new experiences—functions effectively throughout the life span (see Box 3-2).

Since *HPL I* was released, scientists have learned much more about how brain development constrains and supports behavior and learning and about how opportunities to learn in turn influence brain development. For example, research with rats has shown that effects of environmental enrichment can be observed even in mature rats and that they persist well after the adult rats are returned to less-stimulating environments (Briones et al., 2004).

Most of the research regarding the effects of opportunities to learn on changes in brain structure has been conducted in rodents because conducting such studies with humans is obviously more challenging. However, limited research with humans indicates similar effects. To examine how absence of

BOX 3-2 Evidence of Expertise Development and Changes in the Brain

As people acquire knowledge, there are significant changes in their brain activity, brain structure, or both that complement the rapid increase in processing speed and effort needed to use the acquired knowledge (see Chapter 5). Changes that can be detected in gray and white matter provide one form of evidence for this connection between knowledge acquisition and brain structure. For example, Draganski and colleagues (2006) found increased gray matter in the cortices of medical students who had studied extensively for their exams over a 3-month period, compared with control

BOX 3-2 **Continued**

participants who had not experienced this intensive study period. Findings like this suggest a bidirectional relationship between learning and brain development: Learning promotes brain development, and brain development promotes learning.

A number of studies have found that experts in particular disciplines (such as sports or music) have an increase in the density of both gray matter (containing neurons) and white matter (containing neurons' connections to other neurons) that connect task-related regions of their brains, in comparison with nonexperts (Chang, 2014). These changes appear to be associated with long-term training (Roberts et al., 2013). For example, Bengtsson and colleagues (2005) found substantial differences between concert pianists and nonmusicians in the white matter architecture of specific cortical areas. Scholtz and colleagues (2009) found that similar differences resulted from training in the art of juggling. They compared the brains of people who did not know how to juggle, one-half of whom subsequently participated in a 6-week juggling course and one-half of whom did not. The differences before and after training in the two groups did not correlate significantly with the progress the trainees made or their performance levels after the training period, which suggests that the changes might have been related to the amount of time spent training or the effort expended on training, rather than to the achievement of the specific training outcome. Increases in gray matter volume in the frontal lobe have also been found in elite judo players (Jacini et al., 2009) and skilled golfers (Jäncke et al., 2009).

An important point that follows from these findings and is worth reinforcing is that cortical thickness cannot be assumed to be a good measure of expertise, knowledge, and skills. This type of neuroimaging data (brain images from a single imaging session for each subject) is collected at a specific time, and therefore it is difficult to determine whether the observed activation is stable and whether it is attributable to the experimental condition or other factors, such as differences in genetics, experience, strategy, motivation, or even hydration level (Poldrack, 2000). A single measure of cortical thickness thus provides only limited information about this complex process and may not correlate with skill level achieved.

experience (i.e., a lack of opportunity to learn) influences brain development (and therefore learning), researchers have studied the effects of early deprivation experienced by children exposed to institutional rearing. Neuroimaging studies show that early deprivation of learning opportunities of specific kinds (psychosocial, linguistic, sensory, etc.) leads to a dramatic reduction in overall brain volume (both gray and white matter) and to a reduction in electrical activity (Nelson et al., 2009). However, these researchers found that when children who were reared in deprived circumstances were placed in high-quality foster care before the age of 2, their IQs increased significantly (Nelson et al., 2007).

Consistent with the important role of culture and context underscored in Chapter 2, research has demonstrated both culturally unique and culturally universal neurological structures and functions (Ambady and Bharucha, 2009; Kitayama and Uskul, 2011). It is now known that repeated engagement in cultural practices reinforces neural pathways involved in completing such tasks, ultimately leading to changes in neural structure and function (Kitayama and Tompson, 2010).

The use of an abacus for arithmetic operations, a tool-using capability found primarily in Asian cultures, illustrates this point. Even before *HPL I*, research in psychology had suggested that abacus experts use a mental image of an abacus to remember and manipulate large numbers while solving problems (Hatta and Ikeda, 1988). Hanakawa and colleagues (2003) examined the neural correlates underlying mental calculations in abacus experts and found that these experts do in fact recruit different brain areas for mental operations tasks than do non-experts. Another example is long-term engagement in culturally embedded behavioral practices such as meditation, which leads to long-lasting changes in neural structure and function and may in some cases offset age-related cortical thinning (Braboszcz et al., 2013; Creswell and Lindsay, 2014; Davidson and Lutz, 2008; Lazar et al., 2005).

Different models have been developed to describe the conditions under which older adults recruit additional resources (see Table 3-1). Although the neural processes that underlie the observed patterns of compensatory neural recruitment are still being actively investigated, these models all emphasize that even in older age there can be flexibility in how neural networks work together and that task demands can influence the nature of those network connections. Moreover, this research emphasizes the fact that earlier life experiences can set the stage for the ability to compensate effectively (Cabeza, 2002; Kensinger, 2016; Park and Reuter-Lorenz, 2009; Reuter-Lorenz and Cappell, 2008). For example, becoming bilingual when young seems to be associated with more robust cognitive development (Bialystok, 2017) and increased cognitive resilience into old age (Bialystok et al., 2016). The lifelong, persistent demand involved in handling two language systems pushes the cognitive

TABLE 3-1 Models of Age-Related Change in Brain Structures That Affect Learning

Model	Findings
Hemispheric Symmetry Reduction in Older Adults (Cabeza, 2002)	• Older adults often recruit regions bilaterally (from both left and right cerebral hemispheres), especially within the prefrontal cortex, under conditions where younger adults only recruit regions unilaterally (from one hemisphere). • This pattern of bilateral recruitment tends to be associated with better task performance (i.e., the recruitment is compensatory).
Compensation-Related Utilization of Neural Circuits Hypothesis (Reuter-Lorenz and Cappell, 2008)	• Adults of all ages need to recruit additional (often bilateral) regions to achieve task performance. Older adults need to recruit those levels at a lower level of task difficulty than do younger adults. • This difference can lead to many task conditions under which younger adults will recruit regions unilaterally, whereas older adults will recruit regions bilaterally.
Scaffolding Theory of Aging and Cognition (Park and Reuter-Lorenz, 2009)	• Builds on the hemispheric asymmetry reduction model of Cabeza (2002) and the compensation-related utilization of neural circuits hypothesis of Reuter-Lorenz and Cappell (2008). • Emphasizes way that earlier life experiences (genetic predisposition, education, life stressors, etc.) can increase or decrease availability of compensatory resources in older age.

SOURCE: Kensinger (2016).

boundaries to accommodate this social and linguistic need (Kroll et al., 2012). The committee discusses age-related changes in learning further in Chapter 7.

Although changes in brain structures have not been directly linked to learning throughout the life span, we note several points from this research. First, although the brain is able to change and adapt throughout the life span, environmental influences in the early years lay the neural scaffolding for later learning and development (Amedi et al., 2007; Keuroghlian and Knudsen, 2007). Second, many (though not all) of the age-related changes in brain structure are gradual effects that occur throughout middle age and older adulthood. That is, not all age-related changes in brain structure are linear effects of age (e.g., Raz et al., 2005, 2010), and changes in structure can begin well before older age (e.g., Bendlin et al., 2010; de Frias et al., 2007). We also note that the age-related changes in brain structure do not affect all brain regions equally: some regions and networks of the brain are affected more substantially by age than others.

Finally, although cortical thickness, mass, and connectivity do appear to decrease with age, older adults are able to compensate for declines in some abilities by recruiting different or additional neural mechanisms. Neural plasticity, which is the ability of the brain to reorganize itself physically and functionally across the life span in response to the environment, individual behavior, thinking, and emotions—in effect, what is colloquially called "wisdom" (Sternberg, 2004)—may partly explain how older adults are able to compensate (see, e.g., Reuter-Lorenz and Cappell, 2008). Even the earliest studies comparing young and older adults' neural activation during task performance (e.g., Grady et al., 1994) revealed that older adults recruited different regions than young adults did while performing tasks. Indeed, there are few studies that have found reduced levels of neural activity generally in older adults; most studies have found reduced levels of activity in some regions but increased activity in others (Kensinger, 2016).

CONCLUSIONS

In this chapter, we examined some of the diverse types of learning that humans must orchestrate in response to the complex social and cultural environments in which they develop. We emphasized that these types of learning are not discrete functions that operate independently but aspects of a complex, interactive process. The learner shapes that process through decisions and capacities to orchestrate his learning, but many aspects of learning occur below the level of consciousness. Different situations, contexts, and pedagogical strategies promote different types of learning. We saw that many kinds of learning are promoted when the learner engages actively rather than passively, by developing her own models, for example, or deliberately developing a habit or modeling an observed behavior. We saw that learning is predicated on learners' understanding and adopting the learning goal.

In addition, we have explored structural changes that occur in the brain in response to learning and experience throughout life, as well as the processes characteristic of different life stages. We have noted that environmental influences in the early developmental years lay the foundation for later learning and development, that synaptic pruning and other neurological developments through adolescence shape and are shaped by the learner's experiences, and that the brain adapts to age-related declines in some functions by recruiting other mechanisms.

We have shown that the relation between brain development and learning is reciprocal: learning occurs through interdependent neural networks at the same time that learning and development involve the continuous shaping and reshaping of neural connections in response to stimuli and demands. Development of the brain influences behavior and learning, and in turn, learning influences brain development and brain health. We highlight three broad conclusions from this work.

> **CONCLUSION 3-1:** The individual learner constantly integrates many types of learning, both deliberately and unconsciously, in response to the challenges and circumstances he encounters. The way a learner integrates learning functions is shaped by his social and physical environment but also shapes his future learning.

> **CONCLUSION 3-2:** The brain develops throughout life, following a trajectory that is broadly consistent for humans but is also individualized by every learner's environment and experiences. It gradually matures to become capable of a vast array of complex cognitive functions and is also malleable in adapting to challenges at a neurological level.

> **CONCLUSION 3-3:** The relationship between brain development and learning is reciprocal: learning occurs through interdependent neural networks, and at the same time learning and development involves the continuous shaping and reshaping of neural connections in response to stimuli and demands. Development of the brain influences behavior and learning, and in turn, learning influences brain development and brain health.

4

Processes That Support Learning

Learning is supported by an array of cognitive processes that must be coordinated for successful learning to occur. This chapter examines key processes that support learning. We first look at the ways that learners orchestrate processes essential to learning, such as attention, emotion regulation, and inhibition of incorrect or inappropriate responses. We then discuss memory—an essential component of most, if not all, types of learning.

The committee has drawn on both laboratory- and classroom-based research for this chapter. The research related to executive function and self-regulation draws on a mix of field- and classroom-based research from cognitive science and education involving learners of various ages, as well as on laboratory-based studies. Historically, much of the research on memory was conducted with adult populations, primarily in college settings, though younger populations have also been studied. There are historical reasons why college populations have been heavily relied on in research on memory (see Appendix C). Psychology departments recruit thousands of students in introductory psychology classes to participate in experiments, and memory has been a particularly popular subject for such experiments (Benassi et al., 2014; Pashler et al., 2007). Much of the research on memory discussed in this chapter is based on college student populations, but the committee also examined available research that included more diverse populations and learning contexts.

ORCHESTRATING LEARNING

In Chapters 2 and 3, we discussed many of the resources on which learners draw and suggested that learners are able to coordinate these varied capacities—both consciously and unconsciously—as they are needed to meet learning challenges. How do people orchestrate their own learning? Three key ways are through metacognition, executive function, and self-regulation.

Metacognition is the ability to monitor and regulate one's own cognitive processes and to consciously regulate behavior, including affective behavior. The term, which derives from cognitive theory, encompasses the awareness individuals have of their own mental processes (cognitive and affective) and their consequent ability to monitor, regulate, and direct their thinking to achieve a desired objective. This capacity has been studied since the early 1980s, and *How People Learn: Mind Brain, Experience, and School: Expanded Edition* (*HPL I[1]*) noted how important it is for educators to teach learners strategies for increasing their awareness of their learning and their capacity to direct it.

Also important is *executive function,* which is more frequently addressed by psychologists and neuroscientists and refers to cognitive and neural processing that involves the overall regulation of thinking and behavior and the higher-order processes that enable people to plan, sequence, initiate, and sustain their behavior toward some goal, incorporating feedback and making adjustments.

Self-regulation refers to learning that is focused by means of metacognition, strategic action, and motivation to learn. Self-regulation is seen as involving management of cognitive, affective, motivational, and behavioral components that allow the individual to adjust actions and goals to achieve desired results.

Understanding the integration and interplay of these various levels of processing is important to understanding how learners orchestrate their learning in the context of their complex cognitive and social environments. The integration and interrelation of these dimensions of processing is also critical for *deeper or higher-order learning*, and for the development of complex skills and knowledge such as reasoning, problem solving, and critical thinking.

Executive Function

The processes involved in executive function include the abilities to hold information in mind, inhibit incorrect or premature responses, and sustain or switch attention to meet a goal. These processes are highly interrelated: successful application of executive function requires that the processes operate

---

[1] As noted in Chapter 1, this report uses the abbreviation "*HPL I*" for *How People Learn: Brain, Mind, Experience, and School: Expanded Edition* (National Research Council, 2000).

in coordination with one another. Many of the same processes are involved in socioemotional development, which contributes to children's classroom success (Institute of Medicine and National Research Council, 2015). Like Kayla, the hypothetical geometry student we discussed in Chapter 3, all learners need to choose among competing interests and then sustain attention to the chosen ones long enough to make progress, hold in mind multiple pieces of information (e.g., the equation Kayla had to apply and the symbolic notation that was the target for application), manipulate them productively, and monitor their own progress.

The fundamental neural bases of executive function are relatively well known. Early research suggested that the frontal lobes were the site of this capacity (Chung et al., 2014; Damasio, 1994), but more recent neuroimaging research has shown that the various components of executive function use many areas and networks across the brain (Collette et al., 2006, Jurado and Rosselli, 2007; Marvel and Desmond, 2010). Like the positive and negative changes in prefrontal cortical thickness and connectivity with other neural structures described in Chapter 3, the component processes of executive function develop rapidly during the preschool years, continue to develop into adolescence and even beyond, and undergo characteristic changes throughout adulthood.

Executive function is a focus of intense interest—as well as targeted educational interventions (see Box 4-1)—because impaired executive function is a feature of several conditions that may negatively affect learning, including learning disabilities (both reading and mathematical disabilities); attention deficit/hyperactivity disorder, and autism. Conversely, well-developed cognitive control is correlated with numerous positive developmental outcomes, including physical health and socioeconomic status—and even absence of a criminal conviction by age 32 (Moffitt et al., 2011). Moreover, recent research suggests that executive function (indicated by behaviors such as paying attention and following rules, for example) may be a better predictor of school readiness and academic achievement than general intelligence is (e.g., Blair and Razza, 2007; Eigsti et al., 2006; McClelland et al., 2007). Interventions that target social and emotional learning may be beneficial in part because they improve executive function (Riggs et al., 2006).

Other work on executive functioning focuses on so-called "intrinsic" executive control, or a person's ability to direct herself, change course when needed, and strategize in the absence of explicit rules to follow. For example, one study showed that 9-year-old middle-class children from Denver, Colorado, who spent more time in adult-led activities (such as piano lessons and playing on coached sports teams), and less time in self-directed and peer-negotiated activities (such as playing "pick up" sports games with other children) showed worse intrinsic executive functioning (Barker et al., 2014). The researchers concluded that the time these children spent in structured learning activities

BOX 4-1 A Curriculum-Based Executive Function Intervention

Tools of the Mind is a math and literacy program for young children specifically designed to improve executive function (Bodrova and Leong, 2007). The curriculum emphasizes social interaction in shared activities with teachers and peers. Teachers model and scaffold the use of tools for learning, such as language, number systems, and diagramming or mapping. Children interact and practice self-regulation through symbolic play and codevelopment of learning plans and goals. For example, the Numerals Game fosters cognitive set-shifting. In this math activity, children alternate in the roles of "doers" and "checkers." The activity requires that the doer count out plastic teddy bears to match a number card. The checker places the bear on a checking sheet that displays a numeral and corresponding number of dots. If the bears cover the dots and no bears remain, the children know that the number is correct. Research suggests that the use of this curriculum is related to decreases in reported behavioral problems and to improved scores on executive function tasks (Barnett et al., 2008; Diamond et al., 2007).

limited their opportunities to learn to manage themselves in natural and informal learning contexts, which are critical for effective learning in the real world. Components of executive function develop and decline in neither linear nor binary (all or nothing) fashion. Both positive and negative age-related neurocognitive changes depend on the specific executive processes being engaged (Spreng et al., 2010; Turner and Spreng, 2012). Across many domains, older adults often achieve good performance by recruiting different processes than those engaged by younger adults.

Self-Regulation of Learning

The capacity to understand and direct one's own learning is important not only in school but also throughout life. When learners are self-regulated, they have more control over the strategies and behaviors they use to learn. Self-regulation allows them to more effectively direct their cognitive activity by voluntarily setting learning goals, identifying methods for achieving them, actively pursuing those methods, and tracking progress toward the goals. Regulating one's learning requires monitoring of activities, thoughts, and emotions and making the adjustments necessary to achieve goals (Loyens et al., 2008). It also is facilitated when the expectations of educators accommodate learners' interests and developmentally appropriate work, so that learners take responsibility for their goals and perceive that they have the power to make important decisions related to their mode of learning (Patall, 2013).

Self-regulation is a key element of the broader concept of metacognition, the capacity to reflect on and monitor one's own cognitive processes. Monitoring and regulating cognition are sets of interrelated processes. Monitoring processes are those involved in assessing one's own cognitive activities, including learning and memory. The processes of regulation allow the individual to control the decision processes and actions in ways directed by his monitoring (Bjork et al., 2013; Dunlosky and Metcalfe, 2009).

The growing body of research in this area has highlighted how difficult it is for people to regulate their own learning in formal educational settings and the corresponding value of training to improve this capacity. The complex processes involved have been the subject of a considerable amount of theoretical and experimental work in the past decade (Vohs and Bauminster [2017] is a comprehensive handbook of recent research). A number of models have been proposed to characterize self-regulation processes, which suggest directions for interventions to improve learners' capacity to direct their learning (Panadero, 2017). For example, Hattie and Donoghue (2016) identified more than 400 strategies found in the research literature on learning strategies. This body of work has explored the basic regulatory processes and the influence of emotion, desire, and habits; the role of personality traits; the physiological processes involved in self-regulation and how they develop; and many other issues. (Ways that educators can foster self-regulation in their students are discussed in Chapter 7.)

Growing understanding of the variety of variables that contribute to an individual's capacity to regulate her learning complicates the task of succinctly defining what is involved. Nevertheless, the concept is generally understood to encompass personal characteristics, learning contexts, and motivational and regulatory processes, and all of these factors influence learning outcomes. Self-regulation is both a self-directive process and a set of thought patterns through which learners organize their activities to build skills. Successful self-regulated learners have developed the skills and habits to be effective learners, exhibiting effective learning strategies, effort, and persistence.

In one formulation, self-regulation is described as the interplay of the will to invest in learning, curiosity and a willingness to explore what one does not know, and the skills to pursue a deeper understanding of content (Hattie and Donoghue, 2016). Put another way, it is the "self-corrective adjustments [that] are taking place as needed [for the learner] to stay on track, whatever [the learner's] purpose is" (Carver and Scheier, 2017, p. 3). This capacity is driven from within, by intrinsic goals and responses to experience. Many factors influence self-regulation, ranging from sleep to personality traits to social and cultural influences and beyond. Research is ongoing in this field and continues to enlarge the picture of the importance and complexity of self-regulation for learning.

MEMORY

HPL I summarized research by neuroscientists and cognitive scientists on memory processes (National Research Council, 2000). This work had shown that memory is not a unitary construct that occurs in a single area of the brain. Instead, it comprises distinct types of processes associated with different memory functions. Not only are the processes of memory complex in themselves; but they also interact with other learning processes, such as the capacity to generalize (e.g., discrimination, categorization) and reason (e.g., comprehension, sense-making, causal inference).

A metaphor people commonly use to think about encoding and retrieving memories is that of spatial storage and search (Roediger, 1980). In this metaphor, the mind is imagined as a physical space and bits of knowledge (memories) are imagined as objects stored in that space. For instance, the knowledge might be pictured as a collection of books stored on shelves in a library, files stored in cabinets, or digital files stored on a computer hard drive. Accordingly, learning is imagined as a process of creating and storing new files containing different sorts of knowledge, with the hope that those files can be found when needed.

This mental file cabinet view of the mind and memory is compelling, but researchers have rejected the idea that knowledge (memories) consists of copies of experiences stored in one's mind. Instead, learning and memory systems give people the ability to produce knowledge without storing copies of it. Many other systems of the body work in a similar way. For instance, the visual system gives us the ability to perceive objects in the world, but copies of those objects are not stored in the eye. Sensory systems give us the ability to experience a wide variety of sensations without storing them in the body. Consider what happens if you were to pinch your arm and experience pain. It would be strange to say that when your arm was pinched, the pain was "retrieved" from some place where it was "stored" in your arm. Instead, sensory systems provide the appropriate architecture to convey information to the brain, which then constructs the sensory stimulation into an experience.

Reconstructing Memories

What the storage metaphor does not capture is the fact that learning actually involves skills for *reconstructing* memories based on past experiences and cues in the present environment, rather than reproducing copies of an experience. Reconstruction is made possible by the way memories are encoded and stored throughout the brain. Each individual processes memories from a subjective perspective, so that his own memories of the same information or episode will not be identical to those of another person. An important point is that reconstruction of some kinds of knowledge is so implicit and automatic that it feels fluent rather than rebuilt: for a skilled reader and writer, for example, it is not necessary to continually, consciously reconstruct memories of grammar (see Chapter 3 for discussion of types of learning).

When an individual constructs an experience, a *representation* of that experience is left behind in the brain that she may be able to draw upon in the future. The representation is not a perfect copy of the world but rather a partial record of the individual's subjective interpretation and perception, which is in turn shaped by prior knowledge, experiences, perceptual capabilities, and brain processes. The processes involved in transforming "what happens" into mental representations are known as *encoding*. Over time and with sleep, an encoded memory may be *consolidated*, a process whereby the neural connections associated with it are strengthened and the memory, or representation of the experience, is stabilized, or stored. *Retrieval* refers to the processes involved in reconstructing memories of past experiences. Retrieval processes are triggered and guided by *retrieval cues* in the learner's environment (e.g., prompts, questions, or problems to be solved) or in the learner's mind (other thoughts or ideas that have some relationship to the memory).

For example, in practicing the guitar, a student's eyes pass over the spots of ink on the sheet music and visual inputs register in the primary visual areas at the back of the brain, creating the visual part of the pattern of the music. At the same time, the sounds the student creates as he strums the guitar contribute to the pattern by registering in his auditory areas, some of which are consonant with the spots on the page and others less so. Somatosensory areas also contribute to the pattern by registering the position of the fingers on the neck of the guitar as the student plays. Although the inputs from each of the sense modalities register in different areas of the brain (together called the information-processing system), they are pulled together in what are called association areas, contributing to the unified experience of "playing music." At the same time, the association and sensory-motor brain areas contain traces of patterns remaining from previous experiences of playing the guitar and other activities and knowledge, and these are *retroactivated,* allowing the current guitar-playing experience to be enriched by the person's prior learning and expectations. For long-term skill development and learning to occur, the distributed pattern of inputs contributing to the current experience (visual, motor, auditory, emotional, etc.) must be consolidated and integrated with stored memory representations from prior experiences. This is why deliberate practice is needed for long-term robust learning.

Because they are reconstructed, memories are not frozen in time; they are reconstructed anew each time a person recalls something, and the reconstruction takes into account current knowledge, expectations, and context. For this reason, memories are not fixed but instead morph over time, and they may omit details or include fabricated details that did not occur. This is especially evident when people repeatedly remember the same event: what people report will change over time as new information and suggestions become incorporated into the rich, potentially multisensory tapestry of representations physically consolidated across the brain.

Reconstructive processes are at work even when a person remembers highly emotional and unique events, such as the attack in the United States on September 11, 2001 (9/11), as a study by Hirsch and colleagues demonstrates (Hirst et al., 2015). These researchers asked people to report on their memories of 9/11: the circumstances in which they learned about the event as well as details about the attack itself. People were surveyed about their memories at four intervals beginning approximately 1 week after the event and concluding approximately 10 years later. The researchers found that the study participants forgot many of the details they reported during the first year and that their reports, even of emotionally charged and distinctive "flashbulb memories," changed as time passed.

However, it is not only complex knowledge and events that must be reconstructed through the processes of memory. Even a simple task such as remembering a short list of words for a short amount of time requires active reconstruction. For example, when people were asked in a 1995 study to listen to short lists of related words, such as *bed, rest, tired, awake, dream,* and *snooze,* and later recall as many of the words as they could, they were highly likely to recall related words that were not on the list, such as *sleep* (Roediger and McDermott, 1995). This study showed that rather than simply reproducing encoded copies of the words, the study participants actively attempted to reconstruct even an event as simple as encountering a short word list.

The fact that the processes involved in reconstructing knowledge are driven by cues is well established in the study of memory. As early as 1923, a researcher demonstrated differences in people's capacity to recall the (then 48) U.S. states when asked to do so twice at a 30-minute interval: the only difference in the two tests was the retrieval context (Brown, 1923). The retrieval cues available in a learner's environment are critical for what she will be able to recall, and changing the retrieval context and cueing environment changes what a person expresses at any given moment in time (Tulving and Thomson, 1973). Thus, if a person fails to remember a fact or skill at a particular time, that does not necessarily mean he does not possess the necessary knowledge.

The importance of retrieval cueing has been shown for complex as well as simple learning scenarios. In another classic study, Anderson and Pichert (1978) had students read a story about a series of events in a house and then recall details from the story from one of two perspectives: the perspective of a burglar or the perspective of a person buying a home. When students shifted perspectives, they recalled new information that they had not recalled the first time. Only the retrieval conditions had changed. Students had encoded and stored the same story, but what they recalled depended on the cues to which they were attending. In a similar study, Gick and Holyoak (1980, 1983) showed that people's ability to solve a problem differed significantly with changes in the retrieval environment—in this case the instructions they received about how to use the materials they were to draw on in solving the problem.

There are two related implications of this work for educators and others interested in assessing people's learning. First, undue weight should not be placed on any single assessment of a learner's knowledge and skills. Second, memories are reconstructed more easily in situations that feel conducive and relevant to the content of the memory. The way a learner will retrieve particular knowledge and skills varies with the cues that trigger the reconstruction; the cues, in turn, are partly dependent on the emotional, social, and cognitive state of the learner at that moment. For example, a student who prides herself on baseball skills may have no trouble calling up knowledge of statistics during a game but may draw a blank in a high-stakes math test. In part to circumvent this problem, some researchers have proposed the use of dynamic assessments that present learners with multiple assessments and that may allow some form of instruction or feedback between attempts (Koedinger et al., 2012). Another strategy is to help learners recognize and leverage their strengths in other contexts. For example, an educator might remind a baseball player to think about baseball when he has trouble remembering what he knows about statistics during a math test, or encourage a young child who helps with cooking at home to connect her understanding of the proportions of ingredients to call on this knowledge when learning about formal proportionality in math class.

Working and Long-Term Memory

Information may be rehearsed in the mind just for short periods of time, for use in a particular activity, or it may be retained long term so it can be retrieved together with other experiences far in the future. Long-term memory has obvious importance for learning, but short-term, or working, memory also plays a prominent role in complex cognitive tasks and daily activities, such as mental arithmetic (e.g., calculating a tip) and reading (Moscovitch, 1992).

Working Memory

In practice, working memory is associated with academic achievement, including both math and reading skills (e.g., Bull and Scerif, 2001; Nevo and Breznitz, 2011). Keeping information temporarily in mind and manipulating it is necessary for key learning tasks such as remembering lengthy instructions or keeping track of a problem being solved, and low working-memory capacity puts children at risk for poor academic progress (Alloway and Gathercole, 2006; Alloway et al., 2009). Low working memory has also been associated with learning disabilities (e.g., Gathercole et al., 2006; Geary et al., 2012; Smith-Spark and Fisk, 2007; Wang and Gathercole, 2013) and such developmental disorders as attention deficit/hyperactivity disorder (e.g., Willcutt et al., 2005), specific language impairment (e.g., Briscoe and Rankin, 2009), and autism (e.g., Williams et al., 2006).

Working-memory performance declines beginning in middle age (Bopp and Verhaeghen, 2005; Park et al., 2002; Verhaeghen and Salthouse, 1997). The primary cause of this decline seems to be age-related difficulty in attentional control (Fabiani et al., 2006; Hasher et al., 2008). Individual differences in working-memory capacity are relatively stable over time, but recent studies suggest that intervention during childhood may have benefits for specific working-memory outcomes (Holmes et al., 2009; Thorell et al., 2009).

Long-Term Memory

There are three types of long-term memory: procedural, episodic, and semantic. Procedural or implicit memory is unconscious, but the other two involve conscious awareness of past events as episodes in one's individual history (e.g., episodic memory of meeting a friend for the first time) or facts and concepts not drawn from personal experience (e.g., semantic memory of state capitals). A complex operation such as learning to play the guitar involves the gradual and incremental processes of motor learning (using implicit memory) to improve finger work, as well as the episodic memory processes involved in trying to internalize and later repeat specific skills taught in a lesson, such as playing a particular chord sequence, semantic memory for information such as key signatures, and emotional memories of successfully playing beautiful music.

Although some memories may last a lifetime, all are reworked over time, and most fall victim to disruption and interference and are rapidly forgotten. If at some later time, the guitar student is reminded of a particular practice episode by a relevant cue or prompt and tries to recall it, he will not be able to recreate the entire episode in his memory or to play as he did before because some of the necessary representations and motor sequences will no doubt have been weakened or lost. Moreover, he will have experienced other, similar episodes of music and of playing the guitar; his memory of the practice episode may feature bits of information that were not actually part of that particular episode but are consistent with it.

The fact that new learning starts off as a distributed pattern of neural activation that must be stabilized and integrated with existing knowledge stores to be retained as long-term memory contributes to challenges for young learners. One reason is that the neural machinery they have available to register the experiences, stabilize and integrate them, and later retrieve the stored products, is relatively immature and therefore works less efficiently and effectively. Young learners (and beginners in a domain) also have fewer memories of previous experiences in similar situations to call upon, or retroactivate. Metaphorically, although the learning experience itself may be richly textured, by the time it is processed through an immature neural architecture, with a less well-developed set of cognitive, cultural, and social-emotional expectations or schema, it may lose many of its attributes and features, so that the representation of the experience (the memory) is impoverished. An adult's more mature neural structures and networks manage to retain many more of the features of the original experience. For this reason, for many domains of formal learning, young learners generally require more support, relative to older learners. At the same time, young learners may be exquisitely sensitive to certain kinds of learning, such as what they learn from parents' emotional reactions to their behaviors.

Cultural differences in long-term memory capacities have been observed, such as in several studies that compared the capacity for detailed recall of specific events among European Americans, Asians, and Asian Americans (Han et al., 1998; Mullen, 1994; Wang, 2004; Wang and Conway, 2004; for a review, see Wang and Ross, 2007, but also see Ji et al., 2009, for the opposite pattern in an academic context). These researchers have identified differences in recall in preschoolers through adults and have suggested several hypotheses to explain them. Among the hypotheses are that cultural traditions and differences, such as in the way adults talk with preschoolers about personal experiences, may lead learners to attend to different aspects of events they experience (e.g., Leichtman et al., 2000; Wang, 2009) or to tend to use personal memories differently—for example, to guide decisions or to learn moral lessons and norms (e.g., Alea and Wang, 2015; Alea et al., 2015; Basso, 1996; Kulkofsky et al., 2009; Maki et al., 2015; Nile and Van Bergen, 2015; Wang and Conway, 2004).

This research has not definitively established the existence of or basis for cultural differences, and we note the risk of overgeneralizing between-group differences. However, it does suggest that the nature and form of memory for episodes may be influenced by culture.

Memory for Episodes of Learning

Memory for episodes of new learning is critically important because it allows for rapid, even one-trial, learning and retention of new information (e.g., Bauer and Varga, 2015). It is one of the building blocks for cognitive growth during development and throughout the life span. One of the most significant changes learners experience in the first two decades of life is an increase in the amount of information they remember. As young learners develop, their memories also become more deliberate and strategic and they impose increased organization on the material they are learning (e.g., Bjorklund et al., 2009). The organizations they use to conceptualize material and to focus on different features and processes depend on their development and their environment and are therefore deeply cultural and situated. Children become increasingly aware of their own and others' memory processes as they develop (i.e., their *metamemory* improves), which enables them to recruit information-processing resources to assist with increased memory demands (see Box 4-2).

Though many memories of distinct learning episodes persist even into old age, people tend to have increased difficulty in forming memories of new episodes as they age. Normal aging is accompanied by a gradual decline in episodic memory that begins as early as the twenties and accelerates precipitously after the age of 60 (Salthouse, 2009). This decline is associated with degradation in a key aspect of episodic memory: the ability to anchor or bind an event to one's personal past and to a location (e.g., Fandakova et al., 2014; Wheeler et al., 1997). This deficit can be manifested in a number of ways.

BOX 4-2 **Helping Children Develop Memory Skills**

A few researchers have explored techniques to support memory in young children by fostering cognitive activities that increase the depth at which information is processed (Coffman et al., 2008). These techniques include making strategy suggestions, posing metacognitive questions, and structuring instructional activities in particular ways that support elaboration and connection to prior knowledge (Coffman et al., 2008). Coffman and colleagues studied the use of such techniques in first-grade classrooms and found evidence of benefits that lasted beyond the instructional year in which they were used, suggesting that the early experiences had produced an enduring change in the children's memory structures (Ornstein et al., 2010). Another study showed similar results with second-grade students (Grammer et al., 2013). Some teachers used an instructional script rich in features to help learners remember, while others used an instructional script not designed to foster strategies for remembering, as shown in the table below. The children who experienced the first type of instruction showed significant gains in problem-solving ability that persisted as much as 1 month after the intervention.

BOX 4-2 Continued

Memory-Relevant Instructional Techniques

	Definition	Example
Instructional Techniques		
Strategy Suggestions	Recommending that a child adopt a method or procedure for remembering or processing information	"If you are having trouble thinking of ways to connect the wheel and axle, you can look at the diagram to help you."
Metacognitive Questions	Requesting that a child provide a potential strategy, a utilized strategy, or a rationale for a strategy she has indicated using	"How did you figure out which pieces you would need to build a sturdy structure? How did you know that would work?"
Instructional Techniques Co-occurring with Deliberate Memory Demands		
Instructional Activities	Requesting information from memory *and* the presentation of instructional information by the teacher	"Today we will be building our own cars. Who knows the first step we take when building a new structure?"
Cognitive Structuring Activities	Requesting information from memory *and* teacher instruction that could impact the encoding and retrieval of information, such as focusing attention or organizing material	"All of these modes of transportation have wheels. What is another vehicle that you have seen around town that also has wheels?"
Metacognition	Requesting information from memory *and* the provision or solicitation of metacognitive information	"What kind of gear is this? What clue did you use to figure that out?"

SOURCE: Grammer et al. (2013, p. 21).

Older adults are more likely than younger adults to forget where or when an event occurred or to erroneously combine elements from different events (Spencer and Raz, 1995). Older adults may also be more likely than younger adults to bind irrelevant details (Campbell et al., 2010).

As people grow older, changes in memory consolidation and retrieval processes also may affect learning. Aging affects the ability to integrate information together as a memory is consolidated. These deficits can emerge even while information is still being held within working memory, which suggests that the deficits may at least in part reflect a lowered ability to maintain and encode the features of an experience into consolidated representations (e.g., Mitchell et al., 2000; Peich et al., 2013; van Geldorp et al., 2015). The finding that deficits in older adults' binding can be reduced when they are given strategies that enhance memory consolidation supports this idea (e.g., Craik and Rose, 2012; Naveh-Benjamin and Kilb, 2012; Naveh-Benjamin et al., 2007; Old and Naveh-Benjamin, 2012). Another possible explanation is that older adults have a bias toward *pattern completion*: the process by which a partial or degraded memory cue triggers an individual to use other prior knowledge and experiences to reconstitute a complete memory representation (Stark et al., 2010).

Binding and pattern completion are likely to be part of the explanation for why older adults are more likely than younger adults to retain the "gist" of an event but not its specific details. For instance, after reading a list of associated words, older adults will be less likely than younger adults to remember each individual word presented on the list, but they will be at least as likely as younger adults to remember the themes of the list or to falsely remember nonpresented words that are thematically associated with the presented words (reviewed by Schacter et al., 1997). Similarly, older adults are more likely to remember the moral of a story rather than its details (Adams et al., 1990) and to report general rather than specific details of past autobiographical events (e.g., Schacter et al., 2013). Studies show that declines in the specificity of memory likely begin in middle age, with increases in gist-based false memory already apparent by the time an adult is in her 50s (Alexander et al., 2015).

Although these age differences are often framed as deficits, they do not always result in declines and can in fact be useful. The shift toward gist-based memory with age can lead older adults to be more likely than younger adults to remember the "big picture" or important implications (McGinnis et al., 2008). The shift toward pattern completion also may enable older adults to note connections among events and to integrate across experiences, abilities that often are considered part of the wisdom that is acquired with age (Baltes and Staudinger, 2000).

CONCLUSIONS

Executive function and self-regulation are critical processes for supporting learning. Both involve sets of processes that are related to success in school. Self-regulation involves many complex components, and researchers are actively working to understand how these components interact and how to support their development.

Memory is an important foundation for most types of learning. People's learning and memory systems give them the ability to use past experiences to adapt and solve problems in the present. This ability to use the past by retrieving memories when they are needed is reconstructive in nature. It is not a process of searching for stored copies of mental representations of information and experiences but a set of processes triggered by cues in the learner's environment through which he reconstructs these experiences and forges new connections for them. The retrieval cues available in a learner's environment are critical for what she will be able to recall and also play a role in the way the learner begins to integrate new information as knowledge.

CONCLUSION 4-1: Successful learning requires coordination of multiple cognitive processes that involve different networks in the brain. In order to coordinate these processes, an individual needs to be able to monitor and regulate his own learning. The ability to monitor and regulate learning changes over the life span and can be improved through interventions.

CONCLUSION 4-2: Memory is an important foundation for most types of learning. Memory involves reconstruction rather than retrieval of exact copies of encoded mental representations. The cues available in a learner's environment are critical for what she will be able to recall; they also play a role in the way the learner begins to integrate new information as knowledge.

5

Knowledge and Reasoning

This chapter examines the development of knowledge as a primary outcome of learning and how learning is affected by accumulating knowledge and expertise. *HPL I*[1] emphasized these topics as well, but subsequent research has refined and extended understandings in a variety of learning domains. The first section of this chapter describes the problem of knowledge integration from the perspective of learning scientists and illustrates with research findings how people integrate their knowledge at different points in their development and in different learning situations. The second section describes what is known about the effects of accumulated knowledge and expertise on learning. The second half of the chapter discusses strategies for supporting learning. The committee has drawn on both laboratory- and classroom-based research for this chapter.

HPL I noted that the mind works actively to both store and recall information by imposing structure on new perceptions and experiences (National Research Council, 2000). A central focus of *HPL I* was how experts structure their knowledge of a domain in ways that allow them to readily categorize new information and determine its relevance to what they already know. Because novices lack these frameworks, they have more difficulty assimilating and later recalling new information they encounter. This chapter expands on these themes from *HPL I*, citing relevant research reported since that study.

---

[1] As noted in Chapter 1, this report uses the abbreviation *"HPL I"* for *How People Learn: Brain, Mind, Experience, and School: Expanded Edition* (National Research Council, 2000).

BUILDING A KNOWLEDGE BASE

Knowledge integration is a process through which learners put together different sorts of information and experiences, identifying and establishing relationships and expanding frameworks for connecting them. Learners must not only accumulate knowledge from individual episodes of experience but also integrate the knowledge they gain across time, location, circumstances, and the various formats in which knowledge appears (Esposito and Bauer, 2017). How knowledge acquired in discrete episodes is integrated has been debated for decades (Karmiloff-Smith, 1986, 1990; Mandler, 1988; Nelson, 1974). Some researchers have suggested that infants are born with foundational knowledge that provides the elements necessary for learning and reasoning about their experiences (Spelke, 2004; Spelke and Kinzler, 2007) or that infants can build from basic inborn reflexes to actively engage with the world and gradually build skills and knowledge (Fischer and Bidell, 2006). Others have argued that all knowledge is generated through an individual's direct experience with the world (Greeno et al., 1996; Packer, 1985).

More recent work suggests that the integration of knowledge is a natural byproduct of the formation and consolidation of episodic memories (Bauer, 2009; Bauer et al., 2012). As described in Chapter 4, when a memory is consolidated, the learner associates representations of the elements of the experience (e.g., sights, sounds, tactile sensations) and these associations serve to help stabilize that memory. At the same time, these representations may also be linked with older memories from previous experiences that have already been stored in long-term memory (Zola and Squire, 2000). The fact that old and new memory traces can be integrated shows that these traces are not fixed. Instead, elements common to the new and stored memory traces reactivate the old memory and, as the new memory is consolidated, the old memory may be reconstructed and undergo consolidation again (Nader, 2003). When information from either learning episode is later retrieved, elements of both memory traces will be reactivated and will be simultaneously available for reintegration. As memory traces with common elements are simultaneously activated and linked, knowledge is expanded and memories are iteratively reworked. Figure 5-1 illustrates how this happens.

These linked traces may then be integrated with additional new information that comes to the learner later, and another new memory trace undergoes consolidation. Interestingly, it is exactly this process of integration of information from different episodes that may explain why people are sometimes unable to explain when and where they gained particular knowledge. Because the information generated by memory integration was not actually experienced as a single event, the information was not tagged with its origin (Bauer and Jackson, 2015).

The studies of knowledge acquisition in children and college students presented in Box 5-1 illustrate the capacity to integrate unconnected infor-

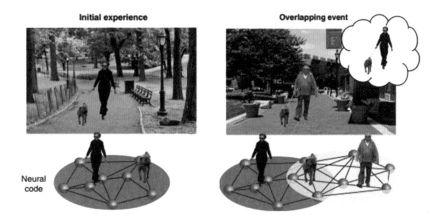

FIGURE 5-1 *Depiction of memory integration.*
NOTE: Imagine that while walking in the park you encounter a woman walking her dog (initial experience). This experience is connected to a group of neurons that are activated simultaneously by it (this neural representation is represented by the blue disc). Later, you encounter the same dog while walking in the city, but this time a man is walking the dog (perceptually overlapping event). The dog (common element) triggers reactivation of your initial experience in the park. This reactivation allows connections of neural representations to be formed regarding the dog, the woman, and the man, such that the events are linked across time. This integration of memories allows you to create new knowledge. That is, you have learned that there is a relationship between the man and the woman, though you have not seen the man and the woman together. SOURCE: Adapted from Schlichting and Preston (2015, Fig. 1).

mation and retain this knowledge starting at a very young age. These studies underscore the active role of the learner; that is, even young children do not simply accrue knowledge from what they have experienced directly but build knowledge from the many things that they have figured out on their own, which, over time, they can do with less repetition and external support.

As discussed in Chapter 2, adequate sleep is important for integration and learning. The brain continues the work of encoding and consolidation during sleep and facilitates generalizations across learning episodes (Coutanche et al., 2013; Van Kesteren et al., 2010). Specifically, activation of the hippocampus (which plays a key role in memory integration) during sleep seems to allow connections between memory traces to be formed across the cortex. This process promotes the integration of new information into existing memory traces, allows for abstraction across episodes (Lewis and Durant, 2011), and leads to the possibility of building novel connections, which may be both creative and insightful or may be bizarre (Diekelmann and Born, 2010).

BOX 5-1 Examples of Developmental Differences in the Process of Knowledge Acquisition

Children as young as age 4 are able to generate new factual knowledge by integrating separate yet related episodes of new learning, and this capacity shows measurable improvement as children age (Bauer and San Souci, 2010; Brown et al., 1986; Holyoak et al., 1984).

Bauer and San Souci (2010) set out to determine whether information learned in different episodes became linked in the memory of 4- and 6-year-olds and if the process for the accumulation of knowledge was the same or different for children at these two ages. The children in the study listened to a pair of related passages that contained two novel facts that could be integrated to generate a third novel fact. One passage included the fact that the largest volcano in the world is in Hawaii and the other noted that Mauna Loa is the largest volcano in the world. By integrating the two, the children could answer where Mauna Loa is located. When presented with an open-ended question that could stimulate the integration of knowledge ("where is Mauna Loa located?"), two-thirds of the 6-year-olds were able to correctly answer the questions. Among the 4-year-olds, 13 percent were able to select the correct answer from a set of choices and 62 percent were able to recognize the correct answer. In a control condition in which only one of the passages was presented, children did not produce the integration facts, which showed that integration and self-generation are the source of the new knowledge. The children who generated the integrated facts also were likely to recall both of the novel facts that were presented to them.

Further, at the age of 6, children are less dependent on repetition and external support to integrate and recall facts from different episodes of learning. Possible reasons why the older children had an easier time integrating and recalling facts include faster processing speed (Kail and Miller, 2006), a larger knowledge base that made the connections more obvious (Chi et al., 1989a), and more deliberate use of prior knowledge and new information (Bjorklund et al., 2009).

Similar research has shown that young children also retain newly self-generated information over time (Bauer and Larkina, 2016; Varga and Bauer, 2013). This high level of retention for information that is self-generated through integration demonstrates its potential as a mechanism for rapid accumulation of semantic knowledge at a young age (in the case of these studies, demonstrated through knowledge of basic facts such as the names of colors) (Bauer and Varga, 2015; see also Varga et al., 2016).

BOX 5-1 **Continued**

A similar study of a college-age population also examined self-generation of new factual knowledge through integration of separate yet related episodes (Bauer and Jackson, 2015). In this study, the students read a large number of true facts they had not previously known and were tested on their capacity to integrate knowledge from the information presented. For trials in which the correct responses could be derived through integration of the facts presented, students selected the correct response 56 percent of the time. In contrast, in trials where integration of previous facts was not possible (such as in novel word trials), they selected the correct response only 27 percent of the time (approximately the rate expected by chance).

The researchers also used measurements of scalp-recorded electrical changes in the brain that are associated with the firing of neurons in response to a stimulus to examine this process in a separate group of college students (Bauer and Jackson, 2015). Again, the students were asked to read lists of facts and were tested on their capacity to integrate knowledge. The measurements showed that the subjects quickly converted the newly self-generated facts to the status of knowledge that is already well known (see Figure 5-1-1). In other words, the newly integrated information had become incorporated into the students' knowledge base.

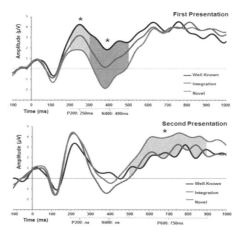

FIGURE 5-1-1 *Mean amplitude of the neural response at the centro-parietal sites to well-known, novel, and integration facts during first and second presentation. SOURCE: Bauer and Jackson (2015).*

KNOWLEDGE AND EXPERTISE

When people repeatedly engage with similar situations or topics, they develop mental representations that connect disparate facts and actions into more effective mental structures for acting in the world. For example, when people first move to a new neighborhood, they may learn a set of discrete routes for traveling between pairwise locations, such as from home to school and from home to the grocery store. Over time, people naturally develop a mental representation of spatial relationships, or mental map, that stitches these discrete routes together. Even if they have never traveled between the school and the grocery store, they can figure out the most efficient route by consulting their mental map (Thorndyke and Hayes-Roth, 1982). The observation that experts in a domain have developed frameworks of information and understanding through long experiences in a particular area was a central focus of *HPL I*. In this section, we briefly describe some of the benefits of expert knowledge (a more detailed discussion of the benefits of expertise appears in *HPL I*) and then discuss the knowledge-related biases that may come with expertise.

Benefits of Expertise

One of the most well-documented benefits of the acquisition of knowledge is an increase in the speed and accuracy with which people can complete recurrent tasks: remembering a solution is faster than problem solving. Another benefit is that people who develop expertise can handle increasingly complex problems. One way this occurs is that people master substeps, so that each substep becomes a chunk of knowledge that does not require attention (e.g., Gobet et al., 2001). People also learn to handle complexity by developing mental representations that make specific tasks easier to complete. When Hatano and Osawa (1983) studied abacus masters, they found that even without an abacus in front of them, the masters had prodigious memories for numbers and could carry out addition problems with very large numbers because they had developed a mental representation of an abacus, which they manipulated virtually. These abacus masters did not show similarly superior ability to remember or keep track of letters or fruits—tasks that were not aided by manipulating a virtual abacus.

A third benefit is an increase in the ability to extract relevant information from the environment. Experts not only have better-developed knowledge representations than novices have but also can perceive more information that is relevant to those representations. For example, radiologists are able to see telling patterns in an x-ray that appear merely as shadows to a novice (Myles-Worsley et al., 1988). The ability to discern more precise information complements a more-differentiated mental representation of those phenomena.

An implication of this ability is that students need to learn to see the relevant information in the environment to help differentiate concepts, such as the difference between a positive and a negative curvilinear slope (Kellman et al., 2010).

A fourth benefit of acquiring expert knowledge is that it helps people use their environment as a resource. Using what is known as distributed cognition, people can offload some of the cognitive demands of a task onto their environment or other people (Hollan et al., 2000). For instance, a major goal of learning is to develop knowledge of where to look for resources and help, and this is still important in the digital age. Experts typically know which tools are available and who in their network has specialized expertise they can call upon.

Finally, acquiring knowledge helps people gain more knowledge by making it easier to learn new and related information. Although some cognitive abilities related to learning novel information decline, on average, with age, these declines are offset by increases in knowledge accumulated through the life span, which empowers new learning. For example, in a study of young adults and older adults (in their 70s) who listened to a broadcast of a baseball game, the older adults who knew a lot about baseball recalled more of the broadcast than the young adults who knew less about baseball. This occurred despite the fact that the younger adults had superior executive functioning (Hambrick and Engle, 2002).

Bias as a Natural Side Effect of Knowledge

As people's knowledge develops, their thinking also becomes biased. But the biases may be either useful or detrimental to learning. The word "bias" often has negative connotations, but bias as understood by psychologists is a natural side effect of knowledge acquisition. Learning biases are often implicit and unknown to the individuals who hold them. They appear relatively early in knowledge acquisition, as people begin to form schemas (conceptual frameworks) for how the world operates and their place within it. These schemas help individuals know what to expect and what to attend to in particular situations (e.g., in a doctor's office versus at a friend's party) and help them develop a sense of cultural fluency—that is, to know how things work "around here" (Mourey et al., 2015).

Psychologists distinguish two types of bias: one is intrinsic to learning and primarily useful and empowering to the learner; the second occurs when prior experiences or beliefs undermine the acquisition of new knowledge and skills.

An aphorism from the context of medical diagnosis illustrates the two types of bias: "When you hear hoof-beats, think of horses not zebras." In the United States, horses are much more common than zebras so one is much more likely to encounter the common "horses" than the rare "zebras." Of course, one should modify assumptions in light of additional evidence: if the large mammal from which the hoof-beats emanate has black and white stripes, it is much more likely to be a zebra than a horse. Thus, if one sees a striped animal in a zoo but insists that it is a horse and not a zebra, this resistance to new information is a strong form of the limiting effects of bias on learning. A person may fail even to notice the zebra at the zoo because he was so strongly expecting to see a horse instead and was attuned to notice only that kind of animal.

Making matters even more complicated, two people who have different prior levels of expertise, or different beliefs, might legitimately have different interpretations when initially presented with the same information. But if sufficient additional information suggests a particular interpretation, they should converge on an answer, especially if the higher level of expertise is brought to bear.

Beliefs about human-caused global climate change are a good example of the biases that blind individuals to new evidence. Despite nearly universal consensus among climate scientists that global climate change is taking place and that this change is induced by humans' behavior, a considerable proportion of adults in the United States do not accept these interpretations of the evidence. One might expect that higher levels of science literacy would be associated with greater agreement with the scientific consensus. However, Kahan and colleagues (2012) found that it is among the individuals with the highest levels of science literacy that the most stark polarization is apparent. Those who only seek out and attend to information consistent with their prior beliefs will create an "echo-chamber" that further biases their learning. Often this echo-chamber effect is socially reinforced, as individuals prefer to discuss the topic in question with others whom they know hold beliefs similar to their own.

Stereotypes perpetuate themselves through learned bias, but not all learning biases are considered to have negative consequences. For example, some positive biases promote well-being and mental health (Taylor and Brown, 1988), some may promote accuracy in perceptions of other people (Funder, 1995), and others may be adaptive behaviors—for example, selective attention and action in situations in which errors have a high cost (Haselton and Buss, 2000; Haselton and Funder, 2006). Hahn and Harris (2014) have written a useful historical overview of research on bias in human cognition.

Still other biases refine perception and serve to blur distinctions within categories that are not meaningful while highlighting subtle cross-category distinctions that may be important. For example, very young infants respond equally to phonological contrasts that matter in their language (e.g., "r" and "l" if the baby lives in an English-speaking context) and those that do not matter (e.g., "r" and "l" in a Japanese-speaking context). Over time, infants lose this discriminatory capability. This loss is actually a benefit, reflecting the baby's increasing efficiency in processing his own language context, and is a mark of learning (Kuhl et al., 1992). In the other direction, dermatologists may learn from experience and formal training to distinguish subtle features of moles and skin growths that signal malignancy, features that to an untrained eye are indistinguishable from those of benign growths.

Biases affect the noncognitive aspects of learning as well. In a variable world, highly stable task environments are not guaranteed and so training to high efficiency may actually create a mindset that makes new learning more difficult, impeding motivation and interest in continuous growth and development. For instance, a person who has learned how to organize her schedule using a specific tool may be reluctant to learn a new tool because of the perception that it will take too much time to learn to use it, even though it may be more efficient in the long run. In this example, it is not that the person is unable to learn the new tool; rather, her beliefs about the amount of effort required affect her motivation and interest in learning. This kind of self-attribution, or prior knowledge of oneself, can have a large influence on how people approach future learning opportunities, which in turn influences what they will learn (Blackwell et al., 2007).

KNOWLEDGE INTEGRATION AND REASONING

We have seen that building a knowledge base requires doing three things: accumulating information (in part by noticing what matters in a situation and is therefore worth attending to); tagging this information as relevant or not; and integrating it across separate episodes. These three activities can happen relatively quickly and automatically, or they can happen slowly through deliberate reflection. However, these processes alone are not sufficient for integrating and extending knowledge. Learners of all ages know many things that were not explicitly taught or directly experienced. They routinely generate their own novel understanding of the information they are accumulating and productively extend their knowledge.

Inferential Reasoning

Inferential reasoning refers to making logical connections between pieces of information in order to organize knowledge for understanding and to drawing conclusions through deductive reasoning, inductive reasoning, and abductive reasoning (Seel, 2012). Inferential thinking is needed for such processes as generalizing, categorizing, and comprehending. The act of reading a text is a good example. To comprehend a text, readers are required to make inferences regarding information that is only implied in the text (see, e.g., Cain and Oakhill, 1999; Graesser et al., 1994; Paris and Upton, 1976). Some types of inferences help readers track the meaning of a text by integrating different information it supplies, for example by recognizing anaphoric references (words in a text that require the reader to refer back to other ideas in the text for their meaning). Other types of inferences allow a reader to fill in gaps in the text by recruiting information from beyond it (i.e., background knowledge), in order to understand information within the text. Though these types of inferences are essential for understanding, they are thought to survive in working memory only long enough to aid comprehension (McKoon and Ratcliff, 1992).

Other inferences that learners make survive beyond the bounds of working memory and become incorporated into their knowledge base. For example, a person who knows both that liquids expand with heat and that thermometers contain liquid may integrate these two pieces of information and infer that thermometers work because liquid expands as heat increases. In this way, the learner generates understanding through a productive extension of prior learning episodes.

Effective problem solving typically requires retrieved knowledge to be adapted and transformed to fit new situations; therefore, memory retrieval must be coordinated with other cognitive processes. One way to help people realize that something they have learned before is relevant to their current task is to explicitly give them a hint that it is relevant (Gick and Holyoak, 1980). For example, such hints might be embedded in text, provided by a teacher, or incorporated into virtual learning platforms. Another strategy for helping people realize that they already know something useful is to ask people to compare related problems in order to highlight exactly what they have in common, increasing the likelihood that they will recall previously acquired knowledge with similar properties (Alfieri et al., 2013; Gentner et al., 2009).

Kolodner et al. (2003) gives the example of an architect trying to build an office building with a naturally lit atrium. She realizes that a familiar library's design, which includes an exterior wall of glass, could be reused for the office building, but would fit the building's needs better if translucent glass bricks were used instead of a clear, glass pane. This kind of design-based reasoning is incorporated into problem-based learning (Hmelo-Silver, 2004) activities. Problem-based learning emphasizes that memories are not simply stored to allow future reminiscing, but are formed so that they can be used, reshaped, and flexibly adapted to serve broad reasoning needs. The goal of problem-based learning is to instill in learners flexible knowledge use, effective problem-solving skills, self-directed learning, collaboration, and intrinsic motivation. These goals are in line with several of the goals identified in other contexts as important for success in life and work (National Research Council, 2012b).

Age-Related Changes in Knowledge and Reasoning

People's learning benefits from a steady increase, over many decades, in the accumulation of world knowledge (e.g., Craik and Salthouse, 2008;

Hedden and Gabrieli, 2004). This accumulation makes it easier for older adults not only to retrieve vocabulary and facts about the world (Cavanagh and Blanchard-Fields, 2002) but also to acquire new information in domains related to their expertise. For example, physicians acquire medical expertise, which enables them to comprehend and remember more information from medical texts than novices can (Patel et al., 1986). It is also thought that older adults can compensate for declines in some abilities by using their extensive world knowledge. For instance, medical experts depend less on working memory because they can draw on their expertise to reconstruct only those facts from long-term memory that are relevant to a current need (e.g., Patel and Groen, 1991).

The knowledge learners accumulate throughout the life span is the growing product of the processes of both learning new information from direct experience and generating new information based on reasoning and imagining (Salthouse, 2010). These two cognitive assets together—accumulated knowledge and reasoning ability—are particularly relevant to healthy aging. Reasoning and knowledge abilities tend to be correlated. That is, people who have comparatively higher reasoning capacity are likely to acquire correspondingly more knowledge over the life span than their peers (Ackerman and Beier, 2006; Beier and Ackerman, 2005). Reasoning ability is a major determinant of learning throughout life, and it is through reasoning, especially in contexts that allow people to pursue their interests, that people develop knowledge throughout their life span (Ackerman, 1996; Cattell, 1987).

On average, however, the trajectories of reasoning and knowledge acquisition are different across the life span. A number of research studies have described the general trajectories of age-related changes in ability, using a variety of measures and research designs (cross-sectional and longitudinal), and have shown a fairly consistent trend in which the development of knowledge remains steady as reasoning capacity (the ability to quickly and accurately manipulate multiple distinct pieces of factual information to make inferences) drops off (Salthouse, 2010). However, there is considerable individual variability in the trajectories, which reflect individual health and other characteristics, as well as educational and experiential opportunities and even social engagement. Yet, even though there is an average decline in inferential reasoning capacity through adulthood, there is not a corresponding decline in the ability to make good decisions—a more colloquial use of the word "reasoning." In other words, the research does not suggest that the average 14-year-old reasons better about what to do in a complex or emotional real-world situation than would an average 50-year-old. Instead, it describes the 14-year-old's stronger ability to quickly manipulate multiple distinct pieces of factual information to make logical and combinatorial inferences.

The growth or decline of abilities can be expected to vary not only between individuals but also within the same person over time (Hertzog et al.,

2008). Two 50-year-olds may have extremely different cognitive profiles, such that one may generally have the same ability profile as an average 30-year-old and the other may more closely resemble an average 70-year-old. Within the same person, abilities will decline or grow at varying rates as a function of that individual's continuing use of some skills and intellectual development in particular domains; losses and declines are associated with disuse of other skills. (Factors that influence cognitive aging are discussed in Chapter 9.) As mentioned, new learning depends on both reasoning ability and knowledge acquisition (Ackerman and Beier, 2006; Beier and Ackerman, 2005). Even though reasoning abilities decline with age, knowledge accumulated throughout the life span facilitates new learning, as long as the information to be learned is aligned with existing domain knowledge. When people select environments for education, work, and hobbies that capitalize on their already-established knowledge and skills as they age, their selectivity allows them to capitalize on their repertoire of knowledge and expertise for learning new information (Baltes and Baltes, 1990).

Cognitive abilities change throughout the life span in a variety of ways that may affect a person's ability to learn new things (see Hartshorne and Germine, 2015, for discussion). For instance, as people age, learning may rely more on knowledge and less on reasoning and quick manipulation of factual information. However, examining peoples' cognitive abilities and learning becomes increasingly complex as people develop past the age of formal education. One reason is that the ways in which people learn become increasingly idiosyncratic outside of a standardized educational curriculum, and understanding this process requires assessing knowledge gained through a wide variety of adult experiences that different individuals amass over a lifetime (Lubinski, 2000). The unique complexities of adult learning and development are discussed in Chapter 8.

Effects of Culture on Reasoning

As described in Chapter 2, learning is inherently cultural, given that a person's experiences in a culture affect biological processes that support learning, perception, and cognition. In the area of reasoning, for example, researchers have explored fundamental differences in peoples' reasoning about three basic domains of life: physical events (naïve physics), biological events (naïve biology), and social or psychological events (naïve psychology) (see e.g., Carey, 1985, 2009; Goswami, 2002; Hirschfeld and Gelman, 1994; Spelke and Kinzler, 2007; also see Ojalehto and Medin, 2015c, for a review). These distinctions are compelling in the sense that each reflects a set of intuitive principles and inferences. That is, each domain is defined by entities having the same kind of causal properties. These might be marked, for example, by the way they move: physical entities are set into motion by external forces, while biological entities may propel themselves. These domains are important for understanding cognition because researchers have suggested that whereas the perception of physical causality is universal, causal reasoning in the biological and psychological domains is culturally variable.

Two studies illustrate ways to examine these issues. Morris and Peng (1994) presented two types of animated displays to American and Chinese participants. One set of displays depicted physical interactions (of geometrical shapes), whereas the other set depicted social interactions (among fish). The participants' answers to questions about what they had seen suggested differences in attention to internal and external causes across the groups, but those differences depended on the domain (social or physical). The authors concluded that attribution of causality in the social domain is susceptible to cultural influences but that causality in the physical domain is not.

Beller and colleagues (2009) asked German, Chinese, and Tongan participants to indicate which entity they regarded as causally most relevant for statements such as "The fact that wood floats on water is basically due to . . . ". Ratings varied by the cultural background of respondents and also by the phenomena participants were considering. In general, the German and Chinese participants, but not the Tongan participants, considered a carrier's capability for buoyancy only when the floater was a solid object, such as wood, but not when it was a fluid, such as oil (Beller et al., 2009; see also Bender et al., 2017). This is an area of research that has barely been explored, but results to date suggest that the perception of physical causality may in fact not be universal and may be learned in culturally mediated ways.

STRATEGIES TO SUPPORT LEARNING

People are naturally interested in strengthening their ability to acquire and retain knowledge and in ways to improve learning performance. Researchers have explored a variety of strategies to support learning and memory. They have identified several principles for structuring practice and engaging with information to be learned to improve memory, to make sense of new information, and to develop new knowledge.

Several scholars have looked across the research on the effectiveness of specific strategies for supporting learning (Benassi et al., 2014; Dunlosky et al., 2013; Pashler et al., 2007). The authors of these three studies looked for strategies that (1) have been examined in several studies, using authentic educational materials in classroom settings; (2) show effects that can be generalized across learner characteristics and types of materials; (3) promote learning that is long-lasting; and (4) support comprehension, knowledge application, and problem solving in addition to recall of factual material. These three analyses identified five learning strategies as promising:

1. retrieval practice;
2. spaced practice;
3. interleaved and varied practice;
4. summarizing and drawing; and
5. explanations: elaborative interrogation, self-explanation, and teaching.

Strategies for Knowledge Retention

The first three strategies are ways of structuring practice that are particularly useful for increasing knowledge retention.

Retrieval Practice

Some evidence shows that the act of retrieval itself enhances learning and that when learners practice retrieval during an initial learning activity, their ability to retrieve and use knowledge again in the future is enhanced (Karpicke, 2016; Roediger and Karpicke, 2006b). The benefits of retrieval practice in general have been shown to generalize across individual differences in learners, variations in materials, and different assessments of learning. For example, researchers have found effects across learner characteristics in children (Lipko-Speed et al., 2014; Marsh et al., 2012). Studies have also suggested that retrieval practice can be a useful memory remediation method among older adults (Balota et al., 2006; Meyer and Logan, 2013; also see Dunlosky et al., 2013, for a review of effective learning techniques). However, most of this research has addressed retrieval of relatively simple information (e.g., vocabulary), rather than deep understanding.

Research has also demonstrated the effects of retrieval practice on recall of texts and other information related to school subjects. For example, Roediger and Karpicke (2006a) had students read brief educational texts and practice recalling them. Students in one condition read the texts four times; students in a second group read three times and recalled the texts once by writing down as much as they could remember; and students in a third group read the material once and then recalled it during three retrieval practice periods. On a final test given 1 week after the initial learning session, students who practiced retrieval one time recalled more of the material than students who only read the texts, and the students who repeatedly retrieved the material performed the best. The results suggest that actively retrieving the material soon after studying it is more productive than spending the same amount of time repeatedly reading.

Attempting retrieval but failing has also been shown to promote learning. Failed retrievals provide feedback signals to learners, signaling that they may not know the information well and should adjust how they encode the material the next time they study it (Pyc and Rawson, 2010). The act of failing to retrieve may thus enhance subsequent encoding (Kornell, 2014).

Such studies suggest that self-testing can be an effective way for students to practice retrieval. However, evidence from surveys of students' learning strategies and from experiments in which learners are given control over when and how often they can test themselves suggests that students may not test themselves often or effectively enough (Karpicke et al., 2009; Kornell and Son, 2009). Many students do not engage in self-testing at all, and when students do test themselves, they often do so as a "knowledge check" to see whether they can or cannot remember what they are learning. While this is an important use of self-testing, few learners self-test because they view the act of retrieval as part of the process of learning. Instead, they are likely to retrieve something once and then, believing they have learned it for the long term, drop the item from further practice.

Spaced Practice

Researchers who have compared spaced and massed practice have shown that the way that learners schedule practice can have an impact on learning (Carpenter et al., 2012; Kang, 2016). Massed practice concentrates all of the practice sessions in a short period of time (such as cramming for a test), whereas spaced practice distributes learning events over longer periods of time. Results show greater effects for spacing than for massed practice across learning materials (e.g., vocabulary learning, grammatical rules, history facts, pictures, motor skills) (Carpenter et al., 2012; Dempster, 1996), stimulus formats (e.g., audiovisual, text) (Janiszewski et al., 2003), and for both intentional and incidental learning (Challis, 1993; Toppino et al., 2002). Studies have shown benefits of spaced practice for learners of ages 4 through 76 (Balota et al., 1989; Rea and Modigliani, 1987; Simone et al., 2012; Toppino, 1991). Cepeda and colleagues (2006) found that spaced practice led to greater recall than massed practice regardless of the size of the lag between practice and recall.

There are many possible reasons why spaced practice might be more effective than massed practice. When an item, concept, or procedure is repeated after a spaced interval, learners have to fully engage in the mental operations they performed the first time because of forgetting that has occurred. But when repetitions are immediate and massed together, learners do not fully engage during repetitions. In the case of reading, one possible reason why massed re-readings do not promote learning is that when people reread immediately, they do not attend to the most informative and meaningful portions of the material during the second reading, as illustrated by Dunlosky and Rawson (2005) in a study of self-paced reading.

A few researchers have attempted to identify the spacing intervals that promote the most memory—a "sweet spot" where spaced practice confers benefits before too much forgetting has occurred (Cepeda et al., 2008; Pavlik and Anderson, 2008). For example, a study of vocabulary learning among fifth graders suggested that a 2-week interval showed the best results (Sobel et al., 2011). Another classroom-based study of spacing effects focused on first-grade children learning to associate letters and sounds during phonics instruction (Seabrook et al., 2005). The children who received spaced practice during the 2-week period significantly outperformed the children who received a single massed practice session each day.

In general, the literature on spaced practice suggests that separating learning episodes by at least 1 day, rather than focusing the learning into a single session, maximizes long-term retention of the material. However, it is important to note that wider spacing is not necessarily always better. The optimal distribution of learning sessions depends at least in part on how long the material needs to be retained in memory (i.e., when the material will be recalled or tested). For example, if the learner will be tested 1 month or more after the last learning session, then the learning should be distributed over weeks or months.

Interleaved and Variable Practice

The way information is presented can significantly affect both what is learned (Schyns et al., 1998) and how well it is learned (Goldstone, 1996). Variable learning generally refers to practicing skills in different ways, while interleaving refers to mixing in different activities. Varying or interleaving different skills, activities, or problems within a learning session—as opposed to focusing on one skill, activity, or problem throughout (called blocked learning)—may better promote learning. Both strategies may also involve spaced practice, and both also present learners with a variety of useful challenges, or "desirable difficulties." Researchers have identified potential benefits of variable and interleaved practice learning, but they have also found a few benefits for blocked practice.

Several studies have shown benefits for blocking, at least for category learning (Carpenter and Mueller, 2013; Goldstone, 1996; Higgins and Ross, 2011). Moreover, when given the option, a majority of learners preferred to block their study (Carvalho et al., 2014; Tauber et al., 2013). Interleaving can boost learning of the structure of categories; that is, learning that some objects or ideas belong to the same category and others do not (Birnbaum et al., 2013; Carvalho and Goldstone, 2014a, 2014b; Kornell and Bjork; 2008). Other researchers have examined interleaved practice in mathematical problem-solving domains (Rohrer, 2012; Rohrer et al., 2015).

Carvalho and Goldstone (2014a) found that the effectiveness of the presentation methods (interleaved or blocked) depended on whether the participant engaged in active or passive study. They also found that interleaving concepts improved students' capacity to discriminate among different categories, while blocked practice emphasized similarities within each category. These results suggest that interleaved study improves learning of highly similar categories (by facilitating between-category comparisons), whereas blocked study improves learning of low-similarity categories (by facilitating within-category comparisons).

Interleaved study naturally includes delays between learning blocks and thus easily allows for spaced practice, which has the potential benefits for long-term memory discussed above. However, it may be beneficial because it helps learners to make comparisons among categories, not because it allows time to elapse between learning blocks (Carvalho and Goldstone, 2014b). The mechanisms that underlie the benefits of either interleaved or blocked study (e.g, possible effects on attentional processes) are ongoing topics of research. As with other strategies, the optimal way to present material—interleaved or blocked—and the mechanisms most heavily involved will likely depend on the nature of the study task.

Strategies for Understanding and Integration

The other two strategies for which there is strong evidence—summarizing and drawing and developing explanations—draw on inferential processes that research shows to be effective for organizing and integrating information for learning.

Summarizing and Drawing

Summarizing and drawing are two common strategies for elaborating on what has been learned. To summarize is to create a verbal description that distills the most important information from a set of materials. Similarly, when learners create drawings, they use graphic strategies to portray important concepts and relationships. In both activities, learners must take the material they are learning and transform it into a different representation. There are differences between them, but both activities involve identifying important terms and concepts, organizing the information, and using prior knowledge to create verbal or pictorial representations.

Both summarization and drawing have been shown to benefit learning in school-age children (Gobert and Clement, 1999; Van Meter, 2001; Van Meter and Garner, 2005). Literature reviews by Dunlosky and colleagues (2013) and Fiorella and Mayer (2015a, 2015b) have identified factors that appear to contribute to the effectiveness of summarization and drawing activities.

A few studies have suggested that the quality of students' summaries and drawings is directly related to how much they learn from the activities and that learners do these activities more effectively when they are trained and guided (Bednall and Kehoe, 2011; Brown et al., 1983; Schmeck et al., 2014). For example, the effectiveness of drawing activities is enhanced when learners compare their drawings to author-generated pictures (Van Meter et al., 2006). Similarly, providing learners with a list of relevant elements to be included in drawings and partial drawings helps learners create more complete drawings and bolsters learning (Schwamborn et al., 2010).

A group of researchers compared summarization and drawing and suggested that their effectiveness depends on the nature of the learning materials. For example, Leopold and Leutner (2012) asked high school students who were studying a science text about water molecules, which contained descriptions of several spatial relations, to either draw diagrams, write a summary of the text, or to re-read the text (the control condition). Those who created drawings performed better on a comprehension test than those who re-read the texts. However, those who created written summaries performed *worse* than those who re-read. The authors concluded that the drawing was more effective in this case because the learning involved spatial relations.

Note-taking, either writing by hand or typing on a laptop, is a form of summarizing that has also been studied. For example, Mueller and Oppenheimer (2014) found that students who hand-wrote notes learn more than those who typed notes using a laptop computer. The researchers asked students to take notes in these two ways and then tested their recall of factual details, conceptual understanding, and ability to synthesize and generalize the information. They found that students who typed took more voluminous notes than those who wrote by hand, but the hand-writers had a stronger conceptual understanding of the material and were more successful in applying and integrating the material than the typers. The researchers suggested that because writing notes by hand is slower, students doing this cannot take notes verbatim but must listen, digest, and summarize the material, capturing the main points. Students who type notes can do so quickly and without processing the information.

Mueller and Oppenheimer (2014) also examined the contents of notes taken by college students in these two ways across a number of disciplines. They found that the typed notes—which were closer to verbatim transcriptions—were associated with lower retention of the lecture material. Even when study participants using laptops were instructed to think about the information and type the notes in their own words, they were no better at synthesizing material than students who were not given the warning. The authors concluded that typing notes does not promote understanding or application of the information; they suggested that notes in the students' own words and handwriting may serve as more effective memory prompts by recreating context (e.g., thought processes, conclusions) and content from the original lecture.

Developing Explanations

Encouraging learners to create explanations of what they are learning is a promising method of supporting understanding. Three techniques for doing this have been studied: elaborative interrogation, self-explanation, and teaching.

Elaborative interrogation is a strategy in which learners are asked, or are prompted to ask themselves, questions that invite deep reasoning, such as why, how, what-if, and what-if not (as opposed to shallow questions such as who, what, when, and where) (Gholson et al., 2009). A curious student who applies intelligent elaborative interrogation asks deep-reasoning questions as she strives to comprehend difficult material and solve problems. However, elaborative interrogation does not come naturally to most children and adults; training people to use this skill—and particularly training in asking deep questions—has been shown to have a positive impact on comprehension, learning, and memory (Gholson et al., 2009; Graesser and Lehman, 2012; Graesser and Olde, 2003; Rosenshine et al., 1996). For example, in an early study, people were asked either to provide "why" explanations for several unrelated sentences or to read and study the sentences. Both groups were then tested on their memory of the sentences. Those who asked questions performed better than the group that just studied the sentences (Pressley et al., 1987). Studies with children have also shown benefits of elaborative interrogation (Woloshyn et al., 1994), and the benefits of elaborative interrogation can persist over time (e.g., 1 or 2 weeks after learning), though few studies have examined effects of elaborative interrogation on long-term retention.

Most studies conducted by researchers in experimental psychology have used isolated facts as materials in studying the effects of elaboration and have assessed verbatim retention, but researchers in educational psychology have also looked at more complex text content and assessed inference making (Dornisch and Sperling, 2006; Ozgungor and Guthrie, 2004). For example, McDaniel and Donnelly (1996) asked college students to study short descriptions of physics concepts, such as the conservation of angular momentum, and then answer a why question about the concept (e.g., "Why does an object speed up as its radius get smaller, as in conservation of angular momentum?"). A final assessment involved both factual questions and inference questions that tapped into deeper levels of comprehension. The authors found benefits of elaborative interrogation for complex materials and assessments and also found that those who engaged in elaborative interrogation outperformed learners who produced labeled diagrams of the concepts in each brief text.

Self-explanation is a strategy in which learners produce explanations of material or of their thought processes while they are reading, answering questions, or solving problems. In the most general case, learners may simply be asked to explain each step they take as they solve a problem (Chi et al., 1989b; McNamara, 2004) or explain a text sentence-by-sentence as they read it (Chi et al., 1994). Self-explanation involves more open-ended prompts than the specific "why" questions used in elaborative interrogation, but both strategies encourage learners to elaborate on the material by generating explanations. Other examples of this work include self-explanations of physics.

An early study of self-explanation was carried out by Chi and colleagues (1994). Eighth-grade students learned about the circulatory system by reading an expository text. While one group just read the text, a second group of students produced explanations for each sentence in the text. The students who self-explained showed larger gains in comprehension of concepts in the text. A subsequent study showed similar results (Wylie and Chi, 2014). Self-explanation has now been explored in a wide range of contexts, including comprehension of science texts in a classroom setting (McNamara, 2004), learning of chess moves (de Bruin et al., 2007), learning of mathematics concepts (Rittle-Johnson, 2006), and learning from worked examples on problems that require reasoning (Nokes-Malach et al., 2013). Self-explanation prompts have been included in intelligent tutoring systems (Aleven and Koedinger, 2002) and systems with game components (Jackson and McNamara, 2013; Mayer and Johnson, 2010). However, relatively few studies have examined the effects of self-explanation on long-term retention or explored the question of how much self-explanation is needed to produce notable results (Jackson and McNamara, 2013).

A few studies have explored the relationship between self-explanation and prior knowledge in learning (Williams and Lombrozo, 2013). For example, Ionas and colleagues (2012) investigated whether self-explanation was beneficial to college students who were asked to do chemistry problems. They found that prior knowledge moderated the effectiveness of self-explanation and that the more prior knowledge of chemistry the students reported having, the more self-explanation appeared to help them learn. Moreover, for students who had just a little prior knowledge, using self-explanation seemed to impede rather than support performance. The researchers suggested that learners search for concepts or processes in their prior knowledge to make sense of new material; when the prior knowledge is weak, the entire process fails. They concluded that educators should thoroughly assess the learners' prior knowledge and use other cognitive support tools and methods during the early stages of the learning process, as learners strengthen their knowledge base.

Finally, *teaching* others can be an effective learning experience. When learners prepare to teach they must construct explanations, just as they do in elaborative interrogation and self-explanation activities. However, elaborative interrogation and self-explanation both require that the learner receive fairly specific prompts, whereas the act of preparing to teach can be more open-ended. Teaching others is often an excellent opportunity to hone one's own knowledge (Biswas et al., 2005; Palincsar and Brown, 1984), and learners in this kind of interaction are likely to feel empowered and responsible in a way that they do not feel when they are the passive recipients of knowledge (Scardamalia and Bereiter, 1993). Peers may be able to express themselves to each other in ways that are particularly relevant, immediate, and informative. Although peer learning and teaching are often quite effective, teachers and instructors typically come closer to injunctive norms and provide better models to observe.

A foundational study of the effects of teaching on learning by Bargh and Schul (1980) has served as a template for subsequent studies. Bargh and Schul asked participants to study a set of materials and either prepare to teach the material to a peer or simply study it for an upcoming test. Both groups were tested on the material without teaching it; only the expectation to teach had been manipulated. Students who prepared to teach others performed better on the assessment than students who simply read and studied the material. Effects of preparing to teach have been replicated in studies since Bargh and Schul's foundational work (e.g., Fiorella and Mayer, 2014).

The benefits of teaching are evident in other contexts. For example, research on tutoring has shown that while students certainly learn by being tutored, the tutors themselves learn from the experience (see Roscoe and Chi, 2007). Reciprocal teaching is another strategy, used primarily in improving students' reading comprehension (Palincsar, 2013; Palincsar and Brown, 1984). In reciprocal teaching, students learn by taking turns teaching material to each other. The students are given guidance: training in four strategies to help them recognize and react to signs of comprehension breakdown (questioning, clarifying, summarizing, and predicting) (Palincsar, 2013).

The research suggests several possible reasons why teaching may benefit learners. Preparing to teach requires elaborative processing because learners need to generate, organize, and integrate knowledge. Also, as mentioned, the explanations that people create may promote learning in the same way that elaborative interrogation and self-explanations promote learning. The process of explaining to others is active and generative, and it encourages learners to focus on deeper questions and levels of comprehension. Explaining in a teaching context also involves retrieval practice, as the teacher actively engages in retrieving knowledge in order to explain instructional content and answer questions. Although researchers have documented benefits of explanation, there are cautions to bear in mind. For example, a few researchers in this area have noted that in developing explanations learners may tend to make broad generalizations at the expense of significant specifics (Lombrozo, 2012; Williams and Lombrozo, 2010; Williams et al., 2013). Children tend to prefer a single explanation for two different phenomena (e.g., a toy that both lights up and spins), even when there are two independent causes (Bonawitz and Lombrozo, 2012). Likewise, when diagnosing diseases based on observable symptoms, adults tend to attribute the two symptoms to a single disease, even when it is more likely that there are two separate diseases (Lombrozo, 2007;

Pacer and Lombrozo, 2017). The tendency to prefer simple, broad explanations over more complex ones may affect what people learn and the inferences they draw. For each of the different types of explanation strategies, researchers have noted reasons for educators to plan carefully when and how they can be used most effectively.

CONCLUSIONS

Learners identify and establish relationships among pieces of information and develop increasingly complex structures for using and categorizing what they have learned. Accumulating bodies of knowledge, structuring that knowledge, and developing the capacity to reason about the knowledge one has are key cognitive assets throughout the life span.

Strategies for supporting learning include those that focus on retention and retrieval of knowledge as well as those that support development of deeper and more sophisticated understanding of what is learned. The strategies that have shown promise for promoting learning help learners to develop the mental models they need to retain knowledge so they can use it adaptively and flexibly in making inferences and solving new problems.

> **CONCLUSION 5-1: Prior knowledge can reduce the attentional demands associated with engaging in well-learned activities, and it can facilitate new learning. However, prior knowledge can also lead to bias by causing people to not attend to new information and to rely on existing schema to solve new problems. These biases can be overcome but only through conscious effort.**

> **CONCLUSION 5-2: Learners routinely generate their own novel understanding of the information they are accumulating and productively extend their knowledge by making logical connections between pieces of information. This capacity to generate novel understanding allows learners to use their knowledge to generalize, categorize, and solve problems.**

> **CONCLUSION 5-3: The learning strategies for which there is evidence of effectiveness include ways to help students retrieve information and encourage them to summarize and explain material they are learning, as well as ways to space and structure the presentation of material. Effective strategies to create organized and distinctive knowledge structures encourage learners to go beyond the explicit material by elaborating**

and to enrich their mental representation of information by calling up and applying it in various contexts.

CONCLUSION 5-4: The effectiveness of learning strategies is influenced by such contextual factors as the learner's existing skills and prior knowledge, the nature of the material, and the goals for learning. Applying these approaches effectively therefore requires careful thought about how their specific mechanisms could be beneficial for particular learners, settings, and learning objectives.

6

Motivation to Learn

Motivation is a condition that activates and sustains behavior toward a goal. It is critical to learning and achievement across the life span in both informal settings and formal learning environments. For example, children who are motivated tend to be engaged, persist longer, have better learning outcomes, and perform better than other children on standardized achievement tests (Pintrich, 2003). Motivation is distinguishable from general cognitive functioning and helps to explain gains in achievement independent of scores on intelligence tests (Murayama et al., 2013). It is also distinguishable from states related to it, such as engagement, interest, goal orientation, grit, and tenacity, all of which have different antecedents and different implications for learning and achievement (Järvelä and Renninger, 2014).

HPL I[1] emphasized some key findings from decades of research on motivation to learn:

- People are motivated to develop competence and solve problems by rewards and punishments but often have intrinsic reasons for learning that may be more powerful.
- Learners tend to persist in learning when they face a manageable challenge (neither too easy nor too frustrating) and when they see the value and utility of what they are learning.
- Children and adults who focus mainly on their own performance (such as on gaining recognition or avoiding negative judgments) are

---

[1] As noted in Chapter 1, this report uses the abbreviation "*HPL I*" for *How People Learn: Brain, Mind, Experience, and School: Expanded Edition* (National Research Council, 2000).

less likely to seek challenges and persist than those who focus on learning itself.

- Learners who focus on learning rather than performance or who have intrinsic motivation to learn tend to set goals for themselves and regard increasing their competence to be a goal.
- Teachers can be effective in encouraging students to focus on learning instead of performance, helping them to develop a learning orientation.

In this chapter, we provide updates and additional elaboration on research in this area. We begin by describing some of the primary theoretical perspectives that have shaped this research, but our focus is on four primary influences on people's motivation to learn. We explore research on people's own beliefs and values, intrinsic motivation, the role of learning goals, and social and cultural factors that affect motivation to learn. We then examine research on interventions and approaches to instructional design that may influence motivation to learn, and we close with our conclusions about the implications of this research.

The research we discuss includes both laboratory and field research from multiple disciplines, such as developmental psychology, social psychology, education, and cognitive psychology.

THEORETICAL PERSPECTIVES

Research on motivation has been strongly driven by theories that overlap and contain similar concepts. A comprehensive review of this literature is beyond the scope of this report, but we highlight a few key points. *Behavior-based theories of learning,* which conceptualized motivation in terms of habits, drives, incentives, and reinforcement schedules, were popular through the mid-20th century. In these approaches, learners were assumed to be passive in the learning process and research focused mainly on individual differences between people (e.g., cognitive abilities, drive for achievement). These differences were presumed to be fixed and to dictate learners' responses to features in the learning environment (method of instruction, incentives, and so on) and their motivation and performance.

Current researchers regard many of these factors as important but have also come to focus on learners as active participants in learning and to pay greater attention to how learners make sense of and choose to engage with their learning environments. Cognitive theories, for example, have focused on how learners set goals for learning and achievement and how they maintain and monitor their progress toward those goals. They also consider how physical aspects of the learning environment, such as classroom structures (Ames, 1986) and social interactions (e.g., Gehlbach et al., 2016), affect learning through their impacts on students' goals, beliefs, affect, and actions.

Motivation is also increasingly viewed as an *emergent phenomenon*, meaning it can develop over time and change as a result of one's experiences with learning and other circumstances. Research suggests, for example, that aspects of the learning environment can both trigger and sustain a student's curiosity and interest in ways that support motivation and learning (Hidi and Renninger, 2006).

A key factor in motivation is an individual's *mindset*: the set of assumptions, values, and beliefs about oneself and the world that influence how one perceives, interprets, and acts upon one's environment (Dweck, 1999). For example, a person's view as to whether intelligence is fixed or malleable is likely to link to his views of the malleability of his own abilities (Hong and Lin-Siegler, 2012). As we discuss below, learners who have a fixed view of intelligence tend to set demonstrating competence as a learning goal, whereas learners who have an incremental theory of intelligence tend to set mastery as a goal and to place greater value on effort. Mindsets develop over time as a function of learning experiences and cultural influences. Research related to mindsets has focused on patterns in how learners construe goals and make choices about how to direct attention and effort. Some evidence suggests that it is possible to change students' self-attributions so that they adopt a growth mindset, which in turn improves their academic performance (Blackwell et al., 2007).

Researchers have also tried to integrate the many concepts that have been introduced to explain this complex aspect of learning in order to formulate a more comprehensive understanding of motivational processes and their effects on learning. For example, researchers who study psychological aspects of motivation take a *motivational systems perspective*, viewing motivation as a set of psychological mechanisms and processes, such as those related to setting goals, engagement in learning, and use of self-regulatory strategies (Kanfer, 2015; Linnenbrink-Garcia and Patall, 2016; Yeager and Walton, 2011).

LEARNERS' BELIEFS AND VALUES

Learners' ideas about their own competence, their values, and the preexisting interests they bring to a particular learning situation all influence motivation.

Self-Efficacy

When learners expect to succeed, they are more likely to put forth the effort and persistence needed to perform well. *Self-efficacy theory* (Bandura, 1977), which is incorporated into several models of motivation and learning, posits that the perceptions learners have about their competency or capabilities are critical to accomplishing a task or attaining other goals (Bandura, 1977).

According to self-efficacy theory, learning develops from multiple sources, including perceptions of one's past performance, vicarious experiences, performance feedback, affective/physiological states, and social influences. Research on how to improve self-efficacy for learning has shown the benefits of several strategies for strengthening students' sense of their competence for learning, including setting appropriate goals and breaking down difficult goals into subgoals (Bandura and Schunk, 1981) and providing students with information about their progress, which allows them to attribute success to their own effort (Schunk and Cox, 1986). A sense of competence may also foster interest and motivation, particularly when students are given the opportunity to make choices about their learning activities (Patall et al., 2014).

Another important aspect of self-attribution involves beliefs about whether one belongs in a particular learning situation. People who come from backgrounds where college attendance is not the norm may question whether they belong in college despite having been admitted. Students may misinterpret short-term failure as reflecting that they do not belong, when in fact short-term failure is common among all college students. These students experience a form of stereotype threat, where prevailing cultural stereotypes about their position in the world cause them to doubt themselves and perform more poorly (Steele and Aronson, 1995).

A recent study examined interventions designed to boost the sense of belonging among African American college freshmen (Walton and Cohen, 2011). The researchers compared students who did and did not encounter survey results ostensibly collected from more senior college students, which indicated that most senior students had worried about whether they belonged during their first year of college but had become more confident over time. The students who completed the activity made significant academic gains, and the researchers concluded that even brief interventions can help people overcome the bias of prior knowledge by challenging that knowledge and supporting a new perspective.

Another approach to overcoming the bias of knowledge is to use strategies that can prevent some of the undesirable consequences of holding negative perspectives. One such strategy is to support learners in trying out multiple ideas before settling on the final idea. In one study, for example, researchers asked college students either to design a Web page advertisement for an online journal and then refine it several times or to create several separate ones (Dow et al., 2010). The researchers posted the advertisements and assessed their effectiveness both by counting how many clicks each generated and by asking experts in Web graphics to rate them. The authors found that the designs developed separately were more effective and concluded that when students refined their initial designs, they were trapped by their initial decisions. The students who developed separate advertisements explored the possibilities more thoroughly and had more ideas to choose from.

Values

Learners may not engage in a task or persist with learning long enough to achieve their goals unless they value the learning activities and goals. *Expectancy-value theories* have drawn attention to how learners choose goals depending on their beliefs about both their ability to accomplish a task and the value of that task. The concept of value encompasses learners' judgments about (1) whether a topic or task is useful for achieving learning or life goals, (2) the importance of a topic or task to the learner's identity or sense of self, (3) whether a task is enjoyable or interesting, and (4) whether a task is worth pursuing (Eccles et al., 1983; Wigfield and Eccles, 2000).

Research with learners of various ages supports the idea that those who expect to succeed at a task exert more effort and have higher levels of performance (Eccles and Wigfield, 2002). However, some studies have suggested that task valuation seems to be the strongest predictor of behaviors associated with motivation, such as choosing topics and making decisions about participation in training (Linnenbrink-Garcia et al., 2008). Such research illustrates one of the keys to expectancy-value theory: the idea that expectancy and value dimensions work together. For example, a less-than-skilled reader may nevertheless approach a difficult reading task with strong motivation to persist in the task if it is interesting, useful, or important to the reader's identity (National Research Council, 2012c). As learners experience success at a task or in a domain of learning, such as reading or math, the value they attribute to those activities can increase over time (Eccles and Wigfield, 2002).

Interest

Learners' interest is an important consideration for educators because they can accommodate those interests as they design curricula and select learning resources. Interest is also important in adult learning in part because students and trainees with little interest in a topic may show higher rates of absenteeism and lower levels of performance (Ackerman et al., 2001).

Two forms of learner interest have been identified. Individual or *personal interest* is viewed as a relatively stable attribute of the individual. It is characterized by a learner's enduring connection to a domain and willingness to re-engage in learning in that domain over time (Schiefele, 2009). In contrast, *situational interest* refers to a psychological state that arises spontaneously in response to specific features of the task or learning environment (Hidi and Renninger, 2006). Situational interest is malleable, can affect student engagement and learning, and is influenced by the tasks and materials educators use or encourage (Hunsu et al., 2017). Practices that engage students and influence their attitudes may increase their personal interest and intrinsic motivation over time (Guthrie et al., 2006).

Sometimes the spark of motivation begins with a meaningful alignment of student interest with an assignment or other learning opportunity. At other times, features of the learning environment energize a state of wanting to know more, which activates motivational processes. In both cases, it is a change in mindset and goal construction brought about by interest that explains improved learning outcomes (Barron, 2006; Bricker and Bell, 2014; Goldman and Booker, 2009). For instance, when learner interest is low, students may be less engaged and more likely to attend to the learning goals that require minimal attention and effort.

Many studies of how interest affects learning have included measures of reading comprehension and text recall. This approach has allowed researchers to assess the separate effects of topic interest and interest in a specific text on how readers interact with text, by measuring the amount of time learners spend reading and what they learn from it. Findings from studies of this sort suggest that educators can foster students' interest by selecting resources that promote interest, by providing feedback that supports attention (Renninger and Hidi, 2002), by demonstrating their own interest in a topic, and by generating positive affect in learning contexts (see review by Hidi and Renninger, 2006).

This line of research has also suggested particular characteristics of texts that are associated with learner interest. For example, in one study of college students, five characteristics of informational texts were associated with both interest and better recall: (1) the information was important, new, and valued; (2) the information was unexpected; (3) the text supported readers in making connections with prior knowledge or experience; (4) the text contained imagery and descriptive language; and (5) the author attempted to relate information to readers' background knowledge using, for example, comparisons and analogies (Wade et al., 1999). The texts that students viewed as less interesting interfered with comprehension in that they, for example, offered incomplete or shallow explanations, contained difficult vocabulary, or lacked coherence.

A number of studies suggest that situational interest can be a strong predictor of engagement, positive attitudes, and performance, including a study of students' essay writing (Flowerday et al., 2004) and other research (e.g., Alexander and Jetton, 1996; Schraw and Lehman, 2001). These studies suggest the power of situational interest for engaging students in learning, which has implications for the design of project-based or problem-based learning. For example, Hoffman and Haussler (1998) found that high school girls displayed significantly more interest in the physics related to the working of a pump when the mechanism was put into a real-world context: the use of a pump in heart surgery.

The perception of having a choice may also influence situational interest and engagement, as suggested by a study that examined the effects of classroom practices on adolescents enrolled in a summer school science course

(Linnenbrink-Garcia et al., 2013). The positive effect learners experience as part of interest also appears to play a role in their persistence and ultimately their performance (see, e.g., Ainley et al., 2002).

Intrinsic Motivation

Self-determination theory posits that behavior is strongly influenced by three universal, innate, psychological needs—autonomy (the urge to control one's own life), competence (the urge to experience mastery), and psychological relatedness (the urge to interact with, be connected to, and care for others). Researchers have linked this theory to people's intrinsic motivation to learn (Deci and Ryan, 1985, 2000; Ryan and Deci, 2000). Intrinsic motivation is the experience of wanting to engage in an activity for its own sake because the activity is interesting and enjoyable or helps to achieve goals one has chosen. From the perspective of self-determination theory (Deci and Ryan, 1985, 2000; Ryan and Deci, 2000), learners are intrinsically motivated to learn when they perceive that they have a high degree of autonomy and engage in an activity willingly, rather than because they are being externally controlled. Learners who are intrinsically motivated also perceive that the challenges of a problem or task are within their abilities.

External Rewards

The effect of external rewards on intrinsic motivation is a topic of much debate. External rewards can be an important tool for motivating learning behaviors, but some argue that such rewards are harmful to intrinsic motivation in ways that affect persistence and achievement.

For example, some research suggests that intrinsic motivation to persist at a task may decrease if a learner receives extrinsic rewards contingent on performance. The idea that extrinsic rewards harm intrinsic motivation has been supported in a meta-analysis of 128 experiments (Deci et al., 1999, 2001). One reason proposed for such findings is that learners' initial interest in the task and desire for success are replaced by their desire for the extrinsic reward (Deci and Ryan, 1985). External rewards, it is argued, may also undermine the learner's perceptions of autonomy and control.

Other research points to potential benefits. A recent field study, for example, suggests that incentives do not always lead to reduced engagement after the incentive ends (Goswami and Urminsky, 2017). Moreover, in some circumstances external rewards such as praise or prizes can help to encourage engagement and persistence, and they may not harm intrinsic motivation over the long term, provided that the extrinsic reward does not undermine the individual's sense of autonomy and control over her behavior (see National Research Council, 2012c, pp. 143–145; also see Cerasoli et al.,

2016; Vansteenkiste et al., 2009). Thus, teaching strategies that use rewards to capture and stimulate interest in a topic (rather than to drive compliance), that provide the student with encouragement (rather than reprimands), and that are perceived to guide student progress (rather than just monitor student progress) can foster feelings of autonomy, competence, and academic achievement (e.g., Vansteenkist et al., 2004). Praise is important, but what is praised makes a difference (see Box 6-1).

Other work (Cameron et al., 2005) suggests that when rewards are inherent in the achievement itself—that is, when rewards for successful completion of a task include real privileges, pride, or respect—they can spur intrinsic motivation. This may be the case, for example, with videogames in which individuals are highly motivated to play well in order to move to the next higher level. This may also be the case when learners feel valued and respected for their demonstrations of expertise, as when a teacher asks a student who correctly completed a challenging homework math problem to explain his solution to the class. Extrinsic rewards support engagement sufficient for learning, as shown in one study in which rewards were associated with enhanced memory consolidation but only when students perceived the material to be boring (Murayama and Kuhbandner, 2011). Given the prevalence

BOX 6-1 **What You Praise Makes a Difference**

Praise received after success influences students' later achievement motivation but perhaps not in the way intended. Mueller and Dweck (1998) conducted two studies in which students received praise for their performance on a reasoning test. Some students were praised for their ability ("*well done for being so smart*") and others for their effort ("*well done for working so hard*"). Students who received praise for ability were more likely to adopt performance goals on a subsequent test, whereas those praised for effort were more likely to adopt mastery goals. Further, when given the choice, a higher proportion (86%) of students praised for ability chose to examine a folder they were told contained average scores of other test takers, rather than a folder they were told contained new interesting strategies for solving similar test problems. In stark contrast, less than one-quarter (24%) of those praised for effort opted for performance information. Students praised for ability engaged in behaviors that may have boosted their self-esteem but were not likely to facilitate more learning or preparation for test-taking in the future.

of different performance-based incentives in classrooms (e.g., grades, prizes), a better, more integrated understanding is needed of how external rewards may harm or benefit learners' motivation in ways that matter to achievement and performance in a range of real-world conditions across the life span.

Effects of Choice

When learners believe they have control over their learning environment, they are more likely to take on challenges and persist with difficult tasks, compared with those who perceive that they have little control (National Research Council, 2012c). Evidence suggests that the opportunity to make meaningful choices during instruction, even if they are small, can support autonomy, motivation, and ultimately, learning and achievement (Moller et al., 2006; Patall et al., 2008, 2010).[2]

Choice may be particularly effective for individuals with high initial interest in the domain, and it may also generate increased interest (Patall, 2013). One possible reason why exercising choice seems to increase motivation is that the act of making a choice induces cognitive dissonance: a feeling of being uncomfortable and unsure about one's decision. To reduce this feeling, individuals tend to change their preferences to especially value and become interested in the thing they chose (Izuma et al., 2010). Knowing that one has made a choice ("owning the choice") can protect against the discouraging effects of negative feedback during the learning process, an effect that has been observed at the neurophysiological level (Murayama et al., 2015). The perception of choice also may affect learning by fostering situational interest and engagement (Linnenbrink-Garcia et al., 2013).

THE IMPORTANCE OF GOALS

Goals—the learner's desired outcomes—are important for learning because they guide decisions about whether to expend effort and how to direct attention, foster planning, influence responses to failure, and promote other behaviors important for learning (Albaili, 1998; Dweck and Elliot, 1983; Hastings and West, 2011).

Learners may not always be conscious of their goals or of the motivation processes that relate to their goals. For example, activities that learners perceive as enjoyable or interesting can foster engagement without the learner's

---

[2] The 2008 study was a meta-analysis, so the study populations are not described. The 2010 study included a total of 207 (54% female) high school students from ninth through twelfth grade. A majority (55.5%) of the students in these classes were Caucasian, 28 percent were African American, 7 percent were Asian, 3 percent were Hispanic, 1.5 percent were Native American, and 5 percent were of other ethnicities.

conscious awareness. Similarly, activities that learners perceive as threatening to their sense of competence or self-esteem (e.g., conditions that invoke stereotype threat, discussed below[3]) may reduce learners' motivation and performance even (and sometimes especially) when they intend to perform well.

HPL I made the point that having clear and specific goals that are challenging but manageable has a positive effect on performance, and researchers have proposed explanations. Some have focused on goals as motives or reasons to learn (Ames and Ames, 1984; Dweck and Elliott, 1983; Locke et al., 1981; Maehr, 1984; Nicholls, 1984). Others have noted that different types of goals, such as mastery and performance goals, have different effects on the cognitive, affective, and behavioral processes that underlie learning as well as on learners' outcomes (Ames and Archer, 1988; Covington, 2000; Dweck, 1986). Research has also linked learners' beliefs about learning and achievement, or mindsets, with students' pursuit of specific types of learning goals (Maehr and Zusho, 2009). The next section examines types of goals and research on their influence.

Types of Goals

Researchers distinguish between two main types of goals: *mastery goals,* in which learners focus on increasing competence or understanding, and *performance goals*, in which learners are driven by a desire to appear competent or outperform others (see Table 6-1). They further distinguish between *performance-approach* and *performance-avoidance* goals (Senko et al., 2011). Learners who embrace performance-avoidance goals work to avoid looking incompetent or being embarrassed or judged as a failure, whereas those who adopt performance-approach goals seek to appear more competent than others and to be judged socially in a favorable light. Within the category of performance-approach goals, researchers have identified both *self-presentation goals* ("wanting others to think you are smart") and *normative goals* ("wanting to outperform others") (Hulleman et al., 2010).

Learners may simultaneously pursue multiple goals (Harackiewicz et al., 2002; Hulleman et al., 2008) and, depending on the subject area or skill domain, may adopt different achievement goals (Anderman and Midgley, 1997). Although students' achievement goals are relatively stable across the school years, they are sensitive to changes in the learning environment, such as moving from one classroom to another or changing schools (Friedel et al., 2007). Learning environments differ in the learning expectations, rules, and

---

[3] When an individual encounters negative stereotypes about his social identity group in the context of a cognitive task, he may underperform on that task; this outcome is attributed to stereotype threat (Steele, 1997).

TABLE 6-1 Mindsets, Goals, and Their Implications for Learning

Mindsets	
Fixed mindset—*you are born with a certain amount of intelligence*	Growth mindset—*intelligence can be acquired through hard work*
Goals	
Performance goal—*works to look good in comparison to others*	Mastery goal—*works to learn/ master the material or skill*
Learning Behaviors	
Avoids challenges—*prioritizes areas of high competence*	Rises to challenges—*prioritizes areas of new knowledge*
Quits in response to failure— *expends less effort*	Tries harder in response to failure—*puts forth more effort*
Pursues opportunities to bolter self-esteem—*seeks affirming social comparisons*	Pursues opportunities to learn more— *seeks more problem-solving strategies*

structure that apply, and as a result, students may shift their goal orientation to succeed in the new context (Anderman and Midgley, 1997).

Dweck (1986) argued that achievement goals reflect learners' underlying theories of the nature of intelligence or ability: whether it is fixed (something with which one is born) or malleable. Learners who believe intelligence is malleable, she suggested, are predisposed toward adopting mastery goals, whereas learners who believe intelligence is fixed tend to orient toward displaying competence and adopting performance goals (Burns and Isbell, 2007; Dweck, 1986; Dweck and Master, 2009; Mangels et al., 2006). Table 6-1 shows how learners' mindsets can relate to their learning goals and behaviors.

Research in this area suggests that learners who strongly endorse mastery goals tend to enjoy novel and challenging tasks (Pintrich, 2000; Shim et al., 2008; Witkow and Fuligni, 2007; Wolters, 2004), demonstrate a greater willingness to expend effort, and engage higher-order cognitive skills during learning (Ames, 1992; Dweck and Leggett, 1988; Kahraman and Sungur, 2011; Middleton and Midgley, 1997). Mastery students are also persistent—even in the face of failure—and frequently use failure as an opportunity to seek feedback and improve subsequent performance (Dweck and Leggett, 1988).

Learners' mastery and performance goals may also influence learning and achievement through indirect effects on cognition. Specifically, learners with mastery goals tend to focus on relating new information to existing knowledge as they learn, which supports deep learning and long-term memory for the information. By contrast, learners with performance goals tend to focus on learning individual bits of information separately, which improves speed of learning and immediate recall but may undermine conceptual learning and long-term recall. In this way, performance goals tend to support better immediate retrieval of information, while mastery goals tend to support better long-term retention (Crouzevialle and Butera, 2013). Performance goals may in fact undermine conceptual learning and long-term recall. When learners with mastery goals work to recall a previously learned piece of information, they also activate and strengthen memory for the other, related information they learned. When learners with performance goals try to recall what they learned, they do not get the benefit of this retrieval-induced strengthening of their memory for other information (Ikeda et al., 2015).

Two studies with undergraduate students illustrate this point. Study participants who adopted performance goals were found to be concerned with communicating competence, prioritizing areas of high ability, and avoiding challenging tasks or areas in which they perceived themselves to be weaker than others (Darnon et al., 2007; Elliot and Murayama, 2008). These students perceived failure as a reflection of their inability and typically responded to failure with frustration, shame, and anxiety. These kinds of performance-avoidance goals have been associated with maladaptive learning behaviors including task avoidance (Middleton and Midgley, 1997; sixth-grade students), reduced effort (Elliot, 1999), and self-handicapping (Covington, 2000; Midgley et al., 1996).

The adoption of a mastery goal orientation to learning is likely to be beneficial for learning, while pursuit of performance goals is associated with poor learning-related outcomes. However, research regarding the impact of performance goals on academic outcomes has yielded mixed findings (Elliot and McGregor, 2001; Midgley et al., 2001). Some researchers have found positive outcomes when learners have endorsed normative goals (a type of performance goal) (Covington, 2000; Linnenbrink, 2005). Others have found that achievement goals do not have a direct effect on academic achievement but operate instead through the intermediary learning behaviors described above and through self-efficacy (Hulleman et al., 2010).

Influence of Teachers on Learners' Goals

Classrooms can be structured to make particular goals more or less salient and can shift or reinforce learners' goal orientations (Maehr and Midgley, 1996). Learners' goals may reflect the classroom's goal structure or the values teachers communicate about learning through their teaching practices (e.g., how the chairs are set up or whether the teacher uses cooperative learning groups) (see Kaplan and Midgley, 1999; Urdan et al., 1998). When learners perceive mastery goals are valued in the classsroom, they are more likely

TABLE 6-2 Achievement Goals and Classroom Climate

Climate Dimension	Mastery Goal	Performance Goal
Success Defined as…	Improvement, progress	High grades, high normative performance
Value Placed on…	Effort/learning	Normatively high ability
Reasons for Satisfaction…	Working hard, challenge	Doing better than others
Teacher Oriented toward…	How students are learning	How students are performing
View of Errors/Mistakes…	Part of learning	Anxiety eliciting
Focus of Attention…	Process of learning	Own performance relative to others
Reasons for Effort…	Learning something new	High grades, performing better than others
Evaluation Criteria…	Absolute, progress	Normative

SOURCE: Adapted from Ames and Archer (1988, Tbl. 1, p. 261).

to use information-processing strategies, self-planning, and self-monitoring strategies (Ames and Archer, 1988; Schraw et al., 1995). A mastery-oriented structure in the classroom is positively correlated with high academic competency and negatively related to disruptive behaviors. Further, congruence in learners' perceptions of their own and their school's mastery orientation is associated with positive academic achievement and school well-being (Kaplan and Maehr, 1999).

Teachers can influence the goals learners adopt during learning, and learners' perceptions of classroom goal structures are better predictors of learners' goal orientations than are their perceptions of their parents' goals. Perceived classroom goals are also strongly linked to learners' academic efficacy in the transition to middle school. Hence, classroom goal structures are a particularly important target for intervention (Friedel et al., 2007; Kim et al., 2010). Table 6-2 summarizes a longstanding view of how the prevailing classroom goal structure—oriented toward either mastery goals or performance goals—affects the classroom climate for learning. However, more experimental research is needed to determine whether interventions designed to influence such mindsets benefit learners.

Learning Goals and Other Goals

Academic goals are shaped not only by the immediate learning context but also by the learners' goals and challenges, which develop and change throughout the life course. Enhancing a person's learning and achievement requires an understanding of what the person is trying to achieve: what goals the individual seeks to accomplish and why. However, it is not always easy to determine what goals an individual is trying to achieve because learners have multiple goals and their goals may shift in response to events and experiences. For example, children may adopt an academic goal as a means of pleasing parents or because they enjoy learning about a topic, or both. Teachers may participate in an online statistics course in order to satisfy job requirements for continuing education or because they view mastery of the topic as relevant to their identity as a teacher, or both.

At any given time, an individual holds multiple goals related to achievement, belongingness, identity, autonomy, and sense of competence that are deeply personal, cultural, and subjective. Which of these goals becomes salient in directing behavior at what times depends on the way the individual construes the situation. During adolescence, for example, social belongingness goals may take precedence over academic achievement goals: young people may experience greater motivation and improved learning in a group context that fosters relationships that serve and support achievement. Over the life span, academic achievement goals also become linked to career goals, and these may need to be adapted over time. For example, an adolescent who aspires to become a physician but who continually fails her basic science courses may need to protect her sense of competence by either building new strategies for learning science or revising her occupational goals.

A person's motivation to persist in learning in spite of obstacles and setbacks is facilitated when goals for learning and achievement are made explicit, are congruent with the learners' desired outcomes and motives, and are supported by the learning environment, as judged by the learner; this perspective is illustrated in Box 6-2.

Future Identities and Long-Term Persistence

Long-term learning and achievement tend to require not only the learner's interest, but also prolonged motivation and persistence. Motivation to persevere may be strengthened when students can perceive connections between their current action choices (present self) and their future self or possible future identities (Gollwitzer et al., 2011; Oyserman et al., 2015). The practice of displaying the names and accomplishments of past successful students is one way educators try to help current students see the connection.

Researchers have explored the mechanisms through which such experiences affect learning. Some neurobiological evidence, for example, suggests that compelling narratives that trigger emotions (such as admiration elicited by a story about a young person who becomes a civil rights leader for his community) may activate a mindset focused on a "possible future" or values

BOX 6-2 Learners' Perceptions of the Learning Environment Can Inadvertently Undermine Motivation

Consider the following letter, written by an elementary school student:

> Every day starts off new, but when I step in the class room I see the bad behavior chart, every single day. This fackt has always bothered me, and makes me feel like the expectations of me are low. Infackt I almost feel like the teacher is daring me to talk or do something bad. Its also like she wants me to test her limits. All of this really makes me uncomfrotble, especaly when I feel that my expectations are low.

Why does a standard chart meant to help the teachers monitor, reward, and correct students' behavior seem to undermine this boy's enthusiasm for school? The chart refers to a color-coded scheme for monitoring behavior with three levels: green (successful), yellow (warning), and red (call parent). The teacher reported that from March through September this student was judged consistently as green (successful) because he worked hard and interacted appropriately with others. So, what was the problem?

This letter suggests that although the student came to school ready to engage with his teacher about interesting ideas and to learn new academic skills, the teacher's strategy for managing the class caused him to infer that his teacher's main goal was to control his behavior, rather than to help him learn. This example is a reminder that sometimes the materials and strategies that teachers intend to support learning can have the opposite effect for some students.

SOURCE: Adapted from Immordino-Yang (2015).

(Immordino-Yang et al., 2009). Similar research also points to an apparent shifting between two distinct neural networks that researchers have associated with an "action now" mindset (with respect to the choices and behaviors for executing a task during learning) and a "possible future/values oriented" mindset (with respect to whether difficult tasks are ones that "people like me" do) (Immordino-Yang et al., 2012). Students who shift between these two mindsets may take a reflective stance that enables them to inspire themselves and to persist and perform well on difficult tasks to attain future goals (Immordino-Yang and Sylvan, 2010).

Practices that help learners recognize the motivational demands required and obstacles to overcome for achieving desired future outcomes also may support goal attainment, as suggested in one study of children's attempts to learn foreign-language vocabulary words (Gollwitzer et al., 2011). Research is needed, however, to better establish the efficacy of practices designed to shape learners' thinking about future identities and persistence

SOCIAL AND CULTURAL INFLUENCES ON MOTIVATION

All learners' goals emerge in a particular cultural context. As discussed in Chapter 2, the way individuals perceive and interpret the world and their own role in it, and their expectations about how people function socially, reflect the unique set of influences they have experienced. The procedures people use to complete tasks and solve problems, as well as the social emotional dispositions people bring to such tasks, are similarly shaped by context and experience (Elliott et al., 2001; Oyserman, 2011). In this section, the committee discusses three specific lines of research that illustrate the importance of culturally mediated views of the self and social identities to learners' perceptions of learning environments, goals, and performance.

Cross-Cultural Differences in Learners' Self-Construals

Over the past several decades, researchers have attempted to discern the influence of culture on a person's self-construal, or definition of herself in reference to others. In an influential paper, Markus and Kitayama (1991) distinguished between independent and interdependent self-construals and proposed that these may be associated with individualistic or collectivistic goals. For example, they argued that East Asian cultures tend to emphasize collectivistic goals, which promote a comparatively interdependent self-construal in which the self is experienced as socially embedded and one's accomplishments are tied to the community. In contrast, they argued, the prevailing North American culture tends to emphasize individualistic goals and an individualistic self-construal that prioritizes unique traits, abilities, and accomplishments tied to the self rather than to the community.

Although assigning cultural groups to either a collectivist or individualistic category oversimplifies very complex phenomena, several large-sample survey studies have offered insights about the ways learners who fit these two categories tend to vary in their assessment of goals, the goals they see as relevant or salient, and the ways in which their goals relate to other phenomena such as school achievement (King and McInerney, 2016). For example, in cross-cultural studies of academic goals, Dekker and Fischer (2008) found that gaining social approval in achievement contexts was particularly important for students who had a collectivist perspective. This cultural value may predispose students to adopt goals that help them to avoid the appearance of incompetence or negative judgments (i.e., performance-avoidance goals) (Elliot, 1997, 1999; Kitayama, Matsumoto, and Norasakkunkit, 1997).

More recent work has also explored the relationships between such differences and cultural context. For example, several studies have compared students' indications of endorsement for performance-avoidance goals and found that Asian students endorsed these goals to a greater degree than European American students did (Elliot et al., 2001; Zusho and Njoku, 2007; Zusho et al., 2005). This body of work seems to suggest that though there were differences, the performance avoidance may also have different outcomes in societies in which individualism is prioritized than in more collectivistic ones. These researchers found that performance-avoidance goals can be adaptive and associated with such positive academic outcomes as higher levels of engagement, deeper cognitive processing, and higher achievement. (See also the work of Chan and Lai [2006] on students in Hong Kong; Hulleman et al. [2010]; and the work of King [2015] on students in the Philippines.)

Although cultures may vary on average in their emphasis on individualism and collectivism, learners may think in either individualistic and collectivistic terms if primed to do so (Oyserman et al., 2009). For example, priming interventions such as those that encourage participants to call up personal memories of cross-cultural experiences (Tadmor et al., 2013) have been used successfully to shift students from their tendency to take one cultural perspective or the other. Work on such interventions is based on the assumption that one cultural perspective is not inherently better than the other: the most effective approaches would depend on what the person is trying to achieve in the moment and the context in which he is operating. Problem solving is facilitated when the salient mindset is well matched to the task at hand, suggesting that flexibility in cultural mindset also may promote flexible cognitive functioning and adaptability to circumstances (Vezzali et al., 2016).

This perspective also suggests the potential benefits of encouraging learners to think about problems and goals from different cultural perspectives. Some evidence suggests that these and other multicultural priming interventions improve creativity and persistence because they cue individuals to think of problems as having multiple possible solutions. For instance, priming learners to adopt a multicultural mindset may support more-divergent thinking about multiple possible goals related to achievement, family, identity, and friendships and more flexible action plans for achieving those goals. Teachers may be able to structure learning opportunities that incorporate diverse perspectives related to cultural self-construals in order to engage students more effectively (Morris et al., 2015).

However, a consideration for both research and practice moving forward is that there may be much more variation within cultural models of the self than has been assumed. In a large study of students across several nations that examined seven different dimensions related to self-construal (Vignoles et al., 2016), researchers found neither a consistent contrast between Western and non-Western cultures nor one between collectivistic and individualistic cultures. To better explain cultural variation, the authors suggested an ecocultural perspective that takes into account racial/ethnic identity.

Social Identity and Motivation Processes

Identity is a person's sense of who she is. It is the lens through which an individual makes sense of experiences and positions herself in the social world. Identity has both personal and social dimensions that play an important role in shaping an individual's goals and motivation. The personal dimensions of identity tend to be traits (e.g., being athletic or smart) and values (e.g., being strongly committed to a set of religious or political beliefs). Social dimensions of identity are linked to social roles or characteristics that make one recognizable as a member of a group, such as being a woman or a Christian (Tajfel and Turner, 1979). They can operate separately (e.g., "an African American") or in combination ("an African American male student") (Oyserman, 2009).

Individuals tend to engage in activities that connect them to their social identities because doing so can support their sense of belonging and esteem and help them integrate into a social group. This integration often means taking on the particular knowledge, goals, and practices valued by that group (Nasir, 2002). The dimensions of identity are dynamic, malleable, and very sensitive to the situations in which people find themselves (Oyserman, 2009; Steele, 1997). This means the identity a person takes on at any moment is contingent on the circumstances

A number of studies indicate that a positive identification with one's racial or ethnic identity supports a sense of school belonging, as well as greater interest, engagement, and success in academic pursuits. For example, African American adolescents with positive attitudes toward their racial/ethnic group express higher efficacy beliefs and report more interest and engagement in school (Chavous et al., 2003). The value of culturally connected racial/ethnic identity is also evident for Mexican and Chinese adolescents (Fuligni et al., 2005). In middle school, this culturally connected identity is linked to higher grade-point averages among African American (Altschul et al., 2006; Eccles et al., 2006), Latino (Oyserman, 2009), and Native American students in North

BOX 6-3 Basketball, Mathematics, and Identity

In a study by Nasir and McKinney de Royston (2013), students were asked to solve problems involving averages and percentages in the context of either basketball or classroom math. When speaking about basketball, players spoke like experts—they "were confident; they sat up straight and answered in relaxed, even vocal tones. . . ." In stark contrast, when asked to solve the problems in classroom math terms, "players were visibly distressed. They shrunk down in their seats; they hemmed and hawed; they told the researcher how poor they were at mathematics" (Nasir and McKinney de Royston, 2013, p. 275). One explanation for these findings is that a sense of competence emerges from identity: as players, students felt competent to calculate scoring averages and percentages, but because they did not identify as math students, they felt ill-equipped to solve the same problems in the classroom context.

America (Fryberg et al., 2013). The research described in Box 6-3 illustrates the potential and powerful influence of social identity on learners' engagement with a task.

Stereotype Threat

The experience of being evaluated in academic settings can heighten self-awareness, including awareness of the stereotypes linked to the social group to which one belongs and that are associated with one's ability (Steele, 1997). The effects of social identity on motivation and performance may be positive, as illustrated in the previous section, but negative stereotypes can lead people to underperform on cognitive tasks (see Steele et al., 2002; Walton and Spencer, 2009). This phenomenon is known as *stereotype threat*, an unconscious worry that a stereotype about one's social group could be applied to oneself or that one might do something to confirm the stereotype (Steele, 1997). Steele has noted that stereotype threat is most likely in areas of performance in which individuals are particularly motivated.

In a prototypical experiment to test stereotype threat, a difficult achievement test is given to individuals who belong to a group for whom a negative stereotype about ability in that achievement domain exists. For example, women are given a test in math. The test is portrayed as either gender-neutral (women and men do equally well on it) or—in the threat condition—as one at which women do less well. In the threat condition, members of the stereotyped group perform at lower levels than they do in the gender-neutral condition. In the case of women and math, for instance, women perform more poorly on the math test than would be expected given their actual ability (as demonstrated in other contexts) (Steele and Aronson, 1995). Several studies have replicated this finding (Beilock et al., 2008; Dar-Nimrod and Heine, 2006; Good et al., 2008; Spencer et al., 1999), and the finding is considered to be robust, especially on high-stakes tests such as the SAT (Danaher and Crandall, 2008) and GRE.

The effects of negative stereotypes about African American and Latino students are among the most studied in this literature because these stereotypes have been persistent in the United States (Oyserman et al., 1995). Sensitivity to these learning-related stereotypes appears as early as second grade (Cvencek et al., 2011) and grows as children enter adolescence (McKown and Strambler, 2009). Among college-age African Americans, underperformance occurs in contexts in which students believe they are being academically evaluated (Steele and Aronson, 1995). African American school-age children perform worse on achievement tests when they are reminded of stereotypes associated with their social group (Schmader et al., 2008; Wasserberg, 2014). Similar negative effects of stereotype threat manifest among Latino youth (Aronson and Salinas, 1997; Gonzales et al., 2002; Schmader and Johns, 2003).

Stereotype threat is believed to undermine performance by lowering executive functioning and heightening anxiety and worry about what others will think if the individual fails, which robs the person of working memory resources. Thus, the negative effects of stereotype threat may not be as apparent on easy tasks but arise in the context of difficult and challenging tasks that require mental effort (Beilock et al., 2007).

Neurophysiological evidence supports this understanding of the mechanisms underlying stereotype threat. Under threatening conditions, individuals show lower levels of activation in the brain's prefrontal cortex, reflecting impaired executive functioning and working memory (Beilock et al., 2007; Cadinu et al., 2005; Johns et al., 2008; Lyons and Beilock, 2012; Schmader and Jones, 2003) and higher levels of activation in fear circuits, including, for example, in the amygdala (Spencer et al., 1999; Steele and Aronson, 1995).

In the short term, stereotype threat can result in upset, distraction, anxiety, and other conditions that interfere with learning and performance (Pennington et al., 2016). Stereotype threat also may have long-term deleterious effects because it can lead people to conclude that they are not likely to be successful in a domain of performance (Aronson, 2004; Steele, 1997). It has been suggested that the longer-term effects of stereotype threat may be one cause of longstanding achievement gaps (Walton and Spencer, 2009). For example, women for whom the poor-at-math stereotype was primed reported

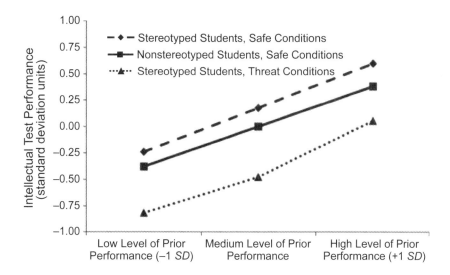

FIGURE 6-1 *Effect of supportive, safe conditions in reducing stereotype threat.*
NOTE: SD refers to standard deviation.
SOURCE: Walton and Spencer (2009, Fig. 1).

more negative thoughts about math (Cadinu et al., 2005). Such threats can be subtly induced. In one classroom study, cues in the form of gendered objects in the room led high school girls to report less interest in taking computer science courses (Master et al., 2015).

Students can maintain positive academic self-concepts in spite of negative stereotypes when supported in doing so (Anderman and Maehr, 1994; Graham, 1994; Yeager and Walton, 2011). For example, a study by Walton and Spencer (2009) illustrates that under conditions that reduce psychological threat, students for whom a stereotype about their social group exists perform better than nonstereotyped students at the same level of past performance (see Figure 6-1).

These findings highlight an important feature of stereotype threat: it is not a characteristic solely of a person or of a context but rather a condition that results from an interaction between the two. To be negatively affected, a person must be exposed to and perceive a potential cue in the environment and be aware of a stereotype about the social group with which he identifies (Aronson et al., 1999). For example, in a study of African American children in an urban elementary school, introduction of a reading test as an index of ability hampered performance only among students who reported being aware of racial stereotypes about intelligence (Walton and Spencer, 2009).

It also appears that the learner must tie her identity to the domain of skills being tested. For example, students who have a strong academic identity and value academic achievement highly are more vulnerable to academic stereotype threat than are other students (Aronson et al., 1999; Keller, 2007; Lawrence et al., 2010; Leyens et al., 2000; Steele, 1997).

Researchers have identified several actions educators can take that may help to manage stereotype threat. One is to remove the social identity characteristic (e.g., race or gender) as an evaluating factor, thereby reducing the possibility of confirming a stereotype (Steele, 1997). This requires bolstering or repositioning dimensions of social identity. Interventions of this sort are likely to work not because they reduce the perception of, or eliminate, stereotype threat, but because they change students responses to the threatening situation (Aronson et al., 2001; Good et al., 2003). For example, learners can be repositioned as the bearers of knowledge or expertise, which can facilitate identity shifts that enable learners to open up to opportunities for learning (Lee, 2012). In research that confronted women with negative gender-based stereotypes about their performance in mathematics but prompted them to think of other aspects of their identity, the women performed on par with men and appeared to be buffered against the deleterious effects of gender-based stereotypes. Women who did not receive the encouragement performed worse than their male counterparts (Gresky et al., 2005). Such findings suggest that having opportunities to be reminded of the full range of dimensions of one's identity may promote resilience against stereotype threats. Notably, interventions that have addressed stereotype threat tend to target and support identity rather than self-esteem. However, clear feedback that sets high expectations and assures a student that he can reach those expectations are also important (Cohen and Steele, 2002; Cohen et al., 1999).

Values-affirmation interventions are designed to reduce self-handicapping behavior and increase motivation to perform. Enabling threatened individuals to affirm their talents in other domains through self-affirmations has in some situations strengthened students' sense of self (McQueen and Klein, 2006). Values-affirmation exercises in which students write about their personal values (e.g., art, sports, music) have bolstered personal identity, reduced threat, and improved academic performance among students experiencing threat (Cohen et al., 2006, 2009; Martens et al., 2006). In randomized field experiments, self-affirmation tasks were associated with better grades for middle school students (Cohen et al., 2006, 2009)[4] and college students (Miyake et al., 2010). However, other studies have not replicated these findings (e.g., Dee, 2015; Hanselman et al., 2017), so research is needed to determine for whom and under which conditions values-affirmation approaches may be effective.

Although research suggests steps that educators can take that may help to

---

[4] The 2006 study included 119 African American and 119 European American students; the 2009 study was a 2-year follow-up with the same sample.

eliminate stereotype threat, much of this research has been in highly controlled settings. The full range of factors that may be operating and interacting with one another has yet to be fully examined in real-world environments. However, educators can take into account the influences that research has identified as potentially causing, exacerbating, or ameliorating the effects of stereotype threat on their own students' motivation, learning, and performance.

INTERVENTIONS TO IMPROVE MOTIVATION

Many students experience a decline in motivation from the primary grades through high school (Gallup, Inc., 2014; Jacobs et al., 2002; Lepper et al., 2005). Researchers are beginning to develop interventions motivated by theories of motivation to improve student motivation and learning.

Some interventions focus on the psychological mechanisms that affect students' construal of the learning environment and the goals they develop to adapt to that environment. For example, a brief intervention was designed to enhance student motivation by helping learners to overcome the negative impact of stereotype threat on social belongingness and sense of self (Yeager et al., 2016). In a randomized controlled study, African American and European American college students were asked to write a speech that attributed adversity in learning to a common aspect of the college-adjustment process rather than to personal deficits or their ethnic group (Walton and Cohen, 2011). After 3 years, African American students who had participated in the intervention reported less uncertainty about belonging and showed greater improvement in their grade point averages compared to the European American students.

One group of interventions to address performance setbacks has focused on exercises to help students shift from a fixed view of intelligence to a growth theory of intelligence. For example, in 1-year-long study, middle school students attended an eight-session workshop in which they either learned about study skills alone (control condition) or both study skills and research on how the brain improves and grows by working on challenging tasks (the growth mindset condition). At the end of the year, students in the growth mindset condition had significantly improved their math grades compared to students who only learned about study skills. However, the effect size was small and limited to a small subset of underachieving students (Blackwell et al., 2007).

The subjective and personal nature of the learner's experiences and the dynamic nature of the learning environment require that motivational interventions be flexible enough to take account of changes in the individual and in the learning environment. Over the past decade, a number of studies have suggested that interventions that enhance both short- and long-term motivation and achievement using brief interventions or exercises can be effective (e.g., Yeager and Walton, 2011). The interventions that have shown sustained effects on aspects of motivation and learning are based on relatively brief activities and exercises that directly target how students interpret their experiences, particularly their challenges in school and during learning.

The effectiveness of brief interventions appears to stem from their impact on the individual's construal of the situation and the motivational processes they set in motion, which in turn support longer-term achievement. Brief interventions to enhance motivation and achievement appear to share several important characteristics. First, the interventions directly target the psychological mechanisms that affect student motivation rather than academic content. Second, the interventions adopt a student-centric perspective that takes into account the student's subjective experience in and out of school. Third, the brief interventions are designed to indirectly affect how students think or feel about school or about themselves in school through experience, rather than attempting to persuade them to change their thinking, which is likely to be interpreted as controlling. Fourth, these brief interventions focus on reducing barriers to student motivation rather than directly increasing student motivation. Such interventions appear particularly promising for African American students and other cultural groups who are subjected to negative stereotypes about learning and ability. However, as Yeager and Walton (2011) note, the effectiveness of these interventions appears to depend on both context and implementation.

Studies such as these are grounded in different theories of motivation related to the learners' cognition, affect, or behavior and are intended to affect different aspects of motivation. Lazowski and Hulleman (2016) conducted a meta-analysis of research on such interventions to identify their effects on outcomes in education settings. The studies included using measures of authentic education outcomes (e.g., standardized test scores, persistence at a task, course choices, or engagement) and showed consistent, small effects across intervention type.

However, this meta-analysis was small: only 74 published and unpublished papers met criteria for inclusion, and the included studies involved a wide range of theoretical perspectives, learner populations, types of interventions, and measured outcomes. These results are not a sufficient basis for conclusions about practice, but further research may help identify which interventions work best for whom and under which conditions, as well as factors that affect implementation (such as dosage, frequency, and timing). Improvements in the ability to clearly define, distinguish among, and measure motivational constructs could improve the validity and usefulness of intervention research.

CONCLUSIONS

When learners want and expect to succeed, they are more likely to value learning, persist at challenging tasks, and perform well. A broad constellation of factors and circumstances may either trigger or undermine students' desire to learn and their decisions to expend effort on learning, whether in the moment or over time. These factors include learners' beliefs and values, personal goals, and social and cultural context. Advances since the publication of *HPL I* provide robust evidence for the importance of both an individual's goals in motivation related to learning and the active role of the learner in shaping these goals, based on how that learner conceives the learning context and the experiences that occur during learning. There is also strong evidence for the view that engagement and intrinsic motivation develop and change over time—these are not properties of the individual or the environment alone.

While empirical and theoretical work in this area continues to develop, recent research does strongly support the following conclusion:

> **CONCLUSION 6-1: Motivation to learn is influenced by the multiple goals that individuals construct for themselves as a result of their life and school experiences and the sociocultural context in which learning takes place. Motivation to learn is fostered for learners of all ages when they perceive the school or learning environment is a place where they "belong" and when the environment promotes their sense of agency and purpose.**

More research is needed on instructional methods and how the structure of formal schooling can influence motivational processes. What is already known does support the following general guidance for educators:

> **CONCLUSION 6-2: Educators may support learners' motivation by attending to their engagement, persistence, and performance by:**
>
> - **helping them to set desired learning goals and appropriately challenging goals for performance;**
> - **creating learning experiences that they value;**
> - **supporting their sense of control and autonomy;**
> - **developing their sense of competency by helping them to recognize, monitor, and strategize about their learning progress; and**
> - **creating an emotionally supportive and nonthreatening learning environment where learners feel safe and valued.**

7

Implications for Learning in School

What does the research we have discussed mean for learning in school? Our charge was to build on *HPL I*[1] with a synthesis of research on learning from birth through adulthood, in both formal and informal settings. This body of work has implications for the work of educators in schools, particularly those who teach at the kindergarten to twelfth grade (K-12) levels.

In previous chapters, we discussed the cultural nature of learning and the growing recognition that culture fundamentally shapes all aspects of learning, from the wiring of the brain to the way that communities and societies organize learning opportunities. We saw that there are many types of learning, which are supported by a suite of cognitive processes that the learner needs to coordinate and organize. We examined research on knowledge and reasoning, which indicates that developing expert knowledge brings both advantages and biases and that simple accumulation of knowledge is insufficient for tackling sophisticated learning tasks and approaching novel problems and situations. Finally, we described how an individual's beliefs, values, interests, and identities play an integral role in learning and are themselves shaped by the learner's experiences at home and in their communities.

All of these insights have implications for the way schools and classrooms are organized. In this chapter, we draw on findings from previous chapters to consider four implications for K-12 educators. First, we consider why attention to the cultural nature of learning is critical to the quality of every learner's educational experience and examine research that illustrates specific impli-

---

[1] As noted in Chapter 1, this report uses the abbreviation "*HPL I*" for *How People Learn: Brain, Mind, Experience, and School: Expanded Edition* (National Research Council, 2000).

cations for instruction. Second, we briefly describe current thinking about how learning in different academic content areas requires approaches that take into account both general findings about learning and subject-specific differences. Third, we discuss instructional approaches that both engage and empower learners. Finally, we consider how understanding of the processes of learning has been brought to bear on the design of educational assessment.

CULTURE AND LEARNING IN SCHOOL

The findings in *HPL I* remain valid today. However, as we discussed in Chapter 2, work from a variety of fields has contributed to a more nuanced understanding of the cultural nature of learning. The authors of *HPL I* recognized the importance of considering how culture influences knowledge transfer, noting, for example, that "school failure may be partly explained by the mismatch between what students have learned in their home cultures and what is required of them in school" (National Research Council, 2000, p. 72). What has since emerged from synthesis of work in fields including anthropology, cultural psychology, cognitive science, and neuropsychology is recognition of the cultural nature of learning and development for all learners and throughout life. For educators, this is important because the influences of environment and culture, from the molecular level to that of the broadest social and historical trends, affect what takes place in every classroom and every student. The characteristics of the learning environment, of educators, and of the students themselves are all shaped by their cultural context.

In Chapter 2, we explained that taking a sociocultural view of learning means taking into account the social, emotional, motivational, cognitive, developmental, biological, and temporal contexts in which learning occurs. In short, the study of learning is the study of the relationships between learners and their environments. If taken seriously, these ideas can influence education practice in very specific ways. Ideally, educators play a key role in determining the nature of the learning experiences available to their students, and they can also shape their students' inclination and capacity to take advantage of their learning environments.

A thorough review of the theoretical and research literature on the role of culture in education would require at least another book-length report. We note here that for some students the culture and practices of school are not markedly different from those they experience outside of school, while for others going to school is a cross-cultural experience that can bring challenges. Thus, we highlight a few points about school and classroom contexts that illustrate the fundamental importance of attention to culture in providing all students an equitable opportunity to learn and for redressing opportunity gaps (Ladson-Billings, 2006).

When learners tackle a new task, they bring a wealth of previous knowl-

BOX 7-1 Do Students Have a Dominant Learning Style?

Some ways of taking individual variation into account in instruction do not have empirical support. For example, the concept of *learning styles* reflects the belief that if the modes of presentation that are most effective for learners can be identified (e.g., visual versus oral presentation of new material), instructors can individualize presentations accordingly (Pashler et al., 2008). The appeal of this approach, which has gotten substantial public attention, is the premise that all students can succeed if the instruction is customized. However, experimental research has consistently shown that learning styles do not exist as described by the concept's proponents, so categorizing and teaching children according to such styles is problematic (Dembo and Howard, 2007; Pashler et al., 2008).

edge and personal experience to the learning context. They often seek an entry point into the new material by attempting to connect to what they already know and to leverage existing strengths (e.g., knowledge and experience). Because learners share some experiences, knowledge, and goals but also bring unique perspectives, experiences, strengths, and skills, there will be variation in how learners engage with new tasks and demonstrate their learning (see Box 7-1). Learning happens as people move in and across the practices of everyday life (including home, school, and neighborhood), and people apply all sorts of learning as they navigate new situations and problems.

Optimal learning environments support this productive variation among learners in part by providing room for learners to interpret tasks and assessments in ways that broadly leverage their individual strengths, experiences, and goals. A theoretical framework for this idea was put forward in a landmark 1995 paper (Ladson-Billings, 1995). Since that time, educators and researchers have explored what it means to make teaching and learning relevant and responsive to the languages, literacies, and cultural practices of all students (see, e.g., discussion of culturally sustaining pedagogy in Paris [2012]).

School and Classroom Contexts

Culture shapes every learning environment and the experience of each learner within that environment: learners who find the classroom environment unfamiliar, confusing, unwelcoming, or unsupportive will be at a disadvantage. It has been well established elsewhere that attention to children's and adolescents' opportunity to learn—which is in large part determined by their educational environments—is critical to addressing disparities among population subgroups (see, e.g., Boykin and Noguera, 2011; Duncan and Murnane, 2011; Reardon, 2011; Tate, 2001). Opportunity to learn is a multidimensional construct that encompasses not only the content available to students but also what teachers do in the classroom, the activities in which students engage, and the materials and other resources that are used to support instruction. These features of the learning environment are shaped by the broader culture in which educators are prepared and policy decisions are made—and those factors, in turn, are shaped by even broader cultural influences.

Learning Environments

A learning environment is structured to promote particular ways of engaging in a specific set of activities, and the features of every learning environment reflect the cultural context in which it is situated. A classroom's culture is reflected in, for example, its physical features; the placement of chairs and desks or tables, the materials on the walls, and the resources available for use and reference all send signals about what is expected. Activities are structured to facilitate learning in a particular way in specific knowledge domains. The artifacts present in the room reinforce values, and researchers have suggested that cultural artifacts can have powerful cumulative effects on both adults and children (Azevedo and Aleven, 2013; Bell et al., 2012; Delpit, 1995).

One small example of this can be seen in the displays of the alphabet illustrated with animals (aardvark to zebra) that are ubiquitous in preschool and elementary classrooms. These educational resources, which are likely to show the animals as stylized representations or human-like characters—rather than in their natural habitats—reflect a particular cultural orientation. If the animals were shown in their typical habitats and engaged in natural behaviors, these kinds of representations might well encourage children to think "ecologically." These sorts of subtle factors may affect how children organize their knowledge about animals (Medin and Bang, 2013; Winkler-Rhoades et al., 2010).

As another example, Bang and colleagues (in press), examined cultural differences in the illustrations in children's books that either were or were not written and illustrated by Native Americans. They analyzed several features of the illustrations: the subjective distance from the reader to the illustrated object, established by the framing of the illustration (standard voyeur versus up-close or panoramic); perspective angle (straight-on view versus viewed from above or below); and the use of devices to encourage perspective taking, such as an "over-the-shoulder" view (see Libby et al., 2009, for evidence that these devices are effective). The Native American–constructed illustrations were more likely to have up-close views, included a greater range of angles and distances, and were more likely to encourage perspective-taking (often from the perspective of an animal actor). The illustrations not created by Native Americans predominantly took a voyeur perspective, placing the reader outside of the scene and looking in.

These differences in illustrations parallel cultural differences some have observed between Native Americans and European Americans in whether experience of nature is foregrounded (e.g., a walk in the woods) or backgrounded (e.g., playing baseball outdoors) (Bang et al., 2007). They also parallel differences some have observed between the two cultures in typical goals for children or grandchildren in relation to the biological world. A European American goal might be, "I want my children to know they must respect nature and have a responsibility to take care of it," whereas a Native American goal might be, "I want my children to realize that they are a part of nature." Cultural differences like these can have consequences for students who do not come from European American backgrounds and encounter a classroom that implicitly endorses European American perspectives.

There are also rules, explicit and implicit, to be followed in classrooms. They guide students' sense about who can speak, when they can speak, and what are acceptable or valued forms of speech, as well as what it is appropriate to say (Lee, 2001). Students and teachers also bring to a culturally defined classroom context their own individual cultural meaning system, derived from their out-of-school experiences in homes, neighborhoods, and communities. Students not already familiar with the rules inherent in the classroom culture are at a distinct disadvantage, compared with those who are (Rogoff, 2003; Serpell and Boykin, 1994; Tyler et al., 2006).

Some research has explored the larger context of schooling and the structures and practices that characterize classroom and school environments. Researchers have proposed, for example, that the structures of rules, assignment of classes, and grading in secondary schools match poorly with adolescents' needs for more space in which to make and take responsibility for decisions about actions and to practice self-regulation (Eccles and Midgley, 1989; Eccles et al., 1991, 1993a, 1993b; MacIver and Epstein, 1993). Research covering a broader age range suggests that ability grouping and other related practices may have negative effects on resilience and self-regulation (Blumenfeld et al., 1987; Guthrie et al., 1996; Urdan et al., 1998; Wilkinson and Fung, 2002).

Moreover, students who appear to be unmotivated may see themselves for various reasons as marginalized in a community (e.g., MacLeod, 1987, 1995; Willis, 1977). More recent work has examined three school phenomena that are related to delinquency (academic failure, suspension, and drop-out) at the elementary, middle, and high school levels (Christle et al., 2005). The researchers found that school characteristics, such as supportive leadership, dedicated and collegial staff, schoolwide behavior management, and effective academic instruction, helped to minimize the risk of delinquency. Furthermore, students who reported a sense of belonging and connection with school were less likely to fail, be suspended, or be expelled.

Negative Consequences of Bias

Much has been written in the past two decades about the subtle ways that unrecognized assumptions about cultural differences affect learning (see, e.g., Banks and McGee, 2010; Erickson, 2010). This effect of cultural differences may be extremely negative. For example, teachers' unexamined biases regarding gender and race may influence their expectations and interpretations of even very young children's behavior, as research on disparities in the use of serious disciplinary measures such as suspension and expulsion in preschool settings suggests (Gilliam et al., 2016). Variation in the application of such serious disciplinary actions across racial groups is well documented among older students and has been associated with teachers' mindsets (Okonofua et al., 2016). As Erickson (2010, p. 34) noted, the way teachers "choose to frame cultural difference has a profound influence on students' understanding of what is being asked of them instructionally and their motivation to learn."

The effects of culturally based expectations may be even more subtle and potentially harmful. We have discussed in Chapter 2 and 3 evidence that observed differences in many cognitive processes and functions, such as attention and memory, have a cultural basis. Recent work by Heidi Keller (2017) has highlighted the extent to which expectations about learners' development reflect unexamined assumptions that the pathways typical in middle-class western populations are the normal healthy ones, the benchmark against which children from other cultures should be assessed. This work suggests that "evaluating the development in one pathway with the principles and standards of the other is unscientific and unethical" (Keller, 2017, p. 833).

The effects of such expectations is illustrated by controversy over the relationship between the richness of a mother's speech and her child's vocabulary development and academic outcomes such as grades, a relationship known as the word gap (Huttenlocher et al., 2002). Efforts to encourage parents to talk more with their children (e.g., the Thirty Million Words Initiative[2]) have been based on this finding. However, it is important to recognize that speaking continuously to one's child—which is typical among middle-class parents in the United States—is just one of many ways to foster learning (see Avineri et al., 2015). Children also learn through engaging in creative play on their own, interacting with others, and observing cultural norms (e.g., Lareau, 2011; Rogoff, 2003).

Shifting from "Deficit" to "Asset" Models

Learning in school may be facilitated if the out-of-school cultural practices of students are viewed as resources, tools, or assets. If the cultural

---

[2] See http://thirtymillionwords.org [November 2017].

practices recognized and accepted in one context are recognized and accepted in another, that consonance will facilitate engagement and learning. This idea has sometimes been associated with a "deficit" model of cultural difference, in which consideration of cultural differences among students is conceived as a way to compensate for academic disadvantages that some groups may share. We want to highlight the importance of shifting away from this model to a view that each student brings a unique combination of assets to the classroom and that every student's learning is fostered in an environment that takes those assets into account.

A key dimension of creating equitable classrooms involves building a classroom environment where all students' ideas are valued. In such classrooms, teachers support students as they explicate their ideas, make their thinking public and accessible to the group, use evidence, coordinate claims and evidence, and build on and critique one another's ideas (Michaels and O'Connor, 2012). Group norms of participation, respect for others, a willingness to revise one's ideas, and equity are all critical elements of this kind of classroom environment (Calabrese Barton and Tan, 2009; Duschl and Osborne, 2002; Osborne et al., 2004; Radinsky et al., 2010; Sandoval and Reiser, 2004).

One way to integrate culture as a resource is the *cultural modeling* approach to classroom instruction (Lee et al., 2003). This model is designed to engage students from nondominant backgrounds by guiding them to see connections between their own cultural experiences and the disciplinary ideas and ways of thinking being taught.

In one study of cultural modeling, Lee (2006) investigated how African American students can be encouraged to apply their understanding of everyday narratives with which they were familiar (e.g., rap lyrics) to their reading of material being taught in class. Teachers who were able to explicitly make these links guided their students to focus on *how* readers figure out what texts mean. The students' knowledge about the meaning of the everyday texts allowed them to act as interpretive authorities and then apply that experience in approaching other material. By making familiar home- or community-based practices visible in the classroom, this approach helps students feel comfortable with learning objectives and view them as accessible.

There is also evidence that when cultural practices are regarded as assets in the classroom, students' motivation and achievement may increase (Boykin and Noguera, 2011). For example, researchers have found that many African American students prefer communal learning contexts (Dill and Boykin, 2000; Hurley et al., 2005), and when school instruction incorporates opportunities for students to work together, their learning can show striking improvements (Boykin et al., 2004; Hurley et al., 2005, 2009; Serpell et al., 2006).

The *Funds of Knowledge* framework, originally developed in the 1990s, has been an influential example of using detailed analysis of skills and knowledge students are familiar with to link their unique experiences to instruction

(Moll et al., 1992). This framework emerged out of collaborations between teacher-researchers and families of students living on the United States–Mexico border. Funds of knowledge, as described by Moll and colleagues (1992), are the valuable understandings, skills, and tools that students maintain as a part of their identity. Families have funds of knowledge from aspects of everyday life, such as fixing cars, working in a business, or building homes. Though often overlooked by teachers and the school community, students' funds of knowledge can be used as valuable resources in the classroom if the teacher solicits and incorporates them in the classroom. More recent work has built on this idea, exploring how this practice can capture students' imaginations and foster deeper understanding of domain knowledge (Lee, 2001; Rogoff, 2003) and how the skills, abilities, and ideas students have developed outside of school can be applied in a range of school contexts.

Another way to capitalize on the connections between cultural life and the classroom is to create *third spaces*: social environments that emerge through genuine dialogue between teachers and students. These environments are co-constructed by teachers and students and provide a space for students to elaborate on and incorporate their own personal narratives and experiences into the larger classroom space (Gutiérrez, 2008; Gutiérrez et al., 1995). These kinds of shared spaces can establish links between the types of knowledge and discourse (funds of knowledge) students experience outside of school and the conventional knowledge and discourses valued by schools (Moje et al., 2004). An ethnographic study of students in a middle school science classroom showed not only that students' funds of knowledge can be valuable resources for making sense of school texts but also how often students needed to be prompted and encouraged to draw on these funds in classroom contexts (Moje et al., 2004). Another ethnographic study, of critical literacy among male African American high school students, illustrates this point (Kirland, 2008). In this study, students who explored themes of revenge, racism, xenophobia, and the social consequences of difference and intolerance through close reading of scenes from the Iliad and comic strips such as Batman and X-Men demonstrated rich and sophisticated understanding.

Research in out-of-school contexts has the potential to expand educators' understanding of students' repertoires of knowledge and skill. For example, Morrell (2008) documents how youth in under-resourced communities gained academic and other skills through research projects related to educational equity and youth empowerment. Gutiérrez (2008) describes a long-term project with youth from migrant farmworker backgrounds, which was designed to build their academic and personal goals. Pinkard and colleagues (2017) found similar benefits in a study of Digital Youth Divas,[3] an out-of-school program

---

[3] See http://digitalyouthnetwork.org/project/digital-divas [November 2017].

that supports middle school girls' interests in science, technology, engineering, and mathematics activities through virtual and real-world communities.

DISCIPLINE-SPECIFIC LEARNING

Academic disciplines each involve characteristic ways of thinking and intellectual challenges, and an important goal in both K-12 and postsecondary education is to develop students' facility with the modes of thought in the subjects they study. Without becoming conversant with the academic language used within and across content areas, students cannot readily engage in the type of deep learning that will enable them to go beyond the memorization of facts (Gee, 2004). For example, scholars have identified what it means to "talk science" (Lemke, 1990) or to participate in "the discourse of mathematics" (Cobb and Bauersfeld, 1995; also see, e.g., National Research Council, 2005, 2007).

Goldman and colleagues (2016) conducted a "conceptual meta-analysis" in which they identified the reading, reasoning, and inquiry practices associated with the disciplines of literature, science, and history. They used the following five core constructs to characterize knowledge across disciplines:

1. Epistemology, that is, beliefs about the nature of knowledge and the nature of knowing
2. Inquiry practices and strategies of reasoning
3. Overarching concepts, themes, and frameworks
4. Forms of information representation, including different types of texts
5. Discourse practices, including the oral and written language used to convey information

Whereas each of these five constructs can be found across disciplines, the particular forms of a construct typical of a discipline—that is, the paradigms of the construct used in that discipline—differ from one to another. Therefore, knowing which forms of a construct are essential to the way a discipline organizes and conveys information helps educators teach in discipline-specific ways.

To illustrate, when learning history in a discipline-specific manner, students are supported in experiencing history as a process of investigation. Students might construct interpretations of historical events as they read primary and secondary texts, attending to the perspectives of the texts' authors, the contexts in which the texts were generated, and the ways in which the texts corroborate, or fail to corroborate, one another (see Bain, 2006). Similarly, when learning science in a discipline-specific manner, students might generate and test explanations for scientific phenomena through investigations in which they collect and analyze data or interpret data collected by others

(Chin and Osborne, 2012). In literary reasoning, readers draw on a repertoire of beliefs, experiences, rhetorical knowledge, and knowledge of literature to engage in argumentation about the meanings of literary texts (Lee et al., 2016).

These variations across subject areas in the structure of knowledge, epistemologies, and disciplinary practices are as important to the design of effective learning experiences for students as the general principles of learning discussed in previous chapters. Indeed, the growing bodies of evidence related to learning in specific disciplines are supporting current efforts to improve K-12 education. These accounts of disciplinary learning are informed by insights from the learning sciences that becoming more proficient in a domain is not simply a matter of acquiring knowledge. Rather, learning in a content area involves a process of engaging in disciplinary practices that require learners to use knowledge in the context of discipline-specific activities and tasks.

A summary of promising approaches in each of the subjects taught in school is beyond the scope of this chapter. Several reports by National Academies study committees have summarized some of the major findings related to learning in the disciplines. These include a follow-on volume to *HPL I* titled *How Students Learn* (National Research Council, 2005) that explored learning in history, mathematics, and science; *America's Lab Report: Investigations in High School Science* (National Research Council, 2006), *Taking Science to School: Learning and Teaching Science in Grades K-8* (National Research Council, 2007), *Adding It Up: Helping Children Learn Mathematics* (National Research Council, 2001b), and *Mathematics Learning in Early Childhood: Paths Toward Excellence and Equity* (National Research Council, 2011b). In the section below, we give a broad overview of learning in the disciplines of mathematics, science, and history drawing on these resources.

Mathematics

The components that constitute proficiency in mathematics were articulated in the National Academies report *Adding It Up* (2001b, p. 107). The five strands of mathematical proficiency are

1. Conceptual understanding, which refers to the student's comprehension of mathematical concepts, operations, and relations
2. Procedural fluency, or the student's skill in carrying out mathematical procedures flexibly, accurately, efficiently, and appropriately
3. Strategic competence, the student's ability to formulate, represent, and solve mathematical problems
4. Adaptive reasoning, the capacity for logical thought and for reflection on, explanation of, and justification of mathematical arguments
5. Productive disposition, which includes the student's habitual inclination to see mathematics as a sensible, useful, and worthwhile subject

to be learned, coupled with a belief in the value of diligent work and in one's own efficacy as a doer of mathematics

These five strands are interwoven and interdependent in the development of proficiency in mathematics. This means that instruction in mathematics needs to address all five strands. Traditional instruction in mathematics, however, has typically focused on procedural fluency (National Research Council, 2001b). In order to develop mathematical proficiency as described above, significant instructional time needs to be devoted to developing concepts and strategies, engaging in discussions, and practicing with feedback (National Research Council, 2001b). Discussions in the classroom need to build on students' thinking, and attend to relationships between problems and solutions and to the nature of justification and mathematical argument (National Research Council, 2001b).

Science

Similarly, a report from the National Research Council on learning science in kindergarten through eighth grade (National Research Council, 2007) described four strands of scientific proficiency.

1. Know, use, and interpret scientific explanations of the natural world
2. Generate and evaluate scientific evidence and explanations
3. Understand the nature and development of scientific knowledge
4. Participate productively in scientific practices and discourse

The four strands work together in the process of learning such that advances in one strand support and advance those in another. The strands are not independent or separable in the practice of science or in the teaching and learning of science (National Research Council, 2007).

In contrast to these four strands, traditional views of science learning focused on individual learners' mastery of factual knowledge. As a result, lecture, reading, and carrying out pre-planned laboratory exercises to confirm already established findings were common instructional strategies (National Research Council, 2007, 2012a). Contemporary views of science learning and teaching instead emphasize engaging students in the practices of a science framework including asking questions, developing and using models, carrying out investigations, analyzing and interpreting data, constructing explanations, and engaging in argumentation (National Research Council, 2012a).

This kind of approach is reflected in the "Guided Inquiry Supporting Multiple Literacies" model, which engages early elementary school students in scientific inquiry and the use of scientific practices (Hapgood et al., 2004). In a classroom-based study, the researchers designed a scientist's notebook that was used to introduce children to the ways in which a scientist formulates research activities that could answer questions about a real-world phenomenon, models the phenomenon, systematically gathers and interprets data, tests his ideas with scientific colleagues, and revises claims based on challenges from peers and new data (Magnusson and Palincsar, 2005; Palincsar and Magnusson, 2001). They found that second-grade students taught with this approach improved their ability to use data as evidence, to interpret multiple representations, and to model scientific phenomena (e.g., the relationship between mass and momentum).

History

As noted in *HPL I*, learning history requires students to learn about the assumptions historians make when connecting events into a narrative. Students must learn to determine why particular events were singled out from among all possible ones as being significant; in doing so they understand not only the interpretive nature of history, but also that history is an evidentiary form of knowledge.

De La Paz and colleagues (2017) explored the use of an apprenticeship model to support eighth-grade students in historical writing, which they define as "an interpretation based on evidence that makes an argument about another place and time" (p. 2). They enlisted teachers in a large urban district to participate in the treatment condition and identified another group who participated in a comparison condition. The intervention began with teachers modeling and thinking aloud about the ways historians engage in historical thinking and writing. Students then engaged in such disciplinary practices as identifying and contextualizing primary sources, discussing and evaluating evidence, examining and developing historical claims and arguments, and writing narrative accounts of their work. The students' writing products were evaluated for their general quality and for specific attributes of historical writing. On all writing measures, students in the treatment group outperformed students in the comparison condition; this finding applied to both higher-proficiency-level readers and those who struggled academically.

Stoel and colleagues (2015) developed a pedagogical framework to foster students' ability to reason causally about history. The framework was designed to include five pedagogical strategies: (1) inquiry tasks, (2) social interaction, (3) situational interest, (4) teaching domain-specific strategies for history, and (5) epistemological reflections on history knowledge and reasoning. In this quasi-experimental study, students were taught explicit disciplinary practices through strategy instruction, concept instruction, and introduction to the epistemological underpinnings of history. For a control group of students, there was no explicit attention to historical thinking.

Both sets of students worked cooperatively in groups of three on an inquiry task in which they investigated the outbreak of World War I. The researchers found that both the students who were taught using the pedagogical framework and the control students gained first-order knowledge, defined as concrete and abstract knowledge about the past and the event being studied (VanSledright and Limón, 2006). However, only the students taught using the disciplinary strategies gained second-order knowledge: knowledge of the concepts historians use to construct narratives and arguments about the past.

Reisman (2012) designed a quasi-experimental study to measure the impact of a curriculum intervention for juniors and seniors in secondary school on historical reading, content knowledge, and reasoning. The students in the study, from five urban high schools, were taught using a curriculum called "Reading Like a Historian," in which document-based lessons on a historical problem are the basis for student investigations. Each lesson followed a repeated sequence that included development of background knowledge on the topic, independent or small group reading and analysis of historical documents, and whole-class discussion of the documents and their meaning. As in other history-specific interventions, the study teachers explicitly taught corroboration, contextualization, and sourcing. Students in the treatment condition repeatedly applied these strategies in reading historical documents. They outperformed their control-group peers on several outcome measures, including measures of generic reasoning, reading comprehension, and historical reading (Reisman, 2012).

Nokes and colleagues (2007) tested the effect on students' historical content learning and disciplinary approaches to reading in history of four interventions, which used (1) traditional textbooks and content instruction, (2) traditional textbooks with heuristics (teaching of strategies) for reading historical documents, (3) multiple texts and content instruction, or (4) multiple texts with heuristic instruction. The heuristic instruction used in interventions 2 and 4 explicitly guided students in the use of sources, corroboration, and contextualization. More than 200 students from eight classrooms in two high schools were distributed across the four treatment groups. After 3 weeks, students were assessed on their content knowledge and ability to apply discipline-specific approaches to reading in history.

The researchers found that students using multiple documents (interventions 3 and 4) made the greatest gains in content knowledge and the greatest gains in knowledge in the use of the heuristic while reading. Those who learned from and interacted with multiple texts learned more content, had higher reading-comprehension scores, and sourced and corroborated more often that the other two treatment groups in the study. The researchers emphasized that their study "highlights the importance of reading multiple texts to deepen content knowledge and facilitate the use of heuristics that historians typically use" (Nokes et al., 2007, p. 11).

As highlighted throughout this section, the different academic disciplines have characteristic ways of thinking and intellectual challenges that reflect the disciplinary differences in epistemology, discourse, representations, and practices. Acknowledging these distinctions is crucial for disciplinary-specific teaching.

ENGAGING AND EMPOWERING LEARNERS

A part of what is accomplished when educators attend to the culture of the classroom environment and the cultural perspectives students bring to their learning is that learners are better supported in taking charge of their own learning. The authors of *HPL I* touched on the importance of empowering learners. For example, they recommended using a metacognitive approach to instruction to help students take control of their own learning. They advocated that schools and classrooms be "learner-centered" places, where educators pay attention to learners' attitudes and expectations about learning (National Research Council, 2000, p. 24). Many of the topics we have discussed in this report build on these ideas. Strategies we have discussed for fostering specific types and functions of learning are primarily ways of supporting the learner in actively making progress and improvements for herself.

In the committee's discussions of learning types and the developing brain (Chapter 3), processes supporting learning (Chapter 4), knowledge and reasoning (Chapter 5), and motivation to learn (Chapter 6), we identified a number of specific implications of learning research for learners. A theme in these findings is that people learn better when they are aware of and direct their own learning and when they engage in learning activities that pose a challenge:

- In Chapters 3 and 4, we noted that teachers can guide learners in developing sound academic habits by offering rewards, that effective feedback targets the specific stage a learner has reached and offers guidance the learner can immediately apply, and that helping learners establish connections with knowledge they already have assists them in learning new material. We noted that when learners are guided in constructing conceptual models for themselves, such models are particularly useful in helping them understand and organize what they are learning.
- In Chapter 5, we noted that practices such as summarizing and drawing, developing their own explanations, or teaching others, all help learners remember information they are learning. In that chapter, we concluded that what effective memory strategies share is that they encourage learners to go beyond the explicit material, to enrich their mental representation of information, and to create organized and distinctive knowledge structures.

- In Chapter 6, we described ways to foster students' feelings of autonomy, competence, and academic achievement, such as giving them the opportunity to make meaningful choices during instruction and, more generally, supporting their sense of control and autonomy.

Each of these points contributes to the general finding that educators can foster learning of many kinds and in many situations through strategies that provide enough support so that students can be successful but that also encourage and allow students to take charge in small and large ways of their own learning. In this section, we explore several ways of thinking about how learners become engaged and empowered. We first look briefly at the challenge of regulating one's own learning. We then examine the evidence regarding some instructional strategies for engaging and guiding learners.

Self-Regulated Learning

HPL I noted that the capacity for self-regulation, like the beginnings of other aspects of metacognition, is evident in very young children and develops gradually with their growing knowledge and experience. As part of developing "strategic competence," that report noted, children come to understand "how to go about planning, monitoring, revising, and reflecting upon their learning" (National Research Council, 2000, p. 112). The growing body of research in this area has, however, highlighted not only how difficult it is for people to regulate their own learning but also the corresponding value of training to improve this capacity.

Either accurately monitoring or controlling one's learning poses its own distinct challenges. Learners need effective strategies to accomplish these things, and if metacognitive monitoring is inaccurate, then any decisions or choices the learner makes are likely to be off kilter. Even before *HPL I* was published, researchers had identified strategies that appear to support students in pursuing learning goals. These are ways in which learners process the content to be learned and the skills associated with learning to learn. Methods for teaching these strategies have been characterized as a learning-to-learn approach.

Recent meta-analyses provide overviews of research on learning strategies, including some that relate to self-regulation and others that do not. Hattie and Donoghue (2016) summarized the findings of 228 meta-analyses of the literature. They identified more than 400 learning strategies; for 302 of those strategies, a relationship could be demonstrated between their use and academic achievement outcomes. They found that the critical elements in the effective strategies were (a) the will to invest in learning, (b) curiosity and a willingness to explore what one does not know, and (c) the skills associated with coming to a deeper understanding of content. We note that these authors adopted a very broad definition of "strategy" and included ways of managing the environment (e.g., providing student control over learning and lessons in time management), as well as participation structures (e.g., peer tutoring and collaborative/cooperative learning).

This work does not directly answer the question of how learners might be trained specifically to improve their capacity for self-regulated learning in ways that transfer beyond a particular study skill or strategy. A recent review summarized findings from studies that explored approaches to training for self-regulation in general (not just as it applies to learning), based on three different theoretical models of the primary drivers of self-regulation (Berkman, 2016). The three models focus on (1) strength (self-regulation is a strength or ability that can be deployed in any domain), (2) motivation (the key is developing the motivation or will to regulate one's self), and (3) cognitive processes (the key is mobilizing cognitive functions by, e.g., developing a habit or changing beliefs about self-efficacy). The review found that interventions based on each of these models have shown benefits but only limited indications that they improve self-regulation in general.

The idea of teaching self-regulation is appealing to parents and educators, and numerous sources offer practical tips for doing this.[4] A review article that examined research on teachers' roles in teaching self-regulation concluded that active involvement in one's learning is associated with positive academic outcomes and that teachers can promote this involvement by such measures as guiding students toward meaningful goals and strategies, monitoring their motivation, and providing useful feedback (Moos and Ringdal, 2012). These authors described a slightly different framing of models of self-regulation, reflecting the complexity of this active research domain, but they also highlighted important concepts such as forethought, performance control, self-reflection, cognition, and motivation. Regardless of the model, Moos and Ringdal (2012) suggested, the studies they reviewed support the idea that teachers can foster self-regulation in their students but need training to do so.

The research literature has not yet definitively identified training methods that have been shown to develop learners' self-regulation capacity in a way that transfers beyond the skills directly trained. It has not thoroughly addressed questions about the role of culture in self-regulation processes, suggested by studies such as a recent one on self-concepts and socialization strategies in preschoolers from Cameroon and Germany (Lamm et al., 2017). However, as the author of the overview of research on training noted, "there is disparate yet tantalizing evidence that self-regulation can be improved with training"

---

[4] Examples can be found at https://www.naeyc.org/files/yc/file/201107/Self-Regulation_Florez_OnlineJuly2011.pdf [October 2017]; http://www.pbs.org/parents/adventures-in-learning/2015/11/games-that-teach-self-regulation [October 2017]; http://teacher.scholastic.com/professional/bruceperry/self_regulation.htm [October 2017]; https://iris.peabody.vanderbilt.edu/module/sr/cresource/q1/p02 [October 2017].

(Berkman, 2016, p. 454). We note some promising areas of research on this topic in Chapter 9.

Instructional Approaches for Engaging the Learner

As we learned in the preceding chapters, humans' drive to understand is powerful. People have an innate capacity to impose meaning on their experiences. This propensity has the potential to be a powerful engine for learning if it is directed at suitable tasks and activities. On the other hand, if students are asked to engage in artificial, decontextualized tasks, they will develop coping strategies that make sense for those situations, but such strategies will simply amount to "doing school." In this section, the committee looks briefly at ways to make school activities an "invitation to thinking." Two instructional approaches intended to engage and challenge learners in the ways we have discussed—problem- and project-based learning and collaborative learning— have received considerable attention from researchers.

Problem- and Project-Based Learning

Problem- and project-based learning are strategies that promote learners' engagement in learning challenges by focusing on long-term goals (Shah and Kruglanski, 2000). Problem-based learning began with efforts in medical education to support medical students in mastering a broad range of content knowledge and clinical practice. The term refers to a family of instructional approaches that focus less on the learning outcome than on a learning process organized around a question or problem. The challenge should be one that drives students to grapple with central concepts and principles of a discipline and to develop constructive investigations that resemble projects adults might do outside of school (Condliffe et al., 2016).

Research showing benefits of this approach includes work with students in elementary and middle grades and in a variety of settings, though primarily in social science and science classrooms (see, e.g., Ferretti et al., 2001; Halvorsen et al., 2012; Kaldi et al., 2011; Parsons et al., 2011; Rivet and Krajcik, 2004). In general, these researchers designed project-based units for students that engaged them in challenges, such as figuring out how machines make it easier to build big things or building a model aquarium, and involved them in a wide variety of activities. Researchers used a variety of methods to assess learning outcomes and identify features that were effective and to document positive results. However, Condliffe and colleagues (2016) have noted that while there is a growing research literature, most studies exploring the relationship between project-based learning and student outcomes are not designed in a way that supports causal inferences. They have urged caution in making claims about the efficacy of this approach. We note also that the theoretical frameworks for problem-based learning are relatively abstract and thus do not easily support firm conclusions about how to design and implement problem-based instruction.

Researchers have also examined questions about implementing this approach. For example, there are questions about how much independence it is optimal for students to have, how much guidance and instruction teachers should provide, and whether a problem-based curriculum designed externally and provided to the teacher can yield the same benefits as one devised by the teacher (Barron and Darling-Hammond, 2008; Halvorsen et al., 2012; Thomas, 2000). This debate highlights the time and effort needed to design and execute this kind of instruction, as well as questions about the challenges of meeting required academic objectives with this approach (Herzog, 2007).

Collaborative Learning

Recognition that learning is not an isolated process that occurs solely in the individual learner's mind has focused a number of researchers' attention on the classroom environment as a learning community, and on how students' interactions among themselves and with their teachers influence learning (see, e.g., Brown and Campione, 1995; McCaslin and Burross, 2011). One focus of this work has been on collaborative learning, in which peer members of a group each contribute their thinking as the group executes a complex task (e.g., revising and refining a scientific model), having been given the authority to divide the labor, develop relations of power and authority, and otherwise navigate the task demands (Roschelle, 1992). Many of the features associated with instruction based on collaborative learning align with the findings from earlier chapters we highlighted above. For example, students take responsibility for learning and are encouraged to reflect on their own assumptions and thought processes, facilitated by the teacher (Kirschner and Paas, 2001).

Several meta-analyses have examined the benefits of group learning across content areas (see Slavin et al., 2008, for studies specific to reading, and Slavin and Lake, 2008, for studies specific to mathematics; also see Johnson et al., 2000). Benefits that have been associated with cooperative learning, when contrasted with competitive or individualistic experiences, include positive social acceptance among group members, greater task orientation, greater psychological health, higher self-esteem, and increased perspective taking. These studies indicate that these benefits occur when the group members have mutual learning goals and each member feels responsible for the learning of every member (Johnson et al., 2000).

One particular form of cooperative learning, complex instruction, was designed to promote equity (Cohen and Lotan, 1997; Cohen et al., 1999). In this approach, the groups must be engaged in an open-ended task that is structured such that the participants are interdependent in completing the task. The structure of the task positions students to serve as academic and linguistic resources to one another. An example of such a task would be pursuing the question "Why do people move?" by studying the experiences of various immigrant groups from Central and South America. This question is complex, and addressing it adequately requires assessing a broad range of potential explanatory factors, including relief from economic hardship, seeking political asylum, and the desire for a better life for oneself and/or one's family.

Drawing on multiple resources (e.g., diaries, photographs, journals, news stories, texts), students construct an understanding of the multiple factors that influence immigrants' choices. There is no one right answer; the task is both inherently uncertain and open-ended, both with respect to the responses the students will arrive at regarding the question and the processes they will use to generate their responses. Teachers are guided to pay particular attention to unequal participation of students. For example, the teacher can emphasize that the issues the group is considering are open to interpretation, that there is no one right answer, and that the work group must work to consensus regarding their group product. Furthermore, the activities call on multiple abilities, so that all students can contribute their respective strengths (e.g., in writing, graphics, or information gathering). Teachers also encourage students to explore alternative solutions and examine issues from a variety of perspectives.

Technology, particularly Internet-based resources, has opened up new avenues for collaborative learning and has provided new tools that have given rise to a research focus on computer-supported collaborative learning (Goodyear et al., 2014; Graesser, 2013). Research on collaborative learning that takes place through mediated Internet networks has pointed to the importance of the design of the learning experience and has suggested that successful tasks are those that (a) allow learners to take control of elements of the lesson (Kershner et al., 2010), (b) provide supports and multiple resources for making sense of and connecting complex ideas (Means et al., 2015), and (c) provide learners the means to share multiple representations of their learning (Scardamalia and Bereiter, 2006).

ASSESSING LEARNING

Assessment can drive the process of learning and motivation in a positive direction by providing feedback that identifies possible improvements and marks progress. It is most effective when the design of assessment reflects understanding of how people learn.

Assessments in K-12 education are directed to a range of audiences. Students need information about whether they are learning intended subject matter and skills. Teachers want to know whether their pedagogical approaches are helping individual students learn and helping their classes progress. Parents want to know whether their children are learning important material. Stakeholders—from school, district, and state officials to leaders in postsecondary education, business, and the federal government—need this information to make policy decisions about areas of success, improvement, and needed actions. Assessments provide essential feedback for the improvement of learning and schooling.

Pellegrino (2014) found that assessments in K-12 educational settings are used for the following purposes:

- To assist learning in the classroom (also known as formative assessment). These assessments provide specific information about what an individual student has or has not learned about the material that has been taught. This information provides feedback to students about progress and helps teachers shape instruction to meet the needs of individual students.
- To assess individual achievement or level of competency after completion of a period of schooling such as at the end of a school year or end of course. These are also known as summative assessments.
- To evaluate programs and institutions and monitor learning at the school, district, state, or national level. These assessments are usually more removed from the classroom. They may reflect content of state standards, for example, rather than material covered in any particular classroom.

No one test or assessment can serve all purposes for all audiences. Although tests used for differing purposes can look quite different, they need to be aligned with each other in order to support learning. Systems of assessment need to be carefully designed using a broad range of assessment strategies tailored to these different purposes (National Research Council, 2001a, 2006, 2014).

Providing Feedback to Learners

Formative assessment conducted in classrooms can generate meaningful feedback about learning to guide choices about next steps in learning and instruction (Bennett, 2011; Black and Wiliam, 2009; Valle, 2015). When grounded in well-defined models of learning, assessment information can be used to identify and subsequently narrow the gap between current and desired levels of students' learning and performance. It does so by providing teachers with diagnostic information about student misunderstandings and thus guiding teachers' decisions about how to adjust instruction and students' decisions about how to revise their work and adjust their learning processes.

An overall positive association between formative assessment and student learning has been found in both early influential reviews (Bangert-Drowns et al., 1991; Black and Wiliam, 1998) and more recent meta-analyses (Graham et al., 2015; Kingston and Nash, 2011). The positive effects hold across different age groups, core school subjects, and countries (Chen, 2015).

However, not all kinds of feedback are equally effective (Ruiz-Primo and Li, 2013; Shute, 2008; Van der Kleij et al., 2015; Wiliam, 2010, 2013). Effective formative assessment articulates the learning targets, provides feedback to teachers and students about where they are in relation to those targets, and prompts adjustments to instruction by teachers, as well as changes to learning processes and revision of work products by students (Andrade, 2016). Research suggests that feedback is most effective when it is

- focused on the task and learning targets; that is, detailed and narrative, not evaluative and graded;
- delivered in a way that is supportive and aligned with the learner's progress;
- delivered at a time when the learner can benefit from it; and
- delivered to a receptive learner who has the self-efficacy needed to respond.

Recent studies are contributing to a more nuanced understanding of the features of effective feedback. Feedback may address how tasks are understood and performed. It may address the self-monitoring, regulating, and directing of actions needed to accomplish the tasks, or provide personal evaluations of the learner (Hattie and Timperley, 2007). Because learners' judgments about and capacity to manage their own learning are often imperfect, researchers have explored ways to use accurate feedback to help them learn (Andrade, 2016; Zimmerman, 2002). Examples include strategies for developing students' self-evaluation skills in the context of mathematics and geography (Ross and Starling, 2008; Ross et al., 2002), and for guiding students in using peer- and self-evaluation together (Andrade, 2016; Topping, 2013).

Connecting Assessment to Evidence about How Students Learn

The National Research Council report *Knowing What Students Know* described three necessary components of a valid assessment system: "a model of student cognition and learning in the domain, a set of beliefs about the kinds of observations that will provide evidence of students' competencies, and an interpretation process for making sense of the evidence" (National Research Council, 2001, p. 44). The model of student learning should be consistent with the research about how learners represent knowledge and develop expertise; it serves as the unifying basis for assessment design. The observations consist of identified assessment tasks or situations that will allow students to provide evidence about their learning. The interpretation method provides a way to make sense of the observations and can range from statistical models to intuitive or qualitative judgements. "These three elements—cognition, observation, interpretation—must be explicitly connected and designed as a coordinated whole" (National Research Council, 2001, p. 2).

Ten years later, Brown and Wilson noted that most assessments still lacked an explicit model of cognition, or a theory about how students represent knowledge and develop competence in a subject domain. They argued that without a model of cognition, assessment designers, presumably including classroom teachers, are handicapped by largely implicit knowledge of how understanding develops, with no clear guidance on how to create meaningful assessments. However, recent promising developments have suggested ways that effective assessments can be designed to align with the growing body of evidence about how students learn.

Assessments Based on Learning Progressions

Also known as a learning trajectory, construct map, or construct model, a learning progression is a model of successively more sophisticated ways of thinking about a topic, typically demonstrated by children as they learn, from naïve to expert (National Research Council, 2007). Based on research and conceptual analysis, learning progressions describe development over an extended period of time (Heritage, 2009). For example, if the learning target is to understand that it gets colder at night because part of Earth is facing away from the sun, the students must first understand that Earth both orbits around the sun and rotates on its own axis. Box 7-2 shows a learning progression for this key concept, which positions the learners at levels 1 through 4.

Although learning progressions are often designed with state and federal standards in mind, they are more detailed than most standards, which do not include the significant intermediate steps within and across grade levels that lead to attainment of the standards (Heritage, 2011). Detailed descriptions of typical learning serve as representations of models of cognition that can guide instruction as well as the design and interpretation of the results of assessment. As shown in Box 7-3, learning progressions can also indicate common misconceptions students have about a topic.

Learning progressions provide a blueprint for instruction and assessment because they represent a goal for summative assessment, indicate a sequence of activities for instruction, and can guide the design of formative assessment processes that provide indicators of students' understanding (Corcoran et al., 2009; Songer et al., 2009). Teachers and districts can design summative assessments with a learning progression in mind, as well as formative assessments that move learning ahead (e.g., Furtak and Heredia, 2014). Questions that target common misconceptions can be designed in advance and delivered

BOX 7-2 Scoring Rubric from Construct Map for Student Understanding of Earth in the Solar System

44 Student is able to coordinate apparent and actual motion of objects in the sky. Student knows that:
- the Earth is both orbiting the Sun and rotating on its axis;
- the Earth orbits the Sun once per year;
- the Earth rotates on its axis once per day, causing the day/night cycle and the appearance that the Sun moves across the sky; and
- the Moon orbits the Earth once every 28 days, producing the phases of the Moon.

COMMON ERROR: Seasons are caused by the changing distance between the Earth and Sun.

COMMON ERROR: The phases of the Moon are caused by a shadow of the planets, the Sun, or the Earth falling on the Moon.

33 Student knows that:
- the Earth orbits the Sun;
- the Moon orbits the Earth; and
- the Earth rotates on its axis.

However, student has not put this knowledge together with an understanding of apparent motion to form explanations and may not recognize that the Earth is both rotating and orbiting simultaneously.

COMMON ERROR: It gets dark at night because the Earth goes around the Sun once a day.

22 Student recognizes that:
- the Sun appears to move across the sky every day; and
- the observable shape of the Moon changes every 28 days.

Student may believe that the Sun moves around the Earth.

COMMON ERROR: All motion in the sky is due to the Earth spinning on its axis.

COMMON ERROR: The sun travels around the Earth.

COMMON ERROR: It gets dark at night because the Sun goes around the Earth once a day.

COMMON ERROR: The Earth is the center of the universe.

BOX 7-2 **Continued**

11 Student does not recognize the systematic nature of the appearance of objects in the sky. Students may not recognize that the Earth is spherical.

COMMON ERROR: It gets dark at night because something (e.g., clouds, the atmosphere, "darkness") covers the Sun.

COMMON ERROR: The phases of the Moon are caused by clouds covering the Moon.

COMMON ERROR: The Sun goes below the Earth at night.

SOURCE: Adapted from Briggs et al. (2006).

BOX 7-3 **Diagnostic Item Based on Construct Map for Student Understanding of Earth in the Solar System**

Which is the best explanation for why it gets dark at night?

A. The Moon blocks the Sun at night. [Level 1 response]
B. The Earth rotates on its axis once a day. [Level 4 response]
C. The Sun moves around the Earth once a day. [Level 2 response]
D. The Earth moves around the Sun once a day. [Level 3 response]
E. The Sun and Moon switch places to create night. [Level 2 response]

SOURCE: Briggs et al. (2006).

verbally or in writing, to individuals or to groups. For example, at a particular point in a unit on the Earth and the solar system, a teacher can ask questions designed to reveal student thinking in relation to a specific learning goal in a progression, such as "How long does it take the Earth to go around the sun, and how do you know?" The students' responses to the questions provide insight into their learning and can guide the teacher's next pedagogical steps.

Diagnostic questions can also be implemented in the form of multiple-choice items (Wylie et al., 2010). Briggs and colleagues (2006) demonstrated that well-designed multiple-choice items can provide teachers with diagnostic information about student understanding. When each of the possible answer choices in an item is linked to developmental levels of student understanding, as in the example in Box 7-3, an item-level analysis of student responses can reveal what individual students and the class as a whole understand. For example, if one-quarter of the students in a class choose option D, which suggests that they believe that darkness is caused by the Earth moving around the sun once a day, the teacher might decide to provide opportunities for structured small group discussions between students who do and do not understand the day-night cycle. More intensive interventions can be implemented for the portion of the class who scored at level 2 or below by selecting options A, C, or E.

According to Pellegrino (2014, p. 70), "research on cognition and learning has produced a rich set of descriptions of domain-specific learning and performance that can serve to guide assessment design, particularly for certain areas of reading, mathematics, and science. . . . That said, there is much left to do in mapping out learning progressions for multiple areas of the curriculum in ways that can effectively guide the design of instruction and assessment."

Evidence-Centered Design Approach to Assessments

Another widely respected contemporary model of assessment is *evidence-centered design* (Mislevy et al., 2003, 2006), which grounds assessments in empirical evidence of cognition and learning. In this model, assessment is considered to be a process of reasoning from evidence to evaluate student learning. The design process begins with examination of research evidence about both expert thinking and novice learning in a given subject area. All the elements associated with learning a subject are analyzed and documented and then used in refining the test during the design process. Assessment experts believe "tests based on such learning science research can better flag when students are successful in engaging in such learning processes, and when they are engaging in counterproductive practices" (Yarnall and Haertel, 2016, p. 3).

In the second, "observation," step of this design process, items or tasks are chosen to try to elicit evidence of the desired knowledge and skills. The observations (based on student responses to these tasks) provide the data that developers need to make inferences about student performance. Unlike conventional test development methods, evidence-centered design starts with evidence about how learning happens in a domain and builds the test from that base. Figure 7-1 illustrates the three essential components of the overall design process. The first step in the process is "defining as precisely as possible the claims that one wants to be able to make about students' knowledge and the ways in which students are supposed to know and understand some particular aspect of a content domain" (National Research Council, 2012a, pp. 52–53). (For more on learning progressions and evidence-centered design, as well as ways of ensuring the reliability and validity of assessments, see National Research Council, 2005, 2012a, 2014; Pellegrino, 2014.)

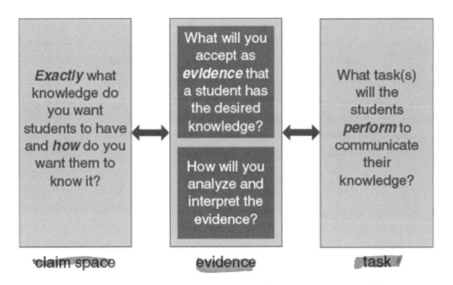

FIGURE 7-1 Simplified representation of three critical components of the evidence-centered design process and their reciprocal relationships.
SOURCE: National Research Council (2014, Fig. 3-2).

CONCLUSIONS

Our synthesis of research on learning supports five conclusions for learning in school.

Conclusion 7-1: Effective instruction depends on understanding the complex interplay among learners' prior knowledge, experiences, motivations, interests, and language and cognitive skills; educators' own experiences and cultural influences; and the cultural, social, cognitive, and emotional characteristics of the learning environment.

CONCLUSION 7-2: A disparate body of research points to the importance of engaging the learner in directing his own learning by, for example, providing targeted feedback and support in developing metacognitive skills, challenges that are well matched to the learner's current capacities, and support in setting and pursuing meaningful goals.

CONCLUSION 7-3: A growing body of research supports adopting an asset model of education in which curricula and instruc-

tional techniques support all learners in connecting academic learning goals to the learning they do outside of school settings and through which learning experiences and opportunities from various settings are leveraged for each learner.

CONCLUSION 7-4: Purposefully teaching the language and practices specific to particular disciplines, such as science, history, and mathematics, is critical to helping students develop deep understanding in these subjects.

CONCLUSION 7-5: Assessment is a critical tool for advancing and monitoring students' learning in school. When grounded in well-defined models of learning, assessment information can be used to identify and subsequently narrow the gap between current and desired levels of students' learning and performance.

8

Digital Technology

Advances in the digital technologies available to support learning are among the most dramatic developments since the publication of *HPL I*.[1] Digital technologies can support learners in meeting a wide range of goals in different contexts, for example:

1. A first-grade teacher concludes that her students are disengaged when working on drill and practice of mathematical operations using digital workbooks. They also rarely complete the associated homework assignments. The teacher introduces a program that targets the same operations in the context of a game. Not only are many of the students excited about the game, but they often choose to play it and have improved their mathematical skills.

2. A manager of an aircraft repair shop receives reports of errors made by workers. The software used to train the workers involves reading and memorizing procedures for troubleshooting, replacing, and repairing the devices they are responsible for. The manager believes that the workers need a deeper understanding (mental model) of the device mechanisms and purchases an intelligent tutoring system that offers individualized instruction and virtual reality simulations; it also explains device mechanisms and common misconceptions. Use of the system results in a significant reduction in errors.

---

[1] As noted in Chapter 1, this report uses the abbreviation "*HPL I*" for *How People Learn: Brain, Mind, Experience, and School: Expanded Edition* (National Research Council, 2000).

3. An individual went bankrupt after his business failed during a major recession. He found a job in a rural area that required a number of new skills, including knowledge of agriculture and statistics. He has completed free online courses to fill these knowledge gaps, has earned a dozen certificates, and now has a leadership role in his new field.

These examples suggest the range of ways technologies can support learning in varied sociocultural contexts. The game in the first example was appropriate for repetitive drill and practice on numerical operations, whereas the intelligent tutoring system was needed to acquire deep mental models of aircraft devices. The free online courses supported self-regulated learning by the individual who needed to change fields. As these examples suggest, learning technology is most useful when it is designed to meet specific needs and contexts.

HPL I noted that technologies may be used to: (1) incorporate real-world problem solving into classroom curricula; (2) scaffold students' learning; (3) provide students and teachers with more opportunities for feedback, reflection, and revision; (4) build local and global communities of individuals who are invested and interested in learning; and (5) expand opportunities for teachers' learning. Since that report was published, new technologies have been developed and researchers have expanded understanding of how digital technology can most effectively be used to foster learning.

In this chapter, we discuss ways to align learning technologies with goals for learning, drawing on research on new technologies that have shown promise for stimulating active learning and supporting learning in school and in the workforce. We also discuss the use of technologies for supporting older learners and close with a discussion of access to learning opportunities.

ALIGNING TECHNOLOGIES WITH LEARNING GOALS

Learning technologies open up significant possibilities for supporting learners. Researchers in the field use the term *affordances* to refer to opportunities that a technology makes possible related to learning and instruction (Collins et al., 2000). In this section we first examine the nature of the affordances of learning technologies and then explore research on how technology can support several aspects of learning.

Affordances of Learning Technologies

An affordance has been defined as a feature or property of an object that makes possible a particular way of relating to the object for the person who uses it (Gibson, 1979; Norman, 2013). For example, a door knob affords its users a way to twist and push, whereas a length of string affords users a means to pull and tie. Contemporary digital environments have features such as multimedia displays with texts, pictures, diagrams, visual highlighting, sound, spoken messages, and input channels (clicking, touching) for entering information that can afford important learning opportunities for users. Box 8-1 summarizes information delivery and input features and other technological

---

BOX 8-1 Key Affordances of Learning Technologies

1. **Interactivity.** The technology systematically responds to actions of the learner. For example, some serious games immerse learners in virtual works through role-playing and interaction with a gaming community. Reading a book, listening to an audiotape, and viewing a film are not interactive technologies because these do not present new information in response to the actions of the learner.

2. **Adaptivity.** The technology presents information that is contingent on the behavior, knowledge, and characteristics of the learner. A technology can be interactive but not adaptive, as in a game that offers the users choices but does not alter the options in response to the users' choices or actions. Conversely, intelligent adaptive learning programs are designed to be adaptive and interactive, so that when learners use the software, it assesses and may respond selectively to every task-related action on the part of the learner, including giving right and wrong answers, length of time taken in making decisions, and the learner's individual decision-making strategies.

3. **Feedback.** The technology gives feedback to the learner on the quality of the learner's performance, sometimes including how the quality could be improved. The feedback can range from a short message that a learner's input or response was correct or incorrect to an explanation of why the input was correct or incorrect. Task-relevant feedback can range from responses to short-term events that last a few seconds to long-term performance extending over (for instance) a school semester.

4. **Choice.** The technology gives students options for what to learn and how to learn so they can regulate their own learning. For example, choice is low for an instruction-oriented technology that pushes an agenda with few options for learner exploration. Choice is high, for

continued

BOX 8-1 **Continued**

instance, when students explore the Internet to find answers to their personal questions.

5. **Nonlinear access.** The technology allows the learner to select or receive learning activities in an order that deviates from a set order. Many commercial learning technologies offer a linear presentation in which material and major concepts are experienced in the same order by all learners. However, other technologies provide nonlinear access to information: the order of presentation depends on the learners' choices or varies by virtue of intelligent adaptivity.

6. **Linked representations.** The technology provides quick connections between representations for a topic that emphasize different conceptual viewpoints, pedagogical strategies, and media, such as between spoken messages, texts, diagrams, videos, and interactive simulations. Such connections support cognitive flexibility and encoding variability to support learning.

7. **Open-ended learner input.** The technology allows learners to express themselves through natural language, drawing pictures, and other forms of open-ended communication that encourage active learning.

8. **Communication with other people.** The learner communicates with one or more other "persons," who may range from peers to subject-matter experts. The communication may include text-based computer-mediated communication (e-mail, chat, discussion rooms), multimedia computer-mediated communication, computer-supported collaborative learning, conversational agents, tutors on demand, and crowd sourcing.

affordances that support learning at deeper levels (this list builds on work by Mayer [2009] and by Moreno and Mayer [2007]).

Learning Through Repetition

We pointed in Chapters 3 and 4 to types of learning that require a significant amount of practice and repetition of items (e.g., perceptual patterns, words, concepts, facts, rules, procedures), including perceptual and motor learning and some kinds of memory learning. We have noted that such learning is most lasting when it takes place in a variety of contexts and on a schedule that is distributed over time (Koedinger et al., 2012; Pashler et al., 2007). Interactivity and feedback are two affordances that are particularly helpful for supporting these types of learning.

Traditional computer-based instruction, or what used to be called "computer-assisted instruction," provides interactivity and feedback. For example, there is a mature industry that provides computer-based vocabulary instruction in which the computer displays a picture and two to four words. The learner selects the word that names the picture and receives immediate feedback (correct versus incorrect). The computer could present thousands of trials with this simple procedure, following particular schedules of item presentation with interactivity and feedback. These training trials have been used in classrooms and labs and to support homework outside of class. The training can be accessible throughout the day if it is available on a mobile device.

One drawback to this type of computer-based instruction is that some learners may lose motivation when using a repetitive format. One way to enhance motivation is to add the affordance of adaptivity. For example, the *FaCT* system is adaptable in that it offers the learner optimally spaced training trials rather than massed training (see Chapter 4 for discussion of spacing) and stops the training on a particular fact if the learner performs correctly on it three times (Pavlik et al., 2016). This approach can result in more efficient learning because learners do not waste time studying facts they already know.

Another approach is to *gamify* the learning by adding expanded feedback (e.g., total score points) and communication with other people in the form of leader boards and competition with partners (Clark et al., 2014; Tobias and Fletcher, 2011; Wouters et al., 2013). Yet another way to sustain motivation is to allow learners to select topics that interest them. Some topics may be very important but unappealing, so a possible downside of allowing too much choice is the risk that learners never get around to acquiring critical knowledge or skills.

Deeper Learning with Models

People need more than the foundations of literacy, numeracy, and other basic skills to handle the complex technologies, social systems, and subject matter typical of 21st century tasks (Autor and Price, 2013; Carnevale and Smith, 2013; Griffin et al., 2012; National Research Council, 2012b). Deeper learning involves understanding complex concepts and systems and is manifested in, for example, the use and construction of models (see Chapter 3), the ability to integrate information from multiple documents and experiences (Wiley et al., 2009), and the ability to explain correct versus incorrect system behavior (VanLehn et al., 2016). Deeper learning is needed for complex problem solving, reasoning, inferential thinking, and transfer of knowledge to new situations (Hattie and Donoghue, 2016).

The technology affordances of linked representations and open-ended learner input are particularly important for this type of learning, as are the interactivity, feedback, and adaptivity affordances of traditional computer-based training. The value of technology for representing a situation from multiple linked perspectives is evident in the example of helping learners understand a system, such as an electronic circuit. An intelligent technology can allow a learner quick access to perspectives, including a picture of the circuit as it appears in a device, a functional diagram of the components and connections, descriptions of the properties of each component, formulas that specify quantitative laws (e.g., Ohm's and Kirchoff's laws), explanations of device behavior, and the simulated behavior of the circuit as a whole when one component in the circuit is modified (see computer systems developed by Dzikovska and colleagues [2014] and Swartout and colleagues [2016]). The quick access will allow the learner to link these elements. Open-ended learner input is also important for conceptual learning with system models. For example, much can be ascertained about the state of a learner's system model and misconceptions about electronics by asking the learner to explain her reasoning through natural-language tutorial dialogue (Graesser, 2016; VanLehn et al., 2007) or to create a circuit to achieve a specified function (VanLehn et al., 2016).

Intelligent tutoring systems can also support deep learning with models (Sottilare et al., 2014; VanLehn, 2011), as has been demonstrated for topics in algebra, geometry, programming languages, engineering, and the sciences. Noteworthy examples in mathematics are the Cognitive Tutors (Anderson et al., 1995; Ritter et al., 2007) and ALEKS (Doignon and Falmagne, 1999; Hu et al., 2012), which have been scaled up for use in thousands of schools. Intelligent tutoring systems have been widely used and have produced impressive learning gains in the areas of digital literacy (Kulik and Fletcher, 2016) and information technology (Mitrovic et al., 2007).

Intelligent tutoring system environments have also shown promise in domains that have strong verbal demands. Such tutoring tools have included open-ended learner input and the ability to communicate with other people, in addition to most of the other affordances. For example, AutoTutor (Graesser, 2016; Graesser et al., 2014; Nye et al., 2014) uses natural language conversations to assist students in learning about a variety of topics. AutoTutor is associated with learning gains in both physics (VanLehn et al., 2007) and computer literacy (Graesser et al., 2004) for college students, beyond the gains associated with reading a textbook for an equivalent amount of time. The agent is a talking head that speaks, points, gestures, and exhibits facial expressions. The learning gains from natural language interactions have been strongest for underachieving college students and for tests that tap deeper inferential reasoning rather than shallow knowledge. However, the research also suggests that conversational interactions with AutoTutor are not ideal for high-achieving college students, who tend to be more autonomous and self-regulated learners, or for use in simulation environments that are intended to push the student to acquire very precise models of the subject matter. AutoTutor is also not the best choice for perceptual, motor, and memory-based learning.

Intelligent tutoring systems have been developed for a wide range of subject matters and proficiencies and have benefited learners in schools, universities, and the workforce. Hundreds of studies have shown the effectiveness of intelligent tutoring systems in promoting deeper learning for some populations of learners on core literacy and numeracy skills, complex STEM topics, and 21st century skills (Kulik and Fletcher, 2016). However, two issues related to implementation have been noted. First, the systems are expensive to build, so using them on a large scale can be a challenge for schools, universities, and workforce programs with limited budgets. Developers of these systems are exploring ways to develop content more quickly and cheaply, as in the U.S. Army's Generalized Intelligent Framework for Tutoring (Sottilare et al., 2014). Second, like any classroom intervention, intelligent tutoring systems need to be integrated adequately into teacher training and curricula in order to have an impact (Dynarsky et al., 2007).

Collaborative and Cooperative Learning

The ability to work effectively in teams is among the 21st century learning objectives that have been identified in a number of venues because of its critical importance in the workplace (National Research Council, 2012b; OECD, 2013). Technologies offer many possibilities for fostering the skills of collaborative and cooperative learning, for example by supporting members of a group in seeking common ground, explaining their ideas, and understanding each other's points of view; all of these processes are associated with successful collaborative problem solving as well as model learning (Chi, 2009; Dillenbourg and Traum, 2006). (See Chapter 7 for further discussion of collaborative learning.)

Collaborative learning can be distinguished from cooperative learning (Dillenbourg et al., 1996; Hesse et al., 2015). Collaborative learning requires *interdependency*, wherein group members work together to plan and organize joint activities to complete a task or solve a problem. The action of each person builds on the actions of others, and an action of one person may be taken up or completed by others in the group. In contrast, cooperative learning involves breaking a task into pieces: group members work separately, although they may coordinate activities that proceed in parallel. The completed pieces are assembled by the group (Hesse et al., 2015).

A variety of general-purpose tools have become available in the past 15 years to support communication and collaboration. These are tools that allow users to, for example, (a) add, change, or delete content with a Web browser on the Internet (such as on a "Wiki Website" or a "Wiki"); (b) upload shared/shareable word processing and spreadsheet files so that others may access, comment on, and edit them (e.g., Google docs); (c) make free voice and video calls; (d) conduct online meetings, with messaging services designed for group use (e.g., Google Hangouts, What's App); (e) store and share electronic files on cloud-based facilities (e.g., Dropbox); or (f) participate in social media (e.g., Facebook, Twitter, and Instagram). Many of these tools are free or very low in cost.

Learning technologies have been designed to promote deeper conceptual learning as part of group collaboration. Two examples for which the developers have shown positive effects are described in Box 8-2. However, the availability of communication technologies for cooperation and collaboration does not necessarily translate into learning gains. For example, Reich and colleagues (2012) studied the use of Wikis in kindergarten through twelfth grade (K-12) classrooms by extracting a random sample of Wikis from a popular site that provides free hosting for education-related Wikis. They assessed the Wikis' development and usage patterns to see whether the students were using them in collaborative knowledge building (and other skills). Nearly three-quarters of the Wikis showed no evidence of student-created content, and only 1 percent featured multimedia content created collaboratively by students. Equally discouraging was their finding that content created by students, as opposed to teachers, was more common among schools serving high-income students than among schools serving less-affluent populations.

Technology-Supported Self-Regulated Learning

Several computer technologies have been developed to train learners to acquire metacognitive and self-regulated learning strategies. Two examples that have shown promise in improving these types of learning are MetaTutor and iDrive.

MetaTutor (Azevedo et al., 2010) is designed to promote self-regulated learning in topics in biology, such as the circulatory system and the digestive system, in a hypermedia learning environment. It uses conversational agents to train students on 13 strategies, such as taking notes, drawing tables or diagrams, re-reading, and making inferences that theory suggests are important for self-regulated learning (Azevedo and Cromley, 2004). Initial studies have shown some positive impacts but not for all learning strategies. One reason may be that the instruction was delivered using a standard script; individualized training adapted to learners may be more effective.

The tool iDRIVE (Instruction with Deep-level Reasoning questions In Vicarious Environments) trains learners to ask deep questions in a STEM context by using computer agents, representing a learner and a teacher, that engage in dialogues in which they model discussion of deep reasoning questions (Craig et al., 2006; Gholson et al., 2009). The student agent asks a series of deep questions about the science content (e.g., *who, how, what-if,* and *what-if-not* questions), and the teacher agent immediately answers each ques-

BOX 8-2 Web-Based Technologies for Group Learning

The Knowledge Forum is a redesign of the Computer-Supported Intentional Learning Environments (CSILE) described in *HPL I*. CSILE provided a multimedia database for groups of students to collaborate by creating and commenting on one another's "notes" to share ideas or information (Scardamalia and Bereiter, 1993). Elementary school classes using CSILE performed better than other classes on both standardized tests and portfolio assessments, and the notes feature gave teachers a window into students' ways of thinking about the topic. Knowledge Forum also offers "views" to help learners organize their notes using tools such as concept maps or diagrams. The capability to link views and notes together into higher-order conceptual frameworks is designed to foster students' deep learning and conceptual growth through collaboration and interactions similar to those of scientists working together on a complex problem (Scardamalia and Bereiter, 2006).

The Web-based Inquiry Science Environment (WISE) is a platform developed by Linn and colleagues (2006) to support collaboration and deep learning of topics in science, technology, engineering, and mathematics (STEM). The technology is designed to help students work as scientists do: comparing viewpoints, generating criteria for selecting potentially fruitful ideas, fitting ideas together into arguments, gathering evidence to test views, and critiquing the arguments of peers. WISE curriculum units combine science investigations and collaborative learning on topics and phenomena in biology, chemistry, Earth sciences, and physics that students often find conceptually difficult. Many WISE projects include interactive simulations, collaborative brainstorming, and scientific papers. Prompts help students identify both confirming and disconfirming evidence and write explanations and arguments that are shared with peers. Students work together to generate and test predictions, develop explanations for what they observe, and move toward consensus on an issue.

tion. Increases in the targeted cognitive activities have been shown (Gholson and Craig, 2006; Rosenshine et al., 1996).

These technologies have two of the important affordances for learning described earlier. They give the learner choice, which seems to optimize motivation, and allow him to communicate with other people, which is especially productive when learners are just beginning to develop self-regulation strategies. However, such approaches have had mixed success, and it usually takes many hours of training with many examples for learners to show appreciable progress (Azevedo et al., 2010; Craig et al., 2006; Gholson et al., 2009).

TECHNOLOGIES THAT STIMULATE ACTIVE LEARNING

We have pointed to the importance of stimulating active student learning rather than merely delivering information to the student through books and lectures (see Chapters 5 and 7). Digital technologies offer a variety of possibilities for stimulating and engaging learners.

Learning Through Game Play

Games are known to capture the attention of players for hours, as the players actively participate for competition or other forms of pleasure. Social media also shares these benefits. It is possible for designers of learning technologies to capitalize on these phenomena and leverage social engagement for academic learning.

Some games were not originally designed with the goal of enhancing academic learning, but case studies have found that they nevertheless provide opportunities for learning and identity formation that can spill over into other aspects of life. These findings have spawned efforts to use technologies such as digital games, social media, and online affinity groups to engage students for academic purposes (Gee, 2009). In other cases, games have been designed specifically to support learning of academic content and skills (O'Neil and Perez, 2008; Shute and Ventura, 2013; Tobias and Fletcher, 2011). Several such online games have been used at scale in both afterschool and classroom settings; examples include Atlantis, Civilization, Crystal Island, Minecraft, Sim City, and Whyville (Dawley and Dede, 2014).

An enthusiastic community of researchers of "serious" games has argued that games have educational benefits because they foster sustained engagement in learning, but a review of this work did not support the claim that skills learned in game playing improve cognition, lead to better performance on cognitive skill tests, or improve cognition (Mayer, 2016). Nevertheless, games may be more effective than alternative approaches for some specific categories of learning outcomes. For example, "shooter" type games have resulted in transferable learning of perceptual attention skills (Mayer, 2016).

More relevant for schooling are the recent reviews of serious games that target specific academic content. A large number of quantitative studies (Clark et al., 2014; Tobias and Fletcher, 2011; Wouters and Van Oostendorp, 2017; Wouters et al., 2013) show a moderate advantage for games over other instructional approaches in fostering knowledge in science, mathematics, and literacy, as well as in promoting productive habits of mind such as intellectual openness, conscientiousness, and positive self-evaluation.

Some researchers have suggested that video games are inherently engaging and motivating to people (Prensky, 2006; Squire, 2011) and that research on video games can provide insights into the design of educational environments (Gee, 2003; Squire, 2011). Malone (1981) argued, for instance, that computer games are intrinsically motivating because they can provide optimal challenge and fantasy, while stimulating curiosity. Malone and Lepper (1987) expanded on the motivating factors of computer games by adding that such games give users a sense of control because their actions affect game outcomes. Gee (2003) identified a taxonomy of motivational factors that could be used to design video games.

However, very little empirical evidence supports these claims (Zusho et al., 2014). Although some studies have linked video game playing to motivation, this possible relationship has not been explored in educational settings. Further, the literature on adult populations (college students and other adults) suggests that users play video games for a variety of cognitive, affective, and social reasons. For instance, such games may satisfy psychological needs for competence, autonomy, and relatedness, which are associated with intrinsic motivation (see Chapter 6), but the applicability of such findings to K-12 populations is unknown (Zusho et al., 2014). Further, it cannot be assumed that gaming, or technology in general, would be inherently motivating to all learners. Whether technology is motivating to people is likely to depend on the learner, the task, and the learning context.

Leveraging Stories and Favorite Characters

The entertainment industry has established the practice of connecting television shows or movies with social media sites, online games, and products based on favorite characters. Educators have found opportunities in this phenomenon for linking education and training programs to popular stories, personalities, and characters (Jenkins et al., 2006) to encourage what some refer to as *transmedia learning,* a "scalable system of messages representing a narrative or core experience that unfolds from the use of multiple media, emotionally engaging learners by involving them personally in the story" (Raybourn, 2014, p. 471). For example, the U.S. Army has used transmedia campaigns that include online games and social messaging for training in cultural literacy.

The U.S. Department of Education's Ready to Learn initiative promoted the development and evaluation of transmedia learning experiences for children ages 2 to 8. Under this program, the Corporation for Public Broadcasting developed PBS Kids Lab, an online portal containing collections of games featuring popular characters from Public Broadcasting System children's shows (such as Sid the Science Kid and Curious George). The games can be played on computers, smartphones, electronic tablets, or smartboards. The PBS Kids Lab Website also helps users link game content related to mathematics and literacy curricula to activities for home, school, or afterschool settings (Herr-Stephenson et al., 2013). For example, designers of the Ready to Learn transmedia experiences have built videos, games, and digital device applications (apps) to support model learning by stimulating discussions between young children and their caretakers and helping children formulate questions and express their ideas (Mihalca and Miclea, 2007). Ready to Learn transmedia interventions that combine media-based and nonmedia activities into coherent curriculum units have shown positive effects on early reading and mathematics skills for preschoolers from homes with low income (Pasnik and Llorente, 2013; Pasnik et al., 2015; Penuel et al., 2012).

Historically, the use of technology with young children has been controversial, largely because of concerns about possible negative effects of extensive screen-viewing time on children's development (American Academy of Pediatrics, 1999). More recently, organizations concerned with young children's health and well-being have taken the position that technology can be designed and used in developmentally appropriate ways that enhance learning (American Academy of Pediatrics, 2015; National Association for the Education of Young Children and Fred Rogers Center, 2012). The American Academy of Pediatrics (2016) has recommended that parents and caregivers develop a family media plan that considers the health, education, and entertainment needs of each child and the entire family. It has offered the following age-based guidelines:

- For children younger than 18 months, avoid use of screen media (with the exception of video-chatting).
- For children 18 to 24 months, parents may introduce digital media. However, they should choose high-quality programming and watch with their children, in order to engage with them and help them understand what they are seeing.
- For children ages 2 to 5, viewing (of high-quality programs) should be limited to less than 1 hour per day. Parents should begin to help their children understand how the material applies to the world around them.

- For children ages 6 and older, parents should place consistent limits on the time spent using media and on the types of media; they should ensure that media use does not take the place of adequate sleep, physical activity, and other behaviors essential to health.

(American Academy of Pediatrics, 2016)

Educators view digital technology as a mixed blessing for academic learning. For example, writing teachers report that online activity has helped equip teen learners to understand multiple points of view, but they worry that the informal style of text messages and Internet posts has crept into students' scholastic writing and that common practices such as "retweeting" and "copy and paste" have desensitized students to the seriousness of plagiarism (Purcell et al., 2013). Another concern is that becoming accustomed to skimming short snippets of online content may reduce students' willingness to read and ponder longer text (Purcell et al., 2013). At present, there is little experimental research that sheds light on whether and how online communication skills and habits transfer to academic settings.

Empowering Learners as Producers and Creators

The Internet allows people without programming skills to create and post content to be shared with millions of people. Consequently, people can create content, collaborate, and critique the ideas and works of others relating to any topic one can imagine. Moreover, a learner can connect quickly with a small community scattered geographically around the world to become knowledgeable about a very specialized topic and develop real expertise.

Studies of informal learning communities, such as those engaged in multiuser online games, suggest that people go through stages in their development as online creators and producers (Dawley, 2009; Kafai, 2010). At first, learners *identify* relevant social networks within and surrounding the virtual world that can serve as a resource for their learning. The learners *lurk* in the virtual worlds and observe more experienced players and the cultural norms and rules for participation. As they become more comfortable with the learning context, the learners *contribute* small amounts of information or time to the network. As they become more experienced and knowledgeable, they *create* their own material, perhaps modifying some aspects of the digital environment or making elaborations to a game. In the final stage, they *lead,* which includes mentoring new learners or managing networks they belong to. In this process, novice players often receive explicit mentoring or tips from fellow players (Shaffer, 2007; Shaffer et al., 2009). With gains in expertise, a player also can gain recognition from fellow players, which may also have positive effects.

For example, a few studies suggest that online learning activity can play a role in the development of a learner's identity, self-concept, and motivation to learn (Ito et al., 2009; Lemke et al., 2015). A review of programs that provide media-rich experiences after school indicates that such activities contribute to a student's social and emotional growth; persistence in the face of obstacles; and skills that support collaboration, provision of mutual support, and inquiry (Lemke et al., 2015).

Wikipedia, the online free encyclopedia, and YouTube, a video- and music-sharing Website, are two examples of online innovations that have blurred the boundary between teacher or expert and learner. In 2013, Wikipedia contained more than 4 million entries in English; it is available in 285 other languages. Authorship of new entries, review, fact checking, and content editing are provided primarily by volunteers, supported by a surprisingly small number of expert editors. YouTube offers a platform for amateurs to develop free learning apps and other resources. Many ventures, such as Khan Academy, which was created by Sal Khan to tutor his young cousin in mathematics, first developed out of altruism or simply as a way to share an interest with others but have evolved into successful companies or nonprofit organizations. Research on the impact of such innovations on learning is still needed, but it is not yet clear how data that would allow for an assessment of their impact can be collected in an environment where the producing and using communities emerge over time with little control and coordination.

Making

Makers are people who engage in building and creating. They use their hands to assemble, build, mold, or modify a physical object. Although the popularity of "making" first arose outside of formal education, making has become increasingly prevalent in formal learning. In universities, making is ingrained in the teaching of engineering, and many institutions have invested significant resources in creating *makerspaces* to support making activities. Makerspaces are physical spaces (e.g., a room or an entire building) where people come together to share resources, knowledge, and equipment to engage in making. Makerspaces may, for example, have tools and machines for use in welding, fabricating, crafting, three-dimensional printing, laser cutting, molding, casting, and sculpting (Barrett et al., 2015; Jordan and Lande, 2014). Makerspaces thus introduce the technology of tools used to build a physical object; these tools create experiences that contribute to their users' understanding of how objects are assembled and how they work.

Making is a form of active learning because it is experiential and engages students in developing their own understanding of a domain through *doing*. Active learning strategies are generally understood to be student-centered, inquiry-based instructional approaches (Kuh, 2008). Although research on making and educational outcomes has only just begun (Jordan and Lande, 2014), the results to date point to the benefits of active, inquiry-based experiences like making for supporting students' learning and persistence in a field (Freeman et al., 2014; National Research Council, 2012a).

Digital versions of making are beginning to flourish. Informally, computer clubhouses are places for students to meet after school to develop computer programs using easy-to-learn computer languages such as Scratch. Other popular digital-making activities include developing wearables, such as jewelry or t-shirts with flashing messages. Digital making is also finding its way into schools. For example, at Design Tech High School in San Mateo, California, students engage in projects in which they identify a problem (such as lighting a campsite at night) and then use Raspberry Pi software and simple peripherals to design and prototype a solution. Wearable technology projects use Flora microcontrollers, conductive materials, sensors, and actuators in designs that respond to student-generated problems. In both cases, students' design work is supported by industry mentors working with teachers in the makerspace.

Embodied Cognition

Another new area of active research, *embodied cognition*, has become closely intertwined with digital technology advances. Embodied cognition is the idea that cognition is shaped by every aspect of an organism's experience, including the bodily system and ways the body interacts with its environment (see Yannier et al., 2016). SMALLab is an example of a technological application of embodied cognition that was designed as a mixed-reality[2] environment for student-centered learning. Students move within a 15 × 15 foot space equipped with a vision-based object tracking system, a top-mounted visual projection system, speakers for surround sound, and (in some applications) glow balls that students can hold or toss. A series of studies conducted using SMALLab in high school classrooms showed positive results for learning about geological layers, chemical titration, and disease transmission, in comparison to instruction without this approach (Birchfield and Johnson-Glenberg, 2010).

The military and corporate sectors have invested resources to develop and test sophisticated embodied-cognition digital technologies not available in typical K-12 and college environments. These capabilities are displayed at the annual Interservice/Industry Training, Simulation and Education Conference.[3] Immersive games and simulation environments are designed to help soldiers improve in several areas that include marksmanship; sensitivity to hazardous signals in combat situations; discharge of weapons under appropriate conditions; and performance on tasks that tap perceptual, motor, memory, and

---

[2]In mixed-reality environments, real and virtual worlds are merged (Milgram and Kishino, 1994). For example, graphics (or other digital components) are projected on a floor or wall and are merged with real-world tangible objects such as trackable handheld wands.

[3]See http://www.iitsec.org [March 2017].

FIGURE 8-1   *The Tactical Language and Culture Training System (TLCTS).*
NOTE: Each TLCTS course incorporates a scenario-based mission game, in which learners
play a character in a three-dimensional virtual world that simulates the target culture. The figure
shows a screenshot from the mission game in Tactical Dari, which was used by U.S. military
service members to learn the Dari language and Afghan culture in preparation for deployment
to Afghanistan. The player (avatar on left, which is controlled by the learner-player) is engaged
in a meeting with a village leader to discuss reconstruction plans for a local school. A transcript
of the conversation to that point is shown in the top center of the screen. The player interacts
with the system through speech. As of 2009, more than 40,000 learner-players had used
TLCTS courses in multiple languages and cultures.
SOURCE: Johnson and Valente (2009, Fig. 2).

basic levels of cognition. Immersive environments also have been developed to train soldiers on equipment maintenance, troubleshooting and repair, and other tasks that require reasoning and more thoughtful deliberation. The technologies have included mixed-reality environments with conversational agents and avatars for the learning of language, social interactions, and collaborations that are culturally appropriate (Johnson and Valente, 2009; Swartout et al., 2013). For example, Figure 8-1 describes the Tactical Language and Culture Training System (TLCTS), which has been used by more than 40,000 learners, mostly in the military. TLCTS is among the few systems that have been assessed on measures of learning, engagement, and learner impressions. The impact of most embodied-cognition digital technologies is difficult to assess because the results typically are not reported outside the business and military environments where they are used.

Conversational Agents

Another new technology that can stimulate active learning is the computerized conversational agent. Digital agents are designed to engage the learner in dialogues that promote reasoning, social interaction, conscious deliberation, and model learning (D'Mello et al., 2014; Lehman et al., 2013). The design allows students to engage in a three-way conversation known as a *trialogue* that includes two computer agents and the student, taking on different roles (e.g., two peers with an expert or a peer with two experts). Figure 8-2 shows two agents on the screen interacting with a human in a trialogue. The results of this particular test of trialogue with conversational agents showed deeper,

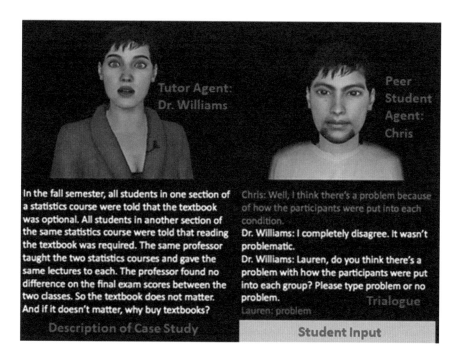

FIGURE 8-2 *Screenshot of conversational agents (a tutor and a peer) discussing an experiment with a student.*
SOURCE: D'Mello et al. (2014).

conceptual learning by the student in conditions where the two agents disagreed, especially for students who experienced confusion.

Research suggests that agent technologies can stimulate active learning by means of several features. A single agent can serve as a tutor (such as AutoTutor; see Graesser, 2016) or as a peer of the learner-player. An ensemble of agents can set up a variety of social situations, which may, for example, (a) model desired behavior and social interaction, (b) stage arguments that invoke reasoning, or (c) pull the learner-player into active contributions through actions and social communication (Graesser et al., 2014). Computerized agent technologies can implement pedagogical approaches with a degree of fidelity that may be difficult or impossible with human agents who are not experts in the pedagogical approach.

TECHNOLOGIES FOR INSTRUCTION

Learning technology can be used to support instruction, and this section explores the evidence for this technology's capability to support three instructional goals: linking formal and informal learning to improve learners' outcomes, orchestrating the complexities of instruction in the classroom, and developing students' writing through interactivity and feedback.

Linking Formal and Informal Learning

Researchers have explored ways educators might recruit the vast bodies of informal knowledge learners acquire from their cultural contexts and self-directed learning to help achieve formal learning objectives in schools and workplaces. Since the publication of *HPL I*, the role of technology in informal learning—and the potential for linking it to formal learning—have only become more salient, as daily life is increasingly mediated by digital and Internet technology. A survey conducted in 2014-2015 found that 88 percent of U.S. teens had access to a smartphone and 86 percent reported going online from a mobile device at least once a day (Lenhart, 2015). Text messages have become a central part of social communication. In this survey, the average teenager reported sending and receiving 30 texts a day. Playing video games online or on their phones was reported by 84 percent of teenage boys and 59 percent of teenage girls.

Educators have explored approaches to capitalize on this pervasive access to these technologies (Bull et al., 2008; U.S. Department of Education, 2010). One approach has been to extend the time for academic learning through mechanisms such as putting WiFi on school buses so that students with long rides can do their homework online. Web-based homework systems give students adaptive practice outside of school hours. Some teachers are experimenting with flipped classrooms by having students watch video presentations of academic content at home as preparation for applying that content to problem-solving activities in the classroom (Siemens et al., 2015).[4] By doing in class what traditionally would have been thought of as homework, students in flipped classrooms have the opportunity to work collaboratively with other students and to get coaching from their teachers when they encounter difficulties applying new knowledge and skills to specific problems.

Online "hangouts" and other informal online groups of students support academic learning for college students in large lecture courses. Early research suggested that membership in study groups can be helpful in a challenging course (Treisman, 1992). More recently, study groups have met online, and the formation and functioning of such groups among people taking massively open online courses (MOOCs) has become a focus of research (Gasevic et al., 2014). Other programs are creating in-person study groups for learners taking courses online. For such programs in public libraries, library staff assist with technical difficulties and scaffold student behaviors intended to help with deeper learning (U.S. Department of Education, 2016).

Technology can support learning outside of school in other ways as well—for example, by providing opportunities for sustained intellectual engagement. Afterschool clubs, youth organizations, museums, and arts programs are examples of settings where technology-supported activities combine learning with entertainment (National Research Council, 2009). Adults can support this type of learning not only by acting as models of technology fluency but also by helping to connect interested children and adolescents with learning-rich out-of-school activities (Barron, 2006). A number of organizations (e.g., Computer Clubhouse, Black Girls Code, 5th Dimension, code.org, and the Digital Youth Network) have developed out-of-school activities to provide mentoring and learning opportunities in digital media and computer programming for low-income, female, and minority youth.

Orchestrating Instruction

K-12 teachers must orchestrate many types of learning to achieve school systems' ambitious goals for college and career readiness. For example, new science standards call on teachers to help their students develop skill in evidence-based argumentation through classroom discussions and related activities that bring out students' initial ideas about science phenomena and confront them with opposing ideas and evidence as a way to trigger conceptual growth. Executing such instructional approaches with classes of 20-40 students is a challenge when students vary markedly in their prior experiences, interests, motivation, and knowledge. Technology can help educators

---

[4]Also see Christensen Institute at http://www.christenseninstitute.org [July 2018] and Kahn Academy at https://www.khanacademy.org [July 2018].

coordinate the many aspects of instruction and navigate the complexities of pedagogy, whether in K-12, college, or corporate settings. Educators may use technology in their personal lives but not be comfortable with integrating it into their teaching (Bakia et al., 2009).

The committee identified three levels at which technology can be integrated into instruction. At a basic level, the educator uses technology to present content or has students use technological tools designed to engage their interest. At the second level, students can use technology to support their individual learning in ways that they, rather than their teachers, direct. At the third level, digital tools allow learners to collaborate with individuals and organizations outside the classroom; these applications require that each participant or group have a network-enabled and connected device.

New technology places additional new demands on teachers, and this in turn places demands on both preservice training and in-service professional development programs. Teacher education programs can model effective integration. Moreover, although the characteristics of effective teacher professional development for technology integration have not been systematically established (Lawless and Pellegrino, 2007), the challenge clearly suggests the importance of devoting considerable training time to that integration, rather than attempting to cover it in a few lectures or a single course. Professional development in technology integration is more successful when it is of extended duration, gives teams of teachers from the same school or program the opportunity to collaborate in using concrete practices and to comment on each other's practice, is coherent with the other practices and change initiatives at their schools, and demonstrates ways to leverage data from digital learning systems for formative purposes (Fishman and Dede, 2016).

Educators and researchers have long recognized that the knowledge transmission model exemplified by lecture-based teaching is less than ideal for many learners and many kinds of learning. It is difficult for educators to build on students' prior understandings when they have no window into the nature of those understandings. Without that connection into "the learner's world," students experiencing a lectured lesson may tune out (Medimorecc et al., 2015). Even when teachers pepper their lectures with questions, the number of students who respond tends to be small. Instructors have limited information to help them identify whether the class is following their explanations, taking notes without thinking, or merely putting on an attentive face. Such concerns, which are particularly strong in college courses that enroll hundreds of students, has inspired the development of technologies that allow each student to respond to a question in a multiple-choice format presented on a small screen or handheld device. Student responses are sent to the instructor, who can then display aggregated responses as histograms (bar charts) for the whole class to see (Abrahamson, 2006; Kay and LeSage, 2009; Mazur, 1997).

Early evidence on the use of this technology showed improvements in student engagement and learning outcomes (Mazur, 1997). The results were attributed to the opportunity for the instructor to identify and address the sources of conceptual confusions common among students in introductory physics. More recent work has shown positive results with similar approaches (Deslauriers et al., 2011). These systems are most heavily used at the post-secondary level, but their use has begun to spread to secondary schools and even elementary school classrooms (Smith et al., 2011).

Another example of the classroom communication concept is Group Scribbles, a network technology designed to support collaborative learning. Group Scribbles works like the student-response systems described above except that students can share notes, sketches, and images, not just numerical responses or selections among multiple-choice response options. Student contributions are displayed (anonymously) on an electronic whiteboard. Group Scribbles has been used in the United States to help students understand fractions, in Spanish primary classrooms (Prieto et al., 2011), and in Singapore to teach science and Chinese language classes (Looi et al., 2009).

Writing Instruction

Software systems for writing instruction and for giving students feedback on their writing are another technological support for classroom communication. These systems can be used to distribute writing assignments and learning resources, provide immediate feedback to students, provide feedback on plagiarism, and allow students to submit their writing to the teacher or to peers for evaluation and feedback. The automated feedback may allow teachers to focus on what a student's writing reveals about a deeper understanding of the material (Cassidy et al., 2016; Warschauer and Grimes, 2008).

Automated writing assessments have also been used to analyze students' writing at deeper levels. For example, Summary Street, a program that analyzes the coherence of sentences and statements within a summary, has shown positive outcomes, such as increases in time spent revising and in depth of content, for elementary school students (Wade-Stein and Kintsch, 2004). Writing Pal (or W-Pal) is a strategy-based training system for middle school ages through adulthood that has game components for improving skills in writing argumentative essays, which are required in some high-stakes assessments (Allen et al., 2016; McNamara et al., 2015). With this digital system, the student generates a thesis statement, supporting statements, and then a conclusion. Pedagogical agents model good writing strategies and give interactive and immediate feedback as the student writes or revises an essay designed to address the student's challenges. The Writing Pal system was based on studies of writing interventions that showed strategy instruction to be a successful form of writing instruction (Graham and Perin, 2007).

There is some evidence that teachers may not view such systems as a substitute for teacher-generated feedback. For example, a study of three writing software systems for use in classrooms, including WriteToLearn, which incorporates Summary Street, found that although teachers appreciated the immediate feedback these systems offer, they still found it important to provide their own feedback on other aspects of their students' writing (Means et al., 2017).

OPPORTUNITIES AND CHALLENGES

Recent technological advances in several areas have yielded both opportunities and challenges. In this section, the committee reviews the issues associated with digital dashboards, distance learning, universal design, mobile devices, and features of technologies that may be addressed through further application of principles from the science of learning.

Digital Dashboard

Digital dashboards allow a learner to monitor his own progress through the learning environment. Open learning environments (Bull and Kay, 2013) allow learners to observe their own performance scores on lessons and skills over time, which can be motivating and help develop metacognitive skills. Teachers can use the dashboards in learning management systems such as Desire to Learn or Blackboard, which provide a quick glimpse of the lessons, how each student is doing on each lesson, and which students need help (Dede and Richards, 2012). The dashboard has options that allow instructors to explore this information in greater detail. For example, they may identify which questions on an assignment were problematic for a student or the extent to which a student is mastering specific areas of skill and knowledge. The dashboard also can provide more general information about a student based on multiple lessons, such as: What percentages of lessons is she completing? How much time is she devoting to the course? How often does the student get stuck and need help? How often does she use digital help facilities? The dashboards also track and display noncognitive characteristics, such as profiles of a student's emotions and social interactions (Siemens et al., 2015).

One example is the ASSISTments system,[5] which allows teachers to create materials for mathematics as well as other topics, to see how well students perform, and to interact with researchers on possible improvements based on the science of learning (Heffernan and Heffernan, 2014). ASSISTment offers three views: The Builder view guides the curriculum designer or teacher in

---

[5]See http://www.assistments.org [January 2018].

creating lessons. The Teacher view shows performance of each student on particular lessons. The Student view guides the student in completing tasks and viewing feedback on performance. In 2015, ASSISTments was used by more than 600 teachers in 43 states and 12 countries, with students completing more than 10 million problems. A randomized field trial of the impact of using ASSISTments for homework problems showed an increase in seventh-graders' scores on end-of-year math achievement tests, compared to a control group that completed homework without the immediate feedback offered by ASSISTments. Lower-achieving students benefited the most from working with ASSISTments (Roschelle et al., 2016).

Digital dashboards are most likely to perform as intended when they are not optional and when users have the time and resources needed to integrate these tools into instruction. Providing the professional development necessary for instructors to use these digital dashboards effectively is a challenge. Many teachers do not yet use digital platforms frequently and systematically in their classrooms. Very simple computer-teacher interfaces may be ignored or quickly abandoned after the novelty of the technology fades (Moeller and Reitzes, 2011). For example, instructors may need a systematic curriculum to facilitate access, use, and monitoring of the digital dashboard interface as a routine part of their courses.

Distance Learning

Distance learning has been defined as "planned learning that normally occurs in a different place from teaching and as a result requires special techniques of course design, special instructional techniques, special methods of communication by electronic and other technology, as well as special organizational and administrative arrangements" (Moore and Kearsley, 1996, p. 2). It does not necessarily require technology, but digital technologies such as e-learning, online learning, or Web-based learning provide many advantages for distance learning (Siemens et al., 2015).

Digital technology can support synchronous communication between instructors and students, such as participating in a live Webinar, using technology-based instruction in the classroom, or corresponding in a course chatroom (instructor and learners spatially separated but interacting in real time). It can also support asynchronous learning, in which the interactions between a human instructor and students are separated in time (and typically also by space), as when the instructor posts a video lecture or lesson on a course learning management system or Website. Technology can also support communication, whether synchronous or asynchronous, such as between the learner and a computer-based teaching agent or with intelligent tutoring systems like those described earlier in this chapter.

Finally, blended learning, which combines one or more forms of distance learning and face-to-face instruction, is facilitated by technology. For example, an instructor could use a learning management system to deliver course material, videos, tests, quizzes, and grades but would periodically interact with students face-to-face (Siemens et al., 2015).

Educators have traditionally been cynical about the effectiveness of distance learning approaches compared to traditional face-to-face synchronous learning (Thompson, 1990), and indeed the early research findings were mixed. The available evidence indicates that modern, technology-rich approaches to distance learning can be as effective as traditional approaches, more effective, or less effective (Bernard et al., 2009; Means et al., 2013). Efficacy depends on the quality of the interactions among the students, the content to be learned, and the instructor.

Technology that encourages students to actively engage with course material and with other students can positively affect cognitive outcomes. In a meta-analysis, blended online and in-person instruction produced better learning outcomes, on average, than conventional face-to-face instruction, but the blended learning conditions in the studies assessed for this analysis also incorporated other changes such as additional learning resources or more time for learning (Means et al., 2013). Based on analyses of the academic progress of students taking fully online courses, a number of researchers have raised concerns about the suitability of fully online learning for less motivated, lower achieving, or less mature learners (Miron et al., 2013; Xu and Jaggers, 2011a, 2011b). Although many students learn successfully with fully online courses, a blend of online and in-person instruction is generally recommended for lower achieving and younger learners (Means et al., 2010).

Social communication has become a ubiquitous feature of modern digital platforms in which instructors, students, and sometimes parents can communicate with each other through chat, email, and discussion boards. Such computer-mediated social support is routinely integrated into MOOCs (Siemens et al., 2015) to compensate for the lack of face-to-face contact with instructors and peers. Most learning management systems include social communication media even in traditional classrooms. However, usage is currently low, with only about 7 percent of the students using it, according to one estimate (Siemens et al., 2015). Social communication may be used more in the future as learning environments become more digitally supported, self-regulated, and socially connected.

Mobile Personal Devices

The use of mobile technologies for learning has exploded in recent years, and this trend is expected to continue (Hirsh-Pasek et al., 2015; Looi et al., 2009). Although mobile technologies share some features with other electronic learning tools, their relatively flexible platforms are unique. Small and easily transportable devices now give users quick and easy ways to search for information, create recordings (pictures, videos, audios), and communicate with others (Looi et al., 2009). This flexibility offers several advantages over standard e-learning. Mobile applications can be adapted for different learning contexts inside and outside of school.

Well-designed mobile applications can also be adapted to a learner's abilities and desires, which may have positive effects on the learning process and peoples' attitudes about their learning experiences (García-Cabot et al., 2015; Hsu et al., 2013). For example, learners who were surveyed reported positive attitudes toward mobile technologies with respect to the amount of effort it takes to use the devices, social norms related to using mobile technologies, perceived playfulness of the devices (i.e., how much fun people will perceive them to be), and the extent to which mobile learning facilitates self-management (Wang et al., 2009). The researchers who conducted the survey reported some gender and age differences in social norms associated with use of mobile devices; their results are consistent with other research on differences in general acceptance of mobile technologies (Magsamen-Conrad et al., 2015).

Despite indications of the potential benefits of mobile devices for learning, systematic research on their effectiveness is limited, and the research that exists often comes from the application developers themselves (Chiong and Shuler, 2010). Downsides also have been reported. For example, if laptops are not used for specific aims and purposes, they can impede students' ability to focus their attention on learning (Fried, 2008; Sana et al., 2013). Adherence to guidelines for the use of mobile devices may help to promote learning in different educational contexts (for an example of guidelines, see Hirsch-Pasek et al., 2015).

Problematic Features of Technology

Educational technologies are replete with features that can facilitate learning in controlled settings but can also serve as a distraction to many students (Gurung and Daniel, 2005). For example, e-textbook developers highlight possibilities for making information available in side-boxes or through embedded links as desirable features that allow students to click out of the reading to pursue learning about certain topics. Yet students may rarely choose to interrupt their reading to do this (Woody et al., 2010). Furthermore, the links can affect fluid reading of narrative and increase the learner's cognitive load. Similarly, text comprehension and metacognition can decrease when readers switch from print to an e-reading format (Ackerman and Goldsmith, 2011). Printed textbooks may use boldface type to support readers' understanding by highlighting key concepts, but some students rely on reading the highlighted material and skip the narrative.

BOX 8-3 **Mayer's Principles to Guide Multimedia Learning**

1. *Coherence Principle.* People learn better when extraneous words, pictures, and sounds are excluded rather than included.

2. *Signaling Principle.* People learn better when cues that highlight the organization of the essential material are added. This allows the learner to focus on the critical material that is presented.

3. *Spatial Contiguity Principle.* People learn better when corresponding words and pictures are presented near to, rather than far from, each other on the page or screen.

4. *Temporal Contiguity Principle.* People learn better when corresponding words and pictures are presented simultaneously rather than successively. This means that the graphic or image should be physically near the text that describes the image.

5. *Segmenting Principle.* People learn better from a multimedia lesson that is presented in user-paced segments rather than as a continuous unit. A simple way to do this is to include a "continue" button allowing the learner to progress through the material at her own pace.

6. *Pretraining Principle.* People learn better from a multimedia lesson when they know the names and characteristics of the main concepts. Pretraining may be most useful to novice learners because learning some of the material before they are exposed to the main lesson allows for improved and quicker learning of the main lesson.

There are ways both teachers and designers can help students benefit from technology. One is to provide adequate instructions for interacting with the technology. Instructions are sometimes poorly presented, such as on a cluttered computer screen, and users often skip them. Design that prioritizes easy engagement for the user and productivity with respect to the intended pedagogical goal is important. Achieving this objective requires substantial testing with users to ensure that the learner is guided to use the technology as intended. Designers can also rely on evidence-based principles supported by decades of research from the fields of human-computer interaction, human factors, and educational technology. Mayer (2001, 2009) identified 12 empirically supported principles to guide learning from multimedia (see Box 8-3). These principles are best viewed as guidelines for the design or selection of a learning technology, rather than as universal rules that apply to all multimedia

7. *Modality Principle.* People learn better from graphics and narrations than from animation and on-screen text. Tindall-Ford and colleagues (1997) found that the modality principle is strongest when the material is complex and the pace is fast and not under the learner's control.

8. *Multimedia Principle.* People learn better from words and pictures than from words alone.

9. *Redundancy Principle.* People learn better from graphics and narration than from the combination of graphics, narration, and on-screen text. Hoffman (2006) notes that the combination of auditory narration and the presentation of visual information can be distracting to the learner; therefore, the presentation of graphics with narration maximizes learning.

10. *Personalization Principle.* People learn better from multimedia lessons when words are in conversational style rather than formal style.

11. *Voice Principle.* People learn better when the narration in multimedia lessons is spoken in a friendly human voice rather than a machine voice.

12. *Image Principle.* People do not necessarily learn better from a multimedia lesson when the speaker's image is added to the screen.

SOURCE: Mayer (2014).

and populations, because implementing them may require tradeoffs among competing objectives.

Universal Design

Universal Design for Learning refers to a framework for drawing on relevant research to design educational experiences that are optimal for all learners, including those with specific learning challenges. Removing obstacles to interacting with technology has been a key objective of Universal Design (Burgstahler, 2015; Meyer et al., 2014). For example, many people benefit from speech-interpretation agents (such as the Siri agent on Apple iPhones) and audio book formats that originated with innovations developed for blind or deaf populations. The core vision of Universal Design is to design technologies "up front" that are accessible for diverse populations, rather than using an accommodation approach, in which features are added later (after the initial design) to allow people with particular disabilities to use the technology. An example of the accommodation approach is a mouth-operated control that allows a person who does not have use of her hands to operate a computer curser.[6]

Burgstahler (2015) identified seven Universal Design principles that have implications for the design of technologies for learning (see Table 8-1). These principles are often violated in typical learning contexts. For example, instructors often rely on a single medium (such as a PowerPoint presentation) instead of attending to cognitive variability and promoting cognitive flexibility through engagement of multiple modalities (Mayer, 2009).

Because people can become reliant on technology, the principles of Universal Design also may be useful in helping learners to adjust when a technology breaks down or is unavailable for other reasons (Burgstahler, 2015; Meyer et al., 2014). For example, it may be desirable to require that the user have some control over the device, rather than the device being fully automated, so the user can acquire some understanding of how the device functions and how to control it and thereby adjust to device malfunctions.

Technology for Learning in Later Life

Several trends suggest digital technologies can support both formal and informal learning in adults. Older adults are increasingly comfortable using technological devices, including tablets and computers (Pew Research Center, 2014). For example, over the past decade, Internet use among people over age 65 has more than doubled, and it is likely to grow as more individuals gain access to computers with Internet connectivity (Pew Research Center, 2014). Despite stereotypes depicting older adults as being uninterested in using Internet resources, many older adults report being interested in using the Internet and are capable of learning to use it (Morrell et al., 2004).

Technologies may support cognition and learning in older adults by providing cognitive aids; expanding their access to content and resources for learning; promoting social connectedness; and providing immersive, multimodal,

---

[6]Early examples of Universal Design for Learning were motivated by the search for ways to help individuals with various disabilities, such as those who are deaf, blind, otherwise physically disabled, or psychologically challenged. Examples of such technological breakthroughs include Braille, American Sign Language, and more recently, text-to-speech generators for the blind and speech-to-text generators for the deaf. Other examples of universal design include ramps and in-vehicle lifts for those in wheel chairs and medication organizers for elderly people. In the United States, federal standards and guidelines for the education of people with disabilities have followed from civil rights mandates, such as the Rehabilitation Act of 1973 and the American Disabilities Act of 1990, with amendments in 2008.

TABLE 8-1 Principles of Universal Design

Universal Design Principle	Example of Universal Design in Higher-Education Practice
Equitable use. The design is useful and marketable to people with diverse abilities.	*Career services.* Job postings in formats accessible to people with a broad range of abilities, disabilities, ages, and racial/ethnic backgrounds.
Flexibility in use. The design accommodates a wide range of individual preferences and abilities.	*Campus museum.* A design that allows a visitor to choose to read or listen to the description of the contents of display cases.
Simple and intuitive. Use of the design is easy to understand, regardless of the user's experience, knowledge, language skills, or current concentration level.	*Assessment.* Testing in a predictable, straightforward manner.
Perceptible information. The design communicates necessary information effectively to the user, regardless of ambient conditions or the user's sensory abilities.	*Dormitory.* An emergency alarm system with visual, aural, and kinesthetic characteristics.
Tolerance of error. The design minimizes hazards and the adverse consequences of accidental or unintended actions.	*Instructional software.* A program that provides guidance when the student makes an inappropriate selection.
Low physical effort. The design can be used efficiently, comfortably, and with a minimum of fatigue.	*Curriculum.* Software with on-screen control buttons that are large enough for students with limited fine motor skills to select easily.
Size and space for approach and use. Appropriate size and space is provided for approach, reach, manipulation, and use, regardless of the user's body size, posture, or mobility (Center for Universal Design, 1997).	*Science job.* An adjustable table and flexible work area that is usable by students who are right- or left-handed and have a wide range of physical characteristics and abilities (Burgstahler, 2015).

SOURCE: Based on Burgstahler (2015) and Center for Universal Design (1997).

and tailored learning environments. Technology can be a cognitive support, for example, by keeping track of grocery lists, upcoming appointments, or medication regimes or by providing easy access to clear explanations of recommended medical procedures (Tait et al., 2014). Older adults are also taking advantage of commercial software and online educational opportunities through universities to enhance their exposure to new fields of study (Gaumer Erickson and Noonan, 2010). Some MOOCs offered by universities serve large numbers of middle-aged and older adults, but research on such online platforms is sparse. Research is needed on the characteristics of older learners and ways to tailor online learning opportunities for them (Kensinger, 2016; Liyanagunawardena and Williams, 2016).

Technology can also bring people together to interact and collaborate virtually, when they might otherwise be isolated in their learning because they live alone or in remote areas or have limited mobility. Social connectedness is linked to successful cognitive aging (Ballesteros et al., 2015), so collaborative learning opportunities may lead to enriched social connections that improve cognition and mitigate cognitive decline.

Providing older adults with the rich, multimodal learning contexts and immersive learning environments that technologies can afford has the potential to optimize learning in later adulthood (Kensinger, 2016). Furthermore, older adults may benefit even more than younger adults from such opportunities as multimodal presentations (Mozolic et al., 2012). Older adults benefit when instruction matches and supports their own intrinsic motivations for learning and when they have the autonomy to guide their own learning. Technology-based experiences that can be tailored to individual learners may be especially useful for older people, whose life experiences and knowledge can be used to engage the individual and scaffold his learning (Kensinger, 2016).

Although older adults may benefit from technology-supported learning and report that technology can improve their quality of life (Delello and McWhorter, 2015), some experience challenges in adopting new technologies (Kensinger, 2016). Many adults need training that focuses both on how to use the technology and on their motivation to learn and the particular benefits the technology offers them (Kensinger, 2016). There is some evidence that participation in training itself can be a beneficial cognitive intervention, a finding consistent with research showing that mentally stimulating activities can benefit older adults' cognitive functions (e.g., Lenehan et al., 2016). For instance, training older adults to use tablet computers has been shown to help episodic memory and increase processing speed more than social activities do (Chan et al., 2014). Another study suggested that training older adults to use online social networking led to gains in executive function (Myhre et al., 2017).

Other age-related challenges associated with technology use pertain to sensory capacities (e.g., font sizes), cognitive capacities (e.g., working memory load imposed by passwords, distractions from pop-up ads), and motor abilities (e.g., ability to control a mouse or to type on a small keyboard) (Pew Research Center, 2014). Older adults who have less income and education are less likely to adopt technologies than those who are more affluent and highly educated (Pew Research Center, 2014), potentially making it more difficult to reach some of the older adults who could most benefit.

The Digital Divide

Policy makers have worried for decades about the "digital divide" between those who do and those who do not have access to a large suite of digital resources (U.S. Department of Commerce, 2014). Significant gaps in technology access related to income and education levels remain a problem. A 2015 survey of a nationally representative sample of adults ages 18 and older reported growth in ownership of smartphones and tablet computers, whereas ownership of other kinds of computing devices (such as laptop and desktop computers) was relatively constant or had fallen (Anderson, 2015b). Smartphones, the most widely used computing devices in 2014, were owned by 68 percent of adults. Smartphone ownership did not differ by racial/ethnic identity but did vary by income level, education, and geographic location. For example, more than 80 percent of adults with at least a bachelor's degree reported smartphone ownership, compared to just 41 percent of those who had not completed high school. The urban-rural difference in smartphone ownership rate was 20 percentage points (72% versus 52%).

Some prefer the term "digital inclusion" rather than "digital divide," to signal that degree of access ranges along a continuum and that the issue is unequal participation in online activities, rather than complete lack of access for certain groups (Livingstone and Helsper, 2007). At this point, for example, access to the Internet is widespread, but the tools to use the current generation of digital learning resources and to create content for online distribution is much less so. This continuum is evident in data about technology use among young people, despite the generalization that young people know how to use technology and learn to do so more easily because they are "digital natives" who have grown up with digital technologies (Warschauer and Matuchniak, 2010). Young people from less-privileged backgrounds who lack technology mentors tend to use their computing devices mainly for texting friends, taking photos, playing simple games, and accessing celebrity Websites, activities that do not develop key digital skills (Anderson, 2015b). Gee (2009) has argued that the digital divide is growing, not shrinking, because those with greater literacy skills and more access to supports for learning continue to accrue larger and larger benefits in areas of learning not available to people of more limited means. Moreover, the most empowering aspect of digital participation—the ability to create or modify online content—lies out of reach for many. Concerns about these digital opportunity gaps have inspired the creation of clubs and community centers with rich technology resources and social supports to enable more of the U.S. population to use a larger range of technologies.

Basic Internet access in U.S. schools has become more consistent over time for students from different backgrounds (Warschauer and Matuchniak, 2010). Moreover, schools that serve students from different income levels differ less in their technology infrastructures than do students' home environments. Although these are positive developments, the infrastructure requirements for the current generation of digital learning applications have risen substantially, and available evidence suggests that schools are not yet positioned to close the digital opportunity gap. The 2016 Broadband Progress Report indicated that 41 percent of U.S. schools did not have Internet access at transmission speeds (bandwidth) capable of supporting digital learning applications (Federal Communications Commission, 2016).

The gap is particularly acute for those living in sparsely populated areas and on tribal lands. Moreover, provision of devices and broadband Internet access is not sufficient: programs of professional support for teachers and leaders in schools who serve low-income students are also necessary (U.S. Department of Education and Office of Educational Technology, 2016). Children who attend schools in more-affluent communities and who have highly educated parents are more likely to use advanced technologies, such as simulations, and to encounter stimulating challenges such as opportunities to create products and address open-ended problems through technology. In contrast, children attending schools in less-privileged communities are more likely to use technology for drill-and-practice and for taking online benchmark assessments (Warschauer and Matuchniak, 2010; Wenglinsky, 2005).

In 2013, the federal government unveiled a plan to provide 99 percent of all public schools with broadband Internet access within 5 years. The plan, called ConnectED, set goals for providing bandwidth to rural areas that would support Internet upload and download speeds needed to access digital resources for learning. For example, with the proposed upgrades, it is envisioned that whole classes would be able to use next-generation learning applications at the same time. The plan called for the preparation of teachers to take advantage of this improved technology infrastructure. It also called on private companies to support the effort by donating computing equipment and support services to the nation's poorest schools.[7] However, the costs of providing bandwidth to sparsely populated areas are large, and debate continues about feasibility and how to pay for the necessary upgrades. It remains to be seen, therefore, whether plans like ConnectED are sufficiently viable to be implemented within the next decade.

A Systematic Approach to Implementation

Effective implementation of digital technology for learning is vital, and failure to properly consider implementation challenges may significantly limit the benefits to be gained from using technology. There is considerable evidence that use of a single instructional technology can lead to different outcomes when used by different learners in different contexts. For example, a large federally funded, randomized controlled trial that investigated the impact of

---

[7]See http://tech.ed.gov/connected/ [March 2017].

reading and mathematics software on students in 132 schools showed positive impacts at some schools and negative impacts at others (Dynarski et al., 2007). Findings such as these show that education policy makers are wise to be cautious about the promise of "single solution" technologies and avoid making major investments in a technology without identifying concrete benchmarks for success and evidence that the technology can meet them. Many factors can affect the impact of a technology when it is used on a large scale, including the characteristics of learners, the sociocultural context, the nature of the affordances the technology provides, the curriculum and materials to be used for learning, the faithfulness with which the technology is implemented, and the involvement of instructors and learners in the implementation process.

Some researchers have advocated taking a "systems approach" in implementing learning technologies, in order to take into account the multiple factors that may affect the impact of the technology. This approach is illustrated by the Texas SimCalc study (Roschelle et al., 2010). SimCalc[8] is a program designed to integrate the use of technology with curriculum goals and teacher professional development, with the goal of improving middle school students' understanding of key mathematics concepts that provide the foundation for algebra and calculus. The program includes a curriculum unit on proportionality, linear functions, and rate that is built around a storyline (managing a soccer team) and calls for small-group work, class discussion, and use of both paper materials and a mathematics software program, The software allows students to see animations of different patterns of motion and link those with corresponding representations in the form of interactive graphs and equations.

The curriculum unit's design emphasizes coherence across these different activities, all related to the unit's theme. The SimCalc curriculum emphasizes repeated applications of key concepts in multiple contexts. The outcome measure in the tests of learning incorporated these deeper levels of understanding. Finally, the role of the classroom instructor in supporting student learning was supported with multiple days of professional development and materials, including a teachers' guide with suggested activities and hints on likely student responses and misconceptions. The researchers found gains in mathematics skills across classrooms that used SimCalc (Roschelle et al., 2010).

A systems approach is also taken in intelligent tutoring systems for mathematics that have been used in thousands of schools, such as Cognitive Tutors (Koedinger et al., 1997; Ritter et al., 2007). Examples such as these suggest that several elements are important to a systems approach. In these cases, the users identified learning goals and matched the use of learning software to those goals. A method for measuring outcomes was identified in advance. The roles each of the actors in the system would play were coordinated. Teachers and other learning facilitators received substantial training.

---

[8]See https://simcalc.sri.com/ [November 2017] for more information.

CONCLUSIONS

The research discussed in this chapter demonstrates that recent advances in technologies for learning can offer significant benefits, but the results will depend on the alignment of goals for learning, contexts, the type of content to be learned, characteristics of learners, and the supports available for learners and instructors. Decision makers responsible for investments in technology need evidence about the many factors that can affect implementation of instructional technologies on a large scale.

From the available evidence on uses of digital technologies in people's learning, we draw two conclusions:

CONCLUSION 8-1: The decision to use a technology for learning should be based on evidence indicating that the technology has a positive impact in situations that are similar with respect to:

- **the types of learning and goals for learning;**
- **characteristics of the learners;**
- **the learning environment;**
- **features of the social and cultural context likely to affect learning; and**
- **the level of support in using the technology to be provided to learners and educators.**

CONCLUSION 8-2: Effective use of technologies in formal education and training requires careful planning for implementation that addresses factors known to affect learning. These factors include alignment of the technology with learning goals, provision of professional development and other supports for instructors and learners, and equitable access to the technology. Ongoing assessment of student learning and evaluation of implementation are critical to ensuring that a particular use of technology is optimal and to identifying needed improvements.

9

Learning Across the Life Span

Individuals learn outside of school and throughout their lives. What is taught in kindergarten through grade 12 (K-12) is relatively circumscribed, leaving relatively little room for individual choice. However, outside of formal schooling, what and how much people learn is increasingly directed by their own choices and circumstances. They may choose to pursue some form of postsecondary formal education or career training or move directly to full employment, raising a family, and other pursuits, and they may combine these options in different ways over time. Regardless of the path, each individual's lifelong development is shaped and constrained by the resources and opportunities afforded in her own complex environment, which is embedded in cultural context, as we discussed in Chapter 2.

The authors of *HPL I*[1] noted that the framework they recommended for K-12 education applied as well to adult learning (National Research Council, 2000). They noted in particular that few professional development programs for teachers met the criteria they outlined for K-12 educational environments. Their report emphasized the importance of the learning context for knowledge transfer but did not elaborate on that point with respect to changes in learning and cognition across the life span.

The learning processes discussed in this report function throughout the life span, but many do change with age, as do the contexts in which people learn and the reasons for engaging in continuous development through their life span. In this chapter, we examine research that addresses learning that

---

[1]As noted in Chapter 1, this report uses the abbreviation "*HPL I*" for *How People Learn: Brain, Mind, Experience, and School: Expanded Edition* (National Research Council, 2000).

takes place outside of compulsory education settings and the changes that occur across the stages of life. We consider how learning abilities are affected by aging and assess ways to preserve cognitive abilities. We also discuss research on learning disabilities that may affect learners throughout life. We then turn to learning in two environments familiar to adults: postsecondary education and the workplace. The chapter closes with a discussion of ways to foster lifelong learning. For this discussion, we rely on laboratory- and field-based cognitive science research.

CHANGES THAT OCCUR WITH AGE

Many changes affect learning as individuals age. Changes occur over time in reasoning processes and cognitive abilities. An individual's knowledge base and motivation for learning also change. These changes reflect variations in the environments in which people learn as they get older and the types of learning activities they are likely to undertake.

Reasoning and Knowledge

Two cognitive resources we discussed in Chapter 5 are particularly important as people age: the reasoning abilities associated with generating, transforming, and manipulating information and the knowledge accumulated through experience and education (the expertise an individual acquires) (Salthouse, 2010). We noted that both reasoning capacity and knowledge accumulation increase up to early adulthood, after which their paths begin to diverge. At that point, reasoning ability begins to decline, while learners retain or increase their base of knowledge as they age. The accumulated knowledge helps learners compensate for the declines in reasoning capacity that come with age.

Research on two knowledge domains that are important to adult learners—personal health and finance—illustrates how existing knowledge facilitates new learning. Researchers tested the hypothesis that older adults who had a base of knowledge about general health could more easily learn new information about heart disease. They found that base knowledge was predictive of new-information retention, particularly for participants who could learn at their own pace, which minimized cognitive load (Beier and Ackerman, 2005). Similarly, prior knowledge of investment products facilitated new learning about managing investments in a self-paced learning environment for adults (Ackerman and Beier, 2006). Very similar results have been found for new learning about technology (Beier and Ackerman, 2005). In general, older people are likely to know more than younger people do, and that knowledge facilitates their learning (Ackerman, 2000; Beier and Ackerman, 2001, 2003, 2005).

This research reinforces a point we made in Chapter 5: as people age and develop expertise in domains associated with their work and other aspects of life, they rely less on reasoning abilities to learn from the experiences of everyday life. However, with new experiences that are more removed from what a learner already knows, he can rely less on his knowledge base and will likely find the learning more challenging. For instance, it would be more difficult for a lawyer or doctor to learn a completely new career, such as K-12 teaching, if she has reached or passed middle age than at a younger age. She could certainly still make this change, by applying knowledge gained through working with other adults to the new challenge of managing a classroom full of children. She would combine prior knowledge about how best to work with others with feedback from the new environment and determine how to transfer the skills she learned with adults to the new challenge.

Although the changes that occur *on average* as people age are well understood, questions about age-related trajectories in learning abilities are complicated by individual variability (Hertzog et al., 2008). That is, different individuals would be expected to grow or decline at varying rates, depending on the characteristics of their environments, exposure to pollutants that affect neurophysiological functioning, health and sleep habits, and many other factors. Every individual's trajectory will be idiosyncratic and depend on his particular experiences with schooling, work, family and community, hobbies, and more. Further, there is not one standard age at which abilities change in a way that affects learning and development. The general age-related trajectories in abilities are a function of regular aging (as opposed to memory impairment that is a function of psychopathology, such as dementia or Alzheimer's disease).

Motivation for Learning

In Chapter 6, we discussed influences on people's motivation to learn that apply in general across the life span, but what people value and other aspects of motivation are likely to change as they age. These changes will influence the goals they pursue and the types of activities they perceive to be important to their sense of competence and well-being (Ebner et al., 2006; Kooij et al., 2011). Developmental activities that do not provide the learner with a sense of growth and accomplishment are unlikely to be sustained as people age (Carstensen et al., 1999). For instance, there is evidence that people's motivation to achieve and to be recognized for that achievement, whether at work or in other environments, tends to decline with age, while their motivation to use their vast repertoire of skills, help others, and preserve their resources and sense of competence tends to increase with age.

Some researchers have suggested that successful aging is a function of *selecting* age-appropriate goals, *optimizing* existing resources, and *compensating* for age-related declines using social or technological resources (Baltes and Baltes, 1990; Heckhausen et al., 2010). Others have pointed out the importance of age-related changes in affective preferences for information during learning (Carstensen et al., 1999). For example, one study suggested that older adults were more likely than younger ones to prefer positive emotional information and to avoid negative emotional information (Wang et al., 2015). Specifically, older workers responded favorably to feedback that was positive, perceived to be of high quality, and delivered in a fair manner. They were also more attentive to the interpersonal nature of feedback, whereas younger workers were more attentive to feedback that provided information on how to improve their performance. Compared to younger learners, older learners have also been shown to be more likely to compensate for age-related changes in reasoning and cognitive abilities when they participate in training and development programs that build on existing knowledge, are well structured, and permit learning to occur in less time-pressured formats (Heckhausen et al., 2010; Maurer et al., 2003).

Taken together, this evidence on motivation during adulthood points to the importance of learning opportunities and environments that take account of age-related changes in learner capacities, motives, and affective preferences. Specifically, research points to the value of training for older learners that enhances the learner's self-efficacy, accommodates age-related differences in cognitive capacities and emotional reactions to feedback, uses content that builds on the trainee's existing knowledge and skills, and has immediate relevance to the trainee.

Learning Activities and Environments

The environments in which people learn also vary as they progress through the life span. Learning in adulthood may occur in connection with formal programs aimed at professional development or when an individual pursues or improves skills such as mathematics literacy or English as a second language. Learning also occurs in connection with the desire to develop avocational interests or to improve health and financial literacy to deal with the challenges of daily life (Kanfer and Ackerman, 2008). Thus, adult learners may be engaged in formal learning environments, such as when a manager working full time enrolls in a continuing education course to learn more about art history in her spare time or when an unemployed maintenance worker engages in workforce software training. But much adult learning—whether in personal life or on the job—takes place in informal training environments: for instance, in learning a new job by executing its tasks without formal training (Tannenbaum et al., 2010) or in the learning that takes place when a person visits a new city or country, reads a newspaper, or plans for retirement.

We also note that people generally adapt their ideas about what they want to learn and do in the future as they age (Carstensen et al., 2003), and they tend to choose environments that align with their established knowledge and

Self-directed (autonomous) development in an informal environment	• Keeping up to date on industry news and events by reading relevant publications • Taking a walking tour of an historical area (e.g., Gettysburg, PA)
Self-directed (autonomous) development in a formal environment	• Taking an online course outside of the workplace to expand relevant knowledge base • Taking a photography class
Required (mandated) development in an informal environment	• Receiving mentoring by a more experienced colleague to learn a job-required skill • Reviewing company policy related to job-specific topics
Required (mandated) development in a formal environment	• Participating in annual employment-wide training to adhere to human resources policies at work • First-aid training for school employees

FIGURE 9-1 *Examples of autonomous (self-directed) and mandated learning in formal and informal settings.*

skills, which makes learning new domain-related information easier (Baltes and Baltes, 1990). Figure 9-1 provides a framework for thinking about the types of learning and development activities in which a person might engage over the life span. It highlights whether the activity is done of the learner's own volition (willingly chosen) and the formality of the learning environment (the extent to which the activity is structured and specifies desired learning outcomes). This figure is useful for framing a discussion of learning environments, but distinctions may not always be clear-cut. For example, if particular training is necessary for a desired promotion, pursuing this training opportunity could be viewed as either autonomous or mandated.

The decoupling of the formality with which training content is delivered from its volitional nature, as shown in Figure 9-1, will likely become increasingly important with the proliferation of educational technology, which has increased access to affordable, self-directed training and development activities at different levels of formality. Participation in such activities may be motivated by an individual's desire to develop workplace skills for a promotion or job change, but they generally include learning goals, a schedule, a curriculum, and possibly a syllabus (Siemens et al., 2015). According to the National Center for Education Statistics, in 2005, more than 39 percent of adults ages 40 to 65 had participated in some form of formal coursework during the previous

12 months,[2] and with the proliferation of online learning experiences such as massive open online courses, the number of people engaging in formal coursework should increase even further. Further work is needed to examine all of the components of lifelong intellectual development.

Cognitive Abilities

There can be substantial variability in the trajectory of people's cognitive ability as they age. At one extreme are "super agers," who perform like younger adults and often have brains that resemble those of people two to three decades younger (e.g., Harrison et al., 2012). At the other extreme are older adults with mild cognitive impairment or dementia. Although coverage of this latter portion of the spectrum is beyond the scope of this report, there has been an increasing interest in examining the factors that may explain some of the variance in functioning among older adults and in using structural and functional neuroimaging methods to better identify what neural differences may relate to that variability in performance (Kensinger, 2016).

Age-related changes in cognition affect the way adults process and maintain information and therefore also affect how adults learn. Although cognitive declines are relevant to learning—because these abilities include the attentional and cognitive resources a person can devote to learning and intellectual development—they are not the same as learning. In adults, the ability to generate and contribute to a knowledge base increases until their 60s and then gradually declines. However, when cognitive abilities are examined separately, a varied age-related trajectory can be seen. In terms of memory, some abilities (e.g., binding pieces of information together in memory, the ability to provide specific memories, metamemory during retrieval) show relative decline with aging while others (collaborative memory, emotional and motivated memory, acquisition and maintenance of existing knowledge base) show relative preservation with aging.

In Chapter 3, we discussed the ways adult brains may compensate for declines in some kinds of cognition by recruiting other resources. Although late adulthood has been associated with decreases in the cognitive abilities associated with learning novel information, memory, and speed, this stage has also been associated with increased skill in solving social dilemmas (Grossman et al., 2010). One interpretation of this increase is that older people may be better able than younger people to evaluate the negative consequences of social decision making. Another view is that older adults focus on the bigger picture of how social conflicts relate to the broader values and feelings of those involved—a shift that can be described as growing "wise" and that plays an important cultural role in society.

---

[2]See https://nces.ed.gov/programs/digest/d14/tables/dt14_507.30.asp [March 2017].

In Western contexts, ideas of "successful aging" (Havighurst, 1961) have incorporated concepts of social engagement as well as cognitive function (Rowe and Kahn, 1987). As a result, there has been increasing interest in understanding why the social connectedness of an individual could influence age-related trajectories (see Antonucci et al., 2001; Berkman, 1985, for reviews). Research has confirmed that factors such as life satisfaction (Waldinger et al., 2015) can mitigate some of the declines associated with aging. Similarly, having a strong social network (Glymour et al., 2008) rather than being lonely (Wilson et al., 2007) can reduce the speed of age-related cognitive decline (Kensinger, 2016).

Some effects of aging can be thought of as interactions between an individual and an environment that unfold over time. These interactions can manifest in two ways. First, age can minimize or exaggerate the effects of culture. For instance, differences in how American and Chinese people categorize information are larger among older adults than among younger adults (Gutchess et al., 2006). Even though this research was cross-sectional (i.e., studying all age groups at once), this result suggests that aging magnifies cultural differences—likely because of the additional time that an older adult has been immersed in the culture. Alternatively, it may indicate a historical change: that cultural differences between these groups were more pronounced at the time when the older participants were young. Conversely, cultural effects may sometimes be minimized with aging; this pattern is thought to occur because effects of culture are minimized as resources become depleted with age (Kensinger, 2016; Park and Gutchess, 2002).

Culture can also influence the types or degree of cognitive changes that are manifested with age. Researchers have explored this idea by examining the effects of more localized environments or subcultures on cognitive aging and asking how the community environment affects the way that cognition changes as a person ages, but these investigations have not yet established a clear answer. That is, effects have been noted in a number of studies, but the magnitude of the effects, as well as the specific domains showing the largest effects, have varied from study to study (e.g., Cassarino et al., 2015; Wu et al., 2015). Moreover, the intersection between the influence of community, social support, and social networks has been under-explored. Although there is still much to learn, the extant research does suggest that community environment, in addition to broader cultural influences, will need to be considered in order to understand the reasons for variation in cognitive aging trajectories (Kensinger, 2016).

LEARNING DISABILITIES

We look next at disabilities that may affect learning at every age. A conservative estimate is that 2 to 5 percent of children in the public school population have learning disabilities, and they are the largest category of children served in special education. However, there is no agreed-upon definition of learning disabilities that applies to adults, so there are not firm estimates of the percentage of U.S. adults who are affected by them (Lindstrom, 2016; Swanson, 2016).

Learning disabilities have been defined as "unexpected, significant difficulties in academic achievement and related areas of learning and behavior in people who have not responded to high-quality instruction" and whose difficulties "cannot be attributed to medical, educational, environmental, or psychiatric causes" (Cortiella and Horowitz, 2014, p. 3). It is important to emphasize that learning disabilities are not the result of poor instruction. They are caused by specific psychological processing problems; neurological inefficiencies with a biological base affect performance on specific tasks such as the acquisition and use of listening, speaking, reading, writing, reasoning, or mathematical abilities, specifically:

- The difficulty is not the result of inadequate opportunity to learn, general intelligence, or significant physical (e.g., hearing impairment), emotional (e.g., stress), or environmental factors (e.g., poverty, family abuse), but of basic disorders in specific psychological processes (such as remembering the association between sounds and letters).
- The difficulty is not manifested in all aspects of learning. The individual's psychological processing deficits depress only a limited aspect of academic behavior.

The most common types of learning disabilities are those that affect learning in reading, mathematics, or written expression. Dyslexia, which is difficulty reading that results from problems in identifying speech sounds and learning how they relate to letters and words, is the most prevalent and easily recognized type of learning disability. Individuals who have disabilities in reading may also have other disorders of attention, language, and behavior, but each affects learning in a different way (Cortiella and Horowitz, 2014). Though learning disabilities share certain features, there is a great deal of variability among the individuals affected by them (Swanson, 2016).

Causes of Learning Disabilities

Learning disabilities arise from neurological differences in brain structure and function and affect a person's ability to receive, store, process, retrieve, or communicate information. While the specific nature of these brain-based disorders is still not well understood, considerable progress has been made in mapping some of the characteristic difficulties to specific brain regions and structures. Evidence suggests that some learning disabilities have a genetic basis. Researchers have documented, for example, that certain learning disabilities, such as attention deficit/hyperactivity disorder and related disorders, occur with considerable frequency within some families (Cortiella and Horowitz, 2014; Lindstrom, 2016).

Learning disabilities may also be a consequence of insults to the developing brain that occur before or during birth, such as significant maternal illness or injury, drug or alcohol use during pregnancy, maternal malnutrition, low birth weight, oxygen deprivation, and premature or prolonged labor. Postnatal events resulting in learning disabilities might include traumatic injuries, severe nutritional deprivation, or exposure to poisonous substances such as lead.

We emphasize that a learning difficulty is not a learning disability if it is caused by visual, hearing, or motor disabilities; intellectual disabilities (formerly referred to as mental retardation); emotional disturbance; cultural factors; limited English proficiency; environmental or economic disadvantages; or inadequate instruction. However, according to Cortiella and Horowitz (2014), there is a higher reported incidence of learning disabilities among people living in poverty, perhaps because of increased risk of exposure to poor nutrition, ingested and environmental toxins (e.g., lead, tobacco and alcohol), and other risk factors during early and critical stages of development. Moreover, given that learning is affected by a complex set of environmental and individual variables, the stigma of learning disabilities is likely to also affect continuing growth and development throughout the life span (Lindstrom, 2016). Here we focus on two subtypes of learning disabilities that have been extensively researched: reading and math disabilities.

Reading Disabilities

It is difficult to know exactly how many children and adolescents are affected by disabilities in reading because available data are not broken down by type of learning disability.[3] Researchers have identified three types of reading disabilities (Flecher et al., 2007): (1) problems in word recognition and spelling; (2) difficulties in reading comprehension; and (3) difficulties in reading fluency and poor automaticity of word reading.[4] Although there are no population-based studies of this disorder, individual studies suggest that approximately 10 percent of samples of children with reading problems have

---

[3]In 2014-2015, 13 percent of public school students received special education services, and 35 percent of those students were classified as having some type of learning disability (see https://nces.ed.gov/programs/coe/indicator_cgg.asp [June 2017]). In 2013, the percentage of children identified by a school official or health professional as having a learning disability was 8 percent (see https://www.childtrends.org/indicators/learning-disabilities [June 2017]). The terms "reading disability," "dyslexia," and "specific learning disorders in reading" are used interchangeably. Most researchers who focus on anatomical abnormalities use the term "dyslexia," whereas researchers interested in cognitive dysfunction use the term "reading disabilities" (Swanson, 2016).

[4]See National Research Council (1998, 1999e) for detailed discussions of learning to read and reading disabilities.

reading comprehension difficulties (Nation et al., 1999; Snowling and Hulme, 2012; Swanson, 2016).

Research suggests that fundamental deficits in verbal abilities (including but not limited to reading disabilities) emerge between the ages of 5 and 18. These findings align with neurological studies that suggest that underactivation of certain brain regions correlates with weak cognitive performance on verbal tasks (Maisog et al., 2008; Richlan, 2012; Richlan et al., 2009, 2013). Because most neuroimaging studies of reading disabilities have been conducted with children or adults who have had years of reading difficulty, it has been impossible to determine whether the brain differences are associated with the underlying neurobiological causes of reading disabilities or are instead the consequence of years of altered and often vastly reduced reading experience (including compensatory alterations in reading networks) (Lindstrom, 2016). However, a variety of research supports the conclusion that underlying brain physiology accounts for some reading disabilities (Fischer and Francks, 2006; Hoeft et al., 2007; Leppänen et al., 2012; Molfese, 2000; Neuhoff et al., 2012; van Zuijen et al., 2013).

Mathematics Disabilities

Although mathematics disabilities have been less thoroughly researched than reading disabilities, they are also common.[5] The fact that some children have disabilities in both areas suggests that a similar cognitive deficit can play a role in both (Geary, 1993, 2013). Like other learning disabilities, those disabilities specifically affecting mathematics learning, often referred to as dyscalculia, are neurodevelopmental disorders of biological origin (American Psychiatric Association, 2013).

A synthesis of the literature on mathematics disabilities (Geary, 1993; also see Geary, 2013, for a review) identified three distinct groups of children with mathematics disabilities. One group is characterized as deficient in semantic memory. These children have disruptions in the ability to retrieve basic facts from long-term memory and high error rates in recall. Further, the characteristics of these retrieval deficits (e.g., slow solution times) suggest that children in this first group do not experience a simple developmental delay but rather have a more persistent cognitive disorder across a broad age span (Swanson, 2016).

Children in the second group have procedural types of math disabilities.

---

[5]As with reading disabilities, measuring the prevalence of math disabilities is challenging. Estimates ranging from 3 to 6 or 7 percent of the school-age population have been suggested (e.g., Geary, 2013; Reigosa-Crespo et al., 2012) but definitions vary. A significant number of children in U.S. schools demonstrate poor achievement in mathematics, and it is likely that disabilities account for some of that deficit (Swanson, 2016).

They generally use developmentally immature procedures in numerical calculations and therefore have difficulties in sequencing multiple steps in complex procedures. Children in the third group have a visual/spatial math disorder. These individuals have difficulties representing numerical information spatially. For example, they may have difficulties representing the alignment of numerals in multicolumn arithmetic problems; may misread numerical signs; may rotate or transpose numbers; may misinterpret spatial placement of numerals; and may have difficulty with problems involving space in areas, as required in algebra and geometry (Lindstrom, 2016).

Children with math disabilities, in contrast to learners characterized as low achievers, show a deficit in number processing, learning of arithmetic procedures, and memorizing basic arithmetic facts. Further, children with math disabilities do not necessarily differ from their peers with normal math ability in the types of strategies they use to solve simple arithmetic problems. However, they do differ in the percentage of retrieval and counting errors they make as a result of incorrect long-term memory of addition facts and lower average working memory capacity. Children with math disabilities have pervasive deficits across all working memory systems, but understanding of the relationship between specific components of working memory and specific mathematical cognition is still in the developmental stages (Geary, 2013; Swanson, 2016).

Few common patterns in anatomical causes of dyscalculia, or math disabilities, have been identified. However, in a meta-analysis of magnetic resonance neuroimaging studies of children diagnosed with developmental dyslexia and/or math disability, Kaufmann and colleagues (2011) found that children's activation patterns were modulated by the type of task performed (symbolic or nonsymbolic; number comparison versus calculation). These findings suggest both areas of commonality and differences; additional research to explore these connections would be useful.

Learning Disabilities in Adults

There is no single, shared method for assessing and counting adults with learning disabilities related to literacy or math skills (Fletcher, 2010; Gregg et al., 2006; MacArthur et al., 2010; Mellard and Patterson, 2008; Sabatini et al., 2010; Swanson, 2016). Thus, it is unclear how many adults have learning disabilities in either area. A conservative estimate is that approximately 3 to 5 percent of the general population has a reading disability (Swanson, 2016). Looking more broadly, it has been estimated that 20 to 30 percent of U.S. adults lack the literacy skills needed to meet the reading and computation demands associated with daily life and work (Kutner et al., 2007).[6] These estimates include people who self-identified as having learning disabilities, primarily in the area of reading (e.g., U.S Department of Education, 1992).

Because there is limited research on reading disabilities in adults (and even less on adults' mathematics disabilities), it is unclear whether adults with reading disabilities have cognitive deficits similar to those that have been noted in children or whether adults' cognitive deficits are the result of other factors, such as relatively lower general intelligence compared to adults not suffering from reading disabilities. In one examination of these issues, Swanson and colleagues (Flynn et al., 2012; Swanson, 2012; Swanson and Hsieh, 2009) synthesized research in which adults with reading disabilities were compared with average-achieving adult readers to determine how they differ from adults without a reading disability on measures related to overall reading competence. These researchers found differences in reading comprehension, reading recognition, verbal intelligence, naming speed, phonological awareness, and verbal memory (Swanson and Hsieh, 2009; Swanson, 2016).

There is also little research on the social and other consequences for adults who have learning disabilities. Existing research mostly focuses on the transition from secondary schooling into the workforce. Researchers have found that, compared to their nondisabled peers, adults with learning disabilities have a greater risk of dropping out of postsecondary schooling (Newman et al., 2009; Rojewski et al., 2014, 2015), lower postsecondary enrollment and attainment (Wagner et al., 2005), restricted labor force participation (Barkley, 2006), and lower earnings (Day and Newburger, 2002). The majority of jobs obtained by adolescents with learning disabilities when they leave school are semiskilled and usually part-time positions (Barkley, 2006; Gregg, 2009; Rojewski, 1999). Although some research (Newman et al., 2010) shows no real differences in earnings for these young people, even when wages were adjusted for inflation, there is evidence that the earning power gap between learning-disabled adults and their nondisabled peers is widening as a result of growing disparities in educational attainment (Day and Newburger, 2002; Swanson, 2016; Wagner et al., 2005).

Adult Literacy

Many adults in the United States and around the world lack basic literacy skills. U.S. adults scored below average in a study of literacy, numeracy, and

---

[6] The Program for the International Assessment of Adult Competencies (PIAAC) collects data on adult literacy and reports it in terms of percentages of adults who score at five different proficiency levels in these areas (see https://nces.ed.gov/surveys/piaac/results/makeselections.aspx [June 2017]).

problem solving in technology-rich environments conducted in 22 countries across Asia, North America, Europe, and Australia (Goodman et al., 2013). More than 50 million adults in the United States do not read at a level sufficient for them to secure a job, yet only a small percentage of these adults (approximately 2 million) were enrolled in federally funded adult education programs to increase their skills (National Research Council, 2012c). Even when adults do enroll in adult education, literacy programs are beset with many obstacles: poor funding; limited professional development for teachers and tutors; high absenteeism and attrition rates; and a wide diversity of students in terms of racial, ethnic, and gender identities, and age (between 16 and 80+), as well as employment, educational, and language status (Greenberg, 2008).

Technology is a key tool for providing access to adult education for learners who have work and family responsibilities that make attending courses in person difficult. Technology also makes it easier to tailor training to suit diverse skills and reading levels (Kruidenier, 2002; National Institute of Literacy, 2008). Adaptive, intelligent tutorial programs can address a range of skills and needs, and programs available online allow students to access the learning environments in their own homes, neighborhood libraries, schools, houses of worship, or locations of employment. Technology can also be used to develop environments that motivate learners, such as social media platforms, computer systems with intelligent conversational agents, and Web-based repositories of readings that target the particular interests of the adult (National Research Council, 2012c).

A significant body of research on adults who read at the third- to eighth-grade levels is available at the Center for the Study of Adult Literacy (CSAL).[7] The research explores interventions to improve reading that can be implemented by teachers or tutors or by means of computer technologies. For example, one promising intervention is based on a successful teacher intervention called PHAST-PACES, which focuses on obstacles to word identification and decoding through a framework of phonologically based remediation (Lovett et al., 2012). CSAL tailored the program, which uses a combination of direct instruction and dialogue-based metacognitive training for adult readers.

We emphasize that interventions to improve adult literacy must optimize a number of factors to be successful; it is important to also consider the prospective participants' motivation, emotions, interests, and social lives, so that the materials used in the intervention have practical value for their lives.

Interventions

Adults and children with learning disabilities are a diverse group, and no general instructional model can be recommended for all of them (Swanson,

---

[7]For more information, see http://csal.gsu.edu [March 2017].

2016). With respect to children, there have been several meta-analyses that examined instructional interventions in domains such as mathematics (e.g., Gersten et al., 2009; Xin and Jitendra, 1999), writing (Graham and Perin, 2007), and reading (e.g., Berkeley et al., 2010; Edmonds et al., 2009; Swanson, 1999; Wanzek et al., 2013).

The results from these studies suggest that children with learning disabilities are generally responsive to intense instruction. For example, controlled experimental studies showed a relatively large improvement after intense instruction using particular models (Swanson et al., 1999). These interventions involved (a) teaching a few concepts and strategies in depth rather than teaching a larger number superficially, (b) teaching students to monitor their performance, (c) teaching students when and where to use the strategy in order to enhance generalization, (d) teaching strategies as an integrated part of an existing curriculum, and (e) providing supervised student feedback and opportunities for practice. The results indicated that explicit strategy instruction (explicit practice, elaboration, strategy cuing) and small group interactive settings yielded the greatest improvement in treatment outcomes (Swanson, 2000).

One might expect these findings to generalize to populations of adults with learning disabilities, but this remains an area ripe for future research (Flynn et al., 2012; Hock, 2012; Mellard and Patterson, 2008; Swanson, 2016). Most of the available work related to adults has been limited to identifying assessment accommodations (e.g., providing extended time for testing) for adults with learning disabilities. Because there is limited research on learning disabilities in adults (including assessment tools), it is unclear whether the cognitive deficits seen in children are similar to those in adults with learning disabilities. Although no general instructional model can be recommended for all adults and children with learning disabilities, children are generally responsive to intense instructional programs.

We note also that many of the difficulties associated with learning disabilities such as dyslexia, dyscalculia, and attention deficit disorders stem from a mismatch between individuals' neuropsychological predispositions and strengths on the one hand and the demands of the learning context on the other (see e.g., McDermott and Varenne, 1996). For example, dyslexic learners' phonological decoding deficits (i.e., problems associating letters with linguistic sounds) are especially problematic in countries that use phonographic (alphabetic) writing systems with complex orthographic conventions, such as English. In countries such as Greece and Germany where the orthographic conventions are more straightforward, there is a lower incidence of dyslexia (Landerl et al., 2013; Vellutino et al., 2004).

The match between learner and context is critical to good outcomes: in conducive contexts and with the right supports, students with learning disabilities and mental illnesses can be successful students. For example, there is evidence that allowing students with attention deficit/hyperactivity disorder to structure their learning environments and resources adaptively can facilitate their learning (Fugate et al., 2013). Individuals with disabilities reflect the same range of human qualities and abilities that others do. Education that capitalizes on an individual student's capacities that are assets for learning (e.g., a dyslexic learner's strengths in pattern recognition and peripheral vision) is thus particularly important for these students (Lorusso et al., 2004; Schneps et al., 2007; von Károlyi et al., 2003; see also Wei et al., 2013, regarding individuals with autism).

POSTSECONDARY EDUCATIONAL EXPERIENCES

Once people complete their compulsory education, they may pursue further education in a variety of settings (e.g., community college, college, university, vocational or technical schools). There are several important differences between K-12 and postsecondary education settings.

First, institutions that educate adults have varied goals. Many academic institutions use prior academic performance and ability to select those they think will succeed and thrive in the academic environment they provide; they do not have responsibility for the success of people whom they do not accept or who do not succeed in their environments. Although there are exceptions, such as adult literacy and retraining programs, for most academic institutions and organizations that are training employees the focus is on recognizing and rewarding talent, rather than raising the performance of those who are struggling. Though academic institutions and educators are increasing their attention to factors that affect their students' performance and persistence (such as adjustment to college life and study skills), it remains true that when students do not perform well in school, colleges are not required to continue to enroll them. In work environments, the outcomes for people who are not able to learn new skills can be even harsher; workers who cannot or will not learn a required skill can expect to be told to look for other employment. These two examples illustrate how vital it is that K-12 experiences prepare students for the developmental demands of college and beyond.

There are also marked differences between the classroom experiences characteristic of K-12 and postsecondary education and those common in training and development in the workplace. In postsecondary situations, students may be expected to complete more of the work outside of the classroom than they had in high school, but they are free to decide how they will prioritize their study time and get work done. In work situations, supervisors will rarely assess whether the employee has learned the necessary skills to execute a task; rather, workers are expected to figure it out on their own and ask questions if they have them. This increased autonomy highlights the importance of interest, motivation, and the capacity to monitor and regulate their own progress.

BOX 9-1 The Meyerhoff Scholars Program

The Meyerhoff Scholars Program at the University of Maryland, Baltimore County, has successfully increased diversity among future leaders in science, engineering, and related fields. Myerhoff Scholars are nominated while they are prospective undergraduate students and plan to pursue doctoral study in the sciences or engineering. These students have shown interest in the advancement of minorities in these scientific fields. The program seeks to establish a tightly knit learning community in which students inspire one another to excel. The program reports that its students are 5.3 times more likely to have graduated from or be currently attending a science, technology, engineering, or mathematics masters or doctoral program than are students who were invited to join the program but declined and attended another university instead (see http://meyerhoff.umbc.edu).

Researchers have not directly assessed the relative importance of interest and motivation among K-12 and postsecondary students. However, there is some empirical evidence that these factors are important for success in post-secondary environments, along with cognitive ability and psychosocial contextual influences such as cultural background (e.g., status as a first-generation college student[8] (see Ackerman et al., 2013; Richardson et al., 2012). Most of this research uses grade-point average as a proxy for learning, though many factors may affect it. This research suggests that cognitive ability (typically measured through standardized tests) and high school performance tend to account for the most variance in college grade point average, but motivational factors such as academic self-efficacy, intrinsic motivation, and goal orientation also have been positively associated with academic performance (Ackerman et al., 2013; Richardson et al., 2012).

Researchers have also begun examining elements of a student's pre-college experiences and cultural background to better understand the factors that lead to success. They have found that the social climate at many colleges and universities does not serve minority and first-generation students well (Stephens et al., 2012). These students often encounter challenges that other students do not face. First-generation students, for instance, tend to come from families

---

[8]A first-generation student is a student who does not have at least one parent who graduated from a 4-year college or university.

with far fewer resources than continuing-generation students, so they are more likely to work for pay at one or more jobs during college in order to pay tuition or living expenses (Phinney and Haas, 2003). They therefore have less time to invest in further opportunities for learning and development, such as unpaid internships (Pascarella et al., 2004).

These challenges are also cultural in that many American universities support middle-class norms of independence (e.g., paving one's own path), which can be at odds with working-class norms of interdependence (e.g., connecting with others; attending to others' needs). Studies of the possible effects of a cultural mismatch for first-generation students suggest that positioning the university culture as independent rendered tasks more difficult for first-generation students, but that representing the culture as interdependent facilitated their performance (Stephens et al., 2012). This is but one example, and although research continues to examine elements of postsecondary educational environments that facilitate or impede student performance, more work in this area is urgently needed. Box 9-1 describes an approach to addressing this problem.

WORKFORCE TRAINING

Formal training accounts for a relatively small percentage of workplace learning, but it is still important for many learners (Tannenbaum et al., 2010). Developing an effective training program requires attention to the needs of the organization and its employees, as well as the constraints in which the organization operates (Goldstein and Ford, 2002).

Some research has examined training performance as people age. Age is generally negatively related to performance in training, in that older learners typically take longer in training and do not perform as well as younger learners after training (Kubeck et al., 1996; Ng and Feldman, 2008). Nonetheless, research does indicate that older adults can learn in training environments if that environment is designed to meet the individual needs of learners (Callahan et al., 2003; Charness and Schumann, 1992). The bottom line is that tailoring instruction to the different motivations and abilities of individual learners is important for workplace training for people of all ages, and the same training intervention will not be equally effective for everyone (Cronbach, 1957; Snow, 1989). The age-related differences in performance that should be considered in planning training for older adults likely relate to the changes in reasoning and motivation discussed above.

Although very little research has examined tailored instruction with working-age adults, the available evidence suggests that older learners may benefit from more structure (i.e., step-by-step instruction) in highly complex training environments (Carter and Beier, 2010; Gully et al., 2002). Nonetheless, research in this area is sparse, and much work remains to be done to identify the best training interventions for individual learners at any age. However, we note that technological advances in training design offer new and easier means of customizing training to individual learners' needs and interests (Snow, 1989; Wolfson et al., 2014). For instance, an employee using an online training tutorial can modify the structure of the program to meet her needs by changing the interface to provide step-by-step instructions when the content to be learned is unfamiliar and perhaps change it back to provide less instruction when the knowledge domain is more familiar. Technology to support tailored instruction has great promise for workplace training and is a topic that merits further research (Gully and Chen, 2010; Wolfson et al., 2014).

Determining Whether People Learn in the Workplace

The effectiveness of workplace training is typically assessed in four ways that derive from an evaluation framework designed to assess an array of outcomes, from trainee reactions to the organization's return on investment (Alliger and Janak, 1989; Kirkpatrick, 1967). First, immediately after training, surveys and other methods can be used to assess trainees' reactions to and satisfaction with different aspects of the training. Second, an evaluation, typically a knowledge test, can be conducted directly after the training has concluded to measure the knowledge acquired by each trainee. Third, the extent to which the trainee has transferred what was learned in training back to the workplace can be assessed, usually by examining workplace behaviors after training has concluded.

The fourth indicator, which can also be measured, is the extent to which the organization benefits over time from the investment in training. Although calculating return on investment can be a complicated process because of the number of different variables other than training (ranging from market trends to myriad organizational initiatives) that can affect organizational success, it is an important outcome for organizations. In 2014, organizations spent an average of just over $1,200 per employee on training and development activities. From the organization's perspective, this money is wasted if trainees do not apply what they learn in training to their performance on the job (Goldstein and Ford, 2002). The economic benefits of employee training may be difficult to assess but it is possible to measure trainees' learning and ability to transfer what they have learned to new situations (Alliger and Janak, 1989).

These four indicators may not provide very complete answers about the effectiveness of training. For example, they may more readily capture trainees' attitudes or capacity to repeat what they just heard in training, rather than actual learning. The third level of assessment, measuring what the employee transfers to the job, arguably comes closest to assessing learning. But this type of assessment is more challenging than assessing attitudes and knowledge directly after training, so it is used less frequently. These challenges are similar to the challenges of assessment in other educational settings: it is easier to find out how much students enjoy classes and perhaps what they know on the last day of class than to assess what learning really sticks.

Training Transfer

The transfer of training, or applying what has been learned in the workplace, is the third level of evaluation discussed above. It has also been widely studied by cognitive psychologists, who have developed a taxonomy that distinguishes between near transfer and far transfer (Barnett and Ceci, 2002). *Near transfer* is using a skill learned in training at another time, outside of the training environment. *Far transfer* is using a trained skill in combination with other elements and/or at a time distant from training. Transfer of skill learning has been studied in other contexts, and findings from that research apply in organizational training contexts. For instance, knowledge learned in training will be more likely to transfer if the training and transfer environments are similar and if the training introduces desirable difficulties (those that pose a manageable level of challenge to a learner but require learners to engage at a high cognitive level) (Schmidt and Bjork, 1992). However, features of the organizational environment, such as how supportive managers and coworkers are when an employee uses a newly learned skill, influence transfer of workplace training back to the job (Blume et al., 2010; Rouiller and Goldstein, 1993).

A meta-analysis of research on workforce training transfer identified characteristics of learners, such as differences in ability or personality (e.g., conscientiousness, dependability) and the training environment that are positively associated with transfer of training (Blume et al., 2010). The authors point to three elements in the work environment that are important:

1. Environmental support for training, including peer and supervisor support
2. Transfer climate, in the form of implicit cues in the environment that using what is learned in training on the job is expected, such as peers who actively transfer their new knowledge
3. Organizational constraints, such as lack of autonomy and other situational factors

They found that environmental support has the largest effect on transfer; organizational constraints also had a modest effect. They found modest evidence that supervisor support in using the new skill may be more important than peer support.

A few examples illustrate how situational cues and opportunities affect training transfer (Blume et al., 2010; Rouiller and Goldstein, 1993). If an employee attends training in the use of a database management software program that he rarely uses on the job, and if he does not have the opportunity to practice the newly learned skills for months, he likely will not be able to effectively transfer what he learned to his work. On the other hand, signals in the environment (situational cues) from coworkers or managers can support the employee in using his new skills. These signals may be perceived by the trainee as consequences: if the employee feels that his attempts to use the new skills or tools learned in training are met with negative consequences, he will be less likely to practice the newly learned skill (Blume et al., 2010; Rouiller and Goldstein, 1993). For example, a new database management software designed to streamline a process that had previously involved multiple spreadsheets may feel difficult, inefficient, and error-prone when the newly trained employee first uses it. Indeed, if the difficulty of implementing this new skill is not acknowledged by supervisors and coworkers and the use of the new program similarly encouraged, the employee may revert to the old approach to meet a deadline. This would be an unfortunate waste of organizational resources. Furthermore, research on skill learning suggests that difficulty using newly trained skills—at least initially—should be expected, but after extensive practice people can be expected to execute complex tasks with expertise (Ackerman, 1988; Anderson, 1982).

Autonomous Workplace Learning

Because workplace learning is diverse, professionals may engage in learning that is incidental and informal (i.e., as a side effect of the work), intentional but nonformal (related to work activities), or formal on-the-job and off-the-job training and education (Tynjälä, 2008). Self-directed, or autonomous, learning at work is the most commonly reported approach for workforce development, but informal methods, such as on-the-job training and peer learning, are largely unstudied (Ellingson and Noe, 2017). One reason is that learning and development are ubiquitous throughout the career span: people often do not realize that the activities in which they are engaging are developmental. Informal development activity is often considered to be a "part of the job" (Tannenbaum, 1997). Such experiences might include learning from failure, mastering new tools to be more efficient at work, or taking on challenging job roles required by a new project. Because learners tend not to view such activities and events as learning experiences, systematic evaluation of this learning is difficult (Boud and Middleton, 2003).

The prevalence of autonomous workplace learning reflects the ways many kinds of careers have changed in industrialized countries over the past 50 years or so. Organizational researchers have remarked that during the mid to late 20th century, many workers could expect to spend the majority of their careers in a single organization and often to retire with a pension plan that rewarded their loyalty. Global competition for the best talent and increased life expectancies, which have extended the average amount of time a person could expect to live past retirement from less than 10 years to more than 20 (Hall and Mirvis, 1995, 2013), have spurred changes in perceptions of a career. Career growth is now exclusively the responsibility of the individual worker, not the organization. Today, most workers can expect to have multiple jobs and even several careers, pursued at many organizations, over the course of their working life. Assuming equal access to opportunities and no age-related bias, people may shift in and out of the labor pool at any age they wish. Successful navigation of a career now requires continuous learning and development, as these contribute to the development of professional skills, interests, and career identity (Hall and Mirvis, 1995, 2013). Organizational scientists call this phenomenon *the Protean career* to reflect its ever-changing nature (Hall and Mirvis, 1995).

The shift to Protean careers highlights the important effects that characteristics of both the individual and the environment have on work trajectories. Individual characteristics, such as worker ability, interests, attitudes, and motivation, will play an increasingly important role in learning and development throughout the span of an individual's working life because of the need to evolve and adapt. The nature of life-span development is essentially individual and is thus driven by each worker's expectations, decisions, interests, persistence, and abilities. These individual factors also interact with contextual factors both at work (e.g., climate and opportunities for development) and outside of work (e.g., life demands outside of work that make it difficult to participate in skill development) to influence continuous learning (Ackerman, 2000; Beier et al., 2017). Consider, for example, how lack of access to child or elder care, libraries, and community events, and even a reliable Internet connection, may interfere with self-directed learning. Access to both formal (e.g., community education programs and participation in massive open online courses) and informal (e.g., books, Websites, and people-networks) opportunities can greatly facilitate self-directed learning (Comings and Cuban, 2000). The effects of support or barriers are not trivial: for example, the support of a spouse, partner, or parent can be more important than career interest and goals in determining whether or not an individual spends time outside of work to develop new skills (Lent et al., 2000; Tang et al., 1999).

Persistence during learning can also be affected by interactions between the environment and individual factors. For instance, an individual who perceives herself as having declining memory abilities with age may be less likely to participate in learning a new job-related skill after a layoff (Maurer et al., 2003). Any environmental barrier to the developmental experience (i.e., lack of Internet connection or limited transportation to attend training) will make participation in developmental activity even less likely.

Research on self-regulation of learning provides another lens for thinking about individuals' workplace learning. For example, a qualitative study examined how knowledge workers in a multinational energy company set and attained their learning and developmental goals to complete a specific project or task (Margaryan et al., 2013). The researchers found that the participants tended to focus on outcome goals (short- and long-term organizational needs relating to the project) rather than process goals, and they tended to be responsive to input from supervisors, mentors, and colleagues when planning and attaining their learning goals. The authors concluded that the participants' direction of their own learning was highly dependent on the social and organizational context.

This work suggests that the organizational environment, or the organization's culture for learning, can play a key role in facilitating employee development (Tannenbaum, 1997). The following are important cultural elements that foster continuous workplace development:

1. *Promoting a "big picture" perspective from which employees know what the goals of the organization are.* This enables workers to align development with organizational goals.
2. *Providing assignments that permit people to stretch beyond their job description.* In learning organizations, people are assigned tasks that provide opportunities to do new things, learn new skills, and apply what they learn back on the job (Ford et al., 1992; Schoorman and Schneider, 1988).
3. *Fostering a climate where people can learn from their mistakes.* In learning organizations, mistakes are tolerated, particularly when people are trying new things in the early stages of learning. Research suggests that error-prone practice can actually enhance learning, so if mistakes are tolerated they can lead to greater development (Keith and Frese, 2008).
4. *Making employees accountable for their own development.* For example, performance evaluations might include ratings for engaging in autonomous career-related professional development.

Another effect of the shift to the Protean career model is that because learning is increasingly a function of individual experiences not controlled by an organization, workers' development is increasingly idiosyncratic. This makes it extremely difficult to conduct any systematic evaluation of autonomous workplace learning and development activity. Nonetheless, the benefits of autonomous learning could be examined on the organizational level by tracking the amount, type, and quality of autonomous learning that occurs within an organization over a period of time and correlating these factors to outcomes such as employee capabilities, retention, and employee perceptions about the culture for learning and development (Tannenbaum et al., 2010). Quantifying the benefits of autonomous workplace learning at the organizational level in this way would help to clarify how it works and why it is beneficial; thus far, however, we are not aware of any research on this.

Although there has been little scientific research on life span learning and development, the importance of autonomous learning is evident to workers themselves. Qualitative research on communities of practice (i.e., workers with common professional interests) within organizations suggests that employees tend not to rely on opportunities for formal training experiences for their own development unless they are interested in a job-specific skill. Instead, workers explore autonomous development opportunities based on their own interest, motivation, and abilities, as well as the people, resources, and time available in their work and home environments (Boud and Middleton, 2003). Indeed, self-initiated learning is pervasive among adult workers. A survey of more than 400 workers across an array of professions identified learning from coworkers and peers, on-the-job training, trial and error, and observing others as the most common methods of workplace learning; classroom learning at college or formal organizational training were far less commonly cited as important for development at work (Tannenbaum, 1997).

With respect to on-the-job training, organizational scientists have studied the effects of jobs themselves. Jobs, particularly those that are cognitively challenging and that afford workers some control over the tasks in which they engage, offer their own learning opportunities (Hackman and Oldham, 1976; Karasek et al., 1998; Morgeson and Humphrey, 2006). Jobs high in autonomy require employees to make decisions about work methods, work scheduling, and overall decision making, rather than relying on the organization for directives. Jobs high in complexity are challenging, intellectually stimulating, and engaging. Although most research has focused on examining the effect of job characteristics on workplace attitudes and related behaviors (e.g., job satisfaction and turnover) (see Morgeson and Hurphreys, 2006), researchers are beginning to examine learning as an important outcome of these types of job characteristics. For instance, a survey of more than 800 workers between the ages of 18 and 65 from various industries found that job demands and autonomy have a positive relationship with self-reported learning at work (Raemdonck et al., 2014). Future research might consider more-objective learning outcomes such as knowledge acquired, but this initial research on worker self-perceptions is promising.

Self-Regulated Learning in the Workplace

Though workplace training is important, most workplace learning is employee-directed (Tannenbaum, 1997). The employee (i.e., the learner) must manage his own work-related learning by identifying knowledge competencies and gaps, setting learning goals, monitoring progress, and adapting strategies to meet learning requirements. All of these activities are components of self-regulated learning (Schultz and Stamov Roßnagel, 2010; Zimmerman, 2000). Though there is a significant body of work on self-regulation, little is known about how professionals regulate their own learning in the context of daily work. Most research in this area has focused on K-12 students. Moreover, for both adults and children, self-regulated learning has also typically been studied in laboratory conditions, which do not necessarily illuminate the impact of the real-world social and organizational environment on an individual's practices (Margaryan et al., 2013).

However, some work on questions about self-regulation of learning in the workplace suggests that each workplace is a complex system, where individuals' work and learning activities are highly influenced by the workplace community and its social norms. The workplace system and community influence the defining and evaluating of learning goals, adaptation of strategies to social and organizational norms, and the nature of incentives and hindrances to learning (e.g., Siadaty et al., 2012). The distinctive features of a learning environment can also influence whether a learner uses self-regulation practices and whether she achieves desired goals (Boekaerts and Cascallar, 2006; Siadaty et al., 2012; Whipp and Chiarelli, 2004). An example of this work is the qualitative study cited above of how knowledge workers in a multinational energy company set and attained their learning and developmental goals to complete a specific task (Margaryan et al., 2013). The researchers found that learning in this workplace was structured and deeply integrated with the work tasks and priorities and that the focus was on outcomes (short- and long-term organizational needs relating to the project) rather than process goals.

The Importance of Active Engagement

People learn continually through active engagement in their environments, and research has demonstrated that engaging in some activities promotes healthy aging, including performance in cognitive tasks (Bielak et al., 2012). The type of activity matters, however (Bielak, 2010; Carlson et al., 2012; Christensen et al., 1996). For example, an engaged lifestyle was positively associated with a reduction of older adults' risk of cognitive impairment (Carlson et al., 2012), and the activities that had the strongest correlations were physical activities (Gow et al., 2012).

Work activities have also been shown to be important in reducing the risk of cognitive impairment, particularly when they are mentally demanding (Bosma et al., 2002). The effects of job challenges on cognitive functioning have been shown both during employment and after retirement (Fisher et al., 2014). Highly complex work with other people (e.g., mentoring and supervising functions) has been associated with increases in verbal ability in the years leading up to retirement, compared with less complex work that involved interactions with other people (Finkel et al., 2009). Declines in cognitive performance have been observed in individuals who had higher physical or visual job demands (Potter et al., 2006).

Similarly, Potter and colleagues (2008) found that work requiring higher levels of intellectual and social effort was associated with better cognitive outcomes, whereas work requiring greater physical effort was associated with cognitive declines. This finding may seem counter to the finding that physical exercise enhances cognitive abilities (Gow et al., 2012). There has been no definitive research on the topic, but it seems likely that a balance of cognitive demands and physical exercise may preserve abilities. It may also be that physically taxing jobs may not promote the type of physical activity that is associated with enhancing cognitive abilities (e.g., aerobic versus static-strength-type exercises such as lifting) (Hertzog et al., 2008).

Although most research on activities and aging is correlational or observational in nature, some experimental research has demonstrated causal influences of activities on cognitive outcomes. For example, Stine-Morrow and colleagues (2008) found benefits for a program that involved team competition and problem solving on a reasoning ability measure. Another study found benefits of active engagement on episodic memory for older adults (Park et al., 2014).

FOSTERING LIFELONG LEARNING

Researchers have explored ways to foster learning across the life span. They have not identified particular educational and learning interventions for people at specific ages, but the research does suggest factors that support continued learning.

Working collaboratively with others is both a challenge and an opportunity that learners encounter in many contexts. Teams are key to planning, problem solving, and decision making in many contexts (National Research Council, 2011). The importance of collaborative problem solving to economic stability and growth is reflected in the decision of OECD to include this capacity in its 2015 survey of student skills and knowledge (OECD, 2013). Group- and project-based training and collaboration are also recognized as among key 21st century skills (Care et al., 2016; National Research Council, 2011c, 2012b). There is little research on learning in these contexts, but the research on team performance can suggest inferences about learning. For example, in team training it may be that having some team members who dominate the learning environment could be detrimental to learning outcomes.

Collaboration can allow for a more effective division of labor, and solutions developed collaboratively incorporate multiple sources of knowledge, perspectives, and experiences. However, the literature is mixed on whether the quality of solutions from a group is better than a collection of solutions from individuals working independently. On the positive side, problem-solving solutions by a group are sometimes better than the sum of the solutions of the individual members (Aronson and Patnoe, 1997; Dillenbourg, 1996; Schwartz, 1995). Better solutions can emerge when differences of opinion, disagreements, conflicts, and other forms of social disequilibrium are explored and addressed. However, when there is chronic discord, one person overly dominates the team, some team members do not contribute adequately, or effort is wasted in irrelevant communication, the benefits of working in teams are reduced (Dillenbourg, 1996; Rosen and Rimor, 2009).

The success of a team can be threatened by an uncooperative member or a counterproductive alliance, and it can be facilitated by a strong leader who ensures that all team members are contributing. Studies have shown that skilled collaboration and social communication facilitate productivity in the general workplace (Klein et al., 2006; Salas et al., 2008) and, more specifically, in engineering and software development work (Sonnentag and Lange, 2002), in mission control in aviation (Fiore et al., 2014), and in interdisciplinary research among scientists (Nash et al., 2003).

People benefit from training in when and how best to apply collaboration skills (Care et al., 2016; Mullins et al., 2011). For example, the ground rules of the collaborative situation must be understood by the group members if they are to optimize their interactions and solutions. Students need to know when, why, and which aspects of collaboration are fruitful for improving the knowledge to be acquired and the problem to be solved. When is it best to focus on disagreements? When is it better to negotiate a consensus? How can the group find common ground on task goals and team organization? What tasks are best conducted individually versus with a tightly coordinated team? For highly interdependent tasks (i.e., those that are impossible to achieve individually), what is the schedule and communication protocol for initiating actions and completing objectives? How are tasks distributed among group members in the team organization? How are potential problems monitored and repaired?

Research on training for these critical teamwork skills is just beginning. One framework, the Collaborative Problem Solving framework used by the Programme for International Student Assessment, identifies three core collaborative competencies: (1) establishing and maintaining a shared understanding, (2) taking appropriate action to solve the problem, and (3) establishing and maintaining team organization (OECD, 2013). These competences are crossed with problem-solving competencies: exploring and understanding; formulating a representation of the problem; planning and executing the plan; and monitoring and reflecting on the problem solution. A 2015 computer-based assessment of the program could be the basis for improvements in curricula in this area (see OECD, 2015).

CONCLUSIONS

Individuals continue to learn throughout their lives, but once they complete the compulsory portion of their education, what and how much they learn is largely directed by their own choices and circumstances. Both reasoning and knowledge increase up to early adulthood, when their paths begin to diverge: abilities to quickly generate, transform, and manipulate factual information begin to decline, while knowledge levels remain stable or increase. We note that because conducting either randomized controlled trials or quasi-experimental research on the effectiveness of training interventions in environments outside of K-12 settings is difficult, the research does not yet support strong conclusions about interventions. However, we offer two broad conclusions about lifelong learning.

> **CONCLUSION 9-1: People continue to learn and grow throughout the life span, and their choices, motivation, and capacity for self-regulation, as well as their circumstances, influence how much and how well they learn and transfer their learning to new situations.**

> **CONCLUSION 9-2: People learn continually through active engagement across many settings in their environments; learning that occurs outside of compulsory educational environments is a function of the learner's motivation, interests, and opportunities. Engagement with work (especially complex work that involves both intellectual and social demands), social engagement, physical exercise, and adequate sleep are all associated with lifelong learning and healthy aging.**

10

Research Agenda

We began this report with a discussion of how all learners grow and learn in culturally defined ways in culturally defined contexts. In Chapter 2, the committee laid out a sociocultural view of learning and noted the application of work from the literature on developmental and cross-cultural psychology to understanding learning and education. This discussion set the stage for the discussions of research from cognitive science, neuropsychology, and other fields on numerous processes and functions of learning, specific influences on learning, and applications of this knowledge for lifelong learning and education. Our review has pointed to strengthening connections among these research domains, and how these connections have supported improved understanding of the dynamic nature of learning. In this chapter, we briefly tie together themes from this body of work. We close with a research agenda we hope will guide researchers and funders of research in pursuing even deeper understanding of human learning.

THE DYNAMIC NATURE OF LEARNING

Learning is a dynamic, ongoing process that is simultaneously biological and cultural. Each individual learner functions within a complex developmental, cognitive, physical, social, and cultural system. Factors that are relevant to learning include influences from the microscopic level to the characteristics of the learner's neighborhood, community, and the time period in which he lives. Further, even at the most basic individual level, evidence shows that brain development and cognition (and the connectivity between cortical areas) are influenced and organized by cultural, social, emotional, and physiological experiences that contribute to both age-related and individual variability in learning.

Learning involves the orchestration of interconnected networks. There is no learned skill that uses only one part of the brain, and these various brain systems support each aspect of the human experience: social, cognitive, emotional, and cultural functioning and even health and physiological survival. Thus, attention to both individual factors (such as developmental stage; physical, emotional, and mental health; and interests and motivations) and factors external to the individual (such as the environment in which the learner is situated, social and cultural contexts, and opportunities available to learners) is necessary to develop a complete picture of the nature of learning.

We have highlighted research on specific ways that culture interacts with learning—not as an external influence but as a central aspect of being human. For example, studies have illustrated cultural differences in areas of learning including the effects of different numeric systems on brain organization, conceptual models such as one's model of time, and expectations about learning. Research suggests that cultural differences may contribute to differences in memory, expectations that guide causal reasoning, and other cognitive processes. Cultural values may influence a learner's mindset and goals, and it has long been established that cultural stereotypes and values can affect a learner's self-construal, or definition of herself in reference to others; her confidence and expectations as a learner; her goals; and her performance. Culture is reflected in the procedures people use to complete tasks and solve problems, as well as the social emotional dispositions people bring to such tasks. Positive cultural identification can foster engagement with learning and achievement. Culture is also associated with the type or degree of cognitive changes that are manifest with age, and it partly accounts for the significant variety in the trajectories of individual learners.

We have also described many illustrations of the idea, introduced in Chapter 1, that "to learn" is an active verb naming a dynamic process through which humans continuously adapt, through conscious and unconscious physiological and cognitive responses, to the unique circumstances and experiences they encounter. We have focused on key ideas that can be distilled from a diverse body of work to build on the picture of how people learn as it stood in 2000, when *HPL I* was published.[1] That picture has grown more sophisticated, but there is still much more to learn.

---

[1]As explained in Chapter 1, *HPL I* refers to *How People Learn: Brain, Mind, Experience, and School: Expanded Edition* (National Research Council, 2000).

RESEARCH AGENDA

Much is known about the science and practice of how people learn, but this exploration of the diverse and fast-moving research communities that are contributing to this knowledge base has highlighted frontiers where more work is needed. The committee has identified needed research in two broad areas: understanding and embracing variability in learning and the potential uses and impacts of technology for learning. Advances in these areas will not only expand on what is known about how people learn but also support the work of educators in formal and informal learning settings and in workplace training. We describe specific research goals within each of these two broad categories, and we hope they will be useful guides for researchers and funders of research as they set priorities for future work.

Strategic investments in the work described here will undoubtedly require integration across levels of analysis, methods, and theoretical frameworks. We note that new data sources that could be relevant for understanding learning beyond formal schooling (such as administrative records) could provide new research avenues, and that partnerships across fields can spur innovations in the analysis of information from a variety of sources. We hope this report advances that effort by highlighting both robust findings from current research and opportunities to advance knowledge.

> **Research Area 1:** Meeting the needs of all learners by connecting research on internal mechanisms of learning with the shaping forces of contextual variation, including culture, social context, instruction, and time of life.

Though the body of research on how people learn is vast, it remains limited in terms of study populations, combinations of contexts, and other important factors. Laboratory science does not adequately reflect the circumstances of learning in the classroom, and the classroom application of lessons from laboratory science is often blunt and insufficiently nuanced. At the most fundamental level, more resources are needed to initiate and then maintain the translation of basic research into translation research for the learning sciences, while also allowing discoveries in situ to be brought back to basic research for exploration. In addition, means of establishing and sustaining truly collaborative and interdisciplinary efforts should be sought.

Several streams of research can address these limitations. One is interdisciplinary research that examines how individual variation and developmental and contextual factors, including social, emotional, environmental, institutional, and experiential factors, influence the lifelong learning process and learning outcomes. These research efforts should include the examination of the cross-level effects of social, emotional, and physiological responses to educational activities and their effects on proximal and distal learning outcomes. In addition, these efforts should address cross-level effects as they occur over different time scales, in order to coordinate short- and long-term supportive effects on different learning outcomes, and they should elucidate the pathways and temporal trajectories associated with events that facilitate or inhibit learning effort and outcomes.

The committee also notes the need for research focused on the ways distinct cultural communities organize learning; how learners adapt across different cultural systems (such as between home and school); and the learning needs of distinct populations, including those with learning disabilities and aging learners. Specific areas of focus should include the following:

Study populations The generalizability and robustness of findings from research on learning are often limited because of oversampling of certain cultural and socioeconomic communities in study populations. Research efforts that include more-diverse study populations are needed to supplement laboratory-based learning research, with the aim of improving its applicability to real-life classroom settings. Moreover, narrowly identifying study participants by, for example, a single race, culture, or ethnicity, should be avoided. Studies that examine cultural and demographic variables and within-group variation will improve understanding of how cultural and individual variability can be maintained and supported in learning situations.

Interest in learning Additional study is needed of the factors that influence situational interest. These factors include the individual's prior experiences, the role of different learning structures and extrinsic incentives on sustaining interest, mindset orientation, and learning progress over time. Also needed is additional study of the factors and processes by which individuals allocate effort and time across competing and complementary life and educational goals over time.

Role of identity in learning Research is needed to more precisely explain the ways in which beliefs about one's cognitive abilities modify learning goals and identities. Research is also needed on how different learning experiences combine to shape learning identity and whether there are particular periods of human development during which learning identity is more or less malleable. Finally, additional research is needed to explain how learners integrate perceived sociocultural norms associated with their present and future identities to arrive at learning goals and how these perceptions influence the use of different learning strategies.

Motivation to learn A more unified understanding of motivation is needed that both distinguishes and integrates the many interrelated and often overlapping factors that have been shown to play a role in motivation and learning. These factors include psychological processes, social interactions, and aspects of culture. Research is needed to explore the boundary conditions of current knowledge: To whom do current understandings about motivation apply and under what circumstances? Research is also needed in ways to influence motivation and support learning across the life span, in order to evaluate practices and test hypotheses derived from theories of motivation and learning in the context of everyday learning environments (schools, homes, and workplaces). Most research on motivation has focused on psychological processes and dyadic or group interactions between peers or between students and teachers during instruction and in the context of a specific activity or task. More research attention is needed to explore how formal school structures and other influences affect psychological motivational processes and how best to promote engagement, persistence, and goal attainment for learners, including through changes to formal education structures.

Self-regulated learning Self-regulation is best understood in the context of specific learning environments and objectives. Three streams of developmental research are needed: (1) studies that explore the development of self-regulation across time and across domains and disciplines, (2) studies that examine effective instruction in self-regulation in respect to individual development, and (3) studies of environments that lend themselves to the autonomous discovery and development of a broad repertoire of self-regulated strategies. Results from such studies could elucidate whether self-regulation is a skill that is fundamental to academic and life success, whether the development of self-regulation can be sustained over time, and at what developmental time period(s) practitioners might most effectively target self-regulation interventions. Research is needed to better explain the relationship between teaching strategies that promote self-regulation and discipline-specific tools for thinking and reasoning within and across subject areas.

Influence of learning environments Further study is needed of how the culture of the learning environment influences learners' sense of belonging, adaptability, agency, and learning outcomes. Researchers should identify the types of learning associated with particular learning tasks and environments and should track the predicted consequences for learning, motivation, emotion, and social interaction. Finally, research is needed to explain how methods of instruction prime a positive connection between current learning efforts and desired future outcomes.

Learning across the life span The committee advocates the creation of several large-scale pilot studies to create longitudinal databases that span learning experiences and outcomes from infancy to older adulthood. Similar in kind to health databases maintained in Iceland and Sweden, these databases will be an investment in future discovery and the goal of supporting lifelong learning, mental health, productivity, and informed citizenship. The development of comprehensive databases will require decisions about the granularity and content of the database entries that are relevant to a person's experiences as a learner, as well as considerations of privacy. Because the median age of the U.S. population is increasing, research is needed on ways to optimize interventions to maintain cognitive and brain health. An immediate goal of such research should be to identify promising interventions and determine their potential efficacy and generalizability. Researchers examining the determinants of learning and development through the life span should look beyond prior achievement and also examine ability, attitude, motivation, and self-regulatory processes for all learners. With respect to postsecondary educational environments, more work is urgently needed on measures that facilitate or impede student performance, as is research on the use of technology to support tailored instruction.

Learning disabilities Advances in experimental design and neuroimaging methods have the potential to substantially improve the ways learning disabilities are defined and diagnosed. Unfortunately, there has been little integration between the field of neuroscience and studies of interventions for learning disabilities. Thus, better merging of data on the results of treatment outcomes and the understanding of underlying conditions provided by the neurosciences is needed to support progress in identifying and remediating disabilities. Technology is also part of the story. Rapidly developing digital, electronic, and mechanical technologies offer promise for the accommodation of a broad set of learning disabilities, but more research is needed to better understand universal design for learning.

> **Research Area 2:** The implications of the science of learning for the design of technology to support learning across the life span; the complex interactions between characteristics of the learner, the content to be learned, and the learning environment; how technology may be influencing the nature of what people need to learn and the psychology of learners; and potential drawbacks.

Since the publication of *HPL I*, the use of digital technology in educational settings has skyrocketed. However, digital learning technologies are not always designed using the science of learning as a guide. Furthermore, the design of learning technologies should be tailored to individual learners who function within multiple sociocultural contexts, and the learner must have access to the appropriate technological tool for the right task, in the right context, at the right time point, in order for the technology to facilitate learning. We suggest several lines of research to help ensure that the benefits of learning technologies are maximized.

Because of the variability in learning contexts, there is a need for methods to determine whether a technology is well suited to the ecological learning niche in which it may be used. Comprehensive, systematic meta-analyses of research on the impacts of different learning technologies (e.g., intelligent tutoring systems, mobile apps for memory practice) and technologies with different features (e.g., dialogues with virtual agent, extensive practice with feedback) for different kinds of learning and for different users can provide the information needed to improve the coordination of learning technologies with desired learning outcomes.

Another issue related to the diversity in learning contexts is the dearth of experimental research shedding light on the transfer of communication skills and habits between online social and academic media. Longitudinal research is needed on the effects of intensive, sustained engagement with online technologies as well as the effects of self-selected online activities on academic learning. This research should examine how online experiences are changing the ways people understand, experience, and engage the world and how these experiences affect academic performance and literacy (e.g., reading, writing, science, mathematics). In terms of the learning environment, some evidence suggests that technology-based learning in informal settings can enhance achievement in school. However, this evidence is not sufficiently strong to guide practice reliably. This gap can be addressed with additional research and development on designs for technology-based interventions linking in-school and out-of-school learning.

There is also a need for research focused on improving the suite of learning technologies available. For example, there is evidence that in an educational setting, very simple computer-teacher interfaces are surprisingly often ignored or quickly abandoned, which would certainly limit their utility in practice. Research and development to investigate the design of digital dashboards and associated instructor training to promote regular and productive use of data from student learning systems to refine instruction will improve classroom utilization of learning technologies. Research should capitalize on (and catalyze) the increasing availability of data from learning technologies and the appearance of new data techniques (e.g., machine learning). These advances will contribute to the design of technologies that support and adapt to variability in the learners who use them in varied contexts.

Likewise, there is currently only limited evidence to support the effectiveness of mobile educational applications or to reliably characterize the impact conversational agents have on learning. Third-party evaluations of the effectiveness of mobile learning applications and subsequent meta-analyses of such studies, once there is a critical mass of evaluation data, can help to address this problem. For example, research is needed on the relative effectiveness of different types of virtual agents, agents with different degrees of domain-specific knowledge, and agents with and without adaptive features, in order to substantiate the utility of such agents in learning environments.

Finally, with respect to learning technologies in the workplace, the committee finds that additional research is needed on the relative effectiveness of supporting embodied cognition through virtual or augmented reality technology and with sensor technologies that can detect nonverbal behaviors, compared to mental manipulation for learning in academic subject areas.

References

Abrahamson, L. (2006). A brief history of networked classrooms: Effects, cases, pedagogy, and implications. In D.A. Banks (Ed.), *Audience Response Systems in Higher Education* (pp. 1-25). Hershey, PA: Information Science.

Ackerman, P.L. (1988). Determinants of individual differences during skill acquisition: Cognitive abilities and information processing. *Journal of Experimental Psychology: General*, *117*(3), 288-318.

Ackerman, P.L. (1996). A theory of adult intellectual development: Process, personality, interests, and knowledge. *Intelligence*, *22*(2), 227-257. doi.org/10.1016/S0160-2896(96)90016-1.

Ackerman, P.L. (2000). Domain-specific knowledge as the "dark matter" of adult intelligence: Gf/Gc, personality and interest correlates. *Journals of Gerontology: Series B: Psychological Sciences and Social Sciences*, *55*(2), P69-P84.

Ackerman, P.L., and Beier, M.E. (2006). Determinants of domain knowledge and independent study learning in an adult sample. *Journal of Educational Psychology*, *98*(2), 366-381.

Ackerman, P.L., Bowen, K.R., Beier, M.B., and Kanfer, R. (2001). Determinants of individual differences and gender differences in knowledge. *Journal of Educational Psychology*, *93*, 797-825.

Ackerman, P.L., Kanfer, R., and Beier, M.E. (2013). Trait complex, cognitive ability, and domain knowledge predictors of baccalaureate success, STEM persistence, and gender differences. *Journal of Educational Psychology*, *105*(3), 911-927. doi.org/10.1037/a0032338.

Ackerman, R., and Goldsmith, M. (2011). Metacognitive regulation of text learning: On screen versus on paper. *Journal of Experimental Psychology: Applied*, *17*(1), 18-32. doi:10.1037/a0022086.

Adams, C., Labouvie-Vief, G., Hobart, C.J., and Dorosz, M. (1990). Adult age group differences in story recall style. *Journal of Gerontology*, *45*(1), P17-P27.

Ader, R., Felten, D.L., and Cohen, N. (2001). *Psychoneuroimmunology* (3rd ed.). San Diego, CA: Academic Press.

Ainley, M., Hidi, S., and Berndorff, D. (2002). Interest, learning, and the psychological processes that mediate their relationship. *Journal of Educational Psychology*, *94*(3), 545-561. doi.org/10.1037/0022-0663.94.3.545.

Albaili, M. (1998). Goal orientations, cognitive strategies and academic achievement among United Arab Emirates college students. *Educational Psychology*, *18*(2), 195-203. doi. org/10.1080/0144341980180205.

Alea, N., and Wang, Q. (2015). Going global: The functions of autobiographical memory in cultural context. *Memory*, *23*(1), 1-10.

Alea, N., Bluck, S., and Ali, S. (2015). Function in context: Why American and Trinidadian young and older adults remember the personal past. *Memory*, *23*(1), 55-68.

Aleven, V., and Koedinger, K.R. (2002). An effective metacognitive strategy: Learning by doing and explaining with a computer-based Cognitive Tutor. *Cognitive Science*, *26*(2), 147-179. doi:10.1016/s0364-0213(02)00061-7.

Alexander, P.A., and Jetton, T.L. (1996). The role of importance and interest in the processing of text. *Educational Psychology Review*, *8*(1), 89-121. doi:10.1007/BF01761832.

Alexander, V., Bahr, M., and Hicks, R. (2015). Ability to recall specific detail and general detail (gist) in young old, middle old, and older adults. *Psychology*, *6*(16), 2071-2080.

Alfieri, L., Brooks, P.J., Aldrich, N.J., and Tenenbaum, H.R. (2011). Does discovery-based instruction enhance learning? *Journal of Educational Psychology*, *103*(1), 1-18. doi:10.1037/a0021017.

Alfieri, L., Nokes-Malach, T.J., and Schunn, C.D. (2013). Learning through case comparisons. *Educational Psychologist*, *48*, 87-113.

Allen, L.K., Snow, E.L., and McNamara, D.S. (2016). The narrative waltz: The role of flexibility on writing performance. *Journal of Educational Psychology*, *108*(7), 911-924. doi. org/10.1037/edu0000109.

Alliger, G.M., and Janak, E.A. (1989). Kirkpatrick's levels of training criteria: Thirty years later. *Personnel Psychology*, *42*(2), 331-342. doi.org/10.1111/j.1744-6570.1989.tb00661.x.

Alloway, T.P., and Gathercole, S.E. (2006). How does working memory work in the classroom? *Educational Research and Reviews*, *1*(4), 134-139.

Alloway, T.P., Gathercole, S.E., Kirkwood, H.J., and Elliott, J.E. (2009). The cognitive and behavioural characteristics of children with low working memory. *Child Development*, *80*(2), 606-621. doi:10.1111/j.1467-8624.2009.01282.x.

Altschul, I., Oyserman, D., and Bybee, D. (2006). Racial–ethnic identity in mid-adolescence: Content and change as predictors of academic achievement. *Child Development*, *77*(5), 1155-1169.

Amalric, M., and Dehaene, S. (2016). Origins of the brain networks for advanced mathematics in expert mathematicians. *Proceedings of the National Academy of Sciences of the United States of America*, *113*(18), 4909-4917. doi:10.1073/pnas.1603205113.

Ambady, N., and Bharucha, J. (2009). Culture and the brain. *Current Directions in Psychological Science*, *18*(6), 342-345. doi:10.1111/j.1467-8721.2009.01664.x.

Amedi, A., Stern, W.M., Camprodon, J.A., Bermpohl, F., Merabet, L., Rotman, S., Hermond, C., Meijer, P., and Pascual-Leone, A. (2007). Shape conveyed by visual-to-auditory sensory substitution activates the lateral occipital complex. *Nature Neuroscience*, *10*(6), 687-689. doi:10.1038/nn1912.

American Academy of Pediatrics. (1999). Media education. *Pediatrics*, *104*(2), 341-343.

American Academy of Pediatrics. (2015). *Media and Children*. Elk Grove Village, IL: Author.

American Academy of Pediatrics. (2016). New recommendations for children's electronic media use. *ScienceDaily*. Available: http:// www.sciencedaily.com/releases/2016/10/161021121843.htm [January 2018].

American Psychiatric Association. (2013). *Diagnostic and Statistical Manual of Mental Disorders* (5th ed.). Washington, DC: Author.

Ames, C. (1986). Conceptions of motivation within competitive and noncompetitive goal structures. In R. Schwarzer (Ed.), *Self-related Cognitions in Anxiety and Motivation* (pp. 229-245). Hillsdale, NJ: Lawrence Erlbaum Associates.

Ames, C. (1992). Achievement goals and adaptive motivation patterns: The role of the environment. In G. Roberts (Ed.), *Motivation in Sport and Exercise* (pp. 161-176). Champaign, IL: Human Kinetics.

Ames, C., and Ames, R. (1984). Goal structures and motivation *The Elementary School Journal, 85*(1), 38-52.

Ames, C., and Archer, J. (1988). Achievement goals in the classroom: Students learning strategies and motivational processes. *Journal of Educational Psychology, 80*(3), 260-267.

Anderman, E.M., and Maehr, M.L. (1994). Motivation and schooling in the middle grades. *Review of Educational Research, 64*(2), 287-309. doi.org/10.2307/1170696.

Anderman, E.M., and Midgley, C. (1997). Changes in achievement goal orientations, perceived academic competence, and grades across the transition to middle level schools. *Contemporary Educational Psychology, 22*(3), 269-298. doi.org/10.1006/ceps.1996.0926.

Andersen, S.L. (2003). Trajectories of brain development: Point of vulnerability or window of opportunity? *Neuroscience and Biobehavioral Reviews, 27*(1-2), 3-18.

Anderson, J.R. (1982). Acquisition of cognitive skill. *Psychological Review, 89*(4), 369-406. doi.org/10.1037/0033-295X.89.4.369.

Anderson, J.R., Corbett, A.T., Koedinger, K.R., and Pelletier, R. (1995). Cognitive tutors: Lessons learned. *Journal of the Learning Sciences, 4*(2), 167-207. doi.org/10.1207/s15327809jls0402_2.

Anderson, M.L. (2015a). *After Phrenology: Neural Reuse and the Interactive Brain*. Cambridge, MA: MIT Press.

Anderson, M.L. (2015b). *Technology Device Ownership: 2015*. Washington, DC: Pew Research Center. Available: http://www.pewinternet.org/2015/10/29/technology-device-ownership-2015 [December 2017].

Anderson, R.C., and Pichert, J.W. (1978). Recall of previously unrecallable information following a shift in perspective. *Journal of Verbal Learning and Verbal Behavior, 17*(1), 1-12. doi.org/10.1016/S0022-5371(78)90485-1.

Andrade, H. (2016, unpublished). *Classroom Assessment and Learning: A Selective Review of Theory and Research*. Paper commissioned by the Committee on the Science of Practice and Learning, National Academies of Sciences, Engineering, and Medicine, Washington, DC.

Antonucci, T.C., Lansford, J.E., Schaberg, L., Baltes, M., Takahashi, K., Dartigues, J.F., Smith, J., Akiyama, H., and Fuhrer, R. (2001). Widowhood and illness: A comparison of social network characteristics in France, Germany, Japan, and the United States. *Psychology and Aging, 16*(4), 655-665.

Aronson, J. (2004). *The Effects of Conceiving Ability as Fixed or Improvable on Responses to Stereotype Threat*. Unpublished manuscript. New York: New York University.

Aronson, E., and Patnoe, S. (1997). *Cooperation in the Classroom: The Jigsaw Method*. New York: Longman.

Aronson, J., and Salinas, M.F. (1997). *Stereotype Threat: Is Low Performance the Price of Self-esteem for Mexican Americans?* Paper presented to the Western Psychological Association Conference, Seattle, WA, April.

Aronson, J., Lustina, M.J., Good, C., Keough, K., Steele, C.M., and Brown, J. (1999). When White men can't do math: Necessary and sufficient factors in stereotype threat. *Journal of Experimental Social Psychology, 35*(1), 29-46.

Aronson, J., Fried, C.B., and Good, C. (2001). Reducing the effects of stereotype threat on African American college students by shaping theories of intelligence. *Journal of Experimental Social Psychology, 38*(2), 113-125. doi:10.1006/jesp.2001.1491.

Autor, D.H., and Price, B. (2013). *The Changing Task Composition of the U.S. Labor Market: An Update of Autor, Levy and Murnane (2003)*. Available: https://economics.mit.edu/files/11600 [December 2017].

Avineri, N., Johnson, E., Brice-Heath, S., McCarty, T., Ochs, E., Kremer-Sadlik, T., Blum, S., Zentella, A.C., Rosa, J., Flores, N., Alim, H.S., and Paris, D. (2015). Invited forum: Bridging the "language gap." *Journal of Linguistic Anthropology, 25*(1), 66-86. doi:10.1111/jola.12071.

Azevedo, R., and Aleven, V. (2013). *International Handbook of Metacognition and Learning Technologies.* New York: Springer.

Azevedo, R., and Cromley, J.G. (2004). Does training on self-regulated learning facilitate students' learning with hypermedia? *Journal of Educational Psychology, 96*(3), 523-535. doi:10.1037/0022-0663.96.3.523.

Azevedo, R., Johnson, A., Chauncey, A., and Burkett, C. (2010). Self-regulated learning with MetaTutor: Advancing the science of learning with MetaCognitive tools. In M.S. Khine and I.M. Saleh (Eds.), *New Science of Learning* (pp. 225-247). New York: Springer.

Bain, R. (2006). Rounding up unusual suspects: Facing the authority hidden in the history classroom. *Teachers College Record, 108*(10), 2080-2114.

Baker, R.D., and F.R. Greer (2010). Diagnosis and prevention of iron deficiency and iron-deficiency anemia in infants and young children (0-3 years of age). *Pediatrics, 126*(5), 1040-1050.

Bakia, M., Means, B., Gallagher, L., Chen, E., and Jones, K. (2009). *Evaluation of the Enhancing Education Through Technology Program: Final Report.* Washington, DC: U.S. Department of Education. Available: http://files.eric.ed.gov/fulltext/ED527143.pdf [December 2017].

Ballesteros, S., Kraft, E., Santana, S., and Tziraki, C. (2015). Maintaining older brain functionality: A targeted review. *Neuroscience & Biobehavioral Reviews, 55*, 453-477. doi:10.1016/j.neubiorev.2015.06.008.

Balota, D.A., Duchek, J.M., and Paullin, R. (1989). Age-related differences in the impact of spacing, lag, and retention interval. *Psychology and Aging, 4*(1), 3-9.

Balota, D.A., Duchek, J.M., Sergent-Marshall, S.D., and Roediger, H.L. (2006). Does expanded retrieval produce benefits over equal-interval spacing? Explorations of spacing effects in healthy aging and early stage Alzheimer's disease. *Psychology and Aging, 21*(1), 19-31. doi:10.1037/0882-7974.21.1.19.

Baltes, P.B., and Baltes, M.M. (1990). Psychological perspectives on successful aging: The model of selective optimization with compensation. In P.B. Baltes and M.M. Baltes (Eds.), *Successful Aging: Perspectives from the Behavioral Sciences* (pp. 1-34). New York: Cambridge University Press.

Baltes, P.B., and Staudinger, U.M. (2000). Wisdom: A metaheuristic (pragmatic) to orchestrate mind and virtue toward excellence. *American Psychologist, 5*(1), 122-136.

Bandura, A. (1965). Influence of models' reinforcement contingencies on the acquisition of imitative responses. *Journal of Personality and Social Psychology, 1*(6), 589-595.

Bandura, A. (1977). *Social Learning Theory.* Englewood Cliffs, NJ: Prentice-Hall.

Bandura, A. (1989). Social cognitive theory. In R. Vasta (Ed.), *Annals of Child Development. Six Theories of Child Development* (vol. 6, pp. 1-60). Greenwich, CT: JAI Press.

Bandura, A., and Schunk, D.H. (1981). Cultivating competence, self-efficacy, and intrinsic interest through proximal self-motivation. *Journal of Personality and Social Psychology, 41*(3), 586-598. doi.org/10.1037/0022-3514.41.3.586.

Bandura, A., Ross, D., and Ross, S.A. (1961). Transmission of aggression through imitation of aggressive models. *Journal of Abnormal and Social Psychology, 63*, 575-582.

Bandura, A., Ross, D., and Ross, S.A. (1963). Imitation of film-mediated aggressive models. *Journal of Abnormal and Social Psychology, 66*, 3-11.

Bang, M., Alfonso, J., Faber, L., Marin, A., Marin, M., Medin, D., Waxman, S., and Woodring, J. (in press). Perspective taking in early childhood books: Implications for early science learning. *Culture Studies in Science Education.*

Bang, M., Medin, D.L., and Atran, S. (2007). Cultural mosaics and mental models of nature. *Proceedings of the National Academy of Sciences of the United States of America, 104*(35), 13868-13874.

Bangert-Drowns, R.L., Kulik, C.C., Kulik, J.A., and Morgan, M.T. (1991). The instructional effect of feedback in test-like events. *Review of Educational Research, 61,* 213–238.

Banks, J.A., and McGee Banks, C.A. (Eds.) (2010). *Multicultural Education: Issues and Perspectives, 7th Edition.* Hoboken, NJ: John Wiley & Sons.

Barab, S., Thomas, M., Dodge, T., Carteaux, R., and Tuzun, H. (2005). Making learning fun: Quest Atlantis, a game without guns. *Educational Technology Research and Development, 53*(1), 86–107.

Bargh, J.A., and Schul, Y. (1980). On the cognitive benefits of teaching. *Journal of Educational Psychology, 72*(5), 593–604. doi:10.1037/0022-0663.72.5.593.

Barker, J.E., Semenov, A.D., Michaelson, L., Provan, L.S., Snyder, H.R., and Munakata, Y. (2014). Less-structured time in children's daily lives predicts self-directed executive functioning. *Frontiers in Psychology, 5,* 1–16. doi.org/10.3389/fpsyg.2014.00593.

Barkley, R.A. (2006). *Attention-Deficit Hyperactivity Disorder: A Handbook for Diagnosis and Treatment* (3rd Edition). New York: Guilford Press.

Barnett, S.M., and Ceci, S.J. (2002). When and where do we apply what we learn? A taxonomy for far transfer. *Psychological Bulletin, 128*(4), 612–637. doi.org/10.1037/0033-2909.128.4.612.

Barnett, W.S., Jung, K., Yarosz, D.J., Thomas, J., Hornbeck, A., Stechuk, R., and Burns, S. (2008). Educational effects of the tools of the mind curriculum: A randomized trial. *Early Childhood Research Quarterly, 23*(3), 299–313.

Barrett, T., Pizzico, M., Levy, B., Nagel, R., Linsey, J., Talley, K., Forest, C.R., and Newstetter, W. (2015). *A Review of University Maker Spaces.* Paper presented at 122nd Annual Conference and Exposition of the American Society Engineering Education, Seattle, WA. Available: https://smartech.gatech.edu/handle/1853/53813 [December 2017].

Barron, B. (2006). Interest and self-sustained learning as catalysts of development: A learning ecology perspective. *Human Development, 49*(4), 193–224.

Barron, B., and Darling-Hammond, L. (2008). Powerful learning: Studies show deep understanding derives from collaborative methods. *Edutopia,* October 8. Available: https://www.edutopia.org/inquiry-project-learning-research [December 2017].

Bassett, D.S., Wymbs, N.F., Porter, M.A., Mucha, P.J., Carlson, J.M., and Grafton, S.T. (2011). Dynamic reconfiguration of human brain networks during learning. *Proceedings of the National Academies of Sciences of the United States of America, 108*(18), 7641–7646. doi:10.1073/pnas.1018985108.

Basso, K.H. (1996). *Wisdom Sits in Places: Landscape and Language among the Western Apache.* Albuquerque, NM: UNM Press.

Bates, E. (1979). *The Emergence of Symbols: Cognition and Communication in Infancy.* New York: Academic Press.

Bauer, P.J. (2009). Neurodevelopmental changes in infancy and beyond: Implications for learning and memory. In O.A. Barbarin and B.H. Wasik (Eds.), *Handbook of Child Development and Early Education: Research to Practice* (pp. 78–102). New York: Guilford Press.

Bauer, P.J., and Jackson, F.L. (2015). Semantic elaboration: ERPs reveal rapid transition from novel to known. *Journal of Experimental Psychology: Learning, Memory, and Cognition, 41*(1), 271–282. doi:10.1037/a0037405.

Bauer, P.J., and Larkina, M. (2016). Predicting remembering and forgetting of autobiographical memories in children and adults: A 4-year prospective study. *Memory (Hove, England), 24*(10), 1345–1368. doi:10.1080/09658211.2015.1110595.

Bauer, P.J., and San Souci, P. (2010). Going beyond the facts: Young children extend knowledge by integrating episodes. *Journal of Experimental Child Psychology, 107*(4), 452–465. doi:10.1016/j.jecp.2010.05.012.

Bauer, P.J., and Varga, N.L. (2015). The developmental cognitive neuroscience of memory: Implications for education. In E. Tardif and P. Doudin (Eds.), *Collective Work on the Topics of Neuroscience, Cognition and Education* (pp. 1–16). Oxford, UK: De Boeck.

Bauer, P.J., King, J.E., Larkina, M., Varga, N.L., and White, E.A. (2012). Characters and clues: Factors affecting children's extension of knowledge through integration of separate episodes. *Journal of Experimental Child Psychology, 111*(4), 681-694. doi:10.1016/j.jeep2011.10.005.

Bednall, T.C., and Kehoe, E.J. (2011). Effects of self-regulatory instructional aids on self-directed study. *Instructional Science, 39*(2), 205-226. doi:10.1007/s11251-009-9125-6.

Beier, M.E., and Ackerman, P.L. (2001). Current events knowledge in adults: An investigation of age, intelligence and non-ability determinants. *Psychology and Aging, 16*(4), 615-628.

Beier, M.E., and Ackerman, P.L. (2003). Determinants of health knowledge: An investigation of age, gender, abilities, personality, and interests. *Journal of Personality and Social Psychology, 84*(2), 439-448.

Beier, M.E., and Ackerman, P.L. (2005). Age, ability, and the role of prior knowledge on the acquisition of new domain knowledge: Promising results in a real-world learning environment. *Psychology and Aging, 20*(2), 341-355. doi.org/10.1037/0882-7974.20.2.341.

Beier, M.E., Torres, W.J., and Gilberto, J.M. (2017). Continuous development throughout a career: A lifespan perspective on autonomous learning. In J.E. Ellingson and R.A. Noe (Eds.), *Autonomous Learning in the Workplace: SIOP Organizational Frontier Series* (pp. 179-200). New York: Routledge.

Beilock, S.L. (2010). *Choke: What the Secrets of the Brain Reveal About Getting it Right When You Have To.* New York: Simon & Schuster

Beilock, S.L., Rydell, R.J., and McConnell, A.R. (2007). Stereotype threat and working memory: Mechanisms, alleviation, and spill over. *Journal of Experimental Psychology: General, 136*(2), 256-276. doi:10.1037/0096-3445.136.2.256.

Beilock, S.L., Lyons, I.M., Mattarella-Micke, A., Nusbaum, H.C., and Small, S.L. (2008). Sports experience changes the neural processing of action language. *Proceedings of the National Academy of Sciences of the United States of America, 105*(36), 13269-13273. doi:10.1073/pnas.0803424105.

Bell, P., Tzou, C., Bricker, L., and Baines, A.D. (2012). Learning in diversities of structures of social practice: Accounting for how, why and where people learn science. *Human Development, 55*(5-6), 269-284.

Beller, S., Bender, A., and Song, J. (2009). Weighing up physical causes: Effects of culture, linguistic cues and content. *Journal of Cognition and Culture, 9*(3), 347-365.

Benassi, V.A., Overson, C.E., and Hakala, C.M. (2014). *Applying Science of Learning in Education: Infusing Psychological Science into the Curriculum.* Washington, DC: Society for the Teaching of Psychology. Available: https://scholars.unh.edu/cgi/viewcontent.cgi?referer=https://www.google.com/&httpsredir=1&article=1286&context=psych_facpub [December 2017].

Bender, A., Beller, S., and Medin, D.L. (2017). Causal cognition and culture. In M.R. Waldmann (Ed.), *The Oxford Handbook of Causal Reasoning.* Oxford, UK: Oxford University Press. doi:10.1093/oxfordhb/9780199399550.013.34.

Bendlin, B.B., Fitzgerald, M.E., Ries, M.L., Xu, G., Kastman, E.K., Thiel, B.W., and Johnson, S.C. (2010). White matter in aging and cognition: A cross-sectional study of microstructure in adults aged eighteen to eighty-three. *Developmental Neuropsychology, 35*(3), 257-277. doi.org/10.1080/87565641003696775.

Bengtsson, S.L., Nagy, Z., Skare, S., Forsman, L., Forssberg, H., and Ullén, F. (2005). Extensive piano practicing has regionally specific effects on white matter development. *Nature Neuroscience, 8*(9), 1148-1150.

Benjamin, A.S., and Tullis, J. (2010). What makes distributed practice effective? *Cognitive Psychology, 61*(3), 228-247. doi:10.1016/j.cogpsych.2010.05.004.

Bennett, R. (2011). Formative assessment: A critical review. *Assessment in Education: Principles, Policy and Practice, 18*(1), 5-25.

Berkeley, S., Scruggs, T.E., and Mastropieri, M.A. (2010). Reading comprehension instruction for students with learning disabilities, 1995-2006: A meta-analysis. *Remedial and Special Education, 31*(6), 423-436. doi:10.1177/0741932509355988.

Berkman, E.T. (2016). Self-regulation training. In K.D. Vohs and R.F. Baumeister (Eds.), *Handbook of Self-Regulation* (3rd ed., pp. 440-457). New York: Guilford Press.

Berkman, L.F. (1985). The relationship of social networks and social support to morbidity and mortality. In S. Cohen and S.L. Syme (Eds.), *Social Support and Health*. New York: Academy Press.

Bernard, R.M., Abrami, P.C., Borokhovski, E., Wade, A., Tamim, R., Surkes, M.A., and Bethel, E.C. (2009). A meta-analysis of three interaction treatments in distance education. *Review of Educational Research*, *79*(3), 1243-1289. doi:10.3102/0034654309333844v1.

Bernstein, I.L., Webster, M.M., and Bernstein, I.D. (1982). Food aversions in children receiving chemotherapy for cancer. *Cancer*, *50*(12), 2961-2963.

Best, J.R. (2010). Effects of physical activity on children's executive function: Contributions of experimental research on aerobic exercise. *Developmental Review*, *30*(4), 331-351.

Bialystok, E. (2017). The bilingual adaptation: How minds accommodate experience. *Psychological Bulletin*, *143*(3), 233-262.

Bialystok, E., Abutalebi, J., Bak, T.H., Burke, D.M., and Kroll, J.F. (2016). Aging in two languages: Implications for public health. *Ageing Research Reviews*, *27*, 56-60. doi:10.1016/j.arr.2016.03.003.

Bielak, A.A.M. (2010). How can we not "lose it" if we still don't understand how to "use it"? Unanswered questions about the influence of activity participation on cognitive performance in older age—a mini-review. *Gerontology*, *56*(5), 507-519. doi.org/10.1159/000264918.

Bielak, A.A.M., Anstey, K.J., Christensen, H., and Windsor, T.D. (2012). Activity engagement is related to level, but not change in cognitive ability across adulthood. *Psychology and Aging*, *27*(1), 219-228. doi.org/10.1037/a0024667.

Birchfield, D., and Johnson-Glenberg, M.C. (2010). A next gen Interface for embodied learning: SMALLab and the geological layer cake. *International Journal of Gaming and Computer-mediated Simulation*, *2*(1), 49-58.

Birnbaum, M.S., Kornell, N., Bjork, E.L., and Bjork, R.A. (2013). Why interleaving enhances inductive learning: The roles of discrimination and retrieval. *Memory & Cognition*, *41*(3), 392-402. doi:10.3758/s13421-012-0272-7.

Biswas, G., Leelawong, K., Schwartz, D., and Vye, N. (2005). Learning by teaching: A new agent paradigm for educational software. *Applied Artificial Intelligence*, *19*(3-4), 363-392. doi:10.1080/08839510590910200.

Bjork, R.A., Dunlosky, J., and Kornell, N. (2013). Self-regulated learning: Beliefs, techniques, and illusions. *Annual Review of Psychology*, *64*, 417-444. doi:10.1146/annurev-psych-113011-143823.

Bjorklund, D.F., Dukes, C., and Brown, R.D. (2009). The development of memory strategies. In M. Courage and N. Cowan (Eds.), *The Development of Memory in Infancy and Childhood* (pp. 145-175). Hove East Sussex, UK: Psychology Press.

Black, P., and Wiliam, D. (1998). Assessment and classroom learning. *Assessment in Education: Principles, Policy & Practice, 5*(1), 7-74.

Black, P., and Wiliam, D. (2009). Developing the theory of formative assessment. *Educational Assessment, Evaluation and Accountability, 21*(1), 5-31.

Blackmore, S. (2000). *The Meme Machine*. Oxford, UK: Oxford University Press.

Blackwell, L.S., Trzesniewski, K.H., and Dweck, C.S. (2007). Implicit theories of intelligence predict achievement across an adolescent transition: A longitudinal study and an intervention. *Child Development*, *78*(1), 246-263.

Blair, C., and Razza, R.P. (2007). Relating effortful control, executive function, and false belief understanding to emerging math and literacy ability in kindergarten. *Child Development*, *78*(2), 647-663.

Blakemore, S.-J. (2010). The developing social brain: Implications for education. *Neuron, 65*(6), 744-747. doi: 10.1016/j.neuron.2010.03.004.

Blume, B.D., Ford, J.K., Baldwin, T.T., and Huang, J.L. (2010). Transfer of training: A meta-analytic review. *Journal of Management, 36*(4), 1065-1105. doi.org/10.1177/0149206309352880.

Blumenfeld, P.C., Mergendoller, J.R., and Swarthout, D.W. (1987). Tasks as heuristics for understanding student learning and motivation. *Journal of Curriculum Studies, 19*(2), 135-148.

Blunden, S., and Galland, B. (2014). The complexities of defining optimal sleep: Empirical and theoretical considerations with a special emphasis on children. *Sleep Medicine Reviews, 18*(5), 371-378.

Bodrova, E., and Leong, D. (2007). *Tools of the Mind: The Vygotskian Approach to Early Childhood Education* (2nd Edition). Upper Saddle River, NJ: Pearson/Merrill Prentice Hall.

Boekaerts, M., and Cascallar, M. (2006). How far have we moved toward the integration of theory and practice in self-regulation? *Educational Psychology Review, 18*(3), 199-210.

Bonawitz, E.B., and Lombrozo, T. (2012). Occam's rattle: Children's use of simplicity and probability to constrain inference. *Developmental Psychology, 48*(4), 1156-1164. doi:10.1037/a0026471.

Bopp, K.L., and Verhaeghen P. (2005). Aging and verbal memory span: A meta-analysis. *Journals of Gerontology, Series B, Psychological Sciences and Social Sciences, 60*(5), 223-233.

Bornstein, M. (2010). *Handbook of Cultural Developmental Science.* New York: Psychology Press.

Bosma, H., van Boxtel, M.P.J., Ponds, R.W.H.M., Jelicic, M., Houx, P., Metsemakers, J., and Jolles, J. (2002). Engaged lifestyle and cognitive function in middle and old-aged, non-demented persons: A reciprocal association? *Zeitschrift Für Gerontologie Und Geriatrie, 35*(6), 575-581. doi.org/10.1007/s00391-002-0080-y.

Boud, D., and Middleton, H. (2003). Learning from others at work: Communities of practice and informal learning. *Journal of Workplace Learning, 15*(5), 194-202.

Bower, G.H., Clark, M.C., Lesgold, A.M., and Winzenz, D. (1969). Hierarchical retrieval schemes in recall of categorized word lists. *Journal of Verbal Learning and Verbal Behavior, 8*(3), 323-343. doi.org/10.1016/S0022-5371(69)80124-6.

Boykin, A.W., Lilja, A., and Tyler, K.M. (2004). The influence of communal vs. individual learning context on the academic performance in social studies of African American 4th and 5th grade children. *Learning Environments Research Journal, 7*(3), 227-244.

Boykin, W., and Noguera, P. (2011). *Creating the Opportunity to Learn: Moving from Research to Practice to Close the Achievement Gap.* Alexandria, VA: ASCD.

Braboszcz, C., Cahn, B.R., Balakrishnan, B., Maturi, R.K., Grandchamp, R., and Delorme, A. (2013). Plasticity of visual attention in Isha yoga meditation practitioners before and after a 3-month retreat. *Frontiers in Psychology, 4,* 914. doi.org/10.3389/fpsyg.2013.00914.

Bricker, L., and Bell, P. (2014). What comes to mind when you think of science? The perfumery! Documenting science-related cultural learning pathways across contexts and timescales. *Journal of Research in Science Teaching. 51*(3), 260-285. doi: 10.1002/tea.21134.

Briggs, D.C., Alonzo, A.C., Schwab, C., and Wilson, M. (2006). Diagnostic assessment with ordered multiple choice items. *Educational Assessment, 11*(1), 33-63.

Briones, T.L., Klintsova, A.Y., and Greenough, W.T. (2004). Stability of synaptic plasticity in the adult rat visual cortex induced by complex environment exposure. *Brain Research, 1018*(1), 130-135. doi:10.1016/j.brainres.2004.06.001.

Briscoe, J., and Rankin, P.M. (2009). Exploration of a "double-jeopardy" hypothesis within working memory profiles for children with specific language impairment. *International Journal of Language & Communication Disorders, 44*(2), 236-250. doi:10.1080/13682820802028760.

Bronfenbrenner, U. (1977). Toward an experimental ecology of human development. *American Psychologist, 32*(7), 513-531.

Bronfenbrenner, U. (1994). Ecological models of human development. In *International Encyclopedia of Education* (2nd ed., vol. 3). Oxford, UK: Elsevier.

Brown, W. (1923). To what extent is memory measured by a single recall? *Journal of Experimental Psychology, 6*(5), 377-382. doi:10.1037/h0073877.

Brown, A.L., and Campione, J.C. (1995). Guided discovery in a community of learners. In E. McGilly (Ed.), *Classroom Learners: Integrated Cognitive Theory and Classroom Practice* (Chapter 9) (pp. 229-249). Cambridge, MA: The MIT Press. Available: http://www.cogsci.ucsd.edu/~deak/classes/EDS115/brown_campione2_ps.pdf [December 2017].

Brown, D., and Clement, J. (1989). Overcoming misconceptions via analogical reasoning: Factors influencing understanding in a teaching experiment. *Instructional Science, 18,* 237-261.

Brown, A.L., Day, J.D., and Jones, R.S. (1983). The development of plans for summarizing texts. *Child Development, 54*(4), 968-979. doi:10.2307/1129901.

Brown, A.L., Kane, M.J., and Echols, C.H. (1986). Young children's mental models determine analogical transfer across problems with a common goal structure. *Cognitive Development, 1*(2), 103-121.

Bruner, J.S. (1961). The act of discovery. *Harvard Educational Review, 31*(1), 21-32.

Bryan, J., Osendarp, S., Hughes, D., Calvaresi, E., Baghurst, K., and van Klinken, J.W. (2004). Nutrients for cognitive development in school-aged children. *Nutrition Reviews, 62*(8), 295-306.

Bubolz, M.M., and Sontag, M.S. (2009). Human ecology theory. In P.G. Boss, W.J. Doherty, R. LaRossa, W.R. Schumm, and S.K. Steinmetz (Eds.), *Sourcebook of Family Theories and Methods: A Contextual Approach* (pp. 419-448). New York: Springer.

Budde, H., Voelcker-Rehage, C., Pietraßyk-Kendziorra, S., Ribeiro, P., and Tidow, G. (2008). Acute coordinative exercise improves attentional performance in adolescents. *Neuroscience Letters, 441*(2), 219-223.

Bull, S., and Kay, J. (2013). Open learner models as drivers for metacognitive processes. In R. Azevedo and V. Aleven (Eds.), *International Handbook of Metacognition and Learning Technologies* (pp. 349-365). New York: Springer.

Bull, R., and Scerif, G. (2001). Executive functioning as a predictor of children's mathematics ability: Inhibition, switching, and working memory. *Developmental Neuropsychology, 19*(3), 273-293.

Bull, G., Thompson, A., Searson, M., Garofalo, J., Park, J., Young, C., and Lee, J. (2008). Connecting informal and formal learning: Experiences in the age of participatory media. *Contemporary Issues in Technology and Teacher Education, 8*(2), 100-107.

Burgstahler, S. (2015). *Equal Access: Universal Design of Instruction. A Checklist for Inclusive Teaching.* Seattle: University of Washington, DO-IT. Available: http://www.washington.edu/doit/Brochures/Academics/equal_access_udi.html [December 2017].

Burkam, D.T., Ready, D.D., Lee, V.E., and LoGerfo, L.F. (2004). Social-class differences in summer learning between kindergarten and first grade: Model specification and estimation. *Sociology of Education, 77*(1), 1-31.

Burns, K.C., and Isbell, L.M. (2007). Promoting malleability is not one size fits all: Priming implicit theories of intelligence as a function of self-theories. *Self and Identity, 6*(1), 51-63. doi:10.1080/15298860600823864.

Bybee, J., and McClelland, J.L. (2005). Alternatives to the combinatorial paradigm of linguistic theory based on domain general principles of human cognition. *Linguistic Review, 22*(2-4), 381-410. doi.org/10.1515/tlir.2005.22.2-4.381.

Cabeza, R. (2002). Hemispheric asymmetry reduction in older adults: The HAROLD model. *Psychology and Aging, 17*(1), 85-100.

Cadinu, M., Maass, A., Rosabianca, A., and Kiesner, J. (2005). Why do women underperform under stereotype threat? Evidence for the role of negative thinking. *Psychological Science, 16*(7), 572-578.

Cajete, G.A. (1999). *The Native American Learner and Bicultural Science Education.* Available: https://files.eric.ed.gov/fulltext/ED427908.pdf [July 2018].

Cain, K., and Oakhill, J.V. (1999). Inference making ability and its relation to comprehension failure in young children. *Reading and Writing, 11*(5-6), 489-503. doi:10.1023/A:1008084120205.

Calabrese Barton, A., and Tan, E. (2009). Funds of knowledge and discourses and hybrid space. *Journal of Research in Science Teaching, 46*(1), 50-73.

Callahan, J.S., Kiker, D.S., and Cross, T. (2003). Does method matter? A meta-analysis of the effects of training method on older learner training performance. *Journal of Management*, *29*(5), 663–680. doi.org/10.1016/S0149-2063(03)00029-1.

Cameron, J., Pierce, W.D., Banko, K.M., and Gear, A. (2005). Achievement-based rewards and intrinsic motivation: A test of cognitive mediators. *Journal of Educational Psychology*, *97*(4), 641–655. doi:10.1037/0022-0663.97.4.641.

Campbell, K.L., Hasher, L., and Thomas, R.C. (2010). Hyper-binding: A unique age effect. *Psychological Science*, *21*(3), 399–405.

Care, E., Scoular, C., and Griffin, P. (2016). Assessment of collaborative problem solving in education environments. *Applied Measurement in Education*, *29*(4), 250–264. doi.org/10.108 0/08957347.2016.1209204.

Carey, S. (1985). *Conceptual Change in Childhood*. Cambridge, MA: The MIT Press.

Carey, S. (2009). *The Origin of Concepts*. New York: Oxford University Press.

Carlson, M.C., Parisi, J.M., Xia, J., Xue, Q.-L., Rebok, G.W., Bandeen-Roche, K., and Fried, L.P. (2012). Lifestyle activities and memory: Variety may be the spice of life. The Women's Health and Aging Study II. *Journal of the International Neuropsychological Society*, *18*(2), 286–294. doi.org/10.1017/S135561771100169X.

Carnevale, A.P., and Smith, N. (2013). *Recovery: Job Growth and Education Requirements through 2020*. Washington, DC: Georgetown University Center on Education and the Workforce. Available: https://cew.georgetown.edu/cew-reports/recovery-job-growth-and-education-requirements-through-2020 [December 2017].

Carpenter, S.K., and Mueller, F.E. (2013). The effects of interleaving versus blocking on foreign language pronunciation learning. *Memory & Cognition*, *41*(4), 671–682. https://doi.org/10.3758/s13421-012-0291-4.

Carpenter, S.K., Cepeda, N.J., Rohrer, D., Kang, S.H.K., and Pashler, H. (2012). Using spacing to enhance diverse forms of learning: Review of recent research and implications for instruction. *Educational Psychology Review*, *24*(3), 369–378. doi:10.1007/s10648-012-9205-z.

Carstensen, L.L., Isaacowitz, D.M., and Charles, S.T. (1999). Taking time seriously: A theory of socioemotional selectivity. *American Psychologist*, *54*(3), 165–181.

Carstensen, L.L., Fung, H.H., and Charles, S.T. (2003). Socioemotional selectivity theory and the regulation of emotion in the second half of life. *Motivation and Emotion*, *27*(2), 103–123.

Carter, M., and Beier, M.E. (2010). The effectiveness of error management training with working-aged adults. *Personnel Psychology*, *63*(3), 641–675. doi.org/10.1111/j.1744-6570.2010.01183.x.

Carvalho, P.F., and Goldstone, R.L. (2014a). Effects of interleaved and blocked study on delayed test of category learning generalization. *Frontiers in Psychology*, *5*(936), 1–11. doi:10.3389/fpsyg.2014.00936.

Carvalho, P.F., and Goldstone, R.L. (2014b). Putting category learning in order: Category structure and temporal arrangement affect the benefit of interleaved over blocked study. *Memory & Cognition*, *42*(3), 481–495. doi:10.3758/s13421-013-0371-0.

Carver, C., and Scheier, M.F. (2017). Self-regulation of action and affect. In K. Vohs and R.F. Bauminster (Eds.), *Handbook of Self-Regulation: Research, Theory, and Applications* (3rd ed., pp. 3–23). New York: Guilford Press.

Cassarino, M., O'Sullivan, B., Keny, R.A., and Setti, A. (2015). Environment and cognitive aging: A cross-sectional study of place of residence and cognitive performance in the Irish longitudinal study on ageing. *Neuropsychology*, *30*(5), 543–557. doi:10.1037/neu0000253.

Cassidy, L., Ortlieb, E., and Grote-Garcia, S. (2016). Beyond the common core: Examining 20 years of literacy priorities and their impact on struggling readers. *Literacy Research and Instruction*, *55*(2), 91–104. doi:10.1080/19388071.2015.1136011.

Caterino, M.C., and Polak, E.D. (1999). Effects of two types of activity on the performance of 2nd, 3rd and 4th grade students on a test of concentration. *Perceptual and Motor Skills*, *89*(1), 245–248.

Cattell, R.B. (1987). *Intelligence: Its Structure, Growth, and Action*. New York: Elsevier Science.

Cavanagh, J.C., and Blanchard-Fields, F. (2002). *Adult Development and Aging* (4th ed.). Belmont, CA: Wadsworth-Thomson.

Cazden, C. (1988). *Classroom Discourse: The Language of Teaching and Learning*. Portmouth, NH: Heinemann.

Center for Universal Design. (1997). *The Principles of Universal Design* (Version 2.0). Raleigh, NC: Author.

Centers for Disease Control and Prevention. (2009). Perceived insufficient rest or sleep among adults—United States, 2008. *Morbidity and Mortality Weekly Report, 58*(42), 1175–1179.

Cepeda, N.J., Pashler, H., Vul, E., Wixted, J.T., and Rohrer, D. (2006). Distributed practice in verbal recall tasks: A review and quantitative synthesis. *Psychological Bulletin, 132*(3), 354–380. doi:10.1037/0033-2909.132.3.354.

Cepeda, N.J., Vul, E., Rohrer, D., Wixted, J.T., and Pashler, H. (2008). Spacing effects in learning: A temporal ridgeline of optimal retention. *Psychological Science, 19*(11), 1095–1102. doi:10.1111/j.1467-9280.2008.02209.x.

Cerasoli, C.P., Nicklin, J.M., and Nassrelgrgawi, A. (2016). Performance, incentives, and needs for autonomy, competence, and relatedness: A meta-analysis. *Motivation & Emotion, 40*(6), 781–813. doi:10.1007/s11031-016-9578-2.

Challis, B.H. (1993). Spacing effects on cued-memory tests depend on level of processing. *Journal of Experimental Psychology: Learning, Memory, and Cognition, 19*(2), 389–396.

Chan, K.-W., and Lai, P.-Y. (2006). *Revisiting the Trichotomous Achievement Goal Framework for Hong Kong Secondary Students: A Structural Model Analysis*. Paper presented at the meeting of Australia Association for Research in Education, Adelaide, Australia, November. Available: https://www.aare.edu.au/publications-database.php/4989/revisiting-the-trichotomous-achievement-goal-framework-for-hong-kong-secondary-students-a-structural.

Chan, M.Y., Haber, S., Drew, L.M., and Park, D.C. (2014). Training older adults to use tablet computers: Does it enhance cognitive function? *The Gerontologist, 56*(3), 475–484. Available: https://doi.org/10.1093/geront/gnu057 [January 2018].

Chang, Y. (2014). Reorganization and plastic changes of the human brain associated with skill learning and expertise. *Frontiers in Human Neuroscience, 8*, 35. doi:10.3389/fnhum.2014.00035.

Charness, N., and Schumann, C.E. (1992). Training older adults in word processing: Effects of age, training technique, and computer anxiety. *International Journal of Technology & Aging, 5*(1), 79–106.

Chaudry, A., Morrissey, T., Weiland, C., and Yoshikawa, H. (2017). *Cradle to Kindergarten: A New Plan to Combat Inequality*. New York: Russell Sage Foundation.

Chavous, T.M., Bernat, D.H., Schmeelk-Cone, K., Caldwell, C.H., Kohn-Wood, L., and Zimmerman, M.A. (2003). Racial identity and academic attainment among African American adolescents. *Child Development, 74*(4), 1076–1090.

Chechik, G., Meilijison, I., and Ruppin, E. (1999). Neuronal regulation: A mechanism for synaptic pruning during brain maturation. *Neural Computation, 11*(8), 2061–2680. doi:10.1162/089976699300016089.

Chen, F. (2015). *The Impact of Criteria-Referenced Formative Assessment on Fifth Grade Students' Theater Arts and English Language Arts Achievement*. Doctoral dissertation. University at Albany—SUNY.

Chi, M.T.H. (2009). Active-constructive-interactive: A conceptual framework for differentiating learning activities. *Topics in Cognitive Science, 1*(1), 73–105. doi:10.1111/j.1756-8765.2008.01005.x.

Chi, M.T.H., Hutchinson, J., and Robin, A. (1989a). How inferences about novel domain-related concepts can be constrained by structured knowledge. *Merrill-Palmer Quarterly, 35*(1), 27–62.

Chi, M.T.H., Bassok, M., Lewis, M.W., Reimann, P., and Glaser, R. (1989b). Self-explanations: How students study and use examples in learning to solve problems. *Cognitive Science, 13*(2), 145–182. doi:10.1207/s15516709cog1302_1.

Chi, M.T.H., De Leeuw, N., Chiu, M.H., and LaVancher, C. (1994). Eliciting self-explanations improves understanding. *Cognitive Science, 18*(3), 439–477.

Chi, M.T.H., Roscoe, R., DSlotta, J., Roy, M., and Chase, M. (2012). Misconceived causal explanations for "emergent" processes. *Cognitive Science, 36*(1), 1–61. doi:10.1111/j.1551-6709. 2011.01207.x.

Chin, C., and Osborne, J. (2012). Supporting argumentation through students' questions: Case studies in science classrooms. *Journal of the Learning Sciences, 19*(2), 230–284. doi. org/10.1080/10508400903530036.

Chiong, C., and Shuler, C. (2010). *Learning: Is There an App for That? Investigations of Young Children's Usage and Learning with Mobile Devices and Apps.* New York: The Joan Ganz Cooney Center at Sesame Workshop. Available: http://pbskids.org/read/files/ cooney_learning_apps.pdf [December 2017].

Christensen, H., Korten, A., Jorm, A.F., Henderson, A.S., Scott, R., and Mackinnon, A.J. (1996). Activity levels and cognitive functioning in an elderly community sample. *Age and Ageing, 25*(1), 72–80.

Christle, C.A., Jolivette, K., and Nelson, C.M. (2005). Breaking the school to prison pipeline: Identifying school risk and protective factors for youth delinquency. *Exceptionality, 13*(2), 69–88.

Chua, H.F., Boland, J.E., and Nisbett, R.E. (2005). Cultural variation in eye movements during scene perception. *Proceedings of the National Academy of Sciences of the United States of America, 102*(35), 12629–12633.

Chung, H.J., Weyandt, L.L., and Swentosky, A. (2014). The physiology of executive functioning. In S. Goldstein and J.A. Naglieri (Eds.), *Handbook of Executive Functioning* (pp. 13–27). New York: Springer.

Cialdini, R.B. (2007). Descriptive social norms as underappreciated sources of social control. *Psychometrika, 72*(2), 263–268.

Cialdini, R.B., Reno, R.R., and Kallgren, C.A. (1990). A focus theory of normative conduct: Recycling the concept of norms to reduce littering in public places. *Journal of Personality and Social Psychology, 58*(6), 1015–1026.

Clark, D., Tanner-Smith, E., Killingsworth, S. (2014). *Digital Games, Design and Learning: A Systematic Review and Meta-Analysis* (Executive Summary). Menlo Park, CA: SRI International. Available: https://www.sri.com/sites/default/files/publications/digital-games-design-and-learning-executive_summary.pdf [December 2017].

Cleeremans, A. (1996). Principles of implicit learning. In D. Berry (Ed.), *How Implicit is Implicit Learning?* (pp. 196–234). Oxford, UK: Oxford University Press.

Clegg, J., Wen, N., Legare, C., Gauthier, I., and Cowan, N. (2017). Is non-conformity WEIRD? Cultural variation in adults' beliefs about children's competency and conformity. *Journal of Experimental Psychology: General, 146*(3), 428–441.

Clement, J. (2000). Model based learning as a key research area for science education. *International Journal of Science Education, 22*(9), 1041–1053.

Cobb, P., and Bauersfeld, H. (Eds.), (1995). *The Emergence of Mathematical Meaning: Interaction in Classroom Cultures.* Hillsdale, NJ: Lawrence Erlbaum Associates.

Coffman, J.L., Ornstein, P.A., McCall, L.E., and Curran, P.J. (2008). Linking teachers' memory-relevant language and the development of children's memory skills. *Developmental Psychology, 44*(6), 1640–1654. doi:10.1037/a0013859.

Cohen, E.G., and Lotan, R.A. (Eds.). (1997). *Working for Equity in Heterogeneous Classrooms: Sociological Theory in Practice.* New York: Teachers College Press.

Cohen, G.L., and Steele, C.M. (2002). A barrier of mistrust: How negative stereotypes affect cross-race mentoring. In J. Aronson (Ed.), *Improving Academic Achievement: Impact of Psychological Factors on Education* (pp. 305–331). San Diego, CA: Academic Press.

Cohen, G.L., Steele, C.M., and Ross, L.D. (1999). The mentor's dilemma: Providing critical feedback across the racial divide. *Personality and Social Psychology Bulletin, 25*(10), 1302–1318.

Cohen, G.L., Garcia, J., Apfel, N., and Master, A. (2006). Reducing the racial achievement gap: A social-psychological intervention. *Science, 313*(5791), 1307–1310. doi:10.1126/science.1128317.

Cohen, G.L., Garcia, J., Purdie-Vaughns, V., Apfel, N., and Brzustoski, P. (2009). Recursive processes in self-affirmation: Intervening to close the minority achievement gap. *Science, 324*(5925), 400–403. doi:10.1126/science.1170769.

Cohen-Kadosh, K., and Johnson, M.H. (2007). Developing a cortex specialized for face perception. *Trends in Cognitive Science, 11*(9), 367–369. doi:10.1016/j.tics.2007.06.007.

Colcombe, S., and Kramer, A.F. (2003). Fitness effects on the cognitive function of older adults: A meta-analytic study. *Psychological Science, 14*(2), 125–130.

Cole, M. (1995). Culture and cognitive development: From cross-cultural research to creating systems of cultural mediation. *Culture & Psychology, 1*, 25–54.

Cole, M. (1998). *Cultural Psychology: A Once and Future Discipline.* Cambridge, MA: Harvard University Press.

Cole, M., and Packer, M. (2005). Culture in development. In M.H. Bornstein and M.E. Lamb (Eds.), *Cognitive Development: An Advanced Textbook* (pp. 67–124). New York: Psychology Press.

Cole, M., and Scribner, S. (1974). *Culture and Thought: A Psychological Introduction.* Oxford, UK: John Wiley & Sons.

Collette, F., Hogge, M., Salmon, E., and Van der Linden, M. (2006). Exploration of the neural substrates of executive functioning by functional neuroimaging. *Neuroscience, 139*(1), 209–221.

Collins, A., Neville, P., and Bielaczyc, K. (2000). The role of different media in designing learning environments. *International Journal of Artificial Intelligence in Education, 11*, 144-162.

Collins, F. (2004). What we do and don't know about "race," "ethnicity," genetics, and health at the dawn of the genome era. *Nature Genetics, 36*(11, Suppl.), S13–S15.

Comings, J.T., and Cuban, S. (2000). *So I Made Up My Mind: Introducing a Study of Adult Learner Persistence in Library Literacy Programs.* Available: http://eric.ed.gov/?id=ED446772 [December 2017].

Condliffe, B., Visher, M.G., Bangser, M.R., Drohojowska, S., and Saco, L. (2016). *Projectbased Learning: A Literature Review.* Available: https://s3-us-west-1.amazonaws.com/ler/MDRC+PBL+Literature+Review.pdf [December 2017].

Cooper, S., Khatib, F., Treuille, A., Barbero, J., Lee, J., Beenen, M., Leaver-Fay, A., Baker, D., and Popovic, Z. (2010). Predicting protein structures with a multiplayer online game. *Nature, 466*(7307), 756–760. doi:10.1038/nature09304.

Cooper, M.M., Kouyoumdjian, H., and Underwood, S.M. (2016). Investigating students' reasoning about acid-base reactions. *Journal of Chemical Education, 93*, 1703-1712.

Corcoran, T., Mosher, F.A., and Rogat, A. (2009). *Learning Progressions in Science: An Evidence-Based Approach to Reform.* Available http://www.cpre.org/images/stories/cpre_pdfs/lp_science_rr63.pdf [July 2018].

Correa-Chávez, M., and Rogoff, B. (2009). Children's attention to interactions directed to others: Guatemalan Mayan and European American patterns. *Developmental Psychology, 45*(3), 630–641.

Cortiella, C., and Horowitz, S.H. (2014). *The State of Learning Disabilities: Facts, Trends and Emerging Issues.* New York: National Center for Learning Disabilities. Available: https://www.ncld.org/wp-content/uploads/2014/11/2014-State-of-LD.pdf [December 2017].

Coutanche, M.N., Gianessi, C.A., Chanales, A.J.H., Willison, K.W., and Thompson-Schill, S.L. (2013). The role of sleep in forming a memory representation of a two-dimensional space. *Hippocampus, 23*(12), 1189–1197. doi:10.1002/hipo.22157.

Covington, M.V. (2000). Goal theory, motivation, and school achievement: An integrative review. *Annual Review of Psychology, 51*(1), 171–200. doi:10.1146/annurev.psych.51.1.171.

Craig, S.D., Sullins, J., Witherspoon, A. and Gholson, B. (2006). Deep-level reasoning questions effect: The role of dialog and deep-level reasoning questions during vicarious learning. *Cognition and Instruction, 24*(4), 563–589.

Craik, F.I.M., and Bialystok, E. (2006). Cognition through the lifespan: Mechanisms of change. *Trends in Cognitive Sciences, 10*(3), 131-138.

Craik, F.I.M., and Rose, N.S. (2012). Memory encoding and aging: A neurocognitive perspective. *Neuroscience & Biobehavioral Reviews, 36*(7), 1729-1739.

Craik, F.I.M., and Salthouse, T.A. (Eds.). (2008). *Handbook of Cognitive Aging* (3rd ed.). New York: Psychology Press.

Craik, F.I.M., and Tulving, E. (1975). Depth of processing and the retention of words in episodic memory. *Journal of Experimental Psychology: General, 104*(3), 268-294. doi:10.1037/0096-3445.104.3.268.

Creswell, J.D., and Lindsay, E.K. (2014). How does mindfulness training affect health? A mindfulness stress buffering account. *Current Directions in Psychological Science, 23*(6), 401-407.

Cronbach, L.J. (1957). The two disciplines of scientific psychology. *American Psychologist, 12*(11), 671-684.

Crone, E.A., and Dahl, R.E. (2012). Understanding adolescence as a period of social-affective engagement and goal flexibility. *Nature Reviews Neuroscience, 13* (9), 636-650. doi:10.1038/nrn3313

Crouch, C.H., and Mazur, E. (2001). Peer instruction: Ten years of experience and results. *American Journal of Physics, 69*, 970-977. doi.org/10.1119/1.1374249.

Crouzevialle, M., and Butera, F. (2013). Performance-approach goals deplete working memory and impair cognitive performance. *Journal of Experimental Psychology: General, 142*(3), 666-678. doi:10.1037/a0029632.

Cvencek, D., Meltzoff, A.N., and Greenwald, A.G. (2011). Math–gender stereotypes in elementary school children. *Child Development, 82*(3), 766-779.

Damasio, A. (1994). *Descartes' Error: Emotion, Reason and the Human Brain.* New York: Random House.

Danaher, K., and Crandall, C.S. (2008). Stereotype threat in applied settings re-examined. *Journal of Applied Social Psychology, 38*(6), 1639-1655. doi:10.1111/j.1559-1816.2008.00362.x.

Darby, K.P., and Sloutsky, V.M. (2015). The cost of learning: Interference effects in memory development. *Journal of Experimental Psychology: General, 144*(2), 410-431. doi:10.1037/xge0000051.

Dar-Nimrod, I., and Heine, S.J. (2006). Exposure to scientific theories affects women's math performance. *Science, 314*(5798), 435.

Darnon, C., Harackiewicz, J., Butera, F., Mugny, G., and Quiamzade, A. (2007). Performance-approach and performance-avoidance goals: When uncertainty makes a difference. *Personality and Social Psychology Bulletin, 33*(6), 813-827.

Davidson, R.J., and Lutz, A. (2008). Buddha's brain: Neuroplasticity and meditation. *IEEE Signal Processing Magazine, 25*(1), 176-174.

Davis, C.L., Tomporowski, P.D., McDowell, J.E., Austin, B.P., Miller, P.H., Yanasak, N.E., Allison, J.D., and Naglieri, JA. (2011). Exercise improves executive function and alters neural activation in overweight children: A randomized controlled trial. *Health Psychology: Official Journal of the Division of Health Psychology, American Psychological Association, 30*(1), 91-98. doi:10.1037/a0021766.

Dawley, L. (2009). Social network knowledge construction: Emerging virtual world pedadogy. *On The Horizon, 17*(2), 109-121.

Dawley, L., and Dede, C. (2014). Situated learning in virtual worlds and immersive simulations. In M. Spector, M.D. Merrill, J. Elen, and M.J. Bishop (Eds.), *Handbook of Research on Educational Communications and Technology* (pp. 723-734). New York: Springer.

Day, J.C., and Newburger, E.C. (2002). *The Big Payoff: Educational Attainment and Synthetic Estimates of Work-Life Earnings.* Washington, DC: U.S. Census Bureau. Available: http://www.census.gov/prod/2002pubs/p23-21pdf [December 2017].

de Bruin, A.B.H., Rikers, R.M.J.P., and Schmidt, H.G. (2007). The effect of self-explanation and prediction on the development of principled understanding of chess in novices. *Contemporary Educational Psychology, 32*(2), 188-205. doi:10.1016/j.cedpsych.2006.01.001.

de Frias, C.M., Dixon, R.A., Fisher, N., and Camicioli, R. (2007). Intraindividual variability in neurocognitive speed: A comparison of Parkinson's disease and normal older adults. *Neuropsychologia, 45*(11), 2499-2507.

De La Paz, S., Monte-Sano, C., Felton, M., Croninger, R., Jackson, C., and Worland, K. (2017). A historical writing apprenticeship for adolescents: Integrating disciplinary learning with cognitive strategies. *Reading Research Quarterly, 52(1),* 31-52. doi:10.1002/rrq.147.

Deci, E.L., and Ryan, R.M. (1985). *Intrinsic Motivation and Self-determination in Human Behavior.* New York: Plenum Press.

Deci, E.L., and Ryan, R.M. (2000). The "what" and "why" of goal pursuits: Human needs and the self-determination of behavior. *Psychological Inquiry,* 11, 227-268.

Deci, E.L., Koestner, R., and Ryan, R.M. (1999). A meta-analytic review of experiments examining the effects of extrinsic rewards on intrinsic motivation. *Psychological Bulletin, 125*(6), 627-668.

Deci, E.L., Koestner, R., and Ryan, R.M. (2001). Extrinsic rewards and intrinsic motivation in education: Reconsidered once again. *Review of Educational Research, 71*(1), 1-27.

Dede, C., and Richards, J. (2012). Synthesis: Next steps in the evolution of digital teaching platforms. In C. Dede and J. Richards (Eds.), *Digital Teaching Platforms: Customizing Classroom Learning for Each Student* (pp. 201-208). New York: Teacher's College Press.

Dee, T.S. (2015). Social identity and achievement gaps: Evidence from an affirmation intervention. *Journal of Research on Educational Effectiveness, 8*(2), 149-168.

Dehaene, S., and Cohen, L. (2011). The unique role of the visual word form area in reading. *Trends in Cognitive Sciences, 15*(6), 254-262.

Dehaene, S., Pegado, F., Braga, L.W., Ventura, P., Nunes Filho, G., Jobert, A., Dehaene-Lambertz, G., Kolinsky, R., Morais, J., and Cohen, L. (2010). How learning to read changes the cortical networks for vision and language. *Science, 330*(6009), 1359-1364.

Dekker, S., and Fischer, R. (2008). Cultural differences in academic motivation goals: A meta-analysis across thirteen societies. *Journal of Educational Research, 102*(2), 99-110. doi.org/10.3200/JOER.102.2.99-110.

Delello, J.A., and McWhorter, R.R. (2015). Reducing the digital divide: Connecting older adults to iPad technology. *Journal of Applied Gerontology, 36*(1), 3-28. doi:10.1177/0733464815589985.

Delpit, L. (1995). *Other Peoples' Children: Cultural Conflict in the Classroom.* New York: The New Press.

Dembo, M.H., and Howard, K. (2007). Advice about the use of learning styles: A major myth in education. *Journal of College Reading and Learning, 37*(2), 101-109.

Dempster, F.N. (1996). Distributing and managing the conditions of encoding and practice. In E.L. Bjork and R.A. Bjork (Eds.), *Handbook of Perception and Cognition* (pp. 317-344). New York: Academic Press.

Deslauriers, L., Schelew, E., and Wieman, C. (2011). Improved learning in a large-enrollment physics class. *Science, 332*(6031), 862-864.

Diamond, A., Barnett, W.S., Thomas, J., and Munro, S. (2007). Preschool program improves cognitive control. *Science (New York, N.Y.), 318*(5855), 1387-1388. doi.org/10.1126/science.1151148.

Diamond, M.C., Krech, D., and Rosenzweig, M.R. (1964). The effects of an enriched environment on the rat cerebral cortex. *Journal of Comparative Neurology, 123*, 111-119.

Diekelmann, S., and Born, J. (2010). The memory function of sleep. *Nature Reviews Neuroscience, 11*, 114-126.

Dill, E., and Boykin, A.W. (2000). The comparative influence of individual, peer tutoring, and communal learning contexts on the text-recall of African American children. *Journal of Black Psychology, 26*(1), 65-78.

Dillenbourg, P. (1996). Some technical implications of the distributed cognition approach on the design of interactive learning environments. *Journal of Artificial Intelligence in Education, 7*(2), 161–180.

Dillenbourg, P., and Traum, D. (2006). Sharing solutions: Persistence and grounding in multi-modal collaborative problem solving. *Journal of the Learning Sciences, 15*(1), 121–151.

Dillenbourg, P., Baker, M., Blaye, A., and O'Malley, C. (1996). The evolution of research on collaborative learning. In E. Spada and P. Reiman (Eds.), *Learning in Humans and Machines: Towards an Interdisciplinary Learning Science* (pp. 189–211). Oxford, UK: Elsevier.

Dirette, D.P. (2014). Questions about race as a research variable. *The Open Journal of Occupational Therapy, 2*(3), 1–7.

D'Mello, S.K., Lehman, B., Pekrun, R., and Graesser, A.C. (2014). Confusion can be beneficial for learning. *Learning and Instruction, 29*(1), 153–170.

Doignon, J.-P., and Falmagne, J.-C. (1999). *Knowledge Spaces*. Berlin: SpringerVerlag.

Dollman, J., Ridley, K., Olds, T., and Lowe, E. (2007). Trends in the duration of school day sleep among 10- to 15-year-old south Australians between 1985 and 2004. *Acta Paediatrica, 96*(7), 1011–1014.

Dornisch, M.M., and Sperling, R.A. (2006). Facilitating learning from technology-enhanced text: Effects of prompted elaborative interrogation. *The Journal of Educational Research, 99*(3), 156–165. doi:10.3200/joer.99.3.156-166.

Dow, S.P., Glassco, A., Kass, J., Schwarz, M., Schwartz, D.L., and Klemmer, S.R. (2010). Parallel prototyping leads to better design results, more divergent creations, and self-efficacy gains. *ACM Transactions on Computer-Human Interaction, 17*(4), 1–24.

Draganski, B., Gaser, C., Busch, V., Schuirer, G., Bogdahn, U., and May, A. (2004). Neuroplasticity: Changes in grey matter induced by training. *Nature, 427*(6972), 311–312. doi:10.1038/427311a.

Draganski, B., Gaser, C., Kempermann, G., Kuhn, H.G., Winkler, J., Buchel, C., and May, A. (2006). Temporal and spatial dynamics of brain structure changes during extensive learning. *Journal of Neuroscience, 26*(23), 6314–6317.

Duncan, G.J., and Murnane, R.J. (Eds.). (2011). *Whither Opportunity*. New York: Russell Sage Foundation.

Dunleavy, M., and Dede, C. (2013). Augmented reality teaching and learning. In J.M. Spector, M.D Merrill, J. Elen, and M.J. Bishop (Eds.), *The Handbook of Research on Educational Communications and Technology* (4th Edition) (pp. 735–745). New York: Springer.

Dunlosky, J., and Metcalfe, J. (2009). *Metacognition*. Thousand Oaks, CA: Sage Publications Inc.

Dunlosky, J., and Rawson, K.A. (2005). Why does rereading improve metacomprehension accuracy? Evaluating the levels-of-disruption hypothesis for the rereading effect. *Discourse Processes, 40*(1), 37–55.

Dunlosky, J., Rawson, K.A., Marsh, E.J., Nathan, M.J., and Willingham, D.T. (2013). Improving students' learning with effective learning techniques: Promising directions from cognitive and educational psychology. *Psychological Science in the Public Interest, 14*(1), 4–58. doi:10.1177/1529100612453266.

Duschl, R.A., and Osborne, J. (2002). Supporting and promoting argumentation discourse in science education. *Studies in Science Education, 38*(1), 39–72.

Dweck, C.S. (1986). Motivational processes affecting learning. *American Psychologist, 41*(10), 1040–1048.

Dweck, C.S. (1999). *Self-Theories: Their Role in Motivation, Personality and Development*. Philadelphia, PA: Psychology Press.

Dweck, C.S., and Elliott, E.S. (1983). Achievement motivation. In P. Mussen and E.M. Hetherington (Eds.), *Handbook of Child Psychology* (Vol. 4) (pp. 643–691). New York: John Wiley & Sons.

Dweck, C.S., and Leggett, E.L. (1988). A social-cognitive approach to motivation and personality. *Psychological Review, 95*(2), 256–273. doi.org/10.1037/0033-295X.95.2.256.

Dweck, C.S., and Master, A. (2009). Self-theories and motivation: Students' beliefs about intelligence. In K.R. Wenzel, and A. Wigfield (Eds.), *Handbook of Motivation at School* (pp. 123–140). New York: Routledge/Taylor and Francis Group.

Dynarski, M., Agodini, R., Heaviside, S. Novak, T. Carey, N., and Campuzano, L. (2007). *Effectiveness of Reading and Mathematics Software Products: Findings from the First Student Cohort. Report to Congress.* NCEE 2007-4005. Washington, DC: U.S. Department of Education.

Dzikovska, M., Steinhauser, N., Farrow, E., Moore, J., and Campbell, G. (2014). BEETLE II: Deep natural language understanding and automatic feedback generation for intelligent tutoring in basic electricity and electronics. *International Journal of Artificial Intelligence in Education, 24*(3), 284–332. doi:10.1007/s40593-014-0017-9.

Ebner, N.C., Freund, A.M., and Baltes, P.B. (2006). Developmental changes in personal goal orientation from young to late adulthood: From striving for gains to maintenance and prevention of losses. *Psychology and Aging, 21*(4), 664–678.

Eccles, J.S., and Midgley, C. (1989). Stage/environment fit: Developmentally appropriate classrooms for early adolescents. In R. Ames and C. Ames (Eds.), *Research on Motivation in Education,* (Vol. 3, pp. 139-181). New York: Academic Press.

Eccles, J.S., and Wigfield, A. (2002). Motivational beliefs, values, and goals. *Annual Review of Psychology, 53,* 109–132. doi.org/10.1146/annurev.psych.53.100901.135153.

Eccles, J.S, Lord, S., and Midgley, C. (1991). What are we doing to early adolescents? The impact of educational contexts on early adolescents. *American Journal of Education, 99*(4), 521–542.

Eccles, J.S., Adler, T.F., Fullerman, R., Goff, S.B., Kaczala, C.M., Meece, J., and Midgley, C. (1983). Expectancies, values and academic behaviors. In J.T. Spence (Ed.), *Achievement and Achievement Motives* (pp. 75–146). San Francisco, CA: W.H. Freeman.

Eccles, J.S., Midgley, C., Wigfield, A., Buchanan, C.M., Reuman, D., Flanagan, C., and Iver, D.M. (1993a). Development during adolescence. The impact of stage-environment fit on young adolescents' experiences in schools and in families. *American Psychologist, 48*(2), 90–101.

Eccles, J.S., Wigfield, A., Harold, R.D., Blumenfeld, P. (1993b). Ontogeny of children's self-perceptions and subjective task values across activity domains during the early elementary school years. *Child Development, 64,* 830–847

Eccles, J.S., Wong, C.A., and Peck, S.C. (2006). Ethnicity as a social context for the development of African-American adolescents. *Journal of School Psychology, 44*(5), 407–426.

Edmonds, M.S., Vaughn, S., Wexler, J., Reutebuch, C., Cable, A., Tackett, K.K., and Schnakenberg, J.W. (2009). A synthesis of reading interventions and effects on reading comprehension outcomes for older struggling readers. *Review of Educational Research, 79*(1), 262–300. doi:10.3102/0034654308325998.

Eigsti, I.M., Zayas, V., Mischel, W., Shoda, Y., Ayduk, O., Dadlani, M.B., Davidson, M.C., Lawrence Aber, J., and Casey, B.J. (2006). Predicting cognitive control from preschool to late adolescence and young adulthood. *Psychological Science, 17*(6), 478–484.

Elbert, T., Pantev, C., Wienbruch, C., Rockstroh, B., and Taub, E. (1995). Increased cortical representation of the fingers of the left hand in string players. *Science, 270*(5234), 307–307.

Ellingson, J.E., and Noe, R.A. (2017). *Autonomous Learning in the Workplace: SIOP Organizational Series* (1st Edition). New York: Routledge.

Elliot, A.J. (1997). Integrating the "classic" and "contemporary" approaches to achievement motivation: A hierarchical model of approach and avoidance motivation. In M. Maehr and P. Pintrich (Eds.), *Advances in Motivation and Achievement* (vol. 10, pp. 143–179). Greenwich, CT: JAI Press.

Elliot, A.J. (1999). Approach and avoidance motivation and achievement goals. *Educational Psychologist, 34*(3), 169–189.

Elliot, A.J., and McGregor, H.A. (2001). A 2 X 2 achievement goal framework. *Journal of Personality and Social Psychology, 80*(3), 501–519.

Elliot, A.J., and Murayama, K. (2008). On the measurement of achievement goals: Critique, illustration, and application. *Journal of Educational Psychology, 100*(3), 613–628.

Elliot, A.J., Chirkov, V.I., Kim, Y., and Sheldon, K.M. (2001). A cross-cultural analysis of avoidance (relative to approach) personal goals. *Psychological Science, 12*(6), 505-510.

Ericsson, K.A. (1996). The acquisition of expert performance: An introduction to some of the issues. In K.A. Ericsson (Ed.), *The Road to Excellence: The Acquisition of Expert Performance in the Arts and Sciences, Sports, and Games* (pp. 1-50). Mahwah, NJ: Lawrence Erlbaum Associates.

Erickson, F. (2010). Culture in society and in educational practices. In J.A. Banks and C.A. McGee (Eds.), *Multicultural Education: Issues and Perspectives* (7th ed., pp. 33-58). Indianapolis, IN: Jossey-Bass.

Esposito, A.G., and Bauer, P.J. (2017). Going beyond the lesson: Self-generating new factual knowledge in the classroom. *Journal of Experimental Child Psychology, 153*, 110-125. doi:10.1016/j.jecp.2016.09.003.

Etnier, J.L., Nowell, P.M., Landers, D.M., and Sibley, B.A. (2006). A meta-regression to examine the relationship between aerobic fitness and cognitive performance. *Brain Research Reviews, 52*(1), 119-130.

Fabiani, M., Low, K.A., Wee, E., Sable, J.J., and Gratton, G. (2006). Reduced suppression or labile memory? Mechanisms of inefficient filtering of irrelevant information in older adults. *Journal of Cognitive Neuroscience, 18*(4), 637-650.

Fandakova, Y., Lindenberger, U., and Shing, Y.L. (2014). Deficits in process-specific prefrontal and hippocampal activations contribute to adult age differences in episodic memory interference. *Cerebral Cortex, 24*(7), 1832-1844.

Farah, M.J. (2010). Mind, brain, and education in socioeconomic context. In M. Ferrari and L. Vuletic (Eds.), *The Developmental Relations among Mind, Brain and Education* (pp. 243-256). Dordrecht, The Netherlands: Springer.

Federal Communications Commission. (2016). *2016 Broadband Progress Report*. Available: https://apps.fcc.gov/edocs_public/attachmatch/FCC-16-6A1.pdf [December 2017].

Ferretti, R.P., MacArthur, C.D., and Okolo, C.M. (2001). Teaching for historical understanding in inclusive classrooms. *Learning Disability Quarterly, 24*(1), 59-71.

Figueroa, P. (1991). *Education and the Social Construction of "Race."* New York: Routledge.

Finkel, D., Andel, R., Gatz, M., and Pedersen, N.L. (2009). The role of occupational complexity in trajectories of cognitive aging before and after retirement. *Psychology and Aging, 24*(3), 563-573. doi.org/10.1037/a0015511.

Fiore, S.M., Wiltshire, T.J., Oglesby, J.M., O'Keefe, W.S., and Salas, E. (2014). Complex collaborative problem solving in mission control. *Aviation, Space, and Environmental Medicine, 85*(4), 456-461.

Fiorella, L., and Mayer, R.E. (2014). Role of expectations and explanations in learning by teaching. *Contemporary Educational Psychology, 39*(2), 75-85. doi:10.1016/j.cedpsych.2014.01.001.

Fiorella, L., and Mayer, R.E. (2015a). Eight ways to promote generative learning. *Educational Psychology Review, 28*(4), 717-741. doi:10.1007/s10648-015-9348-9.

Fiorella, L., and Mayer, R.E. (2015b). *Learning as a Generative Activity: Eight Learning Strategies That Promote Understanding*. New York: Cambridge University Press.

Fischer, K.W., and Bidel, T.R. (2006). Dynamic development of action and thought. In W. Damon and R.M. Lerner (Eds.), *Handbook of Child Psychology* (6th ed., vol. 1, pp. 313-339). New York: John Wiley & Sons.

Fisher, G.G., Stachowski, A., Infurna, F.J., Faul, J.D., Grosch, J., and Tetrick, L.E. (2014). Mental work demands, retirement, and longitudinal trajectories of cognitive functioning. *Journal of Occupational Health Psychology, 19*(2), 231-242. doi.org/10.1037/a0035724.

Fisher, S.E., and Francks, C. (2006). Genes, cognition and dyslexia: Learning to read the genome. *Trends in Cognitive Sciences, 10*(6), 250-257. doi:10.1016/j.tics.2006.04.003.

Fishman, B., and Dede, C. (2016). Teaching and technology: New tools for new times. In D.H. Gitomer and C.A. Bell (Eds.), *Handbook of Research on Teaching* (5th ed.). Washington, DC: American Educational Research Association.

Fjell, A.M., Walhovd, K.B., Fennema-Notestine, C., McEvoy, L.K., Hagler, D.J., Holland, D., Brewer, J.B., and Dale, A.M. (2009). One-year brain atrophy evident in healthy aging. *Journal of Neuroscience, 29*(48), 15223-15231. doi:10.1523/JNEUROSCI.3252-09.2009.

Fletcher, J.M. (2010). Construct validity of reading measures in adults with significant reading difficulties. *Journal of Learning Disabilities, 43*(2), 166-168.

Fletcher, J.M., Lyon, G.R., Fuchs, L.S., and Barnes, M.A. (2007). *Learning Disabilities: From Identification to Intervention.* New York: Guilford Press.

Flowerday, T., Schraw, G., and Stevens, J. (2004). The role of choice and interest in reader engagement. *The Journal of Experimental Education, 72*(2), 93-114.

Flynn, L.J., Zheng, X., and Swanson, H.L. (2012). Instructing struggling older readers: A selective meta-analysis of intervention research. *Learning Disabilities Research and Practice, 27*(1), 21-32. doi:/10.1111/j.1540-5826.2011.00347.x.

Ford, J.K., Quiñones, M.A., Sego, D.J., and Sorra, J.S. (1992). Factors affecting the opportunity to perform trained tasks on the job. *Personnel Psychology, 45*(3), 511-527. doi:10.1111/j.1744-6570.1992.tb00858.x.

Freeman, S., Eddy, S.L., McDonough, M., Smith, M.K., Okoroafor, N., Jordt, H., and Wenderoth, M.P. (2014). Active learning increases student performance in science, engineering, and mathematics. *Proceedings of the National Academy of Sciences of the United States of America, 111*(23), 8410-8415.

Fried. C.B. (2008). In-class laptop use and its effects on student learning. *Computers & Education, 50*(3), 906-914.

Friedel, J.M., Cortina, K.S., Turner, J.C., and Midgley, C. (2007). Achievement goals, efficacy beliefs and coping strategies in mathematics: The roles of perceived parent and teacher goal emphases. *Contemporary Educational Psychology, 32*(3), 434-458. doi:10.1016/j.cedpsych.2006.10.009.

Fryberg, S.A., Troop-Gordon, W., D'Arrisso, A., Flores, H., Ponizovskiy, V., Ranney, J.D., Mandour, T., Tootoosis, C., Robinson, S., Russo, N., and Burack, J.A. (2013). Cultural mismatch and the education of Aboriginal youths: The interplay of cultural identities and teacher ratings. *Developmental Psychology, 49*(1), 72-79. doi:10.1037/a0029056.

Fugate, C.M., Zentall, S.S., and Gentry, M. (2013). Creativity and working memory in gifted students with and without characteristics of attention deficit hyperactive disorder: Lifting the mask. *Gifted Child Quarterly, 57*(4), 234-246.

Fuligni, A.A., Witkow, M., and Garcia, C. (2005). Ethnic identity and the academic adjustment of adolescents from Mexican, Chinese, and European backgrounds. *Developmental Psychology, 41*(5), 799-811.

Funder, D.C. (1995). On the accuracy of personality judgment: A realistic approach. *Psychological Review, 102*(4), 652-670.

Furtak, E.M., and Heredia, S.C. (2014). Exploring the influence of learning progressions in two teacher communities. *Journal of Research in Science Teaching, 51*(8), 982-1020.

Gabbard, C., and Barton, J. (1979). Effects of physical activity on mathematical computation among young children. *Journal of Psychology, 103*(2), 287-288.

Gallup, Inc. (2014). *Gallup Student Poll.* Available: http://www.gallup.com/services/180029/gallup-student-poll-2014-overall-report.aspx [December 2017].

García, J., Kimeldorf, D.J., and Koelling, R.A. (1955). Conditioned aversion to saccharin resulting from exposure to gamma radiation. *Science, 122*(3160), 157-158.

García-Cabot, A., de-Marcos, L., and García-López, E. (2015). An empirical study on m-learning adaptation: Learning performance and learning contexts. *Computers & Education, 82*, 450-459. doi.org/10.1016/j.compedu.2014.12.007.

Gardner, R.C. (1985). *Social Psychology in Second Language Learning: The Role of Attitudes and Motivation.* London, UK: Edward Arnold.

Gasevic, D., Kovanovic, V., Joksimovic, S., and Siemens, G. (2014). Where is research on massive open online courses headed? A data analysis of the MOOC research initiative. *The International Review of Research in Open and Distributed Learning, 15*(5). Available: http://www.irrodl.org/index.php/irrodl/article/view/1954 [December 2017].

Gathercole, S.E., Alloway, T.P., Willis, C.S., and Adams, A.M. (2006). Working memory in children with reading disabilities. *Journal of Experimental Child Psychology, 93*(3), 265-281.

Gaumer Erickson, A.S., and Noonan, P.M. (2010). Late-career adults in online education: A rewarding experience for individuals aged 50 to 65. *MERLOT Journal of Online Learning and Teaching, 6*(2), 388-397.

Gauvain, M. (2009). Social and cultural transactions in cognitive development: A cross-generational view. In A. Sameroff (Ed.), *The Transactional Model of Development: How Children and Contexts Shape Each Other* (pp. 163-182). Washington, DC: American Psychological Association. doi.org/10.1037/11877-009.

Gauvain, M., and Monroe, R.L. (2009). Contributions of societal modernity to cognitive development: A comparison of four cultures. *Child Development, 80*(6), 1628-1642.

Gauvain, M., and Monroe, R.L. (2012). Cultural change, human activity, and cognitive development. *Human Development, 55*(4), 205-228. doi:10.1159/000339451.

Geary, D.C. (1993). Mathematical disabilities: Cognition, neuropsychological and genetic components. *Psychological Bulletin, 114*, 345-362. doi:10.1016/j.lindif.2009.10.008.

Geary, D.C. (2013). Learning disabilities in mathematics: Recent advances. In H.L. Swanson, K. Harris, and S. Graham (Eds.), *Handbook of Learning Disabilities* (2nd ed., pp. 239-255). New York: Guilford Press.

Geary, D.C., Hoard, M.K., Nugent, L., and Bailey, D.H. (2012). Mathematical cognition deficits in children with learning disabilities and persistent low achievement: A five-year prospective study. *Journal of Educational Psychology, 104*(1), 206-223. doi:10.1037/a0025398.

Gee, J.P. (2003). *What Video Games Have to Teach Us About Learning and Literacy*. New York: Palgrave/Macmillan.

Gee, J.P. (2004). *Situated Language And Learning: A Critique of Traditional Schooling*. New York: Routledge.

Gee, J.P. (2009). Games, learning, and 21st century survival skills. *Journal of Virtual Worlds Research, 2*(1), 4-9. doi.org/10.4101/jvwr.v2i1.623.

Gehlbach, H., Brinkworth, M.E., King, A.M., Hsu, L.M., McIntyre, J., and Rogers, T. (2016). Creating birds of similar feathers: Leveraging similarity to improve teacher–student relationships and academic achievement. *Journal of Educational Psychology, 108*(3), 342-352.

Gelfand, M.J. (2012). Culture's contraints: International differences in the strength of social norms. *Current Directions in Psychological Science, 21*(6), 420-424.

Gelfand, M.J., Raver, J.L., Nishii, L., Leslie, L.M., Lun, J., Lim, B.C., Duan, L., Almaliach, A., Ang, S., Arnadottir, J., Aycan, Z., Boehnke, K., Boski, P., Cabecinhas, R., Chan, D., Chhokar, J., D'Amato, A., Ferrer, M., Fischlmayr, I.C., Fischer, R., Fülöp, M., Georgas, J., Kashima, E.S., Kashima, Y., Kim, K., Lempereur, A., Marquez, P., Othman, R., Overlaet, B., Panagiotopoulou, P., Peltzer, K., Perez-Florizno, L.R., Ponomarenko, L., Realo, A., Schei, V., Schmitt, M., Smith, P.B., Soomro, N., Szabo, E., Taveesin, N., Toyama, M., Van de Vliert, E., Vohra, N., Ward, C., and Yamaguchi, S. (2011). Differences between tight and loose cultures: A 33-nation study. *Science, 332*(6033), 1100-1104. doi: 10.1126/science.1197754.

Gentner, D., Loewenstein, J., Thompson, L., and Forbus, K.D. (2009). Reviving inert knowledge: Analogical abstraction supports relational retrieval of past events. *Cognitive Science, 33*, 1343-1382.

Gersten, R., Chard, D.J., Jayanthi, M., Baker, S.K., Morphy, P., and Flojo, J. (2009). Mathematics instruction for students with learning disabilities: A meta-analysis of instructional components. *Review of Educational Research, 79*(3), 1202-1242.

Gesell, A. (1934). *An Atlas of Infant Behavior: A Systematic Delineation of the Forms and Early Growth of Human Behavior Patterns*. New Haven, CT: Yale University Press.

Gholson, B., and Craig, S.D. (2006). Promoting constructive activities that support vicarious learning during computer-based instruction. *Educational Psychology Review, 18*(2), 119-139.

Gholson, B., Witherspoon, A., Morgan, B., Brittingham, J.K., Coles, R., Graesser, A.C., Sullins, J., and Craig, S.D. (2009). Exploring the deep-level reasoning questions effect during vicarious learning among eighth to eleventh graders in the domains of computer literacy and Newtonian physics. *Instructional Science, 37*(5), 487-493.

Gibson, J.J. (1979). *The Ecological Approach to Visual Perception.* Hillsdale, NJ: Lawrence Erlbaum Associates.

Gick M.J., and Holyoak, K.J. (1980). Analogial problem solving. *Cognitive Psychology, 12*, 306-355.

Gick, M.L., and Holyoak, K.J. (1983). Schema induction and analogical transfer. *Cognitive Psychology, 15*(1), 1-38.

Gilbert, C.D., Sigman, M., and Crist, R.E. (2001). The neural basis of perceptual learning. *Neuron, 31*(5), 681-697.

Gilliam, W., Maupin, A.N., Reyes, C.R., Accavitti, M., and Shic, F. (2016). *Do Early Educators' Implicit Biases Regarding Sex and Race Relate to Behavior Expectations and Recommendations of Preschool Expulsions and Suspensions?* A Research Study Brief. New Haven, CT: Yale University Child Study Center. Available: http://ziglercenter.yale.edu/publications/Preschool%20Implicit%20Bias%20Policy%20Brief_final_9_26_276766_5379_v1.pdf [December 2017].

Glymour, M.M., Weuve, J., Fay, M.E., Glass, T., and Berkman, L.F. (2008). Social ties and cognitive recovery after stroke: Does social integration promote cognitive resilience? *Neuroepidemiology, 31*(1), 10-20.

Gobert, J.D., and Clement, J.J. (1999). Effects of student-generated diagrams versus student-generated summaries on conceptual understanding of causal and dynamic knowledge in plate tectonics. *Journal of Research in Science Teaching, 36*(1), 39-53. doi:10.1002/(sici)1098-2736(199901)36:1<39::aid-tea4>3.0.co;2-i.

Gobet, F., Lane, P.C., Croker, S., Cheng, P.C., Jones, G., Oliver, I., and Pine, J.M. (2001). Chunking mechanisms in human learning. *Trends in Cognitive Sciences, 5*(6), 236-243.

Goldin-Meadow, S. (2000). Beyond words: The importance of gesture to researchers and learners. *Child Development, 71*(1), 231-239.

Goldman, S.V., and Booker, A. (2009). Making math a definition of the situation: Families as sites for mathematical practices. *Anthropology and Education Quarterly, 40*(4), 369-387.

Goldman, S.R., Britt, M.A., Brown, W., Cribb, C., George, M.A., Greenleaf, C., Lee, C.D., and Shanahan, C. (2016). Disciplinary literacies and learning to read for understanding: A conceptual framework for disciplinary literacy. *Educational Psychologist, 51*(2), 219-246. doi:10.1080/00461520.2016.1168741.

Goldstein, I.L., and Ford, K. (2002). *Training in Organizations: Needs Assessment, Development, and Evaluation* (4th Edition). Belmont, CA: Wadsworth.

Goldstone, R.L. (1996). Isolated and interrelated concepts. *Memory & Cognition, 24*, 608-628.

Gollwitzer, A., Oettingen, G., Kirby, T.A., Duckworth, A.L., and Mayer, D. (2011). Mental contrasting facilitates academic performance in school children. *Motivation and Emotion, 35*(4), 403-412. doi:10.1007/s11031-011-9222-0.

Gonzales, P., Blanton, H., and Williams, K.J. (2002). The effects of stereotype threat and double-minority status on the test performance of Latino women. *Personality and Social Psychology Bulletin, 28*(5), 659-670.

Good, C., Aronson, J., and Harder, J.A. (2008). Problems in the pipeline: Stereotype threat and women's achievement in high-level math courses. *Journal of Applied Developmental Psychology, 29*(1), 17-28. doi:10.1016/j.appdev.2007.10.004.

Good, C., Aronson, J., and Inzlicht, M. (2003). Improving adolescents' standardized test performance: An intervention to reduce the effects of stereotype threat. *Journal of Applied Developmental Psychology, 24*(6), 645-662. doi:10.1016/j.appdev.2003.09.002.

Goodman, M., Finnegan, R., Mohadjer, L., Krenzke, T., and Hogan, J. (2013). *Literacy, Numeracy, and Problem Solving in Technology-Rich Environments Among U.S. Adults: Results from the Program for the International Assessment of Adult Competencies 2012: First Look.* NCES 2014-008. Washington, DC: National Center for Education Statistics. Available: https://nces.ed.gov/pubs2014/2014008.pdf [December 2017].

Goodwin, C. (1994). Professional vision. *American Anthropologist, 96*(3), 606-633.

Goodyear, P., Jones, C., and Thompson, K. (2014). Computer-supported collaborative learning: Instructional approaches, group processes and educational designs. In J.M. Spector, M.D. Merrill, J. Elen, and M.J. Bishop (Eds.), *Handbook of Research on Educational Communications and Technology* (pp. 439-451). New York: Springer. doi:10.1007/978-1-4614-3185-5_35.

Goswami, U. (2002). *Blackwell Handbook of Childhood Cognitive Development.* Hoboken, NJ: John Wiley & Sons.

Goswami, I., and Urminsky, O. (2017). The dynamic effect of incentives on post-reward task engagement. *Journal of Experimental Psychology: General, 146*(1), 1-19.

Gow, A.J., Mortensen, E.L., and Avlund, K. (2012). Activity participation and cognitive aging from age 50 to 80 in the Glostrup 1914 cohort. *Journal of the American Geriatrics Society, 60*(10), 1831-1838.

Grady, C.L., Maisog, J.M., Horwitz, B., Ungerleider, L.G., Mentis, M.J., Salerno, J.A., Pietrini, P., Wagner, E., and Haxby, J.V. (1994). Age-related changes in cortical blood flow activation during visual processing of faces and location. *Journal of Neuroscience, 14*(3, Pt. 2), 1450-1462.

Graesser, A.C. (2013). Evolution of advanced learning technologies in the 21st century. *Theory Into Practice, 52*(Suppl. 1), 93-101.

Graesser, A.C. (2016). Conversations with AutoTutor help students learn. *International Journal of Artificial Intelligence in Education, 26*(1), 124-132.

Graesser, A.C., and Lehman, B. (2012). Questions drive comprehension of text and multimedia. In M.T. McCrudden, J. Magliano, and G. Schraw (Eds.), *Text Relevance and Learning from Text* (pp. 53-74). Greenwich, CT: Information Age.

Graesser, A.C., and Olde, B.A. (2003). How does one know whether a person understands a device? The quality of the questions the person asks when the device breaks down. *Journal of Educational Psychology, 95*(3), 524-536.

Graesser, A.C., Li, H., and Forsyth, C. (2014). Learning by communicating in natural language with conversational agents. *Current Directions in Psychological Science, 23*(5), 374-380.

Graesser, A.C., Lu, S., Jackson, G.T., Mitchell, H.H., Ventura, M., Olney, A. and Louwerse, M.M. (2004). AutoTutor: A tutor with dialogue in natural language. *Behavior Research Methods, Instruments, & Computers, 36*(2), 180-192. doi:10.3758/BF03195563.

Graesser, A.C., Singer, M., and Trabasso, T. (1994). Constructing inferences during narrative text comprehension. *Psychological Review, 101*(3), 371-395.

Graham, S. (1994). Motivation in African Americans. *Review of Educational Research, 64*(1), 55-117.

Graham, S., and Perin, D. (2007). A meta-analysis of writing instruction for adolescent students. *Journal of Educational Psychology, 99*(3), 445-476.

Graham, S., Hebert, M., and Harris, K.R. (2015). Formative assessment and writing: A meta-analysis. *The Elementary School Journal, 115*(4), 523-547.

Grammer, J., Coffman, J.L., and Ornstein, P. (2013). The effect of teachers' memory-relevant language on children's strategy use and knowledge. *Child Development, 84*(6), 1989-2002. doi.org/10.1111/cdev.12100.

Greenberg, D. (2008). The challenges facing adult literacy programs. *Community Literacy Journal, 3*(1), 39-54.

Greenfield, P.M. (2004). *Weaving Generations Together: Evolving Creativity in the Maya of Chiapas* (1st Edition). Santa Fe, NM: School of American Research Press.

Greenfield, P.M. (2009). Linking social change and developmental change: Shifting pathways of human development. *Developmental Psychology, 45*(2), 401-418.

Greeno, J.G., Collins, A.M., and Resnick, L.B. (1996). Cognition and learning. In D. Beliner and R. Calfee (Eds.), *Handbook of Educational Psychology* (pp. 15–46). New York: Macmillan.

Greenough, W.T., Black, J.E., and Wallace, C.S. (1987). Experience and brain development. *Child Development, 58*(3), 539-559.

Gregg, N. (2009). *Adolescents and Adults with Learning Disabilities and ADHD: Assessment and Accommodation*. New York: Guilford Press.

Gregg, N., Coleman, C., David, M., Lindstrom, W., and Hartwig, J. (2006). Critical issues for the diagnosis of learning disabilities in the adult population. *Psychology in the Schools, 43*(8), 889-899.

Gresky, D.M., Ten Eyck, L.L., Lord, C.G., and McIntyre, R.B. (2005). Effects of salient multiple identities on women's performance under mathematics stereotype threat. *Sex Roles, 53*(9-10), 703-716.

Griffin, P., McGaw, B., and Care, E. (2012). *Assessment and Teaching of 21st Century Skills*. New York: Springer.

Grossman, M., Eslinger, P.J., Troiani, V., Anderson, C., Avants, B., Gee, J.C., McMillan, C., Massimo, L., Khan A., and Antani, S. (2010). The role of ventral medial prefrontal cortex in social decisions: Converging evidence from fMRI and frontotemporal lobar degeneration. *Neuropsychologia, 48*(12), 3505-3512.

Gully, S.M., and Chen, G. (2010). Individual differences, attribute-treatment interactions, and training outcomes. In S.W.J. Kozlowski and E. Salas (Eds.), *Learning, Training, and Development in Organizations* (pp. 3–64). San Francisco, CA: Jossey-Bass.

Gully, S.M., Incalcaterra, K.A., Joshi, A., and Beaubien, J.M. (2002). A meta-analysis of team efficacy, potency, and performance: interdependence and level of analysis as moderators of observed relationships. *Journal of Applied Psychology, 87*(5), 819-832.

Gupta, P.M., Perrine, C.G., Mei, Z., and Scanlon, K.S. (2016). Iron, anemia, and iron deficiency anemia among young children in the United States. *Nutrients, 8*(6), 330. doi.org/10.3390/nu8060330.

Gurung, R.A.R., and Daniel, D. (2005). Evidence-based pedagogy: Do pedagogical features enhance student learning? In D.S. Dunn and S.L. Chew (Eds.), *Best Practices for Teaching Introduction to Psychology* (pp. 41-55). Mahwah, NJ: Lawrence Erlbaum Associates.

Gutchess, A.H., Yoon, C., Luo, T., Feinberg, F., Hedden, T., Jing, Q., Nisbett, R.E., and Park, D.C. (2006). Categorical organization in free recall across culture and age. *Gerontology, 52*(5), 314-323.

Guthrie, J.T., Van Meter, P., McCann, A.D., Wigfield, A., Bennett, L., Punndstone, C.C., Rice, M.E., Faibisch, F.M., Hunt, B., and Mitchell, A.M. (1996). Growth of literacy engagement: Changes in motivations and strategies during concept-oriented reading instruction. *Reading Research Quarterly, 31*, 306-332.

Guthrie, J.T., Hoa, L.W., Wigfield, A., Tonks, S.M., and Perencevich, K. C. (2006). From spark to fire: Can situational reading interest lead to long-term reading motivation? *Reading Research and Instruction, 45*, 91-117.

Gutiérrez, K. (2008). Developing a sociocritical literacy in the third space. *Reading Research Quarterly, 43*(2), 148-164.

Gutiérrez, K.D., and Rogoff, B. (2003). Cultural ways of learning: Individual traits or repertoires of practice. *Educational Researcher, 32*(5), 19-25.

Gutiérrez, K., Rymes, B., and Larson, J. (1995). Script, counterscript, and underlife in the classroom: James Brown versus *Brown vs. Board of Education. Harvard Educational Review, 65*(3), 445-471.

Hackman, D.A., and Farah, M.J. (2009). Socioeconomic status and the developing brain. *Trends in Cognitive Sciences, 13*(2), 65-73.

Hackman, J.R., and Oldham, G.R. (1976). Motivation through the design of work: Test of a theory. *Organizational Behavior and Human Performance, 16*(2), 250-279. doi.org/10.1016/0030-5073(76)90016-7.

Hahn, U., and Harris, A.J.L. (2014). What does it mean to be biased: Motivated reasoning and rationality. In B. Ross (Ed.), *The Psychology of Learning and Motivation* (Vol. 61). London, UK: Elsevier.

Hall, D.T., and Mirvis, P.H. (1995). The new career contract: Developing the whole person at midlife and beyond. *Journal of Vocational Behavior, 47*(3), 269-289. doi.org/10.1006/jvbe.1995.0004.

Hall, D.T., and Mirvis, P.H. (2013). Redefining work, work identity, and career success. In D.L. Blustein (Ed.), *The Oxford Handbook of the Psychology of Working* (pp. 203-217). New York: Oxford University Press.

Halvorsen, A., Duke, N.K., Brugar, K.A., Block, M.K., Strachan, S.L., Berka, M.B., and Brown, J.M. (2012). Narrowing the achievement gap in second-grade social studies and content area literacy: The promise of a project-based approach. *Theory and Research in Social Education, 40*(3), 198-229. doi:10.1080/00933104.2012.705954.

Hambrick, D.Z., and Engle, R.W. (2002). Effects of domain knowledge, working memory capacity, and age on cognitive performance: An investigation of the knowledge-is-power hypothesis. *Cognitive Psychology, 44*, 339-387.

Han, J.J., Leichtman, M.D., and Wang, Q. (1998). Autobiographical memory in Korean, Chinese, and American children. *Developmental Psychology, 34*(4), 701-713.

Hanakawa, T., Honda, M., Okada, T., Fukuyama, H., and Shibasaki, H. (2003). Neural correlates underlying mental calculation in abacus experts: A functional magnetic resonance imaging study. *Neuroimage, 19*(2, Pt. 1), 296-307.

Hanselman, P., Rozek, C.S., Grigg, J., and Borman, G.D. (2017). New evidence on self-affirmation effects and theorized sources of heterogeneity from large-scale replications. *Journal of Educational Psychology, 109*(3), 405-424. doi.org/10.1037/edu0000141.

Hapgood, S., Magnusson, S.J., and Palincsar, A.S. (2004). A very science-like kind of thinking: How young children make meaning from first- and second-hand investigations. *Journal of the Learning Sciences, 13*(4), 455-506.

Harackiewicz, J.M., Barron, K.E., Pintrich, P.R., Elliot, A.J., and Thrash, T.M. (2002). Revision of achievement goal theory: Necessary and illuminating. *Journal of Educational Psychology, 94*(3), 638-645. doi.org/10.1037/0022-0663.94.3.638.

Harrison, T.M., Weintraub, S., Mesulam, M., and Rogalski, E. (2012). Superior memory and higher cortical volumes in unusually successful cognitive aging. *Journal of the International Neuropsychological Society, 18*(6), 1081-1085. doi:10.1017/S1355617712000847.

Hartshorne, J.K., and Germine, L.T. (2015). When does cognitive functioning peak? The asynchronous rise and fall of different cognitive abilities across the life span. *Psychological Science, 26*(4), 1-11. doi.org/10.1177/0956797614567339.

Haselton, M.G., and Buss, D.M. (2000). Error management theory: A new perspective on biases in cross-sex mind reading. *Journal of Personality and Social Psychology, 78*(1), 81-91.

Haselton, M.G., and Funder, D.C. (2006). The evolution of accuracy and bias in social judgment. In M. Schaller, J.A. Simpson, and D.T. Kenrick (Eds.), *Evolution and Social Psychology* (pp. 15-37). New York: Psychology Press.

Hasher, L., Lustig, C., and Zacks, R. (2008). Inhibitory mechanisms and the control of attention. In A. Conway, C. Jarrold, M. Kane, A. Miyake, and J. Towse (Eds.), *Variation in Working Memory* (pp. 227-249). New York: Oxford University Press.

Hastings, E.C., and West, R.L. (2011). Goal orientation and self-efficacy in relation to memory in adulthood. *Aging, Neuropsychology, and Cognition, 18*(4), 471-493. doi:10.1080/13825585.2011.575926.

Hatano, G., and Inagaki, K. (1986). Two courses of expertise. In H. Stevenson, J. Azuma, and K. Hakuta (Eds.), *Child Development and Education in Japan* (pp. 262-272). New York: W. H. Freeman & Co.

Hatano, G., and Osawa, K. (1983). Digit memory of grand experts in abacus-derived mental calculation. *Cognition, 15*(1), 95-110.

Hatano, G., and Oura, Y. (2003). Commentary: Reconceptualizing school learning using insight from expertise research. *Educational Researcher, 32,* 26-29.

Hatta, T., and Ikeda, K. (1988). Hemispheric specialization of abacus experts in mental calculation: Evidence from the results of time-sharing tasks. *Neuropsychologia, 26*(6), 877-893. doi.org/10.1016/0028 3932(88)90056-5.

Hattie, J.A.C., and Donoghue, G.M. (2016). Learning strategies: A synthesis and conceptual model. *NPJ Science of Learning, 1*(16013). doi:10.1038/npjscilearn.2016.13.

Hattie, J.A.C., and Timperley, H. (2007). The power of feedback. *Review of Educational Research, 77*(1), 81-112.

Havighurst, R.J. (1961). Successful aging. *The Gerontologist, 1*(1), 8-13. doi:10.1093/geront/1.1.8.

Heckhausen, J., Wrosch, C., and Schulz, R. (2010). A motivational theory of life-span development. *Psychological Review, 117*(1), 32-60.

Hedden, T., and Gabrieli, J.D. (2004). Insights into the ageing mind: A view from cognitive neuroscience. *Nature Reviews Neuroscience, 5*(2), 87-96.

Heffernan, N., and Heffernan, C. (2014). The ASSISTments Ecosystem: Building a Platform that Brings Scientists and Teachers Together for Minimally Invasive Research on Human Learning and Teaching. *International Journal of Artificial Intelligence in Education, 24*(4), 470-497. doi:10.1007/s40593-014-0024-x.

Henderson, L.M., Weighall, A.R., Brown, H., and Gaskell, M.G. (2012). Consolidation of vocabulary is associated with sleep in children. *Developmental Science, 15*(5), 674-687. doi:10.1111/j.1467-7687.2012.01172.x.

Henrich, J., Heine, S.J., and Norenzayan, A. (2010a). Most people are not WEIRD. *Nature, 466*(7302), 29. doi:10.1038/466029a.

Henrich, J., Heine, S.J., and Norenzayan, A. (2010b). The weirdest people in the world? *Behavioral and Brain Sciences, 33*(2-3), 61-83.

Heritage, M. (2009). *The Case for Learning Progressions.* San Francisco, CA: Stupski Foundation.

Heritage, M. (2011). *Developing learning progressions.* Paper presentation at the annual conference of the American Educational Research Association. New Orleans, LA.

Herr-Stephenson, B., Alper, M., Reilly, E. and Jenkins, H. (2013). *T Is for Transmedia: Learning through Transmedia Play.* Los Angeles and New York: USC Annenberg Innovation Lab and The Joan Ganz Cooney Center at Sesame Workshop. Available: http://joanganzcooneycenter. org/wp-content/uploads/2013/03/t_is_for_transmedia.pdf [December 2017].

Hersher, R. (2012). FoldIt game's next play: Crowdsourcing better drug design. *Spoonful of Medicine: A Blog from Nature Medicine,* April 13. Available: http://blogs.nature.com/ spoonful/2012/04/foldit-games-next-play-crowdsourcing-better-drug-design.html?WT. mc_id=TWT_NatureBlogs [November 2017].

Hertzog, C., Kramer, A.F., Wilson, R.S., and Lindenberger, U. (2008). Enrichment effects on adult cognitive development: Can the functional capacity of older adults be preserved and enhanced? *Psychological Science in the Public Interest, 9*(1), 1-65. doi. org/10.1111/j.1539-6053.2009.01034.x.

Herzog, N.B. (2007). Transporting pedagogy: Implementing the project approach in two first grade classrooms. *Journal of Advanced Academics, 18*(4), 530-564.

Hesse, F., Care, E., Buder, J., Sassenberg, K., and Griffin, P. (2015). A framework for teachable collaborative problem solving skills. In P. Griffin and E. Care (Eds.), *Assessment and Teaching of 21st Century Skills* (pp. 37-56). Dordrecht, The Netherlands: Springer.

Heyn, P., Abreu, B.C., and Ottenbacher, K.J. (2004). The effects of exercise training on elderly persons with cognitive impairment and dementia: A meta-analysis. *Archives of Physical Medicine and Rehabilitation, 85*(10), 1694-1704.

Hidi, S., and Renninger, K.A. (2006). The four-phase model of interest development. *Educational Psychologist, 24*(2), 111-127. doi.org/10.1207/s15326985ep4102_4.

Higgins, E., and Ross, B. (2011) Comparisons in category learning: How best to compare for what. In: *Proceedings of the 33rd Annual Conference of the Cognitive Science Society*. Cognitive Science Society, Austin, pp. 1388-1393.

Hillman, C.H., Erickson, K.I., and Kramer, A.F. (2008). Be smart, exercise your heart: Exercise effects on brain and cognition. *Nature Reviews Neuroscience, 9*(1), 58-65.

Hillman, C.H., Pontifex, M.B., Raine, L.B., Castelli, D.M., Hall, E.E., and Kramer, A.F. (2009). The effect of acute treadmill walking on cognitive control and academic achievement in preadolescent children. *Neuroscience, 159*(3), 1044-1054. doi:10.1016/j.neuroscience.2009.01.057.

Hirschfeld, L.A., and Gelman, S.A. (1994). *Mapping the Mind: Domain-Specificity in Culture and Cognition*. New York: Cambridge University Press.

Hirsh-Pasek, K., Zosh, J.M., Golinkoff, R.M., Gray, J.H., Robb, M.B., and Kaufman, J. (2015). Putting education in "educational" apps lessons from the science of learning. *Psychological Science in the Public Interest, 16*(1), 3-34. doi:10.1177/1529100615569721.

Hirshkowitz, M., Whiton, K., Albert, S.M., Alessi, C., Bruni, O., DonCarlos, L., Hazen, N., Herman, J., Katz, E.S., Kheirandish-Gozal, L., Neubauer, D.N., O'Donnell, A.E., Ohayon, M., Peever, J., Rawding, R., Schdeva, R.C., Setters, B., Vitiello, M.V., Ware, J. C., and Hillard, P.J.A. (2015). National Sleep Foundation's sleep time duration recommendations: Methodology and results summary. *Sleep Health: Journal of the National Sleep Foundation, 1*(1), 40-43. Available: https://sleepfoundation.org/sites/default/files/STREPchanges_1.png [December 2017].

Hirst, W., Phelps, E.A., Meksin, R., Vaidya, C.J., Johnson, M.K., Mitchell, K.J., Buckner, R.L., Budson, A.E., Gabrieli, J.D., Lustig, C., Mather, M., Ochsner, K.N., Schacter, D., Simons, J.S., Lyle, K.B., Cuc, A.F., and Olsson, A. (2015). A ten-year follow-up of a study of memory for the attack of September 11, 2001: Flashbulb memories and memories for flashbulb events. *Journal of Experimental Psychology: General, 144*(3), 604-623. doi:10.1037/xge0000055.

Hmelo-Silver, C.E. (2004). Problem-based learning: What and how do students learn? *Educational Psychology Review, 16*, 235-266.

Hock, M.F. (2012). Effective literacy instruction for adults with specific learning disabilities: Implications for adult educators. *Journal of Learning Disabilities, 45*(1), 64-78. doi.org/10.1177/0022219411426859.

Hoeft, F., Meyler, A., Hernandez, A., Juel, C., Taylor-Hill, H., Martindale, J.L., McMillon, G., Kolchugina, G., Black, J.M., Faizi, A., Deutsch, G.K., Siok, W.T., Reiss, A.L., Whitfield-Gabrieli, S., and Gabrieli, J.E. (2007). Functional and morphometric brain dissociation between dyslexia and reading ability. *Proceedings of the National Academy of Sciences of the United States of America, 104*(10), 4234-4239. doi:10.1073/pnas.0609399104.

Hoffman, B. (2006). *The Encyclopedia of Educational Technology*. San Diego, CA: Montezuma Press.

Hoffmann, L., and Haussler, P. (1998). An intervention project promoting girls' and boys' interest in physics. In L. Hoffmann, A. Krapp, K.A. Renninger, and J. Baumert (Eds.), *Interest and Learning: Proceedings of the Seeon Conference on Interest and Gender* (pp. 301-316). Kiel, Germany: IPN.

Hofstede, G. (1997). *Cultures and Organizations: Software of the Mind*. New York: McGraw Hill.

Hollan, J., Hutchins, E., and Kirsh, D. (2000). Distributed cognition: Toward a new foundation for human-computer interaction research. *ACM Transactions on Computer-Human Interaction (TOCHI), 7*(2), 174-196.

Holmes, J., Gathercole, S.E., and Dunning, D. (2009). Adaptive training leads to sustained enhancement of poor working memory in children. *Developmental Science, 12*(4), F9-F15. doi:10.1111/j.1467-7687.2009.00848.x.

Holyoak, K.J., Junn, E.N., and Billman, D.O. (1984). Development of analogical problem-solving skill. *Child Development, 55*(6), 2042-2055.

Hong, H.Y., and Lin-Siegler, X. (2012). How learning about scientists' struggles influences students' interest and learning in physics. *Journal of Educational Psychology, 104*(2), 469-484.

Hsu, C.-K., Hwang, G.-J., and Chang, C.-K. (2013). A personalized recommendation-based mobile learning approach to improving the reading performance of EFL students. *Computers & Education, 63*, 327-336. doi.org/10.1016/j.compedu.2012.12.004.

Hu, X., Craig, S.D., Bargagliotti A.E., Graesser, A.C., Okwumabua, T., Anderson, C., Cheney, K.R., and Sterbinsky, A. (2012). The effects of a traditional and technology-based after-school program on 6th grade students' mathematics skills. *Journal of Computers in Mathematics and Science Teaching, 31*(1), 17-38.

Hulleman, C.S., Durik, A.M., Schweigert, S., and Harackiewicz, J.M. (2008). Task values, achievement goals, and interest: An integrative analysis. *Journal of Educational Psychology, 100*(2), 398-416.

Hulleman, C.S., Schrager, S.M., Bodmann, S.M., and Harackiewicz, J.M. (2010). A meta-analytic review of achievement goal measures: Different labels for the same constructs or different constructs with similar labels? *Psychological Bulletin, 136*(3), 422-449. doi:10.1037/a0018947.

Hunsu, N.J., Adesope, O., and Van Wie, B.J. (2017). Engendering situational interest through innovative instruction in an engineering classroom: What really mattered? *Instructional Science, 45*(6), 789-804. doi.org/10.1007/s11251-017-9427-z.

Hurley, S., and Chater, N. (Eds.). (2005). *Perspectives on Imitation: From Neuroscience to Social Science.* Cambridge, MA: MIT Press.

Hurley, E.A., Boykin, W.A., and Allen, B.A. (2005). Communal versus individual learning of a math-estimation task: African-American children and the culture of learning contexts. *Journal of Psychology, 139*(6), 513-527.

Hurley, E.A., Allen, B.A., and Boykin, A.W. (2009). Culture and the interaction of student ethnicity with reward structure in group learning. *Cognition and Instruction, 27*(2), 121-164.

Huttenlocher, J., Vasilyeva, M., Cymerman, E., and Levine, S. (2002). Language input and child syntax. *Cognitive Psychology, 45*(3), 337-374.

Iglowstein, I., Jenni, O.G., Molinari, L., and Largo, R.H. (2003). Sleep duration from infancy to adolescence: Reference values and generational trends. *Pediatrics, 111*(2), 302-307.

Ikeda, K., Castel, A.D., and Murayama, K. (2015). Mastery-approach goals eliminate retrieval-induced forgetting: The role of achievement goals in memory inhibition. *Personality and Social Psychology Bulletin, 41*(5), 687-695. doi.org/10.1177/0146167215575730.

Immordino-Yang, M.H. (2015). *Emotions, Learning and the Brain: Exploring the Educational Implications of Affective Neuroscience.* New York: W.W. Norton and Company.

Immordino-Yang, M.H., and Damasio, A.R. (2007). We feel, therefore we learn: The relevance of affective and social neuroscience to education. *Mind, Brain and Education, 1*(1), 3-10.

Immordino-Yang, M.H., and Fischer, K.W. (2010). Brain development. In I. Weiner and E. Craighead (Eds.), *Corsini Encyclopedia of Psychology* (4th ed., pp. 254-256). New York: John Wiley & Sons.

Immordino-Yang, M.H., and Gotlieb, R. (2017). Embodied brains, social minds, cultural meaning: Integrating neuroscientific and educational research on social-affective development. *American Educational Research Journal: Centennial Issue, 54*(1), 344S-367S. Available: http://journals.sagepub.com/doi/abs/10.3102/0002831216669780 [November 2017].

Immordino-Yang, M.H., and Sylvan, L. (2010). Admiration for virtue: Neuroscientific perspectives on a motivating emotion. *Contemporary Educational Psychology, 35*(2), 110-115.

Immordino-Yang, M.H., McColl, A., Damasio, H., and Damasio, A. (2009). Neural correlates of admiration and compassion. *Proceedings of the National Academy of Sciences of the United States of America, 106*(19), 8021-8026.

Immordino-Yang, M.H., Christodoulou, J., and Singh, V. (2012). Rest is not idleness: Implications of the brain's default mode for human development and education. *Perspectives on Psychological Science, 7*(4), 352-364.

Immordino-Yang, M.H., Yang, X., and Damasio, H. (2014). Correlations between social-emotional feelings and anterior insula activity are independent from visceral states but influenced by culture. *Frontiers in Human Neuroscience, 8*, 728. doi:10.3389/fnhum.2014.00728.

Institute of Medicine. (2000). *From Neurons to Neighborhoods: The Science of Early Childhood Development*. Washington, DC: National Academy Press.

Institute of Medicine. (2006). *Sleep Disorders and Sleep Deprivation: An Unmet Public Health Problem*. Washington, DC: The National Academies Press.

Institute of Medicine. (2011). *Early Childhood Obesity Prevention Policies*. Washington, DC: The National Academies Press.

Institute of Medicine and National Research Council. (2015). *Transforming the Workforce for Children Birth Through Age 8: A Unifying Foundation*. Washington, DC: The National Academies Press.

Ionas, I.G., Cernusca, D., and Collier, H.L. (2012). Prior knowledge influence on self-explanation effectiveness when solving problems: An exploratory study in science learning. *International Journal of Teaching and Learning in Higher Education, 24*(3), 349-358.

Ito, M., Baumer, S., Bittanti, M., Boyd, D., Cody, R., Herr-Stephenson, R., Horst, H.A., Lange, P.G., Mahendran, D., Martínez, K.,Z., Pascoe, C.J., Perkel, D., Robinson, L., Sims, C., and Tripp, L. (2009). *Hanging Out, Messing Around, Geeking Out: Living and Learning with New Media*. Cambridge, MA: MIT Press.

Izuma, K., Saito, D.N., and Sadato, N. (2010). Processing of the incentive for social approval in the ventral striatum during charitable donation. *Journal of Cognitive Neuroscience, 22*(4), 621-631. doi:10.1162/jocn.2009.21228.

Jacini, W.F., Cannonieri, G.C., Fernandes, P.T., Bonilha, L., Cendes, F., and Li, L.M. (2009). Can exercise shape your brain? Cortical differences associated with judo practice. *Journal of Science and Medicine in Sport, 12*(6), 688-690. doi:10.1016/j.jsams.2008.11.004.

Jackson, G.T., and McNamara, D.S. (2013). Motivation and performance in a game-based intelligent tutoring system. *Journal of Educational Psychology, 105*(4), 1036-1049. doi.org/10.1037/a0032580.

Jackson, M.L., Gunzelmann, G., Whitney, P., Hinson, J.M., Belenky, G., Rabat, A., and Van Dongen, H.P. (2013). Deconstructing and reconstructing cognitive performance in sleep deprivation. *Sleep Medicine Reviews, 17*(3), 215-225.

Jacobs, J., Lanza, S., Osgood, D. W., Eccles, J.S., and Wigfield, A. (2002). Changes in children's self-competence and values: Gender and domain differences across grades one through twelve. *Child Development, 73*(2), 509-527.

Jäncke, L., Koeneke, S., Hoppe, A., Rominger, C., and Hänggi, J. (2009) The architecture of the golfer's brain. *PLoS One, 4*(3), e4785. doi.org/10.1371/journal.pone.0004785.

Janiszewski, C., Noel, H., and Sawyer, A.G. (2003). A meta-analysis of spacing effect in verbal learning: Implications for research on advertising repetition and consumer memory. *Journal of Consumer Research, 30*(1), 138-149.

Järvelä, S., and Renninger, K.A. (2014). Designing for learning: Interest, motivation, and engagement. In R.K. Sawyer (Ed.), *Cambridge Handbook of the Learning Sciences* (2nd ed., pp. 668-685). New York: Cambridge University Press.

Jenkins, H., Purushotma, R., Clinton, K., Weigel, M., and Robison, A.J. (2006). *Confronting the Challenges of Participatory Culture: Media Education for the 21st Century*. Chicago, IL: MacArthur Foundation.

Ji, L.-J., Guo, T., Zhang, Z., and Messervey, D. (2009). Looking into the past: Cultural differences in perception and representation of past information. *Journal of Personality and Social Psychology, 96*(4), 761-769. doi:10.1037/a0014498.

John-Steiner, V., and Mahn, H. (1996). Sociocultural approaches to learning and development: A Vygotskian framework. *Educational Psychologist, 31*(3/4), 191-206.

Johns, M., Inzlicht, M., and Schmader, T. (2008). Stereotype threat and executive resource depletion: Examining the influence of emotion regulation. *Journal of Experimental Psychology: General, 137*(4), 691-705. doi.org/10.1037/a0013834.

Johnson, D.W., Johnson, R.T., and Stanne, M.E. (2000). *Cooperative Learning Methods: A Meta-Analysis.* Minneapolis: University of Minnesota, Cooperative Learning Center. Available: https://www.researchgate.net/profile/David_Johnson50/publication/220040324_Cooperative_learning_methods_A_meta-analysis/links/00b4952b39d258145c000000/Cooperative-learning-methods-A-meta-analysis.pdf [December 2017].

Johnson, W.L., and Valente, A. (2009). Tactical language and culture training systems: Using AI to teach foreign languages and cultures. *AI Magazine, 30*(2), 72-83.

Jones, P.D., and Holding, D.H. (1975). Extremely long-term persistence of the McCollough effect. *Journal of Experimental Psychology: Human Perception and Performance, 1*(4), 323-327.

Jordan, S., and Lande, M. (2014). Might young makers be the engineers of the future? In *Proceedings of the IEEE Frontiers in Education (FIE) Conference* (pp. 1-4). Available: http://ieeexplore.ieee.org/document/7044218 [December 2017]. doi.org/10.1109/FIE.2014.7044218.

Jurado, M.B., and Rosselli, M. (2007). The elusive nature of executive functions: A review of our current understanding. *Neuropsychology Review, 17*(3), 213-233.

Kafai, Y.B. (2010). The world of Whyville: Living, playing, and learning in a tween virtual world. *Games and Culture, 5*(1), 3-22. doi:10.1177/1555412009351264.

Kahan, D.M., Peters., E., Wittlin, M., Slovic, P., Ouellette, L.L., Braman, D., and Mandel, G. (2012). The polarizing impact of science literacy and numeracy on perceived climate change risks. *Nature Climate Change, 2*, 732-735. doi:10.1038/nclimate1547.

Kahraman, N., and Sungur, S. (2011). The contribution of motivational beliefs to students' metacognitive strategy use. *Education and Science, 36*(160), 3-10.

Kail, R.V., and Miller, C.A. (2006). Developmental changes in processing speed: Domain specificity and stability during childhood and adolescence. *Journal of Cognition and Development, 7*(1), 119-137. doi.org/10.1207/s15327647jcd0701_6.

Kalakoski, V., and Saariluoma, P. (2001). Taxi drivers' exceptional memory of street names. *Memory & Cognition, 29*(4), 634-638.

Kaldi, S., Filippatou, D., and Govaris, C. (2011). Project-based learning in primary schools: Effects on pupils' learning and attitudes. *Education, 39*(1), 35-47. doi:10.1080/03004270903179538.

Kanfer, R. (2015). Motivation. *Wiley Encyclopedia of Management, 11*, 1-8.

Kanfer, R., and Ackerman, P.L. (2008). Aging and work motivation. In C. Wankel (Ed.) *Handbook of 21st Century Management* (pp. 106-109). Thousand Oaks, CA: Sage.

Kang, S.H.K. (2016). Spaced repetition promotes efficient and effective learning: Policy implications for instruction. *Policy Insights from the Behavioral and Brain Sciences, 3*(1), 12-19. doi:10.1177/2372732215624708.

Kaplan, A., and Maehr, M.L. (1999). Achievement goals and student well-being. *Contemporary Educational Psychology, 24*(4), 330-358.

Kaplan, A., and Midgley, C. (1999). The relationship between perceptions of the classroom goal structure and early adolescents' affect in school: The mediating role of coping strategies. *Learning and Individual Differences, 11*(2), 187-212. doi.org/10.1016/S1041-6080(00)80005-9.

Karasek, R., Brisson, C., Kawakami, N., Houtman, I., Bongers, P., and Amick, B. (1998). The Job Content Questionnaire (JCQ), An instrument for internationally comparative assessments of psychosocial job characteristics. *Journal of Occupational Health Psychology, 3*(4), 322-355. doi.org/10.1037/1076-8998.3.4.322.

Karasik, L.B., Adolph, K.E., Tamis-LeMonda, C.S., and Bornstein, M.H. (2010). WEIRD walking: Cross-cultural research on motor development. *The Behavioral and Brain Sciences, 33*(2-3), 95-96.

Karmiloff-Smith, A. (1986). From meta-processes to conscious access: Evidence from children's metalinguistic and repair data. *Cognition, 23*(2), 95-147.

Karmiloff-Smith, A. (1990). Constraints on representational change: Evidence from children's drawing. *Cognition, 34*(1), 57-83.

Karpicke, J.D. (2016). A powerful way to improve learning and memory: Practicing retrieval enhances long-term, meaningful learning. *American Psychological Association Psychological Science Agenda*, June. Available: http://www.apa.org/science/about/psa/2016/06/learning-memory.aspx [December 2017].

Karpicke, J.D., Butler, A.C., and Roediger, H.L. (2009). Metacognitive strategies in student learning: Do students practice retrieval when they study on their own? *Memory, 17*(4), 471-479. doi:10.1080/09658210802647009.

Kataria, S., Swanson, M.S., and Trevathan, G.E. (1987). Persistence of sleep disturbances in preschool children. *Journal of Pediatrics, 110*(4), 642-646.

Kaufmann, L., Wood, G., Rubinsten, O., and Henik, A. (2011). Meta-analyses of developmental fMRI studies investigating typical and atypical trajectories of number processing and calculation. *Developmental Neuropsychology, 36*(6), 763-787. doi.org/10.1080/87565641.2010.549884.

Kay, R.H., and LeSage, A. (2009). A strategic assessment of audience response systems used in higher education. *Australian Journal of Educational Technology, 25*(2), 235-249.

Keeley, T.J., and Fox, K.R. (2009). The impact of physical activity and fitness on academic achievement and cognitive performance in children. *International Review of Sport and Exercise Psychology, 2*(2), 198-214.

Keith, N., and Frese, M. (2008). Effectiveness of error management training: A meta-analysis. *Journal of Applied Psychology, 93*(1), 59-69. doi.org/10.1037/0021-9010.93.1.59.

Keller, H., Borke, J., Staufenbiel, T., Yovsi, R.D., Abels, M., Papaligoura, Z., Jensen, H., Lohaus, A., Chaudhary, N, Lo, W., and Su, Y. (2009). Distal and proximal parenting as alternative parenting strategies during infants' early months of life: A cross-cultural study. *International Journal of Behavioral Development, 33*, 412-420.

Keller, J. (2007). Stereotype threat in classroom settings: The interactive effect of domain identification, task difficulty and stereotype threat on female students' maths performance. *British Journal of Educational Psychology, 77*(Pt. 2), 323-338. doi:10.1348/000709906X113662.

Keller, H. (2017). Culture and development: A systematic relationship. *Perspectives on Psychological Science, 12*(5), 833-840. doi.org/10.1177/1745691617704097.

Kellman, P.J., Massey, C.M., and Son, J.Y. (2010). Perceptual learning modules in mathematics: Enhancing students' pattern recognition, structure extraction, and fluency. *Topics in Cognitive Science, 2*(2), 285-305.

Kemmelmeier, M., and Chavez, H.L. (2014). Biases in the perception of Barack Obama's skin tone. *Analyses of Social Issues and Public Policy, 14*, 137-161. doi 10.1111/asap.12061.

Kempton, W. (1986). Two theories of home heat control. *Cognitive Science, 10*(1), 75-90. doi.org/10.1016/S0364-0213(86)80009-X.

Kensinger, E.A. (2016, unpublished). *Learning in Middle and Late Adulthood*. Paper commissioned by the Committee on the Science of Practice and Learning, National Academies of Sciences, Engineering, and Medicine, Washington, DC.

Kershner, R., Mercer, N., Warwick, P., and Kleine Staarman, J. (2010). Can the interactive whiteboard support young children's collaborative communication and thinking in classroom science activities? *Computer-supported Collaborative Learning, 5*(4), 359-383.

Keunen, K., Counsell, S.J., and Benders, M.J.N.L. (2017). The emergence of functional architecture during early brain development. *NeuroImage, 160*, 2-14. doi.org/10.1016/j.neuroimage.2017.01.047.

Keuroghlian, A.S., and Knudsen, E.I. (2007). Adaptive auditory plasticity in developing and adult animals. *Progress in Neurobiology, 82*(3), 109-121. doi:10.1016/j.pneurobio.2007.03.005.

Khatib, F., Dimaio, F., Cooper, S., Kazmierczyk, M., Gilski, M., Krzywda, S., Zabranska, H., Pichova, I., and Thompson, J. (2011). Crystal structure of a monomeric retroviral protease solved by protein folding game players. *Nature Structural & Molecular Biology, 18*(10), 1175-1177. doi:10.1038/nsmb.2119.

Kim, J.I., Schallert, D.L., and Kim, M. (2010). An integrative cultural view of achievement motivation: Parental and classroom predictors of children's goal orientations when learning mathematics in Korea. *Journal of Educational Psychology, 102*(2), 418-437. doi:10.1037/a0018676.

King, R.B. (2015). Examining the dimensional structure and nomological network of achievement goals in the Philippines. *Journal of Adolescence, 44*, 214-218. doi:10.1016/j.adolescence.2015.07.019.

King, R.B., and McInerney, D.M. (2016). Culture and motivation: The road travelled and the way ahead. In K. Wentzel and D. Miele (Eds.), *Handbook of Motivation at School* (2nd Edition) (pp. 275-299). New York: Routledge.

Kingston, N., and Nash, B. (2011). Formative assessment: A meta-analysis and a call for research. *Educational Measurement: Issues and Practice, 30*(4), 28-37.

Kirkland, D.E. (2008). The rose that grew from concrete: Postmodern blackness and New English education. *English Journal, 97*(5), 69-75.

Kirkpatrick, D.L. (1967). Evaluation of training. In R.L. Craig and L.R. Bittel (Eds.), *Training and Development Handbook* (pp. 87-112). New York: McGraw-Hill.

Kirschner, P.A., and Paas, F. (2001). Web-enhanced higher education: A tower of Babel. *Computers in Human Behavior, 17*(4), 347-353.

Kitayama, S., and Cohen, D. (2007). *Handbook of Cultural Psychology*. New York: Guilford.

Kitayama, S., and Park, J. (2010). Cultural neuroscience of the self: Understanding the social grounding of the brain. *Social Cognitive and Affective Neuroscience, 5*(2), 111-129. doi:10.1093/scan/nsq052.

Kitayama, S., and Tompson, S. (2010). Envisioning the future of cultural neuroscience. *Asian Journal of Social Psychology, 13*(2), 92-101.

Kitayama, S., and Uskul, A.K. (2011). Culture, mind, and the brain: Current evidence and future directions. *Annual Review of Psychology, 62*(1), 419-449. doi:10.1146/annurev-psych-120709-145357.

Kitayama, S., Matsumoto, H., and Norasakkunkit, V. (1997). Individual and collective processes in the construction of the self: Self-enhancement in the United States and self-criticism in Japan. *Journal of Personality and Social Psychology, 72*(6), 1245-1267.

Kitayama, S., Yanagisawa, K., Ito, A., Ueda, R., Uchida, Y, and Abe, N. (2017). Reduced orbitofrontal cortical volume is associated with interdependent self-construal. *Proceedings of the National Academy of Sciences of the United States of America, 114*(30), 7969-7974. doi:10.1073/pnas.1704831114.

Klein, C., DeRouin, R.E., and Salas, E. (2006). Uncovering workplace interpersonal skills: A review, framework, and research agenda. In G.P. Hodgkinson and J.K. Ford (Eds.), *International Review of Industrial and Organizorganisational Psychology* (vol. 21, pp. 80-126). New York: John Wiley & Sons.

Koedinger, K.R., Anderson, J.R., Hadley, W.H., and Mark, M.A. (1997). Intelligent tutoring goes to school in the big city. *International Journal of Artificial Intelligence in Education, 8*, 30-43. Available: http://repository.cmu.edu/cgi/viewcontent.cgi?article=1000&context=hcii [December 2017].

Koedinger, K.R., Corbett, A.T., and Perfetti, C. (2012). The knowledge-learning-instruction framework: Bridging the science-practice chasm to enhance robust student learning. *Cognitive Science, 36*(5), 757-798.

Koedinger, K.R., Booth, J.L., and Klahr, D. (2013). Instructional complexity and the science to constrain it. *Science, 342*, 935-937.

Koller, K., Brown, T., Spurgeon, A., and Levy, L. (2004). Recent developments in low-level lead exposure and intellectual impairment in children. *Environmental Health Perspectives, 112*(9), 987-994. doi.org/10.1289/ehp.6941.

Kolodner, J.L., Camp, P.L., Crismond, D., Fasse, B., Gray, J., Holbrook, J., Puntambekar, S., and Ryan, M. (2003). Problem-based learning meets case-based reasoning in the middle school science classroom: Putting Learning by Design™ into practice. *Journal of the Learning Sciences, 4*, 495-547.

Kooij, D.T.A.M., de Lange, A.H., Jansen, P.G.W., Kanfer, R., and Dikkers, J.S.E. (2011). Age and work-related motives: Results of a meta-analysis. *Journal of Organizational Behavior, 32*(2), 197-225. doi:10.1002/job.665.

Kornell, N. (2014). Attempting to answer a meaningful question enhances subsequent learning even when feedback is delayed. *Journal of Experimental Psychology: Learning, Memory, and Cognition, 40*(1), 106-114. doi:10.1037/a0033699.

Kornell, N., and Bjork, R.A. (2008). Learning concepts and categories: Is spacing the "enemy of induction?" *Psychological Science, 19*(6), 585-592. doi:10.1111/j.1467-9280.2008.02127.x.

Kornell, N., and Son, L.K. (2009). Learners' choices and beliefs about self-testing. *Memory, 17*(5), 493-501. doi:10.1080/09658210902832915.

Kroll, J.F., Dussias, P.E., Bogulski, C.A., and Valdes-Kroff, J. (2012). Juggling two languages in one mind: What bilinguals tell us about language processing and its consequences for cognition. In B. Ross (Ed.), *The Psychology of Learning and Motivation* (vol. 56, pp. 229-262). San Diego, CA: Academic Press.

Kronenfeld, D.B., Bennardo, G., de Munck, V.C. and Fischer, M.D. (eds). (2011). *A Companion to Cognitive Anthropology*. Hoboken, NJ: Blackwell.

Kruidenier, J. (2002). *Research-based Principles for Adult Basic Education*. Washington, DC: National Institute for Literacy.

Kubeck, J.E., Delp, N.D., Haslett, T.K., and McDaniel, M.A. (1996). Does job-related training performance decline with age? *Psychology and Aging, 11*(1), 92-107.

Kuh, G.D. (2008). *High-Impact Educational Practices: What They Are, Who Has Access to Them, and Why They Matter*. Washington, DC: Association of American Colleges and Universities. Available: https://keycenter.unca.edu/sites/default/files/aacu_high_impact_2008_final.pdf [December 2017].

Kuhl, P.K., Williams, K.A., Lacerda, F., Stevens, K.N., and Lindblom, B. (1992). Linguistic experience alters phonetic perception in infants by 6 months of age. *Science, 255*(5044), 606-608.

Kulik, J.A., and Fletcher, J.D. (2016). Effectiveness of intelligent tutoring systems: A meta-analytic review. *Review of Educational Research, 86*(1), 42-78. doi:10.3102/0034654315581420.

Kulkofsky, S., Wang, Q., and Koh, J.B.K. (2009). Functions of memory sharing and mother-child reminiscing behaviors: Individual and cultural variations. *Journal of Cognition and Development, 10*(1-2), 92-114.

Kutner, M., Greenberg, E., Jin, Y., Boyle, B., Hsu, Y., Dunleavy, E., and White, S. (2007). *Literacy in Everyday Life: Results from the 2003 National Assessment of Adult Literacy*. NCES 2007-480. Washington, DC: National Center for Education Research.

Ladson-Billings, G. (1995). Toward a theory of culturally relevant pedagogy. *American Educational Research Journal, 32*, 465-491.

Ladson-Billings, G. (2006). From the achievement gap to the education debt: Understanding achievement in U.S. schools. *Educational Researcher, 35*(7), 3-12.

Lake, B.M., Salakhutdinov, R., and Tenenbaum, J.B. (2015). Human-level concept learning through probabilitic program induction. *Science, 350*, 1332-1338.

Lake, B.M., Ullman, T.D., Tenenbaum, J.B., and Gershman, S.J. (2017). Building machines that learn and think like people. *Behavioral and Brain Sciences, e253*. doi:10.1017/S0140525X16001837.

Lamm, B., Keller, H., Teiser, J., Gudi, H., Yovsi, R.D., Freitag, C., Poloczek, S., Fassbender, I., Suhrke, J., Teubert, M., Vöhringer, I., Knopf, M., Schwarzer, G., and Lohaus, A. (2017). Waiting for the second treat: Developing culture-specific modes of self-regulation. *Child Development*. doi:10.1111/cdev.12847.

Landerl, K., Ramus, F., Moll, K., Lyytinen, H., Leppänen, P.H.T., Lohvansuu, K., O'Donovan, M., Williams, J., Bartling, J., Bruder, J., Kunze, S., Neuhoff, N., Tóth, D., Honbolygó, F., Csépe, V., Bogliotti, C., Iannuzzi, S., Chaix, Y., Démonet, J.-F., Longeras, E., Valdois, S., Chabernaud, C., Delteil-Pinton, F., Billard, C., George, F., Ziegler, J.C., Comte-Gervais, I., Soares-Boucaud, I., Gérard, C.-L., Blomert, L., Vaessen, A., Gerretsen, P., Ekkebus, M., Brandeis, D., Maurer, U., Schulz, E., van der Mark, S., Müller-Myhsok, B., and Schulte-Körne, G. (2013), Predictors of developmental dyslexia in European orthographies with varying complexity. *Journal of Child Psychology and Psychiatry, 54*(6), 686-694. doi:10.1111/jcpp.12029.

Lareau, A. (2011). *Unequal Childhoods: Class, Race, and Family Life, with an Update a Decade Later.* Berkeley: University of California Press.

Lauderdale, D.S., Knutson, K.L., Yan, L.L., Rathouz, P.J., Hulley, S.B., Sidney, S., and Liu, K. (2006). Objectively measured sleep characteristics among early-middle-aged adults: The Cardia Study. *American Journal of Epidemiology, 164*(1), 5-16.

Lave, J., and Wenger, E. (1991). *Situated Learning: Legitimate Peripheral Participation.* Cambridge, MA: Cambridge University Press.

Lawless, K.A., and Pellegrino, J.W. (2007). Professional development in integrating technology into teaching and learning: Knowns, unknowns, and ways to pursue better questions and answers. *Review of Educational Research, 77*(4), 575-614.

Lawrence, J.S., Marks, B.T., and Jackson, J.S. (2010). Domain identification predicts black students' underperformance on moderately difficult tests. *Motivation and Emotion, 34*(2), 105-109.

Lazar, S.W., Kerr, C.E., Wasserman, R.H., Gray, J.R., Greve, D.N., Treadway, M.T., McGarvey, M., Quinn, B.T., Dusek, J.A., Benson, H., Rauch, S.L., Moore, C.I., and Fischl, B. (2005). Meditation experience is associated with increased cortical thickness. *Neuroreport, 16*(17), 1893-1897.

Lazowski, R.A., and Hulleman, C.S. (2016). Motivation interventions in education: A meta-analytic review. *Review of Educational Research, 86*(2), 602-640. doi:10.3102/0034654315617832.

Lee, C.D. (2001). Is October Brown Chinese? A cultural modeling activity system for underachieving students. *American Educational Research Journal, 38*(1), 97-141.

Lee, C.D. (2006). "Every good-bye ain't gone": Analyzing the cultural underpinnings of classroom talk. *International Journal of Qualitative Studies in Education, 19*(3), 305-327.

Lee, Y.J. (2012). Identity-based research in science education. In B.J. Fraser., K. Tobin., and C.J. McRobbie (Eds.), *Second International Handbook of Science Education* (pp. 34-45). Dordrecht, The Netherlands: Springer.

Lee, H.S., and Anderson, J.R. (2013). Student learning: What has instruction got to do with it? *Annual Review of Psychology, 64*, 445-469. doi:10.1146/annurev-psych-113011-143833.

Lee, C.D., Spencer, M.B., and Harpalani, V. (2003). Every shut eye ain't sleep: Studying how people live culturally. *Educational Researcher, 32*(5), 6-13.

Lee, C.D., Goldman, S.R., Levine, S., and Magliano, J.P. (2016). Epistemic cognition in literary reasoning. In J. Green, W. Sandoval, and I. Braten (Eds.), *Handbook of Epistemic Cognition* (pp. 165-183). New York: Routledge.

Lehman, B., D'Mello, S., Strain, A., and Graesser, A. (2013). Inducing and tracking confusion with contradictions during complex learning. *International Journal of Artificial Intelligence in Education, 22*(1-2), 85-105.

Leichtman, M.D., Pillemer, D.B., Wang, Q., Koreishi, A., and Han, J.J. (2000). When Baby Maisy came to school: Mothers' interview styles and preschoolers' event memories. *Cognitive Development, 15*(1), 99-114.

Leisman, G. (2011). Brain networks, plasticity, and functional connectivities inform current directions in functional neurology and rehabilitation. *Functional Neurology, Rehabilitation, and Ergonomics, 1*, 315-356.

Leisman, G., Rodriguez-Rojas, R., Batista, K., Carballo, M., Morales, J.M., Iturria, Y., and Machado, C. (2014). Measurement of axonal fiber connectivity in consciousness evaluation. In *Proceedings of the 2014 IEEE 28th Convention of Electrical and Electronics Engineers in Israel.* Minneapolis, MN: IEEE. doi.org/10.13140/2.1.4845.7289.

Leisman, G., Mualem, R., and Mughrabi, S.K. (2015). The neurological development of the child with the educational enrichment in mind. *Psicología Educativa, 21*(2), 79-96. doi. org/10.1016/j.pse.2015.08.006.

Lemke, J.L. (1990). *Talking Science: Language, Learning, and Values.* Norwood, NJ: Ablex.

Lemke, J.L., Lecusay, R., Cole, M., and Michalchik, V. (2015). *Documenting and Assessing Learning in Informal and Media-Rich Environments.* Cambridge, MA: MIT Press.

Lenehan, M.E., Summers, M.J., Saunders, N.L., Summers, J.J., Ward, D.D., Ritchie, K., and Vickers, J.C. (2016). Sending your grandparents to university increases cognitive reserve: The Tasmanian Healthy Brain Project. *Neuropsychology, 30*(5), 525-531. doi:10.1037/neu0000249.

Lenhart, A. (2015). *Teen, Social Media and Technology Overview 2015.* Pew Research Center. Available: http://www.pewinternet.org/2015/04/09/teens-social-media-technology-2015/# [January 2018].

Lenroot, R.K., and Giedd, J.N. (2006). Brain development in children and adolescents: Insights from anatomical magnetic resonance imaging. *Neuroscience Biobehavioral Review, 30*(6), 718-729.

Lent, R.W., Brown, S.D., and Hackett, G. (2000). Contextual supports and barriers to career choice: A social cognitive analysis. *Journal of Counseling Psychology, 47*(1), 36-49.

Leopold, C., and Leutner, D. (2012). Science text comprehension: Drawing, main idea selection, and summarizing as learning strategies. *Learning and Instruction, 22*(1), 16-26. doi:10.1016/j.learninstruc.2011.05.005.

Leppänen, J.M., and Nelson, C.A. (2009). Tuning the developing brain to social signals of emotions. *Nature Reviews Neuroscience, 10,* 37-47.

Leppänen, P.H., Hamalainen, J.A., Guttorm, T.K., Eklund, K.M., Salminen, H., Tanskanen, A., and Lyytinen, H. (2012). Infant brain responses associated with reading-related skills before school and at school age. *Neurophysiologie Clinique, 42*(1-2), 35-41. doi:10.1016/j.neucli.2011.08.005.

Lepper, M.R., Corpus, J.H., and Iyengar, S.S. (2005). Intrinsic and extrinsic motivational orientations in the classroom: Age differences and academic correlates. *Journal of Educational Psychology, 97*(2), 184-196. doi.org/10.1037/0022-0663.97.2.184.

Levine, R. (1997). *A Geography of Time.* New York: Basic Books

Lewis, P.A., and Durrant, S.J. (2011). Overlapping memory replay during sleep builds cognitive schemata. *Trends in Cognitive Sciences, 15*(8), 343-351. doi:10.1016/j.tics.2011.06.004.

Leyens, J., Desert, M., Croizet, J., and Darcis, C. (2000). Stereotype threat: Are lower status and history of stigmatization preconditions of stereotype threat? *Personality and Social Psychology Bulletin, 26*(10), 1189-1199.

Libby, L.K., Shaeffer, E.M., and Eibach, R.P. (2009). Seeing meaning in action: A bidirectional link between visual perspective and action identification level. *Journal of Experimental Psychology: General, 138*(4), 503-516.

Lillie-Blanton, M., and Laveist, T. (1996). Race/ethnicity, the social environment, and health. *Social Science and Medicine, 43*(1), 83-91.

Lindstrom, J.H. (2016, unpublished). *Critical Issues in Learning Disabilities Over the Past Decade: An Evolving Landscape.* Paper commissioned by the Committee on the Science of Practice and Learning, National Academies of Sciences, Engineering, and Medicine, Washington, DC.

Linn, M.C., Lee, H.-S., Tinker, R., Husic, F., and Chiu, J.L. (2006). Teaching and assessing knowledge integration in science. *Science, 313*(5790), 1049-1050.

Linnenbrink, E.A. (2005). The dilemma of performance-approach goals: The use of multiple goal contexts to promote students' motivation and learning. *Journal of Educational Psychology, 97*(2), 197-213.

Linnenbrink-Garcia, L., and Patall, E.A. (2016). Motivation. In E. Anderman and L. Corno (Eds.), *Handbook of Educational Psychology* (3rd ed., pp. 91-103). New York: Taylor & Francis.

Linnenbrink-Garcia, L., Tyson, D.F., and Patall, E.A. (2008). When are achievement goal orientations beneficial for academic achievement? A closer look at moderating factors. *International Review of Social Psychology, 21*(1-2), 19-70.

Linnenbrink-Garcia, L., Patall, E.A., and Messersmith, E. (2013). Antecedents and consequences of situational interest in science. *British Journal of Educational Psychology, 83*(4), 591-614.

Lipko-Speed, A., Dunlosky, J., and Rawson, K.A. (2014). Does testing with feedback help grade-school children learn key concepts in science? *Journal of Applied Research in Memory and Cognition, 3*(3), 171-176. doi:10.1016/j.jarmac.2014.04.002.

Livingstone, S., and Helsper, E. (2007). Gradations in digital inclusion: Children, young people and the digital divide. *New Media and Society, 9*(4), 671-696. doi:10.1177/1461444807080335.

Liyanagunawardena, T.R., and Williams S.A. (2016). Elderly learners and massive open online courses: A review. *Interactive Journal of Medical Research, 5*(1), e1. doi:10.2196/ijmr.4937.

LoBue, V. (2014). Measuring attentional biases for threat in children and adults. *Journal of Visualized Experiments : JoVE, (92)*, 52190. http://doi.org/10.3791/52190.

Locke, E.A., Shaw, K.N., Saari, L.M., and Latham, G.P. (1981). Goal setting and task performance: 1969-1980. *Psychological Bulletin, 90*(1), 125-152.

Lodge, J. (2013). Session I—From the laboratory to the classroom: Translating the learning sciences for use in technology-enhanced learning. *ACER Research Conferences, 16.* Available: https://research.acer.edu.au/research_conference/RC2013/5august/16 [December 2017].

Loewenstein, J. (2017). Structure mapping and vocabularies for thinking. *Topics in Cognitive Science, 9*, 842-858.

Lombrozo, T. (2007). Simplicity and probability in causal explanation. *Cognitive Psychology, 55*(3), 232-257. doi:10.1016/j.cogpsych.2006.09.006.

Lombrozo, T. (2012). Explanation and abductive inference. In K.J. Holyoak and R.G. Morrison (Eds.), *Oxford Handbook of Thinking and Reasoning* (pp. 260-276). Oxford, UK: Oxford University Press. doi:10.1093/oxfordhb/9780199734689.013.0014.

Looi, C.K., Seow, P., Zhang, B.H., So, H.-J., and Chen, W. (2009). Leveraging mobile technology for sustainable seamless learning: A research agenda. *British Journal of Educational Technology, 41*(2), 154-169.

López, I.H. (2006). *White by Law.* New York: New York University Press.

Lorusso, M.L., Facoetti, A., Pescenti, S., Cattaneo, C., Molteni, M., and Gieger, G. (2004). Wider recognition in peripheral vision common to different subtypes of dyslexia. *Vision Research, 44*(20), 2413-2424.

Lövdén, M., Bodammer, N.C., Kühn, S., Kaufmann, J., Schütze, H., Tempelmann, C., Heinze, H.D., Düzel, E., Schmiedek, F., and Lindenberger, U. (2010). Experience-dependent plasticity of white-matter microstructure extends into old age. *Neuropsychologia, 48*(13), 3878-3883. doi:10.1016/j.neuropsychologia.2010.08.026.

Lovett, M.W., Lacerenza, L., De Palma, M., and Frijters, J.C. (2012). Evaluating the efficacy of remediation for struggling readers in high school. *Journal of Learning Disabilities, 45*(2), 151-169. doi:10.1177/0022219410371678.

Loyens, S.M.M., Magda, J. and Rikers, R.M.J.P. (2008). Self-directed learning in problem-based learning and its relationships with self-regulated learning. *Educational Psychology Review, 20*(4), 411-427. doi:10.1007/s10648-008-9082-7.

Low, L.K., and Cheng, H.-J. (2006). Axon pruning: An essential step underlying the developmental plasticity of neuronal connections. *Philosophical Transactions of the Royal Society B: Biological Sciences, 361*(1473), 1531-1544. doi:10.1098/rstb.2006.1883.

Lozano, S.C., Hard, B.M., and Tversky, B. (2006). Perspective taking promotes action understanding and learning. *Journal of Experimental Psychology: Human Perception and Performance, 32*(6), 1405-1421.

Lozoff, B. (2007). Iron deficiency and child development. *Food and Nutrition Bulletin, 28*(4 Suppl.), S560-S571.

Lozoff, B. (2011). Early iron deficiency has brain and behavior effects consistent with dopaminergic dysfunction. *Journal of Nutrition, 141*(4), 740S-746S.

Lozoff, B., Castillo, M., Clark, K.M., Smith, J.B., and Sturza, J. (2014). Iron supplementation in infancy contributes to more adaptive behavior at 10 years of age. *The Journal of Nutrition, 144*(6), 838-845. doi:10.3945/jn.113.182048.

Lubinski, D. (2000). Scientific and social significance of assessing individual differences: "Sinking shafts at a few critical points." *Annual Review of Psychology, 51,* 405-444.

Lyall, A.E., Savadjiev, P., Shenton, M.E., and Kubicki, M. (2016). Insights into the brain: Neuroimaging of brain development and maturation. *Journal of Neuroimaging in Psychiatry and Neurology, 1*(1), 10-19. doi.org/10.17756/jnpn.2016-003.

Lyons, I.M., and Beilock, S.L. (2012). When math hurts: Math anxiety predicts pain network activation in anticipation of doing math. *PLoS One, 7*(10), e48076. doi.org/10.1371/journal.pone.0048076.

MacArthur, C.A., Konold, T.R., Glutting, J.J., and Alamprese, J.A. (2010). Reading component skills of learners in adult basic education. *Journal of Learning Disabilities, 43*(2), 108-121.

MacIver, D., and Epstein, J. (1993). Middle grades research: Not yet mature, but no longer a child. *Elementary School Journal, 93,* 519-533.

MacLeod, J. (1987). *Ain't No Making It: Aspirations and Attainment in a Low-Income Neighborhood.* Boulder, CO: Westview Press.

MacLeod, J. (1995). *Ain't No Making It.* Boulder, CO: Westview Press.

Maehr, M.L. (1984). Meaning and motivation: Toward a theory of personal investment. In R. Ames and C. Ames (Eds.), *Research on Motivation in Education* (vol. 1, pp. 39-73). San Diego, CA: Academic Press.

Maehr, M.L., and Midgley, C. (1996). *Transforming School Cultures.* Boulder, CO: Westview Press.

Maehr, M.L., and Zusho, A. (2009). Achievement goal theory: The past, present, and future. In K.R. Wentzel and A. Wigfield (Eds.), *Handbook of Motivation in School* (pp. 77-104). New York: Taylor Francis.

Magnusson, S.J., and Palincsar, A.S. (2005). Teaching to promote the development of scientific knowledge and reasoning about light at the elementary school level. In J. Bransford and S. Donovan (Eds.), *How Students Learn: History, Mathematics, and Science in the Classroom* (pp. 421-474). Washington, DC: National Academies Press.

Magsamen-Conrad, K., Dowd, J., Abuljadail, M., Alsulaiman, S., and Shareefi, A. (2015). *Life-Span Differences in the Uses and Gratifications of Tablets: Implications for Older Adults.* Media and Communications Faculty Publications, Paper 39. Available: http://scholarworks.bgsu.edu/smc_pub/39 [December 2017].

Maisog, J.M., Einbinder, E.R., Flowers, D.L., Turkeltaub, P.E., and Eden, G.F. (2008). A meta-analysis of functional neuroimaging studies of dyslexia. *Annals of the New York Academy of Sciences, 1145,* 237-259. doi:10.1196/annals.1416.024.

Maki, Y., Kawasaki, Y., Demiray, B., and Janssen, S.M. (2015). Autobiographical memory functions in young Japanese men and women. *Memory, 23*(1), 11-24.

Malone, T.W. (1981). Toward a theory of intrinsically motivating instruction. *Cognitive Science, 5*(4), 333-369.

Malone, T., and Lepper (1987). Making learning fun: A taxonomy of intrinsic motivations for learning. In R. Snow and M.J. Farr (Eds.), *Aptitude, Learning, and Instruction Volume 3: Conative and Affective Process Analyses.* Hillsdale, NJ: Lawrence Earlbaum Associates.

Mandler, J.M. (1988). How to build a baby: On the development of an accessible representational system. *Cognitive Development, 3*(2), 113-136.

Mangels, J.A., Butterfield, B., Lamb, J., Good, C., and Dweck, C.S. (2006). Why do beliefs about intelligence influence learning success? A social cognitive neuroscience model. *Social Cognitive and Affective Neuroscience, 1*(2), 75-86.

Margaryan, A., Littlejohn, A., and Milligan, C. (2013). Self-regulated learning in the workplace: Strategies and factors in the attainment of learning goals. *International Journal of Training and Development, 17*(4), 245–259. doi:10.1111/ijtd.12013.

Markus, H.R., and Kitayama, S. (1991). Culture and the self: Implications for cognition, emotion, and motivation. *Psychological Review, 98*(2), 224–253. doi.org/10.1037/0033-295X.98.2.224.

Marsh, E.J., Fazio, L.K., and Goswick, A.E. (2012). Memorial consequences of testing school-aged children. *Memory, 20*(8), 899–906. doi:10.1080/09658211.2012.708757.

Martens, A., Johns, M., Greenberg, J., and Schimel, J. (2006). Combating stereotype threat: The effect of self-affirmation on women's intellectual performance. *Journal of Experimental Social Psychology, 42*(2), 236–243. doi.org/10.1016/j.jesp.2005.04.010.

Marvel, C.L., and Desmond, J.E. (2010). Functional topography of the cerebellum in verbal working memory. *Neuropsychology Review, 20*(3), 271–279.

Master, A., Cheryan, S., and Meltzoff, A.N. (2015). Computing whether she belongs: Stereotypes undermine girls' interest and sense of belonging in computer science. *Journal of Educational Psychology, 108*(3), 424–437.

Maurer, T.J., Weiss, E.W., and Barbeite, F.G. (2003). A model of involvement in work-related learning and development activity: The effects of individual, situational, motivational, and age variables. *Journal of Applied Psychology, 88*(4), 707–724.

Mawdsley, M., Grasby, K., and Talk, A. (2014). The effect of sleep on item recognition and source memory recollection among shift-workers and permanent day-workers. *Journal of Sleep Research, 23*(5), 538–544.

Mayer, R.E. (2001). *Multimedia Learning*. New York: Cambridge University Press

Mayer, R.E. (2004). Should there be a three-strikes rule against pure discovery learning? The case for guided methods of instruction. *American Psychologist, 59*(1), 14–19.

Mayer, R.E. (2009). *Multimedia Learning* (2nd ed.). New York: Cambridge University Press.

Mayer, R.E. (2014). *Computer Games for Learning: An Evidence-based Approach*. Cambridge, MA: MIT Press.

Mayer, R.E. (2016). What should be the role of computer games in education? *Policy Insights from the Behavioral and Brain Sciences, 3*(1), 20–26. doi:10.1177/2372732215621311.

Mayer, R.E., and Johnson, C.I. (2010). Adding instructional features that promote learning in a game-like environment. *Journal of Educational Computing Research, 42*(3), 241–265. doi:10.2190/EC.42.3.a.

Mazur, E. (1997). *Peer Instruction: A User's Manual*. Upper Saddle River, NJ: Prentice Hall.

McCaslin, M., and Burross, H.L. (2011). Research on individual differences within a sociocultural perspective: Co-regulation and adaptive learning. *Teachers College Record, 113*(2), 325–349.

McClelland, M.M., Cameron, C.E., Connor, C.M., Farris, C.L., Jewkes, A.M., and Morrison, F.J. (2007). Links between behavioral regulation and preschoolers' literacy, vocabulary, and math skills. *Developmental Psychology, 43*(4), 947–959.

McCollough, C. (1965). Color adaptation of edge-detectors in the human visual system. *Science, 149*(3688), 1115–1116.

McDaniel, M.A., and Donnelly, C.M. (1996). Learning with analogy and elaborative interrogation. *Journal of Educational Psychology, 88*(3), 508–519. doi:10.1037/0022-0663.88.3.508.

McDermott, R.P., and Varenne, H. (1996). Culture, development, disability. In R. Jessor, A. Colby, and R.A. Shweder (Eds.), *Ethnograpny and Human Development*. Chicago: The University of Chicago Press.

McGinnis, D., Goss, R., Tessmer, C., and Zelinski, E.M. (2008). Inference generation in young, young-old and old-old adults: Evidence for semantic architecture stability. *Applied Cognitive Psychology, 22*(2), 171–192.

McKoon, G., and Ratcliff, R. (1992). Inference during reading. *Psychological Review, 99*(3), 440–466.

McKown, C., and Strambler, M.J. (2009). Developmental antecedents and social and academic consequences of stereotype-consciousness in middle childhood. *Child Development, 80*(6), 1643-1659. doi:10.1111/j.1467-8624.2009.01359.x.

McNamara, D.S. (2004). SERT: Self-explanation reading training. *Discourse Processes, 38*(1), 1-30. doi:10.1207/s15326950dp3801_1.

McNamara, D.S., Jacovina, M.E., and Allen, L.K. (2015). Higher order thinking in comprehension. In P. Afflerbach (Ed.), *Handbook of Individual Differences in Reading: Text and Context* (pp. 164-176). New York: Taylor and Francis, Routledge.

McNaughten, D., and Gabbard, C. (1993). Physical exertion and immediate mental performance of sixth-grade children. *Perceptual and Motor Skills, 77*(3 Suppl.), 1155-1159.

McQueen, A., and Klein, W.M.P. (2006). Experimental manipulations of self-affirmation: A systematic review. *Self and Identity, 5*(4), 289-354. doi.org/10.1080/15298860600805325.

Means, B., Toyama, Y., Murphy, R., Bakia, M., and Jones, K. (2010). *Evaluation of Evidence Based Practices in Online Learning: A Meta-Analysis and Review of Online Learning Studies.* Monograph. Available: http://www.ed.gov/about/offices/list/opepd/ppss/reports.html [November 2017].

Means, B., Toyama, Y., Murphy, R., and Baki, M. (2013). The effectiveness of online and blended learning: A meta-analysis of the empirical literature. *Teachers College Record, 115*, 1-47. Available: https://www.sri.com/sites/default/files/publications/effectiveness_of_online_and_blended_learning.pdf [December 2017].

Means, B., Shear, L., and Roschelle, J. (2015). *Using Technology and Evidence to Promote Cultures of Educational Innovation: The Example of Science and Mathematics Education.* Menlo Park, CA: SRI International.

Means, B., Murphy, R., and Shear, L. (2017). *Pearson | SRI Series on Building Efficacy in Learning Technologies* (Vol. 1). London, UK: Pearson.

Medaglia, J.D., Lynall, M.E., and Bassett, D.S. (2015). Cognitive network neuroscience. *Journal of Cognitive Neuroscience, 27*(8), 1471-1491.

Medimorecc, M.A., Pavlik, P., Olney, A., Graesser, A.C., and Risko, E.F. (2015). The language of instruction: Compensating for challenge in lectures. *Journal of Educational Psychology, 107*(4), 971-990.

Medin, D.L., and Bang, M. (2013). Culture in the classroom. *Phi Delta Kappan, 95*(4), 64-67.

Medin, D.L., and Bang, M. (2014). *Who's Asking? Native Science, Western Science and Science Education.* Cambridge, MA: MIT Press.

Meeusen, R., Piacentini, M.F., and De Meirleir, K. (2001). Brain microdialysis in exercise research. *Sports Medicine, 31*(14), 965-983.

Mellard, D.F., and Patterson, M.B. (2008). Contrasting adult literacy learners with and without specific learning disabilities. *Remedial and Special Education, 29*(3), 133-144. doi.org/10.1177/0741932508315053.

Metcalfe, B. (2013). Metcalfe's law after 40 years of ethernet. *Computer, 46*(12), 26-31. doi:10.1109/MC.2013.374.

Meyer, A.N.D., and Logan, J.M. (2013). Taking the testing effect beyond the college freshman: Benefits for lifelong learning. *Psychology and Aging, 28*(1), 142-147. doi:10.1037/a003089010.1037/a0030890.supp.

Meyer, A., Rose, D.H., and Gordon, D. (2014). *Universal Design for Learning: Theory and Practice.* Wakefield, MA: CAST Professional.

Michaels, S., and O'Connor, C. (2012). *Talk Science Primer.* Available: https://inquiryproject.terc.edu/shared/pd/TalkScience_Primer.pdf [July 2018].

Middleton, M.J., and Midgley, C. (1997). Avoiding the demonstration of lack of ability: An unexplored aspect of goal theory. *Journal of Educational Psychology, 89*(4), 710-718.

Midgley, C., Arunkumar R., and Urdan, T. (1996). If I don't do well tomorrow, there's a reason: Predictors of adolescents' use of academic self-handicapping behavior. *Journal of Educational Psychology, 88*(3), 423-434. doi.org/10.1037/0022-0663.88.3.423.

Midgley, C., Kaplan, A., and Middleton, M.J. (2001). Performance approach goals: Good for what, for whom under what circumstances, and at what cost? *Journal of Educational Psychology, 93*(1), 77-86. doi.org/10.1037/0022-0663.93.1.77.

Mihalca, L., and Miclea, M. (2007). Current trends in educational technology research. *Cognition, Brain, Behavior, 9*(1), 115-129.

Milgram, P., and Kishino, A.F. (1994). Taxonomy of mixed reality visual displays. *IEICE Transactions on Information Systems, E77-D*(12), 1321-1329. Available: http://citeseerx.ist.psu.edu/viewdoc/download?doi=10.1.1.102.4646&rep=rep1&type=pdf [December 2017].

Miron, G., Huerta, L., Cuban, L., Horvitz, B., Gulosino, C., Rice, J.K., and Shafer, S.R. (2013). *Virtual Schools in the U.S. 2013: Politics, Performance, Policy, and Research Evidence.* Boulder, CO: National Education Policy Center. Available: http://nepc.colorado.edu/publication/virtual-schools-annual-2013 [December 2017].

Mislevy, R.J., Steinberg, L.S., and Almond, R.G. (2003). On the structure of educational assessments. *Measurement: Interdisciplinary Research and Perspectives, 1*(1), 3-62.

Mislevy, R.J., Steinberg, L.S., Almond, R.G., and Lukas, J.F. (2006). Concepts, terminology, and basic models of evidence-centered design. In D.M. Williamson, I.I. Bejar, and R.J. Mislevy (Eds.), *Automated Scoring of Complex Tasks in Computer-Based Testing* (pp. 15-48). Mahwah, NJ: Erlbaum.

Mitchell, K.J., Johnson, M.K., Raye, C.L., Mather, M., and D'Esposito, M. (2000). Aging and reflective processes of working memory: Binding and test load deficits. *Psychological Aging, 15*(3), 527-541.

Mitrovic, A., Martin, B., and Suraweera, P. (2007). Intelligent tutors for all: The constraint-based approach. *IEEE Intelligent Systems, 22*(4), 38-45.

Miyake, A., Kost-Smith, L.E., Finkelstein, N.D., Pollock, S.J., Cohen, G.L., and Ito, T.A. (2010). Reducing the gender achievement gap in college science: A classroom study of values affirmation. *Science, 330*(6008), 1234-1237. doi:10.1126/science.1195996.

Moeller, B., and Reitzes, T. (2011). *Education Development Center, Inc. (EDC). Integrating Technology with Student-Centered Learning.* Quincy, MA: Nellie Mae Education Foundation.

Moffitt, T.E., Arseneault, L., Belsky, D., Dickson, N., Hancox, R.J., Harrington, H., Houts, R., Poulton, R., Roberts, B.W., Ross, S., Sears, M.R., Thomson, W.M., and Caspi, A. (2011). A gradient of childhood self-control predicts health, wealth, and public safety. *Proceedings of the National Academy of Sciences of the United States of America, 108*(7), 2693-2698. doi:10.1073/pnas.1010076108.

Moje, E.B., Ciechanowski, K.M., Kramer, K., Ellis, L., Carrillo, R., and Collazo, T. (2004). Working toward third space in content area literacy: An examination of everyday funds of knowledge and discourse. *Reading Research Quarterly, 39*(1), 38-70.

Molfese, D. (2000). Predicting dyslexia at 8 years of age using neonatal brain responses. *Brain & Language, 72*(3), 238-245.

Moll, L., Amanti, C., Neff, D., and Gonzalez, N. (1992). Funds of knowledge for teaching: Using a qualitative approach to connect homes and classrooms. *Theory Into Practice, XXXI*(2), 132-141.

Moller, A.C., Deci, E.L., and Ryan, R.M. (2006). Choice and ego-depletion: The moderating role of autonomy. *Personality and Social Psychology Bulletin, 32*(8), 1024-1036.

Moore, M.G., and Kearsley, G. (1996). *Distance Education: A Systems View.* New York: Wadsworth.

Moos, D., and Rongdal, A. (2012). Self-regulated learning in the classroom: A literature review on the teacher's role. *Education Research International*, Article ID 423284. Available: https://www.hindawi.com/journals/edri/2012/423284 [December 2017]. doi.org/10.1155/2012/423284.

Moreno, R., and Mayer, R.E. (2007). Interactive multimodal learning environments. *Educational Psychology Review, 19*(3), 309-326.

Morgeson, F.P., and Humphrey, S.E. (2006). The Work Design Questionnaire (WDQ), Developing and validating a comprehensive measure for assessing job design and the nature of work. *Journal of Applied Psychology, 91*(6), 1321-1339. doi.org/10.1037/0021-9010.91.6.1321.

Morrell, E. (2008). Six summers of YPAR: Learning, action and change in urban education. In J. Cammarota and M. Fine (Eds.), *Revolutionizing Education: Youth Participatory Action Research in Motion* (pp. 155-184). New York: Routledge.

Morrell, R.W., Mayhorn, C.B., and Echt, K.V. (2004). Why older adults use or do not use the Internet. In D.C. Burdick and S. Kwon (Eds.), *Gerotechnology: Research and Practice in Technology and Aging* (pp. 71-85). New York: Springer..

Morris, M.W., and Peng, K. (1994). Culture and cause: American and Chinese attributions for social and physical events. *Journal of Personality and Social Psychology, 67*(6), 949-971. Available: http://citeseerx.ist.psu.edu/viewdoc/download?doi=10.1.1.320.1966&rep=rep 1&type=pdf [December 2017].

Morris, M.W., Chiu, C., and Liu, Z. (2015). Polycultural psychology. *Annual Reviews of Psychology, 66,* 631-659. doi.org/10.1146/annurev-psych-010814-015001.

Moscovitch, M. (1992). Memory and working-with-memory: A component process model based on modules and central systems. *Journal of Cognitive Neuroscience, 4*(3), 257-267. doi:10.1162/jocn.1992.4.3.257.

Moss, P., and Haertel, E. (2016). Engaging methodological pluralism. In D. Gitomer and C. Bell (Eds.), *Handbook of Research on Teaching* (5th ed., pp. 127-248). Washington, DC: American Educational Research Association.

Mourey, J.A., Lam, B.C.P., and Oyserman, D. (2015). Consequences of cultural fluency. *Social Cognition, 33*(4), 308-344.

Mozolic, J.L., Hugenschmidt, C.E., Peiffer, A.M., and Laurienti, P.J. (2012). Multisensory integration and aging. In M.M. Murray and M.T. Wallace (Eds.), *The Neural Bases of Multisensory Processes* (pp. 381-394). Boca Raton, FL: CRC Press/Taylor & Francis.

Mueller, C.M., and Dweck, C.S. (1998). Praise for intelligence can undermine children's motivation and performance. *Journal of Personality and Social Psychology, 75*(1), 33-52.

Mueller, P.A., and Oppenheimer, D.M. (2014). The pen is mightier than the keyboard. *Psychological Science, 25*(6), 1159-1168. doi:10.1177/0956797614524581.

Mullen, M.K. (1994). Earliest recollections of childhood: A demographic analysis. *Cognition, 52*(1), 55-79.

Mullins, D., Rummel, N., and Spada, H. (2011). Are two heads always better than one? Differential effects of collaboration on students' computer-supported learning in mathematics. *International Journal of Computer-Supported Collaborative Learning, 6*(3), 421-443.

Murayama, K., and Kuhbandner, C. (2011). Money enhances memory consolidation—but only for boring material. *Cognition, 119*(1), 120-124. doi:10.1016/j.cognition.2011.01.001.

Murayama, K., Pekrun, R., Lichtenfeld, S., and Vom Hofe, R. (2013). Predicting long-term growth in students' mathematics achievement: the unique contributions of motivation and cognitive strategies. *Child Developoment, 84*(4), 1475-1490. doi 10.1111/cdev.12036.

Murayama, K., Matsumoto, M., Izuma, K., Sugiura, A., Ryan, R.M., Deci, E.L., and Matsumoto K. (2015). How self-determined choice facilitates performance: A key role of the ventromedial prefrontal cortex. *Cerebral Cortex, 25*(5), 1241-1251. doi:10.1093/cercor/bht317.

Myhre, J.W., Mehl, M.R., and Glisky, E.L. (2017). Cognitive benefits of online social networking for healthy older adults. *Journals of Gerontology. Series B: Psychological Sciences and Social Sciences, 72*(5), 752-760. doi:10.1093/geronb/gbw025.

Myles-Worsley, M., Johnston, W.A., and Simons, M.A. (1988). The influence of expertise on X-ray image processing. *Journal of Experimental Psychology: Learning, Memory, and Cognition, 14*(3), 553-557.

Nader, K. (2003). Memory traces unbound. *Trends in Neurosciences, 26*(2), 65-72.

Nash, J., Collins, B., Loughlin, S.E., Solbrig, M., Harvey, R., Krishnan-Sarin, S., Unger, J., Miner, C., Rukstalis, M., Shenassa, E., Dubé, C., and Spirito, A. (2003). Training the transdisciplinary scientist: A general framework applied to tobacco use behavior. *Nicotine and Tobacco Research, 5*(Suppl. 1), S41-S53.

Nasir, N.S. (2002). Identity, goals, and learning: Mathematics in cultural practice. *Mathematical Thinking and Learning, 4*(2-3), 213-247.

Nasir, N.S., and de Royston, M. (2013). Power, identity, and mathematical practices outside and inside school. *Journal of Research in Mathematics Education, 44*(1), 264-287.

Nasir, N.S., and Hand, V.M. (2006). Exploring Sociocultural perspectives on race, culture, and learning. *Review of Educational Research, 76*, 449-475.

Nasir, N.S., Rosenbery, A.S., Warren, B., and Lee, C.D. (2006). Learning as a cultural process: Achieving equity through diversity. In R.K. Sawyer (Ed.), *The Cambridge Handbook of the Learning Sciences* (pp. 489-504). New York: Cambridge University Press.

Nation, K., Adams, J.W., Bowyer-Crane, C.A., and Snowling, M.J. (1999). Working memory deficits in poor comprehenders reflect underlying language impairments. *Journal of Experimental Child Psychology, 73*(2), 139-158. doi:10.1006/jecp.1999.2498.

National Academies of Sciences, Engineering, and Medicine. (2017). *Promoting the Educational Success of Children and Youth Learning English: Promising Futures*. Washington, DC: The National Academies Press.

National Association for the Education of Young Children and Fred Rogers Center. (2012). *Key Messages of the NAEYC/Fred Rogers Center Position Statement on Technology and Interactive Media in Early Childhood Programs*. Available: https://www.naeyc.org/files/naeyc/file/positions/KeyMessages_Technology.pdf [December 2017].

National Institute for Literacy. (2008). *Investigating the Language and Literacy Skills Required for Independent Online Learning*. Washington, DC: Author. Available: http://eric.ed.gov/PDFS/ED505199.pdf [December 2017].

National Research Council. (1998). *Preventing Reading Difficulties in Young Children*. Washington, DC: National Academy Press.

National Research Council. (1999b). *How People Learn: Brain, Mind, Experience, and School*. Washington, DC: National Academy Press.

National Research Council. (1999c). *How People Learn: Bridging Research and Practice*. Washington, DC: National Academy Press.

National Research Council. (2000). *How People Learn: Brain, Mind, Experience, and School: Expanded Edition*. Washington, DC: National Academy Press.

National Research Council. (2001a). *Knowing What Students Know: The Science and Design of Educational Assessment*. Washington, DC: National Academy Press.

National Research Council. (2001b). *Adding It Up: Helping Children Learn Mathematics*. Washington, DC: National Academy Press.

National Research Council. (2005). *How Students Learn: History, Mathematics, and Science in the Classroom*. Washington, DC: The National Academies Press.

National Research Council. (2006). *America's Lab Report: Investigations in High School Science*. Washington, DC: The National Academies Press.

National Research Council. (2007). *Taking Science to School: Learning and Teaching Science in Grades K-8*. Washington, DC: The National Academies Press.

National Research Council. (2009). *Learning Science in Informal Environments: People, Places, and Pursuits*. Washington, DC: The National Academies Press.

National Research Council. (2011a). *Incentives and Test-based Accountability in Education*. Washington, DC: The National Academies Press.

National Research Council. (2011b). *Mathematics Learning in Early Childhood: Paths toward Excellence and Equity*. Washington, DC: The National Academies Press.

National Research Council. (2011c). *Assessing 21st Century Skills: Summary of a Workshop*. Washington, DC: The National Academies Press. doi:10.17226/13215.

National Research Council. (2012a). *Discipline-Based Education Research: Understanding and Improving Learning in Undergraduate Science and Engineering*. Washington, DC: The National Academies Press.

National Research Council. (2012b). *Education for Life and Work: Developing Transferable Knowledge and Skills in the 21st Century*. Washington, DC: The National Academies Press.

National Research Council. (2012c). *Improving Adult Literacy Instruction: Options for Practice and Research*. Washington, DC: The National Academies Press.

National Research Council. (2014). *Developing Assessments for the Next Generation Science Standards*. Washington, DC: The National Academies Press.

National Research Council and Institute of Medicine. (2009). *Preventing Mental, Emotional, and Behavioral Disorders Among Young People: Progress and Possibilities*. Washington, DC: The National Academies Press.

National Research Council and Institute of Medicine. (2015). *Transforming the Workforce for Children Birth Through Age 8: A Unifying Foundation*. Washington, DC: The National Academies Press.

National Scientific Council on the Developing Child. (2006). *Early Exposure to Toxic Substances Damages Brain Architecture*. Working Paper No. 4. Available: https://developingchild. harvard.edu/resources/early-exposure-to-toxic-substances-damages-brain-architecture [December 2017].

National Sleep Foundation. (2006). *Teens and Sleep*. Washington, DC: National Sleep Foundation. Available: http://www.sleepfoundation.org/article/sleep-america-polls/2006-teens-and-sleep [June 2018].

National Sleep Foundation. (2008). *2008 Sleep in America Poll*. Available: https://sleepfoundation. org/sites/default/files/2008%20POLL%20SOF.PDF [December 2017].

Naveh-Benjamin, M., and Kilb, A. (2012). How the measurement of memory processes can affect memory performance: The case of remember/know judgments. *Journal of Experimental Psychology: Learning, Memory and Cognition, 38*(1), 194–203.

Naveh-Benjamin, M., Brav, T.K., and Levy, O. (2007). The associative memory deficit of older adults: The role of strategy utilization. *Psychology and Aging, 22*(1), 202–208.

Nelson, C.A., Zeanah, C.H., Fox, N.A., Marshall, P.J., Smyke, A.T., and Guthrie, D. (2007). Cognitive recovery in socially deprived young children: The Bucharest Early Intervention Project. *Science, 318*(5858), 1937–1940.

Nelson, C.A., Furtado, E.A., Fox, N.A., and Zeanah, C.H. (2009). The deprived human brain. *American Scientist, 97*, 222–229.

Nelson, C.A., Fox, N.A., and Zeanah, C.H. (2014). *Romania's Abandoned Children: Deprivation, Brain Development and the Struggle for Recovery*. Cambridge, MA: Harvard University Press.

Nelson, K. (1974). Concept, word, and sentence: Interrelations in acquisition and development. *Psychological Review, 81*(4), 267–285. doi.org/10.1037/h0036592.

Neuhoff, N., Bruder, J., Bartling, J., Warnke, A., Remschmidt, H., Müller-Myhsok, B., and Schulte-Körne, G. (2012). Evidence for the late MMN as a neurophysiological endophenotype for dyslexia. *PLoS One, 7*(5), 1–7. doi:10.1371/journal.pone.0034909.

Nevarez, M.D., Rifas-Shiman, S.L., Kleinman, K.P., Gillman, M.W., and Taveras, E.M. (2010). Associations of early life risk factors with infant sleep duration. *Academic Pediatrics, 10*(3), 187–193.

Nevo, E., and Breznitz, Z. (2011). Assessment of working memory components at 6 years of age as predictors of reading achievements a year later. *Journal of Experimental Child Psychology, 109*(1), 73–90. doi.org/10.1016/j.jecp.2010.09.010.

Newman, L., Wagner, M., Cameto, R., and Knokey, A. (2009). *The Post-High School Outcomes of Youth with Disabilities up to 4 Years after High School: A Report from the National Longitudinal Transition Study-2 (NLTS2)*. NCSER 2009-3017. Menlo Park, CA: SRI International.

Newman, L., Wagner, M., Cameto, R., Knokey, A.M., and Shaver, D. (2010). *Comparisons across Time of the Outcomes of Youth with Disabilities up to 4 Years after High School*. Menlo Park, CA: SRI International. Available: www.nlts2.org/reports/2010_09/nlts2_report_2010_09_complete.pdf [December 2017].

Ng, T.W.H., and Feldman, D.C. (2008). The relationship of age to ten dimensions of job performance. *Journal of Applied Psychology, 93*(2), 392–423. doi.org/10.1037/0021-9010.93.2.392.

Nicholls, J.G. (1984). Achievement motivation: Conceptions of ability, subjective experience, task choice and performance. *Psychological Review, 91*(3), 328–346. doi.org/10.1037/0033-295X.91.3.328.

Nielsen, M., Haun, D., Kärtner, J., and Legare, C.H. (2017). The persistent sampling bias in developmental psychology: A call to action. *Journal of Experimental Child Psychology, 162*, 31–38. doi.org/10.1016/j.jecp.2017.04.017.

Nile, E., and Van Bergen, P. (2015). Not all semantics: Similarities and differences in reminiscing function and content between Indigenous and non-Indigenous Australians. *Memory, 23*(1), 83–98.

Nisbett, R.E., Peng, K., Choi, I., and Norenzayan, A. (2001). Culture and systems of thought: Holistic versus analytic cognition. *Psychological Review, 108*(2), 291–310.

Nobel, K.G., Engelhardt, L.E., Brito, N.H., Mack, L.J., Nail, E.J., Angal, J., Barr, R., Fifer, W.P., Elliott, A.J., and in collaboration with the PASS Network. (2015). Socioeconomic disparities in neurocognitive development in the first two years of life. *Developmental Psychobiology, 57*, 535–551.

Nokes, J.D., Dole, J.A., and Hacker, D.J. (2007). Teaching high school students to use heuristics while reading historical texts. *Journal of Educational Psychology, 99*(3), 492–504.

Nokes-Malach, T.J., VanLehn, K., Belenky, D.M., Lichtenstein, M., and Cox, G. (2013). Coordinating principles and examples through analogy and self-explanation. *European Journal of Psychology of Education, 28*(4), 1237–1263. doi:10.1007/s10212-012-0164-z.

Norman, D.A. (2013), *The Design of Everyday Things: Revised and Expanded Edition*. New York: Basic Books.

Norton, E.S., Beach, S.D., and Gabrieli, J.D. (2015). Neurobiology of dyslexia. *Current Opinion in Neurobiology, 30*, 73–78. doi:10.1016/j.conb.2014.09.007.

Núñez, R., and Cooperrider, K. (2013). The tangle of space and time in human cognition. *Trends in Cognitive Sciences, 17*(5), 220–229.

Nye, B.D., Graesser, A.C., and Hu, X. (2014). AutoTutor and family: A review of 17 years of natural language tutoring. *International Journal of Artificial Intelligence, 24*(4), 427–469.

OECD. (2013). *PISA 2015: Draft Collaborative Problem Solving Framework*. Available: https://www.oecd.org/pisa/pisaproducts/Draft%20PISA%202015%20Collaborative%20Problem%20Solving%20Framework%20.pdf [December 2017].

OECD. (2015). *PISA 2015 Released Field Trial Cognitive Items*. Available: www.oecd.org/pisa/pisaproducts/PISA2015-Released-FT-Cognitive-Items.pdf [December 2017].

Öhman, A., and Mineka, S. (2001). Fears, phobia, and preparedness: Toward an evolved module of fear and fear learning. *Psychological Review, 108*(3), 483–522.

Ojalehto, B.L., and Medin, D. (2015a). Emerging trends in culture and concepts. In R. Scott and S. Kosslyn (Eds.), *Emerging Trends in the Social and Behavioral Sciences: An Interdisciplinary, Searchable, and Linkable Resource*. New York: John Wiley & Sons.

Ojalehto, B.L., and Medin, D. (2015b). Perspectives on culture and concepts. *Annual Review of Psychology, 66*, 249–275. doi.org/10.1146/annurev-psych-010814-015120.

Ojalehto, B., and Medin, D.L. (2015c). Theory of mind in the Pacific: Reasoning across cultures. *Ethos, 43*(1), E5–E8.

Okonofua, J.A., Paunesku, D., and Walton, G.M. (2016). Brief intervention to encourage empathic discipline cuts suspension rates in half among adolescents. *Proceedings of the National Academy of Sciences of the United States of America, 113*(9), 5221–5226.

Old, S.R., and Naveh-Benjamin, M. (2012). Age differences in memory for names: The effect of prelearned semantic associations. *Psychology and Aging, 27*(2), 462–473.

Oliver, M., and Conole, G. (2003). Evidence-based practice and e-learning in higher education: Can we and should we? *Research Papers in Education, 18*(4), 385–397. doi:10.1080/026 7152032000176873.

O'Neil, H.F., and Perez, R.S. (2008). *Computer Games and Team and Individual Learning.* Boston, MA: Elsevier.

Ornstein, P.A., Coffman, J.L., Grammer, J.K., San Souci, P.P., and McCall, L.E. (2010). Linking the classroom context and the development of children's memory skills. In J. Meece and J. Eccles (Eds.), *Handbook of Research on Schools, Schooling, and Human Development* (pp. 42–59). New York: Routledge.

Osborne, R., and Freyberg, P. (1985). *Learning in Science: The Implications of Children's Science.* Auckland, New Zealand: Heinneman.

Osborne, J., Erduran, S., and Simon, S. (2004). Enhancing the quality of argumentation in school science. *Journal of Research in Science Teaching, 41*(10), 994–1020.

Oyserman, D. (2011). Culture as situated cognition: Cultural mindsets, cultural fluency, and meaning making. *European Review of Social Psychology, 22*(1), 164–214.

Oyserman, D., Gant, L., and Ager, J. (1995). A socially contextualized model of African American identity: Possible selves and school persistence. *Journal of Personality and Social Psychology, 69*(6), 1216–1232. doi.org/10.1037/0022-3514.69.6.1216.

Oyserman, D., Sorensen, N., Reber, R., and Chen, S.X. (2009). Connecting and separating mindsets: Culture as situated cognition. *Journal of Personality and Social Psychology, 97*(2), 217–235. doi:10.1037/a0015850.

Oyserman, D., Destin, M., and Novin, S. (2015). The context-sensitive future self: Possible selves motivate in context, not otherwise. *Self and Identity, 14*(2), 173–188. doi:10.1080/1529 8868.2014.965733.

Ozgungor, S., and Guthrie, J.T. (2004). Interactions among elaborative interrogation, knowledge, and interest in the process of constructing knowledge from text. *Journal of Educational Psychology, 96*(3), 437–443. doi:10.1037/0022-0663.96.3.437.

Pacer, M., and Lombrozo, T. (2017). Occam's razor cuts to the root: Simplicity in causal explanation. *Journal of Experimental Psychology: General, 146*(12), 1761–1780.

Packer, M.J. (1985). Hermeneutic inquiry in the study of human conduct. *American Psychologist, 40*(10), 1081–1093. doi.org/10.1037/0003-066X.40.10.1081.

Palincsar, A.S. (2013). Reciprocal teaching. In J. Hattie and E. M. Anderman (Eds.), *International Guide to Student Achievement* (pp. 369–371). New York: Routledge/Taylor and Francis Group.

Palincsar, A.S., and Brown, A.L. (1984). Reciprocal teaching of comprehension-fostering and comprehension-monitoring activities. *Cognition and Instruction, 1*(2), 117–175. doi:10.1207/s1532690xci0102_1.

Palincsar, A.S., and Magnusson, S.J. (2001). The interplay of firsthand and text-based investigations to model and support the development of scientific knowledge and reasoning. In S. Carver and D. Klahr (Eds.), *Cognition and Instruction: Twenty Five Years of Progress* (pp. 151–194). Mahwah, NJ: Lawrence Erlbaum.

Panadero, E. (2017). A review of self-regulated learning: Six models and directions for research. *Frontiers in Psychology, 8*, 422. doi:10.3389/fpsyg.2017.00422.

Panksepp, J., and Biven, L. (2012). *The Archaeology of the Mind: Neuroevolutionary Origins of Human Emotions.* New York: W.W. Norton & Company.

Paris, D. (2012). Culturally sustaining pedagogy a needed change in stance, terminology, and practice. *Educational Researcher, 41*(3), 93–97.

Paris, S., and Upton, L. (1976). Children's memory for inferential relationships in prose. *Child Development, 47*(3), 660–668. Available: http://www.jstor.org/stable/1128180 [December 2017].

Park, D.C., and Gutchess, A.H. (2002). Aging, cognition, and culture: A neuroscientific perspective. *Neuroscience & Biobehavioral Reviews, 26*(7), 859-867.

Park, D.C., and Reuter-Lorenz, P.A. (2009). The adaptive brain: Aging and neurocognitive scaffolding. *Annual Review of Psychology, 60,* 173-196. doi:10.1146/annurev.psych.59.103006.093656.

Park, D.C., Lautenschlager, G., Hedden, T., Davidson, N.S., Smith, A.D., and Smith, P.K. (2002). Models of visuospatial and verbal memory across the adult life span. *Psychology and Aging, 17*(2), 299-320.

Park, D.C., Lodi-Smith, J., Drew, L., Haber, S., Hebrank, A., Bischof, G.N., and Aamodt, W. (2014). The impact of sustained engagement on cognitive function in older adults. The Synapse Project. *Psychological Science, 25*(1), 103-112.

Parsons, S.A., Metzger, S.R., Askew, J., and Carswell, A. (2011). Teaching against the grain: One Title I school's journey toward project-based literacy instruction. *Literacy Research and Instruction, 50*(1), 1-14. doi.org/10.1080/19388070903318413.

Pascarella, E., Pierson, C., Wolniak, G., and Terenzini, P. (2004). First-generation college students: Additional evidence on college experiences and outcomes. *Journal of Higher Education, 75*(3), 249-284.

Pashler, H., Bain, P.M., Bottge, B.A., Graesser, A., Koedinger, K., McDaniel, M., and Metcalfe, J. (2007). *Organizing Instruction and Study to Improve Student Learning: A Practice Guide.* NCER 2007-2004. Washington, DC: Institute of Education Sciences.

Pashler, H., McDaniel, M., Rohrer, D., and Bjork, R. (2008). Learning styles concepts and evidence. *Psychological Science in the Public Interest, 9*(3), 105-119.

Pasnik, S., and Llorente, C. (2013). *Preschool Teachers Can Use a PBS KIDS Transmedia Curriculum Supplement to Support Young Children's Mathematics Learning: Results of a Randomized Controlled Trial.* Waltham, MA: Center for Technology in Learning and Menlo Park, CA: SRI International.

Pasnik, S., Llorente, C., Hupert, N., and Moorthy, S. (2015). *Children's Educational Media 2010-2015: A Report to the CPB-PBS Ready to Learn Initiative.* Menlo Park, CA: SRI International and New York: Education Development Center.

Patall, E.A. (2013). Constructing motivation through choice, interest, and interestingness. *Journal of Educational Psychology, 105*(2), 522-534. doi: 10.1037/a0030307.

Patall, E.A., Cooper, H., and Robinson, J.C. (2008). The effects of choice on intrinsic motivation and related outcomes: A meta-analysis of research findings. *Psychological Bulletin, 134*(2), 270-300. doi.org/10.1037/0033-2909.134.2.270.

Patall, E.A., Cooper, H., and Wynn, S.R. (2010). The effectiveness and relative importance of choice in the classroom. *Journal of Educational Psychology, 102*(4), 896-915.

Patall, E.A., Sylvester, B.J., and Han, C.W. (2014). The role of competence in the effects of choice on motivation. *Journal of Experimental Social Psychology, 50*(1), 27-44. doi:10.1016/j.jesp.2013.09.002.

Patel, V.L., and Groen, G.J. (1991). Developmental accounts of the transition from medical student to doctor: Some problems and suggestions. *Medical Education, 25*(6), 527-535.

Patel, V.L., Groen, G.J., and Frederiksen, C.H. (1986). Differences between medical students and doctors in memory for clinical cases. *Medical Education, 20*(1), 3-9.

Pavlik, P.I. Jr., and Anderson, J.R. (2008). Using a model to compute the optimal schedule of practice. *Journal of Experimental Psychology: Applied, 14*(2), 101-117.

Pavlik, P.I. Jr., Kelly, C., and Maass, J.K. (2016). The Mobile Fact and Concept Training System (MoFaCTS). In A. Micarelli, J. Stamper, and K. Panourgia (Eds.), *Intelligent Tutoring Systems. ITS 2016. Lecture Notes in Computer Science* (Vol. 9684). Cham, Switzerland: Springer.

Peich, M.-C., Husain, M., and Bays, P.M. (2013). Age related decline of precision and binding in visual working memory. *Psychology and Aging, 28*(3), 729-743. doi:10.1037/a0033236.

Pellegrino, J.W. (2014). Assessment as a positive influence on 21st century teaching and learning: A systems approach to progress. *Psicología Educativa, 20,* 65-77.

Pennington, C.R., Heim, D., Levy, A.R., and Larkin, D.T. (2016). Twenty years of stereotype threat research: A review of psychological mediators. *PLoS One, 11*(1), 1-25. doi:10.1371/journal.pone.0146487.

Penuel, W.R., Bates, L., Gallagher, L.P., Pasnik, S., Llorente, C., Townsend, E., Hupert, N., Domínguez, X, and VanderBorght, M. (2012). Supplementing literacy instruction with a media-rich intervention: Results of a randomized controlled trial. *Early Childhood Research Quarterly, 27*(1), 115-127. doi.org/10.1016/j.ecresq.2011.07.002.

Pesce, C., Crova, C., Cereatti, L., Casella, R., and Bellucci, M. (2009). Physical activity and mental performance in preadolescents: Effects of acute exercise on free-recall memory. *Mental Health and Physical Activity, 2*(1), 16-22.

Pew Research Center. (2014). *Older Adults and Technology Use.* Available: http://www.pewinternet.org/2014/04/03/older-adults-and-technology-use [December 2017].

Phinney, J.S., and Haas, K. (2003). The process of coping among ethnic minority first-generation college freshman: A narrative approach. *The Journal of Social Psychology, 143*(6), 707-726.

Pinkard, N., Erete, S., Martin, C., and McKinney de Royston, M. (2017). Digital youth divas: Exploring narrative-driven curriculum to trigger middle school girls' interest in computational activities. *Journal of the Learning Sciences, 26*(3), 477-516. doi.org/10.1080/10508406.2017.1307199.

Pintrich, P.R. (2000). Multiple goals, multiple pathways: The role of goal orientation in learning and achievement. *Journal of Educational Psychology, 92*(3), 544-555.

Pintrich, P.R. (2003). A motivational science perspective on the role of student motivation in learning and teaching contexts. *Journal of Educational Psychology, 95*(4), 667-686.

Poldrack, R.A. (2000). Imaging brain plasticity: Conceptual and methodological issues. *Neuroimage, 12*(1), 1-13.

Pollock, J.I. (1994). Night-waking at five years of age: Predictors and prognosis. *Journal of Child Psychology and Psychiatry and Allied Disciplines, 35*(4), 699-708.

Potter, G.G., Plassman, B.L., Helms, M.J., Foster, S.M., and Edwards, N.W. (2006). Occupational characteristics and cognitive performance among elderly male twins. *Neurology, 67*(8), 1377-1382. doi.org/10.1212/01.wnl.0000240061.51215.ed.

Potter, G.G., Helms, M.J., and Plassman, B.L. (2008). Associations of job demands and intelligence with cognitive performance among men in late life. *Neurology, 70*(19), 1803-1808. doi.org/10.1212/01.wnl.0000295506.58497.7e.

Prensky, M. (2006). *Don't Bother Me, Mom, I'm Learning!: How Computer and Video Games are Preparing Your Kids for 21st Century Success and How You Can Help!* St. Paul, MN: Paragon House.

Pressley, M., McDaniel, M.A., Turnure, J.E., Wood, E., and Ahmad, M. (1987). Generation and precision of elaboration: Effects on intentional and incidental learning. *Journal of Experimental Psychology: Learning, Memory, and Cognition, 13*(2), 291-300. doi:10.1037/0278-7393.13.2.291.

Prieto, L.P., Dlab, M.H., Gutiérrez, I., Abdulwahed, M., and Balid, W. (2011). Orchestrating technology enhanced learning: A literature review and a conceptual framework. *International Journal of Technology Enhanced Learning, 3*(6), 583-598.

Pronin, E., Puccio, C., and Ross, L. (2002). Understanding misunderstanding: Social psychological perspectives. In T. Gilovich and D. Griffin (Eds.), *Heuristics and Biases: The Psychology of Intuitive Judgment* (pp. 636-665). New York: Cambridge University Press

Purcell, K., Heaps, A., Buchanan, J., and Friedrich, L. (2013). *The Impact of Digital Tools on Student Writing and How Writing Is Taught in Schools.* Washington, DC: Pew Research Center's Internet and American Life Project.

Pyc, M.A., and Rawson, K.A. (2010). Why testing improves memory: Mediator effectiveness hypothesis. *Science, 330*(6002), 335. doi:10.1126/science.1191465.

Rader, H.B. (2002). 21st century literacy summit. *Library Hi Tech News, 19*(7), 21.

Radinsky, J., Alamar, K., and Oliva, S. (2010). Camila, the earth, and the sun: Constructing an idea as shared intellectual property. *Journal of Research in Science Teaching, 47*, 619-642.

Raemdonck, I., Gijbels, D., and van Groen, W. (2014). The influence of job characteristics and self-directed learning orientation on workplace learning. *International Journal of Training and Development, 18*(3), 188-203. doi.org/10.1111/ijtd.12028.

Rauh, V.A., and Margolis, A.E. (2016). Research review: Environmental exposures, neurodevelopment, and child mental health—new paradigms for the study of brain and behavioral effects. *Journal of Child Psychology and Psychiatry, 57*(7), 775-793. doi:10.1111/jcpp.12537.

Raviv, S., and Low, M. (1990). Influence of physical activity on concentration among junior high-school students. *Perceptual and Motor Skills, 70*(1), 67-74.

Raybourn, E.M. (2014). A new paradigm for serious games: Transmedia learning for more effective training and education. *Journal of Computational Science, 5*(3), 471-481. doi.org/10.1016/j.jocs.2013.08.005.

Raz, N., Lindenberger, U., Rodrigue, K.M., Kennedy, K.M., Head, D., Williamson, A., Dahle, C., Gerstorf, D., and Acker, J.D. (2005). Regional brain changes in aging healthy adults: General trends, individual differences and modifiers. *Cerebral Cortex, 15*(11), 1676-1689.

Raz, N., Ghisletta, P., Rodrigue, K.M., Kennedy, K.M., and Lindenberger, U. (2010). Trajectories of brain aging in middle-aged and older adults: Regional and individual differences. *Neuroimage, 51*(2), 501-511.

Rea, C.P., and Modigliani, V. (1987). The spacing effect in 4- to 9-year-old children. *Memory & Cognition, 15*(5), 436-443.

Reardon, S.F. (2011). The widening academic achievement gap between the rich and the poor: New evidence and possible explanations. In R. Murnane and G. Duncan (Eds.), *Whither Opportunity? Rising Inequality and the Uncertain Life Chances of Low-Income Children* (pp. 91-116). New York: Russell Sage Foundation Press.

Reich, J., Murnane, R., and Willett, J. (2012). The state of wiki usage in U.S. K-12 schools: Leveraging Web 2.0 data warehouses to assess quality and equity in online learning environments. *Educational Researcher, 41*(1), 7-15.

Reigosa-Crespo, V., Valdés-Sosa, M., Butterworth, B., Estévez, N., Rodríguez, M., Santos, E., and Lage, A. (2012). Basic numerical capacities and prevalence of developmental dyscalculia: The Havana survey. *Developmental Psychology, 48*(1), 123-135. doi.org/10.1037/a0025356.

Reisman, A. (2012). Reading like a historian: A document-based history curriculum intervention in urban high schools. *Cognition and Instruction, 30*, 86-112.

Renier, L.A., Anurova I., De Volder A.G., Carlson S., VanMeter J., and Rauschecker J.P. (2010). Preserved functional specialization for spatial processing in the middle occipital gyrus of the early blind. *Neuron, 68*(1), 138-148.

Renninger, K.A., and Hidi, S. (2002). Student interest and achievement: Developmental issues raised by a case study. In A. Wigfield and J.S. Eccles (Eds.), *Development of Achievement Motivation* (pp. 173-195). New York: Academic Press.

Reuter-Lorenz, P.A., and Cappell, K.A. (2008). Neurocognitive aging and the compensation hypothesis. *Current Directions in Psychological Science, 17*(3), 177-182.

Richardson, M., Abraham, C., and Bond, R. (2012). Psychological correlates of university students' academic performance: A systematic review and meta-analysis. *Psychological Bulletin, 138*(2), 353-387. doi:10.1037/a0026838.

Richlan, F. (2012). Developmental dyslexia: Dysfunction of a left hemisphere reading network. *Frontiers in Human Neuroscience, 6*, 120. doi:10.3389/fnhum.2012.00120.

Richlan, F., Kronbichler, M., and Wimmer, H. (2009). Functional abnormalities in the dyslexic brain: A quantitative meta-analysis of neuroimaging studies. *Human Brain Mapping, 30*(10), 3299-3308. doi:10.1002/hbm.20752.

Richlan, F., Kronbichler, M., and Wimmer, H. (2013). Structural abnormalities in the dyslexic brain: A meta-analysis of voxel-based morphometry studies. *Human Brain Mapping, 34*(11), 3055-3065. doi:10.1002/hbm.22127.

Riggs, N.R., Jahromi, L.B., Razza, R.P., Dillworth, J.E., and Mueller, U. (2006). Executive function and the promotion of social-emotional competence. *Journal of Applied Developmental Psychology, 27*(4), 300-309. doi:10.1016/j.appdev.2006.04.002.

Ritter, S., Anderson, J.R., Koedinger, K, and Corbett, A. (2007). Cognitive tutor: Applied research in mathematics education. *Psychonomic Bulletin and Review, 14*(2), 249-255.

Rittle-Johnson, B. (2006). Promoting transfer: Effects of self-explanation and direct instruction. *Child Development, 77*(1), 1-15. doi:10.1111/j.1467-8624.2006.00852.x.

Rivet, A.E., and Krajcik, J.S. (2004). Achieving standards in urban systemic reform: An example of a sixth grade project-based science curriculum. *Journal of Research in Science Teaching, 41*(7), 669-692. doi:10.1002/tea.20021.

Roberts, R.E., Anderson, E.J., and Husain, M. (2013). White matter microstructure and cognitive function. *The Neuroscientist, 19*(1), 8-15.

Roediger, H.L. (1980). Memory metaphors in cognitive psychology. *Memory & Cognition, 8*(3), 231-246. doi:10.3758/bf03197611.

Roediger, H.L., and Karpicke, J.D. (2006a). Test-enhanced learning: Taking memory tests improves long-term retention. *Psychological Science, 17*(3), 249-255. doi:10.1111/j.1467-9280.2006.01693.x.

Roediger, H.L., and Karpicke, J.D. (2006b). The power of testing memory: Basic research and implications for educational practice. *Perspectives on Psychological Science, 1*(3), 181-210. doi:10.1111/j.1745-6916.2006.00012.x.

Roediger, H.L., and McDermott, K.B. (1995). Creating false memories: Remembering words not presented in lists. *Journal of Experimental Psychology: Learning, Memory, and Cognition, 21*(4), 803-814. doi:10.1037/0278-7393.21.4.803.

Rogoff, B. (2003). *The Cultural Nature of Human Development*. New York: Oxford University Press.

Rogoff, B. (2015). Human teaching and learning involve cultural communities, not just individuals. *Behavioral and Brain Sciences, 38*, e60. doi:10.1017/S0140525X14000818.

Rogoff, B. (2016). Culture and participation: A paradigm shift. *Current Opinion in Psychology, 8*, 182-189. doi:10.1016/j.copsyc.2015.12.002.

Rogoff, B., and Chavajay, P. (1995). What's become of research on the cultural basis of cognitive development. *American Psychologist, 50*(10), 859-877.

Rohrer, D. (2012). Interleaving helps students distinguish among similar concepts. *Educational Psychology Review, 24*(3), 355-367. doi:10.1007/s10648-012-9201-3.

Rohrer, D., Dedrick, R.F., and Stershic, S. (2015). Interleaved practice improves mathematics learning. *Journal of Educational Psychology, 107*(3), 900-908. doi:10.1037/edu0000001.

Rojewski, J.W. (1999). Occupational and educational aspirations and attainment of young adults with and without LD 2 years after high school completion. *Journal of Learning Disabilities, 32*(6), 533-552.

Rojewski, J.W., Lee, I.H., and Gregg, N. (2014). Intermediate work outcomes for adolescents with high-incidence disabilities. *Career Development and Transition for Exceptional Individuals, 37*(2), 106-118. doi.org/10.1177/2165143412473352.

Rojewski, J.W., Lee, I.H., and Gregg, N. (2015). Causal effects of inclusion on postsecondary education outcomes of individuals with high-incidence disabilities. *Journal of Disability Policy Studies, 25*(4), 210-219. doi.org/10.1177/1044207313505648.

Rosch, E., and Mervis, C.B. (1975). Family resemblance: Studies in the internal structure of categories. *Cognitive Psychology, 7*(4), 573-605. doi.org/10.1016/0010-0285(75)90024-9.

Roschelle, J. (1992). Learning by collaborating: Convergent conceptual change. *The Journal of the Learning Sciences, 2*(3), 235-276.

Roschelle, J., Shechtman, N., Tatar, D., Hegedus, S., Hopkins, B., Empson, S., Knudsen, J., and Gallagher, L. (2010). Integration of technology, curriculum, and professional development for advancing middle school mathematics: Three large-scale studies. *American Educational Research Journal, 44*(4), 833-878.

Roschelle, J., Feng, M., Murphy, R.F., and Mason, C.A. (2016). Online mathematics homework increases student achievement. *AERA Open, 2*(4), 1-12.

Roscoe, R.D., and Chi, M.T.H. (2007). Understanding tutor learning: Knowledge-building and knowledge-telling in peer tutors' explanations and questions. *Review of Educational Research, 77*(4), 534-574. doi:10.3102/0034654307309920.

Rosen, Y., and Rimor, R. (2009). Using collaborative database to enhance students' knowledge construction. *Interdisciplinary Journal of E-Learning and Learning Objects, 5*, 187-195. Available: http://www.ijello.org/Volume5/IJELLOv5p187-195Rosen671.pdf [December 2017].

Rosenshine, B., Meister, C., and Chapman, S. (1996). Teaching students to generate questions: A review of the intervention studies. *Review of Educational Research, 66*(2), 181-221.

Ross, J.A., and Starling, M. (2008). Self-assessment in a technology supported environment: The case of grade 9 geography. *Assessment in Education, 15*(2), 183-199.

Ross, J.A., Hogaboam-Gray, A., and Rolheiser, C. (2002). Student self-evaluation in grade 5-6 mathematics: Effects on problem-solving achievement. *Educational Assessment, 8*(1), 43-58. doi.org/10.1207/S15326977EA0801_03.

Rouiller, J.Z., and Goldstein, I.L. (1993). The relationship between organizational transfer climate and positive transfer of training. *Human Resource Development Quarterly, 4*(4), 377-390. doi.org/10.1002/hrdq.3920040408.

Rowe, J.W., and Kahn, R.L. (1987). Human aging: Usual and successful. *Science, 237*(4811), 143-149. doi:10.1126/ science.3299702.

Ruiz-Primo, M.A., and Li, M. (2013). Examining formative feedback in the classroom context: New research perspectives. In J.H. McMillan (Ed.), *SAGE Handbook of Research on Classroom Assessment* (pp. 215-231). New York: SAGE.

Ryan, R.M., and Deci, E.L. (2000). Intrinsic and extrinsic motivations: Classic definitions and new directions. *Contemporary Educational Psychology, 25*(1), 54-67. doi:10.1006/ ceps.1999.1020.

Sabatini, J.P., Sawaki, Y., Shore, J.R., and Scarborough, H.S. (2010). Relationships among reading skills of adults with low literacy. *Journal of Learning Disabilities, 43*(2), 122-138.

Sadoski, M., and Paivio, A. (2001). *Imagery and Text: A Dual Coding Theory Reading and Writing*. New York: Lawrence Erlbaum Associates.

Saffran, J.R., Aslin, R.N., and Newport, E.L. (1996). Statistical learning by 8-month-old infants. *Science, 274*(5294), 1926-1928.

Salas, E., Cooke, N.J., and Rosen, M.A. (2008). On teams, teamwork, and team performance: Discoveries and developments. *Human Factors, 50*(3), 540-548.

Salthouse, T.A. (2009). When does age-related cognitive decline begin? *Neurobiology of Aging, 30*(4), 507-514. doi:10.1016/j.neurobiolaging.2008.09.023.

Salthouse, T.A. (2010). *Major Issues in Cognitive Aging*. New York: Oxford University Press.

Sana, F., Weston, T., and Cepeda, N.J. (2013). Laptop multitasking hinders classroom learning for both users and nearby peers. *Computers and Education, 62*, 24-31. doi:10.1016/j.compedu.2012.10.003.

Sandoval, W.A., and Reiser, B.J. (2004). Explanation-driven inquiry: Integrating conceptual and epistemic scaffolds for scientific inquiry. *Science Education, 88*(3), 345-372.

Saxe, G.B. (2012a). Approaches to reduction in treatments of culture-cognition relations: Affordances and limitations. Commentary on Gauvain and Munroe. *Human Development, 55*, 233-242. doi:10.1159/000341975.

Saxe, G.B. (2012b). *Cultural Development of Mathematical Ideas: Papua New Guinea Studies*. New York: Cambridge University Press.

Scardamalia, M., and Bereiter, C. (1993). Computer support for knowledge-building communities. *Journal of the Learning Sciences, 3*(3), 265-283.

Scardamalia, M., and Bereiter, C. (2006). Knowledge building: Theory, pedagogy, and technology. In K. Sawyer (Ed.), *Cambridge Handbook of the Learning Sciences* (pp. 97-118). New York: Cambridge University Press.

Schacter, D.L., Koutstaal, W., and Norman, K.A. (1997). False memories and aging. *Trends in Cognitive Sciences, 1*(6), 229-236.

Schacter, D.L., Gaesser, B., and Addis, D.R. (2013). Remembering the past and imagining the future in the elderly. *Gerontology, 59*(2), 143-151.

Schapiro, A.C., and Turk-Browne, N.B. (2015). Statistical learning. In A.W. Toga and R.A. Poldrack (Eds.), *Brain Mapping: An Encyclopedic Reference* (pp. 501-506). London, UK: Academic Press.

Schedlowski, M., Enck, P., Rief, W., and Bingel, U. (2015). Neuro-bio-behavioral mechanisms of placebo and nocebo responses: Implications for clinical trials and clinical practice. *Pharmacological Reviews, 67*(3), 697-730. doi:10.1124/pr.114.009423.

Schiefele, U. (2009). Situational and individual interest. In K.R. Wentzel and A. Wigfield (Eds.), *Handbook of Motivation in School* (pp. 197-223). New York: Taylor Francis.

Schlichting, M.L., and Preston, A.R. (2015). Memory integration: Neural mechanisms and implications for behavior. *Current Opinion in Behavioral Sciences, 1*, 1-8. doi.org/10.1016/j.cobeha.2014.07.005.

Schmader, T., and Johns, M. (2003). Converging evidence that stereotype threat reduces working memory capacity. *Journal of Personality and Social Psychology, 85*(3), 440-452.

Schmader, T., Johns, M., and Forbes, C. (2008). An integrated process model of stereotype threat effects on performance. *Psychological Review, 115*(2), 336-356. doi.org/10.1037/0033-295X.115.2.336.

Schmeck, A., Mayer, R.E., Opfermann, M., Pfeiffer, V., and Leutner, D. (2014). Drawing pictures during learning from scientific text: Testing the generative drawing effect and the prognostic drawing effect. *Contemporary Educational Psychology, 39*(4), 275-286. doi:10.1016/j.cedpsych.2014.07.003.

Schmidt, R.A., and Bjork, R.A. (1992). New conceptualizations of practice: Common principles in three paradigms suggest new concepts for training. *Psychological Science, 3*(4), 207-217.

Schneps, M.H., Rose, L.T. and Fischer, K.W. (2007). Visual learning and the brain: Implications for dyslexia. *Mind, Brain, and Education, 1*(3), 128-139. doi:10.1111/j.1751-228X.2007.00013.x.

Scholz, J., Klein, M.C., Behrens, T.E.J., and Johansen-Berg, H. (2009). Training induces changes in white matter architecture. *Nature Neuroscience, 12*(11), 1370-1371.

Schoorman, F.D., and Schneider, B. (1988). Integration and overview of the research on work facilitation. In F.D. Schoorman and B. Schneider (Eds.), *Facilitating Work Effectiveness* (pp. 215-230). Lexington, MA: Lexington Books/D.C. Heath and Company.

Schraw, G., and Lehman, S. (2001). Situational interest: A review of the literature and directions for future research. *Educational Psychology Review, 13*(1), 23-52. doi:10.1023/A:1009004801455.

Schraw, G., Bruning, R., and Svoboda, C. (1995). Sources of situational interest. *Journal of Reading Behavior, 27*(1), 1-17. Available: http://journals.sagepub.com/doi/pdf/10.1080/10862969509547866 [December 2017].

Schulz, M., and Stamov Roßnagel, C. (2010). Informal workplace learning: An exploration of age differences in learning competence. *Learning and Instruction, 20*(5), 383-399. doi.org/10.1016/j.learninstruc.2009.03.003.

Schultz, W.P., Nolan, J.M., Cialdini, R.B., Goldstein, N.J., and Griskevicius, V. (2007). The constructive, destructive, and reconstructive power of social norms. *Psychological Science, 18*(5), 429-434.

Schunk, D.H., and Cox, P.D. (1986). Strategy training and attributional feedback with learning disabled students. *Journal of Educational Psychology, 78*(3), 201-209. doi.org/10.1037/0022-0663.78.3.201.

Schwamborn, A., Mayer, R.E., Thillmann, H., Leopold, C., and Leutner, D. (2010). Drawing as a generative activity and drawing as a prognostic activity. *Journal of Educational Psychology, 102*(4), 872–879. doi:10.1037/a0019640.

Schwartz, D.L. (1995). The emergence of abstract dyad representations in dyad problem solving. *The Journal of the Learning Sciences, 4*(3), 321–354. doi.org/10.1207/s15327809jls0403_3.

Schwartz, D.L., Martin, T., and Pfaffman, J. (2005). How mathematics propels the development of physical knowledge. *Journal of Cognition and Development, 6*(1), 65–88. doi 10.1207/s15327647jcd0601_5.

Schyns, P.G., Goldstone, R.L., and Thibaut, J.-P. (1998). The development of features in object concepts. *Behavioral and Brain Sciences, 21*, 1–54.

Seabrook, R., Brown, G.D.A., and Solity, J.E. (2005). Distributed and massed practice: From laboratory to classroom. *Applied Cognitive Psychology, 19*(1), 107–122. doi:10.1002/acp.1066.

Seehagen, S., Konrad, C., Herbert, J.S., and Schneider, S. (2015). Timely sleep facilitates declarative memory consolidation in infants. *Proceedings of the National Academy of Sciences of the United States of America, 112*(5), 1625–1629.

Seel, N.M. (2012). *Encyclopedia of the Sciences of Learning.* Boston, MA: Springer.

Segall, M.H., Campbell, D.T., and Herskovits, M.J. (1966). *The Influence of Culture on Visual Perception.* Indianapolis, IN: Bobbs-Merrill Company.

Senko, C., Hulleman, C.S., and Harackiewicz, J.M. (2011). Achievement goal theory at the crossroads: Old controversies, current challenges, and new directions. *Educational Psychologist, 46*(1), 26–47. doi:10.1080/00461520.2011.538646.

Serpell, R., and Boykin, A.W. (1994). Cultural dimensions of cognition: A multiplex, dynamic system of constraints and possibilities. In R.J. Sternberg (Ed.), *Thinking and Problem Solving* (pp. 235–258). San Diego, CA: Academic Press.

Serpell, R., and Boykin, A.W. (1994). Cultural dimensions of cognition: A multiplex, dynamic system of constraints and possibilities. In R.J. Sternberg (Ed.), *Handbook of Perception and Cognition, Vol. 12: Thinking and Problem Solving* (pp. 369–408). San Diego, CA: Academic Press.

Serpell, Z.N., Boykin, A.W., Madhere, S., and Nasim, A. (2006). The significance of contextual factors in African American students' transfer of learning. *Journal of Black Psychology, 32*(4), 418–441.

Shaffer, D.W. (2007). *How Computer Games Help Children Learn.* New York: Palgrave.

Shaffer D.W., Hatfield D., Svarovsky G.N., Nash P., Nulty A., Bagley E., Frank, K., Rupp, A.A., and Mislevy, R. (2009). Epistemic network analysis: A prototype for 21st-century assessment of learning. *International Journal of Learning and Media, 1*(2), 33–53. doi:10.1162/ijlm.2009.0013.

Shah, J.Y., and Kruglanski, A.W. (2000). Aspects of goal networks: Implications for self-regulation. In M. Boekaerts, P.R. Pintrich, and M. Zeidner (Eds.), *Handbook of Self-Regulation* (pp. 85–110). San Diego, CA: Academic Press.

Shim, S.S., Ryan, A.M., and Anderson, C.J. (2008). Achievement goals and achievement during early adolescence: Examining time-varying predictor and outcome variables in growth-curve analysis. *Journal of Educational Psychology, 100*(3), 655–671. doi.org/10.1037/0022-0663.100.3.655.

Shute, V. (2008). Focus on formative feedback. *Review of Educational Research, 78*(1), 153–189.

Shute, V.J., and Ventura, M. (2013). *Measuring and Supporting Learning in Games: Stealth Assessment.* Cambridge, MA: The MIT Press.

Siadaty, M., Gašević, D., Jovanović, J., Pata, K., Milikić, N., Holocher-Ertl, T., Jeremić, Z., Ali, L., Giljanović, A., and Hatala, M. (2012). Self-regulated workplace learning: A pedagogical framework and semantic web-based environment. *Educational Technology and Society, 15*(4), 75–88.

Sibley, B.A., and Etnier, J.L. (2003). The relationship between physical activity and cognition in children: A metaanalysis. *Pediatric Exercise Science, 15*(3), 243-256. doi.org/10.1123/pes.15.3.243.

Siemens, G., Gašević , D., and Dawson, S. (2015*). Preparing for the Digital University: A Review of the History and Current State of Distance, Blended, and Online Learning.* Available: http://linkresearchlab.org/PreparingDigitalUniversity.pdf [December 2017].

Silveri, M.M. (2012). Adolescent brain development and underage drinking in the United States: Identifying risks of alcohol use in college populations. *Harvard Review of Psychiatry, 20*(4), 189-200.

Simone, P.M., Bell, M.C., and Cepeda, N.J. (2012). Diminished but not forgotten: Effects of aging on magnitude of spacing effect benefits. *Journals of Gerontology Series B: Psychological Sciences and Social Sciences, 68*(5), 674-680. doi:10.1093/geronb/gbs096.

Siuda-Krzywicka, K., Bola, L., Paplińska, M., Sumera, E., Jednoróg, K., Marchewka, A., Śilwińska, M.W., Amedi, A., and Szwed, M. (2016). Massive cortical reorganization in sighted Braille readers. *eLife,* 5, e10762. http://doi.org/10.7554/eLife.10762.

Slavin, R.E. (2008). Perspectives on evidence-based research in education: What works? *Educational Researcher, 37*(1), 5-14. doi:10.3102/0012189X08314117.

Slavin, R.E. (2016). *Educational Psychology: Theory and Practice.* London: Pearson.

Slavin, R.E., and Lake, C. (2008). Effective programs in elementary mathematics: A best-evidence synthesis. *Review of Educational Research, 78*(3), 427-515. doi.org/10.3102/0034654308317473.

Smedley, A., and Smedley, B.D. (2005). Race as biology is fiction, racism as a social problem is real: Anthropological and historical perspectives on the social construction of race. *American Psychologist, 60*(1), 16-26.

Smeyers, P., and Depaepe, M. (2013). Making sense of the attraction of psychology: On the strengths and weaknesses for education and educational research. In P. Smeyers and M. Depaepe (Eds.), *Educational Research: The Attraction of Psychology* (pp. 1-10). Dordrecht, The Netherlands: Springer.

Smith, M.K., Wood, W.B., Krauter, K., and Knight, J.K. (2011). Combining peer discussion with instructor explanation increases student learning from in-class concept questions. *CBE-Life Sciences Education, 10*(1), 55-63. doi:10.1187/cbe.10-08-0101.

Smith-Spark, J.H., and Fisk J.E. (2007). Working memory functioning in developmental dyslexia. *Memory, 15*(1), 34-56. doi:10.1080/09658210601043384.

Snow, R.E. (1989). Cognitive-conative aptitude interactions in learning. In R. Kanfer, P.L. Ackerman, and R. Cudeck (Eds.), *Abilities, Motivation, and Methodology: The Minnesota Symposium on Learning and Individual Differences* (pp. 435-474). Hillsdale, NJ: Lawrence Erlbaum Associates.

Snowling, M.J., and Hulme, C. (2012). Annual research review: The nature and classification of reading disorders—a commentary on proposals for DSM-5. *Journal of Child Psychology and Psychiatry, 53*(5), 593-607. doi:10.1111/j.1469-7610.2011.02495.x.

Sobel, H.S., Cepeda, N.J., and Kapler, I.V. (2011). Spacing effects in real-world classroom vocabulary learning. *Applied Cognitive Psychology, 25*(5), 763-767. doi:10.1002/acp.1747.

Songer, N., Kelcey, B., and Gotwals, A. (2009). How and when does complex reasoning occur? Empirically driven development of a learning progression focused on complex reasoning about biodiversity. *Journal for Research in Science Teaching, 46*(6), 610-631.

Sonnentag, S., and Lange, I. (2002). The relationship between high performance and knowledge about how to master cooperative situations. *Applied Cognitive Psychology, 16,* 491-508. Available: https://pdfs.semanticscholar.org/f850/d8a0f6155107149d92edaded7f7cede442c3.pdf [December 2017].

Sottilare, R., Graesser, A., Hu, X., and Goldberg, B. (Eds.). (2014). *Design Recommendations for Intelligent Tutoring Systems* (Vol. 2). Orlando, FL: U.S. Army Research Laboratory. Available: http://ict.usc.edu/pubs/Intelligent%20Tutoring%20Support%20for%20Learners%20Interacting%20with%20Virtual%20Humans.pdf [December 2017].

Spelke, E.S. (2004). Core knowledge. In N. Kanwisher and J. Duncan (Eds.), *Attention and Performance* (Vol. 20). Oxford, UK: Oxford University Press.

Spelke, E.S., and Kinzler, K.D. (2007). Core knowledge. *Developmental Science, 10*(1), 89-96.

Spencer, J.A. (1999). Learner centered approaches in medical education. *British Medical Journal, 318*, 1280-1283. doi.org/10.1136/bmj.318.7193.1280.

Spencer, S.J., Steele, C.M., and Quinn, D.M. (1999). Stereotype threat and women's math performance. *Journal of Experimental Social Psychology, 35*(1), 4-28. doi:10.1006/jesp.1998.1373.

Spencer, W.D., and Raz, N. (1995). Differential effects of aging on memory for content and context: A meta-analysis. *Psychology and Aging, 10*(4), 527-539.

Spilsbury, J.C., Storfer-Isser, A., Drotar, D., Rosen, C.L., Kirchner, L.H., Benham, H., and Redline, S. (2004). Sleep behavior in an urban U.S. sample of school-aged children. *Archives of Pediatrics and Adolescent Medicine, 158*(10), 988-994.

Sporns, O. (2011). *Networks of the Brain*. Cambridge, MA: MIT Press.

Spreng, R.N., Wojtowicz, M., and Grady, C.L. (2010). Reliable differences in brain activity between young and old adults: A quantitative meta-analysis across multiple cognitive domains. *Neuroscience and Biobehavioral Reviews, 34*, 1178-1194.

Squire, K. (2011). *Video Games and Learning: Teaching and Participatory Culture in the Digital Age. Technology, Education—Connections (the TEC series)*. New York: Teachers College Press.

Stark, S.M., Yassa, M.A., and Stark, C.E. (2010). Individual differences in spatial pattern separation performance associated with healthy aging in humans. *Learning & Memory, 17*(6), 284-288.

Steele, C.M. (1997). A threat in the air: How stereotypes shape intellectual identity and performance. *American Psychologist, 52*(6), 613-629.

Steele, C.M., and Aronson, J. (1995). Stereotype threat and the intellectual test performance of African Americans. *Journal of Personality and Social Psychology, 69*(5), 797-811.

Steele, C.M., Spencer, S.J., and Aronson, J. (2002). Contending with group image: The psychology of stereotype and social identity threat. In M. Zanna (Ed.), *Advances in Experimental Social Psychology* (vol. 34, pp. 379-440). New York: Academic Press.

Stephens, N.M., Fryberg, S.A., Markus, H.R., Johnson, C.S., and Covarrubias, R. (2012). Unseen disadvantage: How American universities' focus on independence undermines the academic performance of first-generation college students. *Journal of Personality and Social Psychology, 102*(6), 1178-1197. doi:10.1037/a0027143.

Sternberg, R.J. (2004). Culture and intelligence. *American Psychologist, 59*(5), 325-338. doi.org/10.1037/0003-066X.59.5.325.

Stiles, J., and Jernigan, T.L. (2010). The basics of brain development. *Neuropsychology Review, 20*(4), 327-348. doi.org/10.1007/s11065-010-9148-4.

Stine-Morrow, E.A.L., Parisi, J.M., Morrow, D.G., and Park, D.C. (2008). The effects of an engaged lifestyle on cognitive vitality: A field experiment. *Psychology and Aging, 23*(4), 778-786. doi.org/10.1037/a0014341.

Stoel, G.L., van Drie, J.P., and van Boxtel, C.A.M. (2015). Teaching towards historical expertise. Developing a pedagogy for fostering causal reasoning in history. *Journal of Curriculum Studies, 47*, 49-76.

Stroth, S., Kubesch, S., Dieterle, K., Ruchsow, M., Heim, R., and Kiefer, M. (2009). Physical fitness, but not acute exercise modulates event-related potential indices for executive control in healthy adolescents. *Brain Research, 1269*, 114-124. doi:10.1016/j.brainres.2009.02.073.

Sue, S., and Dhindsa, M.K. (2006). Ethnic and racial health disparities research: Issues and problems. *Health Education and Behavior, 33*(4), 459-469. doi.org/10.1177/1090198106287922.

Super, C.M., and Harkness, S. (1986). The developmental niche: A conceptualization at the interface of child and culture. *International Journal of Behavioral Development, 9*(4), 545-569.

Super, C.M., and Harkness, S. (2010). Culture and infancy. In J.G. Bremner and T.D. Wachs (Eds.), *The Wiley-Blackwell Handbook of Infant Development* (2nd ed., vol. 1). Oxford: Blackwell.

Swanson, H.L. (1999). Reading research for students with LD: A meta-analysis in intervention outcomes. *Journal of Learning Disabilities, 32*(6), 504-532. doi:10.1177/002221949903200605.

Swanson, H.L. (2000). Searching for the best cognitive model for instructing students with learning disabilities: A component and composite analysis. *Educational and Child Psychology, 17*(3), 101-121.

Swanson, H.L. (2012). Adults with reading disabilities: Converting a meta-analysis to practice. *Journal of Learning Disabilities, 45*(1), 17-30. doi.org/10.1177/0022219411426856.

Swanson, H.L. (2016, unpublished). *Learning Disabilities.* Paper commissioned by the Committee on the Science of Practice and Learning, National Academies of Sciences, Engineering, and Medicine, Washington, DC.

Swanson, H.L., and Hsieh, C. (2009). Reading disabilities in adults: A selective meta-analysis of the literature. *Review of Educational Research, 79*(4), 1362-1390.

Swanson, H.L., Hoskyn, M., and Lee, C. (1999). *Interventions for Students with Learning Disabilities: A Meta-analysis of Treatment Outcomes.* New York: Guilford Press.

Swartout, W., Artstein, R., Forbell, E., Foutz, S., Lane, H.C., Lange, B., Morie, J.F., Rizzo, A. S., and Traum, D. (2013). Virtual humans for learning. *AI Magazine, 34*(4), 13-30.

Swartout, W., Nye, B.D., Hartholt, A., Reilly, A., Graesser, A.C., VanLehn, K., Wetzel, J., Liewer, M., Morbini, F., Morgan, B. Wang, L., Benn, G., and Rosenberg, M. (2016). Designing a personal assistant for life-long learning (PAL3). In *Proceedings of the 29th International Florida Artificial Intelligence Research Society Conference, FLAIRS 2016* (pp. 491-496). Palo Alto, CA: AAAI Press.

Swisher, K. (1990). Cooperative learning and the education of American Indian/Alaskan Native Students: A review of the literature and suggestions for implementation. *Journal of American Indian Education, 29*, 2, 36-43.

Tadmor, C.T., Chao, M.M., Hong, Y.Y., and Polzer, J.T. (2013). Not just for stereotyping anymore: Racial essentialism reduces domain-general creativity. *Psychological Science, 24*(1), 99-105. doi:10.1177/0956797612452570.

Tait, A.R., Voepel-Lewis, T., Chetcuti, S.J., Brennan-Martinez, C., and Levine, R. (2014). Enhancing patient understanding of medical procedures: Evaluation of an interactive multimedia program with in-line exercises. *International Journal of Medical Informatics, 83*(5), 376-384.

Tajfel, H., and Turner, J.C. (1979). An integrative theory of intergroup conflict. In W.G. Austin, and S. Worchel (Eds.), *The Social Psychology of Intergroup Relations* (pp. 33-37). Monterey, CA: Brooks/Cole.

Tang, M., Fouad, N.A., and Smith, P.L. (1999). Asian Americans' career choices: A path model to examine factors influencing their career choices. *Journal of Vocational Behavior, 54*(1), 142-157. doi.org/10.1006/jvbe.1998.1651.

Tannenbaum, S.I. (1997). Enhancing continuous learning: Diagnostic findings from multiple companies. *Human Resource Management, 36*(4), 437-452. doi.org/10.1002/(SICI)1099-050X(199724)36:4<437::AID-HRM7>3.0.CO;2-W.

Tannenbaum, S.I., Beard, R.L., McNall, L.A., and Salas, E. (2010). Informal learning and development in organizations. In S W.J. Kozlowski and E. Salas (Eds.), *Learning, Training, and Development in Organizations* (pp. 303-331). New York: Routledge/Taylor and Francis Group.

Taras, H. (2005). Nutrition and student performance at school. *Journal of School Health, 75*(6), 199-213.

Tate, W. (2001). Science education as a civil right: Urban schools and opportunity-to-learn considerations. *Journal of Research in Science Teaching, 38*(9), 1015-1028.

Tauber, S.K., Dunlosky, J., Rawson, K.A., Wahlheim, C.N., and Jacoby, L.L. (2013). Self-regulated learning of a natural category: Do people interleave or block exemplars during study? *Psychonomic Bulletin & Review, 20*, 356-363.

Taylor, S.E., and Brown, J.D. (1988). Illusion and well-being: A social psychological perspective on mental health. *Psychological Bulletin, 103*(2), 193-201.

Tenenbaum, J.B., Kemp, C., Griffiths, T.L., and Goodman, N.D. (2011). How to grow a mind: Statistics, structure, and abstraction. *Science, 331*(6022), 1279-1285.

Thomas, J.W. (2000). *A Review of Research on Project-based Learning.* Available: http://www.bie.org/images/uploads/general/9d06758fd346969cb63653d00dca55c0.pdf [December 2017].

Thompson, G. (1990). How can correspondence-based distance education be improved?: A survey of attitudes of students who are not well disposed toward correspondence study. *International Journal of E-Learning and Distance Education, 5*(1), 53-65.

Thorell, L.B., Lindqvistm, S., Bergmanm, N., Bohlinm, G., and Klingberg, T. (2009). Training and transfer effects of executive functions in preschool children. *Developmental Science, 12*(1), 106-113. doi:10.1111/j.1467-7687.2008.00745.x.

Thorndyke, P.W., and Hayes-Roth, B. (1982). Differences in spatial knowledge acquired from maps and navigation. *Cognitive Psychology, 14*, 560-589.

Thrasher, C., and LoBue, V. (2016). Do infants find snakes aversive? Infants' psychological responses to "fear-relevant" stimuli. *Journal of Experimental Child Psychology, 142*, 382-390. doi: 10.1016/j.jecp.2015.09.013.

Tindall-Ford, S., Chandler, P., and Sweller, J. (1997). When two sensory modes are better than one. *Journal of Experimental Psychology: Applied, 3*(4), 257-287. doi.org/10.1037/1076-898X.3.4.257.

Tobias, S., and Fletcher, J.D. (2011). *Computer Games and Instruction.* Charlotte, NC: Information Age.

Tomasello, M. (2001). *The Cultural Origins of Human Cognition.* Cambridge, MA: Harvard University Press.

Tomasello, M. (2008). *Origins of Human Communication.* Cambridge, MA: MIT Press.

Tomasello, M. (2016). Cultural learning redux. *Child Development, 87*(3), 643-653.

Tomporowski, P.D., and Ellis, N.R. (1984). Preparing severely and profoundly mentally retarded adults for tests of motor fitness. *Adapted Physical Activity Quarterly, 1*(2), 158-163.

Tomporowski, P.D., and Ellis, N.R. (1985). The effects of exercise on the health, intelligence, and adaptive behavior of institutionalized severely and profoundly mentally retarded adults: A systematic replication. *Applied Research in Mental Retardation, 6*(4), 465-473.

Tomporowski, P.D., Lambourne, K., and Okumura, M.S. (2011). Physical activity interventions and children's mental function: An introduction and overview. *Preventive Medicine, 52*(Suppl. 1), S3-S9. doi:10.1016/j.ypmed.2011.01.028.

Topping, K. (2013). Peers as a source of formative and summative assessment. In J. McMillan (Ed.), *SAGE Handbook of Research on Classroom Assessment* (pp. 395-412). New York: SAGE.

Toppino, T.C. (1991). The spacing effect in young children's free recall: Support for automatic-process explanations. *Memory & Cognition, 19*(2), 159-167.

Toppino, T.C., Hara, Y., and Hackman, J. (2002). The spacing effect in the free recall of homogeneous lists: Present and accounted for. *Memory & Cognition, 30*(4), 601-606.

Treisman U. (1992). Studying students studying calculus: A look at the lives of minority mathematics students in college. *The College Mathematics Journal, 23*(5), 362-372. doi:10.2307/2686410.

Tulving, E., and Thomson, D.M. (1973). Encoding specificity and retrieval processes in episodic memory. *Psychological Review, 80*(5), 352-373. doi:10.1037/h0020071.

Turner, G.R., and Spreng, R.N. (2012). Executive functions and neurocognitive aging: Dissociable patterns of brain activity. *Neurobiology of Aging, 33*, 826.e1-826.e13.

Tyler, K.M., Boykin, A.W., and Walton, T.R. (2006). Cultural considerations in teachers' perceptions of student classroom behavior and achievement. *Teaching and Teacher Education, 22*(8), 998-1005. doi.org/10.1016/j.tate.2006.04.017.

Tynjala, P. (2008). Perspectives into learning at the workplace. *Educational Research Review*, 3(2), 130-154.

Urdan, T., Midgley, C., and Anderman, E.M. (1998). The role of classroom goal structure in students' use of self-handicapping strategies. *American Educational Research Journal, 35*(1), 101–122. doi:10.3102/00028312035001101.

U.S. Department of Commerce, National Telecommunications and Information Administration. (2014). *Exploring the Digital Nation: Embracing the Mobile Internet*. Available: https://www.ntia.doc.gov/files/ntia/publications/exploring_the_digital_ nation_embracing_the_mobile_internet_10162014.pdf [December 2017].

U.S. Department of Education. (1992). *Fourteenth Annual Report to Congress on the Implementation of the Individuals with Disabilities Education Act*. Washington, DC: U.S. Government Printing Office.

U.S. Department of Education. (1999). *1992 National Adult Literacy Survey: An Overview*. Working Paper No. 1999-09a. Available: https://nces.ed.gov/pubs99/199909a.pdf [July 2018].

U.S. Department of Education. (2001). *No Child Left Behind Act of 2001*. Washington, DC: Author. Available: http://www2.ed.gov/policy/elsec/leg/esea02/index.html [December 2017].

U.S. Department of Education. (2010). *Beyond the Bubble Tests: The Next Generation of Assessments—Secretary Arne Duncan's Remarks to State Leaders at Achieve's American Diploma Project Leadership Team Meeting*. Available: http://www.ed.gov/news/speeches/beyond-bubble-tests-next-generation-assessments-secretary-arne-duncans-remarks-state-leaders-achieves-american-diploma-project-leadership-team-meeting [December 2017].

U.S. Department of Education. (2016). *Section 1: Engaging and Empowering Learning Through Technology*. Available: https://tech.ed.gov/netp/learning [December 2017].

U.S. Department of Education, and Office of Educational Technology. (2016). *Future Ready Learning: Reimagining the Role of Technology in Education*. Available: https://tech.ed.gov/files/2015/12/NETP16.pdf [December 2017].

U.S. Department of Health and Human Services, and Administration for Children and Families (2010). *Head Start Impact Study*. Final Report. Washington, DC: Author. Available: https://www.acf.hhs.gov/sites/default/files/opre/hs_impact_study_final.pdf [December 2017].

Valle, C. (2015). Effects of criteria-referenced formative assessment on achievement in music. Doctoral dissertation. University at Albany—SUNY.

Van der Kleij, F.M., Feskens, R.C., and Eggen, T.J.H.M. (2015). Effects of feedback in a computer-based learning environment on students' learning outcomes: A meta-analysis. *Review of Educational Research, 85*(4), 475–511.

van Geldorp, B., Heringa, S.M., van den Berg, E., Olde Rikkert, M.G., Biessels, G.J., and Kessels, R.P. (2015). Working memory binding and episodic memory formation in aging, mild cognitive impairment, and Alzheimer's dementia. *Journal of Clinical and Experimental Neuropsychology*, 37(5), 538-548.

Van Kesteren, M.T.R., Fernández, G., Norris, D.G., and Hermans, E.J. (2010). Persistent schema-dependent hippocampal-neocortical connectivity during memory encoding and postencoding rest in humans. *Proceedings of the National Academy of Sciences of the United States of America, 107*(16), 7550-7555. doi.org/10.1073/pnas.0914892107.

Van Meter, P. (2001). Drawing construction as a strategy for learning from text. *Journal of Educational Psychology, 93*(1), 129–140. doi:10.1037/0022-0663.93.1.129.

Van Meter, P., and Garner, J. (2005). The promise and practice of learner-generated drawing: Literature review and synthesis. *Educational Psychology Review, 17*(4), 285–325. doi:10.1007/s10648-005-8136-3.

Van Meter, P., Aleksic, M., Schwartz, A., and Garner, J. (2006). Learner-generated drawing as a strategy for learning from content area text. *Contemporary Educational Psychology, 31*(2), 142-166. doi:10.1016/j.cedpsych.2005.04.001

van Zuijen, T.L., Plakas, A., Maassen, B.M., Maurits, N.M., and van der Leij, A. (2013). Infant ERPs separate children at risk of dyslexia who become good readers from those who become poor readers. *Developmental Science, 16*(4), 554-563. doi:10.1111/desc.12049.

VanLehn, K. (2011). The relative effectiveness of human tutoring, intelligent tutoring systems, and other tutoring systems. *Educational Psychologist, 46*(4), 197-221.

VanLehn, K., Graesser, A.C., Jackson, G.T., Jordan, P., Olney, A., and Rose, C.P. (2007). When are tutorial dialogues more effective than reading? *Cognitive Science, 31*(1), 3-62.

VanLehn, K., Wetzel, J., Grover, S., and van de Sande, B. (2015). Learning how to construct models of dynamic systems: An initial evaluation of the Dragoon intelligent tutoring system. *IEEE Transactions on Educational Technology*. Available: http://ieeexplore.ieee.org/document/7374728 [December 2017]. doi:10.1109/TLT.2016.2514422.

VanLehn, K., Chung, G., Grover, S., Madni, A., and Wetzel, J. (2016). Learning science by constructing models: Can Dragoon increase learning without increasing the time required? *International Journal of Artificial Intelligence in Education, 26*(4), 1033-1068. doi:10.1007/s40593-015-0093-5.

VanSledright, B., and Limón, M. (2006). Learning and teaching social studies: A review of cognitive research in history and geography. In P.A. Alexander and P.H. Winne (Eds.), *Handbook of Educational Psychology* (pp. 545-570). Hillsdale, NJ: Erlbaum.

Vansteenkiste, M., Lens, W., Dewitte, S., De Witte, H, and Deci, E.L. (2004). The "why" and "why not" of job search behavior: Their relation to searching, unemployment experience and well-being. *European Journal of Social Psychology, 34*(3), 345-363. doi:10.1002/ejsp.202.

Vansteenkiste, M., Sierens, E., Soenens, B., Luyckx, K., and Lens, W. (2009). Motivational profiles from a self-determination perspective: The quality of motivation matters. *Journal of Educational Psychology, 101*(3), 671-688. doi.org/10.1037/a0015083.

Varga, N.L., and Bauer, P.J. (2013). Effects of delay on 6-year-old children's self-generation and retention of knowledge through integration. *Journal of Experimental Child Psychology, 115*(2), 326-341. doi:10.1016/j.jecp.2013.01.008.

Varga, N.L., Stewart, R., and Bauer, P.J. (2016). Integrating across episodes: Investigating the long-term accessibility of self-derived knowledge in 4-year-old children. *Journal of Experimental Child Psychology, 145*(1), 48-63. doi:10.1016/j.jcep.2015.11.015.

Vellutino, F.R., Fletcher, J.M., Snowling, M.J., and Scanlon, D.M. (2004). Specific reading disability (dyslexia), What have we learned in the past four decades? *Journal of Child Psychology and Psychiatry, 45*(1), 2-40. doi:10.1046/j.0021-9630.2003.00305.x.

Verhaeghen, P., and Salthouse, T.A. (1997). Meta-analyses of age-cognition relations in adulthood: Estimates of linear and nonlinear age effects and structural models. *Psychological Bulletin, 122*(3), 231-249.

Vezzali, L., Goclowska, M., Crisp, R., and Stathi, S. (2016). On the relationship between cultural diversity and creativity in education: The moderating role of communal versus divisional mindset. *Thinking Skills and Creativity, 21*, 152-157. doi:10.1016/j.tsc.2016.07.001.

Vignoles, V.L., Owe, E., Becker, M., Smith, P.B., Easterbrook, M.J., Brown, R., González, R., Didier, N., Carrasco, D., Cadena, M.P., Lay, S., Schwartz, S.J., Des Rosiers, S.E., Villamar, J.A., Gavreliuc, A., Zinkeng, M., Kreuzbauer, R., Baguma, P., Martin, M., Tatarko, A., Herman, G., de Sauvage, I., Courtois, M., Garðarsdóttir, R.B., Harb, C., Schweiger Gallo, I., Prieto Gil, P., Lorente Clemares, R., Campara, G., Nizharadze, G., Macapagal, M.E., Jalal, B., Bourguignon, D., Zhang, J., Lv, S., Chybicka, A., Yuki, M., Zhang, X., Espinosa, A., Valk, A., Abuhamdeh, S., Amponsah, B., Özgen, E., Güner, E. Ü., Yamakoğlu, N., Chobthamkit, P., Pyszczynski, T., Kesebir, P., Vargas Trujillo, E., Balanta, P., Cendales Ayala, B., Koller, S.H., Jaafar, J.L., Gausel, N., Fischer, R., Milfont, T.L., Kusdil, E., Çağlar, S., Aldhafri, S., Ferreira, M.C., Mekonnen, K.H., Wang, Q., Fülöp, M., Torres, A., Camino, L., Lemos, F.C., Fritsche, I., Möller, B., Regalia, C., Manzi, C., Brambilla, M., and Bond, M.H. (2016). Beyond the "east-west" dichotomy: Global variation in cultural models of selfhood. *Journal of Experimental Psychology: General, 145*(8), 966-1000.

Vohs, K., and Bauminster, R.F. (Eds.). (2017). *Handbook of Self-Regulation: Research, Theory, and Applications* (3rd ed.). New York: Guilford Press.

von Károlyi, C., Winner, E., Gray, W., and Sherman, G.F. (2003). Dyslexia linked to talent: Global visual-spatial ability. *Brain and Language, 85*(3), 427-431. doi:10.1016/S0093-934X(03)00052-X.

Vosniadou, S., and Brewer, W.F. (1992). Mental models of the earth: A study of conceptual change in childhood. *Cognitive Psychology, 24*(4), 535-585. doi.org/10.1016/0010-0285(92)90018-W.

Wade, S.E., Buxton, W.M., and Kelly, M. (1999). Using think-alouds to examine reader–text interest. *Reading Research Quarterly, 34*(2), 194-216.

Wade-Stein, D., and Kintsch, E. (2004). Summary Street: Interactive computer support for writing. *Cognition and Instruction, 22*(3), 333-362.

Wagner, M., Newman, L., Cameto, R., Garza, N., and Levine, P. (2005). *After High School: A First Look at the Postschool Experiences of Youth with Disabilities.* Menlo Park, CA: SRI International. Available: https://files.eric.ed.gov/fulltext/ED494935.pdf [December 2017].

Wahlstrom, K., Dretzke, B., Gordon, M., Peterson, K., Edwards, K., and Gdula, J. (2014). *Examining the Impact of Later School Start Times on the Health and Academic Performance of High School Students: A Multi-Site Study.* Center for Applied Research and Educational Improvement. St. Paul: University of Minnesota.

Waldinger, R.J., Cohen, S., Schulz, M.S., and Crowell, J.A. (2015). Security of attachment to spouses in late life: Concurrent and prospective links with cognitive and emotional wellbeing. *Clinical Psychological Science, 3*(4), 516-529.

Walker, M.P. (2006). Sleep to remember. *American Scientist, 94*, 326-333.

Walton, G.M., and Cohen, G.L. (2011). A brief social-belonging intervention improves academic and health outcomes of minority students. *Science, 331*(6023), 1447-1451.

Walton, G.M., and Spencer, S.J. (2009). Latent ability: Grades and test scores systematically underestimate the intellectual ability of negatively stereotyped students. *Psychological Science, 20*(9), 1132-1139.

Wang, M., Burlacu, G., Truxillo, D.J., James, K., and Yao, X. (2015). Age differences in feedback reactions: The roles of employee feedback orientation on social awareness and utility. *Journal of Applied Psychology, 100*(4), 1296-1308. doi:10.1037/a0038334.

Wang, Q. (2004). The emergence of cultural self-constructs: Autobiographical memory and self-description in European American and Chinese children. *Developmental Psychology, 40*(1), 3-15.

Wang, Q. (2009). Are Asians forgetful? Perception, retention, and recall in episodic remembering. *Cognition, 111*(1), 123-131.

Wang, Q., and Conway, M.A. (2004). The stories we keep: Autobiographical memory in American and Chinese middle-aged adults. *Journal of Personality, 72*(5), 911-938.

Wang, Q., and Ross, M. (2007). Culture and memory. In H. Kitayama and D. Cohen (Eds.), *Handbook of Cultural Psychology* (pp. 645-667). New York: Guilford Press.

Wang, S., and Gathercole, S.E. (2013). Working memory deficits in children with reading difficulties: Memory span and dual task coordination. *Journal of Experimental Child Psychology, 115*(1), 188-197.

Wang, Y.-S., Wu, M.-C., and Wang, H.-Y. (2009). Investigating the determinants and age and gender differences in the acceptance of mobile learning. *British Journal of Educational Technology, 40*(1), 92-118.

Wanzek, J., Vaughn, S., Scammacca, N.K., Metz, K., Murray, C.S., Roberts, G., and Danielson, L. (2013). Extensive reading interventions for students with reading difficulties after grade 3. *Review of Educational Research, 83*(2), 163-195. doi:10.3102/0034654313477212.

Warschauer, M., and Grimes, D. (2008). Automated writing in the classroom. *Pedagogies: An International Journal, 3*, 22-26. doi:10.1080/15544800701771580.

Warschauer, M., and Matuchniak, T. (2010). New technology and digital worlds: Analyzing evidence of equity in access, use, and outcomes. *Review of Research in Education, 34*(1), 179-219.

Wasserberg, M.J. (2014). Stereotype threat effects on African American children in an urban elementary school. *The Journal of Experimental Education, 82*(4), 502-517. doi.org/10.1080/00220973.2013.876224.

Wei, X., Yu, J.W., Shattuck, P., McCracken, M., and Blackorby, J. (2013). Science, technology, engineering, and mathematics (STEM) participation among college students with an autism spectrum disorder. *Journal of Autism and Developmental Disorders, 43*(7), 1539-1546. doi:10.1007/s10803-012-1700-z.

Wenglinsky, H. (2005). *Using Technology Wisely: The Keys to Success in Schools.* New York: Teachers College Press.

Wertsch, J.V. (1991). *Voices of the Mind: A Sociocultural Approach to Mediated Action.* Cambridge, MA: Harvard University Press.

Wheeler, M.A., Stuss, D.T., and Tulving, E. (1997). Toward a theory of episodic memory: The frontal lobes and autonoetic consciousness. *Psychological Bulletin, 121*(3), 331-354.

Whipp, J.L., and Chiarelli, S. (2004). Self-regulation in a Web-based course: A case study. *Educational Technology Research and Development, 52*(4), 5-22.

Wiesel, T.N., and Hubel, D.N. (1965). Extent of recovery from the effects of visual deprivation in kittens. *Journal of Neurophysiology, 28*(6), 1060-1072.

Wigfield, A., and Eccles, J.S. (2000). Expectancy-value theory of achievement and motivation. *Contemporary Educational Psychology, 25*(1), 68-81. https://doi.org/10.1006/ceps.1999.1015.

Wiley, J., Goldman, S., Graesser, A., Sanchez, C., Ash, I., and Hemmerich, J. (2009). Source evaluation, comprehension, and learning in Internet science inquiry tasks. *American Educational Research Journal, 46*(4), 1060-1106.

Wiliam, D. (2010). The role of formative assessment in effective learning environments. In H. Dumont, D. Istance, and F. Benavides (Eds.), *The Nature of Learning: Using Research to Inspire Practice* (pp. 135-159). Paris, France: OECD. doi.org/10.1787/9789264086487-8-en.

Wiliam, D. (2013). Feedback and instructional correctives. In J.H. McMillan (Ed.), *Handbook of Research on Classroom Assessment* (Chapter 12). Thousand Oaks, CA: SAGE. doi.org/10.4135/9781452218649.n12.

Wilkinson, I.A., and Fung, I.Y.,Y. (2002). Small-group composition and peer effects. *International Journal of Educational Research, 37*(5), 425-447.

Willcutt, E.G., Pennington, B.F., Chhabildas, N.A., Olson, R.K., and Hulslander, J.L. (2005). Neuropsychological analyses of comorbidity between RD and ADHD: In search of the common deficit. *Developmental Neuropsychology, 27*(1), 35-78.

Williams, J.J., and Lombrozo, T. (2010). The role of explanation in discovery and generalization: Evidence from category learning. *Cognitive Science, 34*(5), 776-806. doi:10.1111/j.1551-6709.2010.01113.x.

Williams, J.J., and Lombrozo, T. (2013). Explanation and prior knowledge interact to guide learning. *Cognitive Psychology, 66*(1), 55-84. doi:10.1016/j.cogpsych.2012.09.002.

Williams, D.L., Goldstein, G., and Minshew, N.J. (2006). The profile of memory function in children with autism. *Neuropsychology, 20*(1), 21-29.

Williams, J.J., Lombrozo, T., and Rehder, B. (2013). The hazards of explanation: Overgeneralization in the face of exceptions. *Journal of Experimental Psychology: General, 142*(4), 1006-1014. doi:10.1037/a0030996.

Willingham, E.B., Nissen, M.J., and Bullemer, P. (1989). On the development of procedural knowledge. *Journal of Experimental Psychology. Learning, Memory, and Cognition, 15*(6), 1047-1060.

Willis, P. (1977). *Learning to Labour.* Farnborough, UK: Saxon House.

Wilson, R.S., Krueger, K.R., Arnold, S.E., Schneider, J.A., Kelly, J.F., Barnes, L.L., Tang, Y., and Bennett, D.A. (2007). Loneliness and risk of Alzheimer disease. *Archives of General Psychiatry, 64*(2), 234-240.

Winkler-Rhoades, N., Medin, D., Waxman, S.R., Woodring, J., and Ross, N.O. (2010). Naming the animals that come to mind: Effects of culture and experience on category fluency. *Journal of Cognition and Culture, 101*(2), 205-220.

Witkow, M.R., and Fuligni, A.J. (2007). Achievement goals and daily school experiences among adolescents with Asian, Latino, and European American backgrounds. *Journal of Educational Psychology, 99*(3), 584-596. doi.org/10.1037/0022-0663.99.3.584.

Wolfson, N.E., Cavanagh, T.M., and Kraiger, K. (2014). Older adults and technology-based instruction: Optimizing learning outcomes and transfer. *Academy of Management Learning and Education, 13*(1), 26-44. doi.org/10.5465/amle.2012.0056.

Woloshyn, V.E., Paivio, A., and Pressley, M. (1994). Use of elaborative interrogation to help students acquire information consistent with prior knowledge and information inconsistent with prior knowledge. *Journal of Educational Psychology, 86*(1), 79-89. doi:10.1037/0022-0663.86.1.79.

Wolters, C.A. (2004). Advancing achievement goal theory: Using goal structures and goal orientations to predict students' motivation, cognition, and achievement. *Journal of Educational Psychology, 96*(2), 236-250. doi.org/10.1037/0022-0663.96.2.236.

Wood, W., Quinn, J.M., and Kashy, D.A. (2002). Habits in everyday life: Thought, emotion, and action. *Journal of Personality and Social Psychology, 83*(6), 1281-1297. doi:10.1037//0022-3514.83.6.1281.

Woody, W.D., Daniel, D.B., and Baker, C.A. (2010). E-books or textbooks: Students prefer textbooks. *Computers and Education, 55*(3), 945-948. doi.org/10.1016/j.compedu.2010.04.005.

Wouters, P., and van Oostendorp, H. (Eds.). (2017). *Instructional Techniques to Facilitate Learning and Motivation of Serious Games.* CITY: Switzerland: Springer International.

Wouters, P., van Nimwegen, C., van Oostendorp, H., and van der Spek, E.D. (2013). A meta-analysis of the cognitive and motivational effects of serious games. *Journal of Educational Psychology, 105*(2), 249-265.

Wu, Y.T., Prina, A.M., and Brayne, C. (2015). The association between community environment and cognitive function: A systematic review. *Social Psychiatry and Psychiatric Epidemiology, 50*(3), 351-362.

Wylie, R., and Chi, M.T.H. (2014). The self-explanation principle in multimedia learning. In R.E. Mayer (Ed.), *Cambridge Handbooks in Psychology* (2nd ed., pp. 413-432, xvii, 930). New York: Cambridge University Press.

Wylie, C., Ciofalo, J., and Mavronikolas, E. (2010). *Documenting, Diagnosing and Treating Misconceptions: Impact on Student Learning.* Paper presentation at the annual meeting of the American Educational Research Association, Denver, CO.

Xin, Y.P., and Jitendra, A.K. (1999). The effects of instruction in solving mathematical word problems for students with learning problems: A meta-analysis. *The Journal of Special Education, 32*(4), 207-225.

Xu, D., and Jaggars, S.S. (2011a). *Online and Hybrid Course Enrollment and Performance in Washington State Community and Technical Colleges.* CCRC Working Paper No. 31. New York: Columbia University, Teachers College, Community College Research Center.

Xu, D., and Jaggars, S.S. (2011b). The effectiveness of distance education across Virginia's community colleges: Evidence from introductory college-level math and English courses. *Educational Evaluation and Policy Analysis, 33*(3), 360-377.

Yannier, N., Hudson, S.E., Wiese, E.S., and Koedinger, K.R. (2016). Adding physical objects to an interactive game improves learning and enjoyment: Evidence from EarthShake. *ACM Transaction on Computer-Human Interaction, 23*(4), Article 26:1-31.

Yarnall, L., and Haertel, G. (2016). CIRCL Primer: Evidence-Centered Design. In *CIRCL Primer Series.* Available: http://circlcenter.org/evidence-centered-design/ [July 2018].

Yeager, D.S., and Walton, G.M. (2011). Social-psychological interventions in education: They're not magic. *Review of Educational Research, 81*(2), 267-301.

Yeager, D.S., Walton, G.M., Brady, S.T., Akcinar, E.N., Paunesku, D., Keane, L., Kamentz, D., Ritter, G., Duckworth, A.L., Urstein, R., Gomez E., Markus, H.R. Cohen, G.L., and Dweck, C.S. (2016). Teaching a lay theory before college narrows achievement gaps at scale. *Proceedings of the National Academy of Sciences of the United States of America, 113*(24), E3341-E3348.

Zacks, J.M., Tversky, B., and Iyer, G. (2001). Perceiving, remembering, and communicating structure in events. *Journal of Experimental Psychology: General, 130*(1), 29-58.

Zeki, S., Romaya, J.P., Benincasa, D.M., and Atiyah, M.F. (2014). The experience of mathematical beauty and its neural correlates. *Frontiers in Human Neuroscience, 8*, 68. doi.org/10.3389/fnhum.2014.00068.

Zimmerman, B.J. (2000). Attaining self-regulation: A social cognitive perspective. In M. Boekaerts, P.R., Pintrich and M. Zeidner (Eds.), *Handbook of Self Regulation* (pp. 13-39). San Diego, CA: Academic Press.

Zimmerman, B.J. (2002). Achieving self-regulation: The trial and triumph of adolescence. In F. Pajares and T. Urdan (Eds.), *Academic Motivation of Adolescents* (vol. 2, pp. 1-27). Greenwich, CT: Information Age.

Zola, S.M., and Squire, L.R. (2000). The medial temporal lobe and the hippocampus. In E. Tulving and F.I.M. Craik (Eds.), *The Oxford Handbook of Memory* (pp. 485-500). New York: Oxford University Press.

Zusho, A., and Njoku, H. (2007). Culture and motivation to learn: Exploring the generalizability of achievement goal theory. In F. Salili and R. Hoosain (Eds.), *Culture, Motivation, and Learning: A Multicultural Perspective* (pp. 91-113). Charlotte, NC: Information Age.

Zusho, A., Pintrich, P.R., and Cortina, K.S. (2005). Motives, goals, and adaptive patterns of performance in Asian American and Anglo American students. *Learning and Individual Differences, 15*(2), 141-158. doi.org/10.1016/j.lindif.2004.11.003.

Zusho, A., Anthony, J.S., Hashimoto, N., and Robertson, G. (2014). Do video games provide motivation to learn? In F.C. Blumberg (Ed.), *Learning by Playing: Video Gaming in Education* (pp. 69-86). New York: Oxford University Press.

Appendix A
History of the *How People Learn* Studies and Their Use

How People Learn: Brain, Mind, Experience, and School: Expanded Edition (National Research Council, 2000; hereafter, *HPL I*) was the result of the work of two separate committees. *How People Learn: Brain, Mind, Experience, and School*, was the product of a 2-year study conducted by the Committee on Developments in the Science of Learning. This committee was tasked with conducting a study of the research fields that have contributed to the then-current understanding of human learning and cognitive development, in order to distill the knowledge and insight most relevant to education in the elementary and secondary grades. The goal of that study was to convey the most immediately useful developments in the science of learning to teachers, school officials, parents, and policy makers, and the original volume included a research agenda to guide the Office of Educational Research and Improvement in the U.S. Department of Education in developing program directions and funding priorities (National Research Council, 1999b).

Following the 1999 publication of *How People Learn*, a second National Research Council committee, the Committee on Learning Research and Educational Practice, was formed to carry the original report an essential step further by hosting a workshop to bring together practitioners, policy makers, and researchers to react to *How People Learn* and to discuss the issue of translating educational research into everyday school practice. The results of the workshop were captured in *How People Learn: Bridging Research and Practice*, published in June 1999 (National Research Council, 1999c). A subsequent report focused on how people learn in the disciplines of history, mathematics, and science (National Research Council, 2005).

Unifying these first two reports was deemed valuable because the two together revealed critical insights for improving learning in kindergarten-to-grade-12 (K-12) settings. The resulting product, *HPL I,* generated extraordinary interest, especially among groups and individuals responsible for the preparation of teachers. In fact, *HPL I* remains the third most popular report published by the National Academies of Sciences, Engineering, and Medicine, even decades after its publication.

Based on an accumulation of decades-long research, *HPL I* identified a number of key concepts in human cognition and learning that were new at the time of its publication. For example, the importance of drill and practice to students' understanding and application of knowledge came about through a fuller understanding of (1) memory and the structure of knowledge, (2) problem solving and reasoning, (3) the early foundations of learning, (4) metacognitive processes and self-regulatory capabilities, and (5) how symbolic thinking emerges from the culture and community of the learner (National Research Council, 2000).

To demonstrate how these themes contribute to successful learning, *HPL I* drew on key findings from studies of expertise and concluded that experts differ from novices in more than just their general abilities (i.e., memory or intelligence) and the use of general strategies. Instead, experts have acquired extensive knowledge that affects what they notice and how they organize, represent, and interpret information in their environments, which in turn affects their abilities to remember, reason, and solve problems.

Similarly, *HPL I* used research studies on the concept of transfer of learning (i.e., extending what is learned to a new or different context) to understand the long-term impact learning has on other kinds of learning or performance. From the literature, *HPL I* drew the following conclusions:

- Skills and knowledge must be extended beyond the narrow contexts in which they are initially learned in order for deeper learning to occur.
- It is imperative for the learner to develop a sense of the application of the knowledge (or when the knowledge can be used).
- Transfer most likely occurs when the learner knows and understands the underlying general principles that can be applied to problems in different contexts.
- Conceptual knowledge promotes learning.
- Learners are most successful at learning and will sustain their own learning if they are mindful of themselves as learners and thinkers (i.e., use a metacognitive approach to learning and instruction).

The remainder of *HPL I* focused on children as learners, on the development of the mind and brain, and on key concepts for teachers and teaching (such as designed learning environments, subject-specific examples of effective teaching, teacher learning, and technology to support learning). In sum, *HPL I* highlighted that children exhibit capacities that are shaped by environmental experiences and the individuals who care for them. Further, it noted that learning is promoted and regulated by both the biology and ecology of the child: learning produces development. Because learning changes the physical structure of the brain, and the changing structure in turn organizes and reorganizes how the brain functions, different parts of the brain may be ready to learn at different times. Finally, learning and development in childhood are influenced by the interactions between each child's early competencies and environmental supports, interactions through which relevant capacities are strengthened.

Data collected by the National Academies Press on purchases and downloads of *HPL I* show that volume has been one of the most popular reports from the National Academies. The press commissioned market research in 2008 that included a structured telephone survey to determine how educators, in particular, have used *HPL I* in their educational settings, what they found to be its most compelling attributes, and potential new additions they believed would be useful in a revision.

While most survey respondents used *HPL I* as the central text for their courses and made it required reading for their students, others used it to supplement another text for specific topics or as a resource to provide a shared base of common knowledge. Due to the age of the report, many instructors reported supplementing *HPL I* with other materials to give students the most up-to-date information, thereby identifying the limitations of *HPL I* as a central text. As topics to add or update in a revision, *technologies for learning* and *neuroscience* were mentioned most often in the survey. Further, discussions with leading experts on learning from the fields of cognition, learning science, cognitive neuroscience, education, and workforce development suggested similar themes for a revision that would update areas in which significant development has occurred since *HPL I* was published and that may be transformative for understanding learning and the development of learning tools and practices in the next decade.

Appendix B

List of Relevant Reports Published by the National Academies Press

This bibliography consists of reports related to the 2000 National Research Council report, *How People Learn: Brain, Mind, Experience, and School: Expanded Edition,* and prepared under the auspices of the National Research Council, the Institute of Medicine, or the new combined title, National Academies of Sciences, Engineering, and Medicine. It was prepared by conducting a word search on the National Academies Press Website (www.nap.edu) using the following keywords:

21st century skills
Adolescent education/learning
Adult education/learning

Assessment of learning
Cognitive neuroscience of
  learning
Early childhood education
English language learners
Informal learning

Influence of culture on learning
Learning disabilities
Learning in academic domains
  (mathematics, science, literacy)
Motivation for learning
STEM (science, technology,
  engineering, mathematics)
Teacher quality
Technology in education

Dates of publication included in the bibliography are 1999–2016. The search results for each word string are listed below.

21st Century Skills

1. National Research Council. (2010). *Exploring the intersection of science education and 21st century skills: A workshop summary*. Washington, DC: The National Academies Press.
2. National Research Council. (2011). *Assessing 21st century skills: Summary of a workshop*. Washington, DC: The National Academies Press.
3. National Research Council. (2012). *Education for life and work: Developing transferable knowledge and skills in the 21st century*. Washington, DC: The National Academies Press.

Adolescent Education/Learning

1. National Research Council. (1999). *High stakes: Testing for tracking, promotion, and graduation*. Washington, DC: National Academy Press. doi:10.17226/6336.
2. National Research Council. (2000). *Mathematics education in the middle grades: Teaching to meet the needs of middle grades learners and to maintain high expectations: Proceedings of a National Convocation and Action Conferences*. Washington, DC: National Academy Press. doi:10.17226/9764.
3. National Research Council. (2002). *Learning and understanding: Improving advanced study of mathematics and science in U.S. high schools*. Washington, DC: The National Academies Press. doi:10.17226/10129.
4. National Research Council. (2003). *Engaging schools: Fostering high school students' motivation to learn*. Washington, DC: The National Academies Press. doi:10.17226/10421.
5. National Research Council. (2005a). *America's lab report: Investigations in high school science*. Washington, DC: The National Academies Press. doi:10.17226/11311.
6. National Research Council. (2005b). *How students learn: History in the classroom*. Washington, DC: The National Academies Press. doi:10.17226/11100.
7. National Research Council. (2006). *ICT fluency and high schools: A workshop summary*. Washington, DC: The National Academies Press. doi:10.17226/11709.
8. National Research Council. (2009). *Strengthening high school chemistry education through teacher outreach programs: A workshop summary to the chemical sciences roundtable*. Washington, DC: The National Academies Press. doi:10.17226/12533.
9. National Research Council. (2011a). *High school dropout, graduation, and completion rates: Better data, better measures, better decisions*. Washington, DC: The National Academies Press. doi:10.17226/13035.

10. National Research Council. (2011b). *Incentives and test-based accountability in education*. Washington, DC: The National Academies Press. doi:10.17226/12521.

11. Institute of Medicine. (2013). *Educating the student body: Taking physical activity and physical education to school*. Washington, DC: The National Academies Press. doi:10.17226/18314.

12. Institute of Medicine and National Research Council. (2014). *Building capacity to reduce bullying: Workshop summary*. Washington, DC: The National Academies Press. doi:10.17226/18762.

13. National Research Council. (2001). *Understanding dropouts: Statistics, strategies, and high-stakes testing*. Washington, DC: National Academy Press.

14. National Research Council. (2006). *A study of interactions: Emerging issues in the science of adolescence workshop summary*. Washington, DC: The National Academies Press.

15. National Research Council and Institute of Medicine. (1999). *Adolescent decision making: Implications for prevention programs: Summary of a workshop*. Washington, DC: National Academy Press.

16. National Research Council and Institute of Medicine. (2000). *After-school programs that promote child and adolescent development: Summary of a workshop*. Washington, DC: National Academy Press.

Adult Education/Learning

1. National Research Council. (2002a). *The knowledge economy and postsecondary education: Report of a workshop*. Washington, DC: The National Academies Press. doi:10.17226/10239.

2. National Research Council. (2002b). *Performance assessments for adult education: Exploring the measurement issues: Report of a workshop*. Washington, DC: The National Academies Press. doi:10.17226/10366.

3. National Research Council. (2012). *Improving adult literacy instruction: Supporting learning and motivation*. Washington, DC: The National Academies Press. doi:10.17226/13469.

4. Institute of Medicine. (2010). *Redesigning continuing education in the health professions*. Washington, DC: The National Academies Press. doi:10.17226/12704.

Assessment of Learning

1. National Research Council. (1999). *The assessment of science meets the science of assessment: Summary of a workshop*. Washington, DC: National Academy Press. doi:10.17226/9588.

2. National Research Council. (2000a). *Grading the nation's report card: Research from the evaluation of NAEP*. Washington, DC: National Academy Press. doi:10.17226/9751.

3. National Research Council. (2000b). *Inquiry and the national science education standards: A guide for teaching and learning*. Washington, DC: National Academy Press. doi:10.17226/9596.

4. National Research Council. (2001a). *Classroom assessment and the national science education standards*. Washington, DC: National Academy Press. doi:10.17226/9847.

5. National Research Council. (2001b). *Knowing what students know: The science and design of educational assessment*. Washington, DC: National Academy Press. doi:10.17226/10019.

6. National Research Council. (2002). *Performance assessments for adult education: Exploring the measurement issues: Report of a workshop*. Washington, DC: The National Academies Press. doi:10.17226/10366.

7. National Research Council. (2003). *Assessment in support of instruction and learning: Bridging the gap between large-scale and classroom assessment—workshop report*. Washington, DC: The National Academies Press. doi:10.17226/10802.

8. National Research Council. (2004). *Keeping score for all: The effects of inclusion and accommodation policies on large-scale educational assessment*. Washington, DC: The National Academies Press. doi:10.17226/11029.

9. National Research Council. (2005). *Systems for state science assessment*. Washington, DC: The National Academies Press. doi:10.17226/11312.

10. National Research Council. (2008). *Early childhood assessment: Why, what, and how*. Washington, DC: The National Academies Press. doi:10.17226/12446.

11. National Research Council. (2010). *State assessment systems: Exploring best practices and innovations: Summary of two workshops*. Washington, DC: The National Academies Press. doi:10.17226/13013.

12. National Research Council. (2012). *Improving adult literacy instruction: Developing reading and writing*. Washington, DC: The National Academies Press. doi:10.17226/13468.

13. National Research Council. (2015). *Guide to implementing the next generation science standards*. Washington, DC: The National Academies Press. doi:10.17226/18802.

14. National Academy of Engineering. (2009). *Developing metrics for assessing engineering instruction: What gets measured is what gets improved*. Washington, DC: The National Academies Press. doi:10.17226/12636.

Cognitive Neuroscience of Learning

1. Institute of Medicine. (2015). *The neuroscience of gaming: Workshop in brief*. Washington, DC: The National Academies Press. doi:10.17226/21695.

Early Childhood Education

1. National Research Council. (1999). *Improving student learning: A strategic plan for education research and its utilization*. Washington, DC: National Academy Press. doi:10.17226/6488.
2. National Research Council. (2002). *Minority students in special and gifted education*. Washington, DC: The National Academies Press. doi:10.17226/10128.
3. Institute of Medicine and National Research Council. (2005). *Mathematical and scientific development in early childhood: A workshop summary*. Washington, DC: The National Academies Press.
4. Institute of Medicine. (2009). *Strengthening benefit-cost analysis for early childhood interventions: Workshop summary*. Washington, DC: The National Academies Press. doi:10.17226/12777.
5. Institute of Medicine and National Research Council. (2012). *The early childhood care and education workforce: Challenges and opportunities: A workshop report*. Washington, DC: The National Academies Press. doi:10.17226/13238.
6. Institute of Medicine and National Research Council. (2014). *The cost of inaction for young children globally: Workshop summary*. Washington, DC: The National Academies Press. doi:10.17226/18845.
7. Institute of Medicine and National Research Council. (2015a). *Financing investments in young children globally: Summary of a joint workshop by the Institute of Medicine, National Research Council, and the Centre for Early Childhood Education and Development, Ambedkar University, Delhi*. Washington, DC: The National Academies Press. doi:10.17226/18993.
8. Institute of Medicine and National Research Council. (2015b). *Scaling program investments for young children globally: Evidence from Latin America and the Caribbean: Workshop in brief*. Washington, DC: The National Academies Press. doi:10.17226/21748.
9. Institute of Medicine and National Research Council. (2015c). *Transforming the workforce for children birth through age 8: A unifying foundation*. Washington, DC: The National Academies Press. doi:10.17226/19401.

10. National Academies of Sciences, Engineering, and Medicine. (2015). *Using existing platforms to integrate and coordinate investments for children: Summary of a joint workshop by the National Academies of Sciences, Engineering, and Medicine; Centre for Health Education and Health Promotion; and Wu Yee Sun College of the Chinese University of Hong Kong*. Washington, DC: The National Academies Press. doi:10.17226/21799.

11. National Academies of Sciences, Engineering, and Medicine. (2016a). *Moving from evidence to implementation of early childhood programs: Proceedings of a workshop—in brief*. Washington, DC: The National Academies Press. doi:10.17226/23669.

12. National Academies of Sciences, Engineering, and Medicine. (2016b). *Reaching and investing in children at the margins: Summary of a joint workshop by the National Academies of Sciences, Engineering, and Medicine; Open Society Foundations; and the International Step by Step Association (ISSA)*. Washington, DC: The National Academies Press. doi:10.17226/23491.

13. National Academy of Sciences and National Academy of Engineering. (2009). *Nurturing and sustaining effective programs in science education for grades K-8: Building a village in California: Summary of a convocation*. Washington, DC: The National Academies Press.

14. National Research Council. (1999). *Starting out right: A guide to promoting children's reading success*. Washington, DC: National Academy Press.

15. National Research Council. (2000). *Eager to learn: Educating our preschoolers*. Washington, DC: National Academy Press.

16. National Research Council. (2001a). *Adding it up: Helping children learn mathematics*. Washington, DC: National Academy Press.

17. National Research Council. (2001b). *Early childhood development and learning: New knowledge for policy*. Washington, DC: National Academy Press.

18. National Research Council. (2007a). *Ready, set, science!: Putting research to work in K-8 science classrooms*. Washington, DC: The National Academies Press.

19. National Research Council. (2007b). *Taking science to school: Learning and teaching science in grades K-8*. Washington, DC: The National Academies Press.

20. National Research Council. (2008). *Early childhood assessment: Why, what, and how*. Washington, DC: The National Academies Press.

21. National Research Council. (2009). *Mathematics learning in early childhood: Paths toward excellence and equity*. Washington, DC: The National Academies Press.

22. National Research Council and Institute of Medicine. (2000). *After-school programs that promote child and adolescent development: Summary of a workshop*. Washington, DC: The National Academies Press.

English Language Learners

1. National Research Council. (1999). *High stakes: Testing for tracking, promotion, and graduation*. Washington, DC: National Academy Press. doi:10.17226/6336.
2. National Research Council. (2000). *Testing English-language learners in U.S. schools: Report and workshop summary*. Washington, DC: National Academy Press. doi:10.17226/9998.
3. National Research Council. (2002). *Reporting test results for students with disabilities and English-language learners: Summary of a workshop*. Washington, DC: The National Academies Press. doi:10.17226/10410.
4. National Research Council. (2003). *Measuring access to learning opportunities*. Washington, DC: The National Academies Press. doi:10.17226/10673.
5. National Research Council. (2010). *Language diversity, school learning, and closing achievement gaps: A workshop summary*. Washington, DC: The National Academies Press. doi:10.17226/12907.
6. National Research Council. (2011a). *Allocating federal funds for state programs for English language learners*. Washington, DC: The National Academies Press. doi:10.17226/13090.
7. National Research Council. (2011b). *High school dropout, graduation, and completion rates: Better data, better measures, better decisions*. Washington, DC: The National Academies Press. doi:10.17226/13035.
8. National Research Council. (2012). *Improving adult literacy instruction: Options for practice and research*. Washington, DC: The National Academies Press. doi:10.17226/13242.
9. National Academies of Sciences, Engineering, and Medicine. (2016). *Speech and language disorders in children: Implications for the Social Security Administration's supplemental security income program*. Washington, DC: The National Academies Press. doi:10.17226/21872.
10. National Academies of Sciences, Engineering, and Medicine. (2015). *The integration of immigrants into American society*. Washington, DC: The National Academies Press. doi:10.17226/21746.

11. National Academies of Sciences, Engineering, and Medicine. (2016). *Integrating health literacy, cultural competence, and language access services: Workshop summary*. Washington, DC: The National Academies Press. doi:10.17226/23498.

Influence of Culture on Learning

1. National Academies of Sciences, Engineering, and Medicine. (2016). *Barriers and opportunities for 2-year and 4-year STEM degrees: Systemic change to support students' diverse pathways*. Washington, DC: The National Academies Press. doi:10.17226/21739.
2. National Research Council. (2003). *We're friends, right? Inside kids' culture*. Washington, DC: Joseph Henry Press. doi:10.17226/10723.

Informal Learning

1. National Research Council. (2015). *Identifying and supporting productive STEM programs in out-of-school settings*. Washington, DC: The National Academies Press. doi:10.17226/21740.
2. National Academies of Sciences, Engineering, and Medicine. (2016). *Effective chemistry communication in informal environments*. Washington, DC: The National Academies Press. doi:10.17226/21790.
3. National Research Council. (2009). *Learning science in informal environments: People, places, and pursuits*. Washington, DC: The National Academies Press.
4. National Research Council. (2010). *Surrounded by science: Learning science in informal environments*. Washington, DC: The National Academies Press.
5. National Research Council. (2011a). *Chemistry in primetime and online: Communicating chemistry in informal environments*. Washington, DC: The National Academies Press.
6. National Research Council. (2011b). *Learning science through computer games and simulations*. Washington, DC: The National Academies Press.
7. National Academy of Sciences and National Academy of Engineering. (2009). *Nurturing and sustaining effective programs in science education for grades K-8: Building a village in California: Summary of a convocation*. Washington, DC: The National Academies Press. doi:10.17226/12739.

Learning Disabilities

1. National Research Council. (2002a). *Minority students in special and gifted education*. Washington, DC: The National Academies Press. doi:10.17226/10128.
2. National Research Council. (2002b). *Reporting test results for students with disabilities and English-language learners: Summary of a workshop*. Washington, DC: The National Academies Press. doi:10.17226/10410.

Learning in Academic Domains

1. National Research Council. (2001). *Adding it up: Helping children learn mathematics*. Washington, DC: National Academy Press. doi:10.17226/9822.
2. National Research Council. (2002). *Helping children learn mathematics*. Washington, DC: The National Academies Press. doi:10.17226/10434.
3. National Research Council. (2003). *Assessment in support of instruction and learning: Bridging the gap between large-scale and classroom assessment—workshop report*. Washington, DC: The National Academies Press. doi:10.17226/10802.
4. National Research Council. (2005a). *How students learn: Mathematics in the classroom*. Washington, DC: The National Academies Press. doi:10.17226/11101.
5. National Research Council. (2005b). *Measuring literacy: Performance levels for adults*. Washington, DC: The National Academies Press. doi:10.17226/11267.
6. National Research Council. (2011). *Challenges and opportunities for education about dual use issues in the life sciences*. Washington, DC: The National Academies Press. doi:10.17226/12958.
7. National Research Council. (2012). *Improving adult literacy instruction: Developing reading and writing*. Washington, DC: The National Academies Press. doi:10.17226/13468.
8. National Research Council. (2014a). *Developing assessments for the next generation science standards*. Washington, DC: The National Academies Press. doi:10.17226/18409.
9. National Research Council. (2014b). *Literacy for science: Exploring the intersection of the next generation science standards and common core for ELA standards: A workshop summary*. Washington, DC: The National Academies Press. doi:10.17226/18803.
10. National Research Council. (2015). *Guide to implementing the next generation science standards*. Washington, DC: The National Academies Press. doi:10.17226/18802.

11. National Academy of Engineering and National Research Council. (2006). *Tech tally: Approaches to assessing technological literacy*. Washington, DC: The National Academies Press. doi:10.17226/11691.

12. Institute of Medicine. (2009). *Measures of health literacy: Workshop summary*. Washington, DC: The National Academies Press. doi:10.17226/12690.

13. Institute of Medicine. (2011a). *Improving health literacy within a state: Workshop summary*. Washington, DC: The National Academies Press. doi:10.17226/13185.

14. Institute of Medicine. (2011b). *Promoting health literacy to encourage prevention and wellness: Workshop summary*. Washington, DC: The National Academies Press. doi:10.17226/13186.

15. Institute of Medicine. (2013a). *Health literacy: Improving health, health systems, and health policy around the world: Workshop summary*. Washington, DC: The National Academies Press. doi:10.17226/18325.

16. Institute of Medicine. (2013b). *Organizational change to improve health literacy: Workshop summary*. Washington, DC: The National Academies Press. doi:10.17226/18378.

17. Institute of Medicine. (2014a). *Health literacy and numeracy: Workshop summary*. Washington, DC: The National Academies Press. doi:10.17226/18660.

18. Institute of Medicine. (2014b). *Implications of health literacy for public health: Workshop summary*. Washington, DC: The National Academies Press. doi:10.17226/18756.

19. Institute of Medicine. (2015). *Informed consent and health literacy: Workshop summary*. Washington, DC: The National Academies Press. doi:10.17226/19019.

20. National Academies of Sciences, Engineering, and Medicine. (2015a). *Health literacy and consumer-facing technology: Workshop summary*. Washington, DC: The National Academies Press. doi:10.17226/21781.

21. National Academies of Sciences, Engineering, and Medicine. (2015b). *Health literacy: Past, present, and future: Workshop summary*. Washington, DC: The National Academies Press. doi:10.17226/21714.

22. National Academies of Sciences, Engineering, and Medicine. (2015c). *Integrating discovery-based research into the undergraduate curriculum: Report of a convocation*. Washington, DC: The National Academies Press. doi:10.17226/21851.

23. National Academies of Sciences, Engineering, and Medicine. (2016a). *Food literacy: How do communications and marketing impact consumer knowledge, skills, and behavior? Workshop summary*. Washington, DC: The National Academies Press. doi:10.17226/21897.

24. National Academies of Sciences, Engineering, and Medicine. (2016b). *Health literacy and palliative care: Workshop summary.* Washington, DC: The National Academies Press. doi:10.17226/21839.

25. National Academies of Sciences, Engineering, and Medicine. (2016c). *Integrating health literacy, cultural competence, and language access services: Workshop summary.* Washington, DC: The National Academies Press. doi:10.17226/23498.

26. National Academies of Sciences, Engineering, and Medicine. (2016d). *Quality in the undergraduate experience: What is it? How is it measured? Who decides? Summary of a workshop.* Washington, DC: The National Academies Press. doi:10.17226/23514.

27. National Academies of Sciences, Engineering, and Medicine. (2016e). *Science literacy: Concepts, contexts, and consequences.* Washington, DC: The National Academies Press. doi:10.17226/23595.

28. National Research Council. (1999a). *Designing mathematics or science curriculum programs: A guide for using mathematics and science education standards.* Washington, DC: National Academy Press.

29. National Research Council. (1999b). *Grading the nation's report card: Evaluating NAEP and transforming the assessment of educational progress.* Washington, DC: National Academy Press.

30. National Research Council. (1999c). *Improving student learning: A strategic plan for education research and its utilization.* Washington, DC: National Academy Press.

31. National Research Council. (2002a). *Learning and understanding: Improving advanced study of mathematics and science in U.S. high schools: Report of the Content Panel for Chemistry.* Washington, DC: The National Academies Press.

32. National Research Council. (2002b). *Minority students in special and gifted education.* Washington, DC: The National Academies Press.

33. National Research Council. (2003a). *Learning and instruction: A SERP research agenda.* Washington, DC: The National Academies Press.

34. National Research Council. (2003b). *Understanding others, educating ourselves: Getting more from international comparative studies in education.* Washington, DC: The National Academies Press.

35. National Research Council. (2005). *Focusing on assessment of learning: Proceedings and transcripts from mathematics/science partnership workshops.* Washington, DC: The National Academies Press.

36. National Research Council. (2008). *Common standards for K-12 education?: Considering the evidence: Summary of a workshop series.* Washington, DC: The National Academies Press.

37. National Research Council. (2010a). *Language diversity, school learning, and closing achievement gaps: A workshop summary.* Washington, DC: The National Academies Press.

38. National Research Council. (2010b). *Standards for K-12 engineering education.* Washington, DC: The National Academies Press.

39. National Research Council. (2012a). *A framework for K-12 science education: Practices, crosscutting concepts, and core ideas.* Washington, DC: The National Academies Press.

40. National Research Council. (2012b). *Improving measurement of productivity in higher education.* Washington, DC: The National Academies Press.

41. National Research Council. (2012c). *Key national education indicators: Workshop summary.* Washington, DC: The National Academies Press.

42. National Research Council. (2013a). *Adapting to a changing world—Challenges and opportunities in undergraduate physics education.* Washington, DC: The National Academies Press.

43. National Research Council. (2013b). *Next generation science standards: For states, by states.* Washington, DC: The National Academies Press.

44. National Research Council. (2015). *Reaching students: What research says about effective instruction in undergraduate science and engineering.* Washington, DC: The National Academies Press.

45. National Research Council. (2016). *Art, design and science, engineering and medicine frontier collaborations: Ideation, translation, realization: Seed idea group summaries.* Washington, DC: The National Academies Press. doi:10.17226/23528.

Motivation for Learning

1. National Research Council. (2011). *Learning science through computer games and simulations.* Washington, DC: The National Academies Press. doi:10.17226/13078.

2. National Research Council. (2015). *Reaching students: What research says about effective instruction in undergraduate science and engineering.* Washington, DC: The National Academies Press. doi:10.17226/18687.

3. National Research Council. (2003). *Engaging schools: Fostering high school students' motivation to learn.* Washington, DC: The National Academies Press.

STEM

1. National Research Council. (2011). *Successful K-12 STEM education: Identifying effective approaches in science, technology, engineering, and mathematics*. Washington, DC: The National Academies Press. doi:10.17226/13158.

2. National Research Council. (2015). *Identifying and supporting productive STEM programs in out-of-school settings*. Washington, DC: The National Academies Press. doi:10.17226/21740.

3. National Academies of Sciences, Engineering, and Medicine. (2016). *Art, design and science, engineering and medicine frontier collaborations: Ideation, translation, realization: Seed idea group summaries*. Washington, DC: The National Academies Press. doi:10.17226/23528.

4. National Academies of Sciences, Engineering, and Medicine. (2016). *Barriers and opportunities for 2-year and 4-year STEM degrees: Systemic change to support students' diverse pathways*. Washington, DC: The National Academies Press. doi:10.17226/21739.

5. National Academies of Sciences, Engineering, and Medicine. (2015). *Science teachers' learning: Enhancing opportunities, creating supportive contexts*. Washington, DC: The National Academies Press. doi:10.17226/21836.

6. National Academies of Sciences, Engineering, and Medicine. (2016a). *Developing a national STEM workforce strategy: A workshop summary*. Washington, DC: The National Academies Press. doi:10.17226/21900.

7. National Academies of Sciences, Engineering, and Medicine. (2016b). *Promising practices for strengthening the regional STEM workforce development ecosystem*. Washington, DC: The National Academies Press. doi:10.17226/21894.

8. National Academy of Engineering and National Research Council. (2014). *STEM integration in K-12 education: Status, prospects, and an agenda for research*. Washington, DC: The National Academies Press.

9. National Research Council. (2004). *The engineer of 2020: Visions of engineering in the new century*. Washington, DC: The National Academies Press.

10. National Research Council. (2011). *Successful STEM education: A workshop summary*. Washington, DC: The National Academies Press.

11. National Research Council. (2012). *Discipline-based education research: Understanding and improving learning in undergraduate science and engineering*. Washington, DC: The National Academies Press.

12. National Research Council. (2013). *Monitoring progress toward successful K-12 STEM education: A nation advancing?* Washington, DC: The National Academies Press.

13. National Research Council. (2014). *STEM learning is everywhere: Summary of a convocation on building learning systems*. Washington, DC: The National Academies Press.
14. National Research Council and National Academy of Engineering. (2012). *Community colleges in the evolving STEM education landscape: Summary of a summit*. Washington, DC: The National Academies Press.

Teacher Quality

1. National Research Council. (2000). *Educating teachers of science, mathematics, and technology: New practices for the new millennium*. Washington, DC: National Academy Press. doi:10.17226/9832.
2. National Academies of Sciences, Engineering, and Medicine. (2015). *Science teachers' learning: Enhancing opportunities, creating supportive contexts*. Washington, DC: The National Academies Press. doi:10.17226/21836.
3. National Research Council. (1999). *Testing, teaching, and learning: A guide for states and school districts*. Washington, DC: National Academy Press.
4. National Research Council. (2000). *Tests and teaching quality: Interim report*. Washington, DC: National Academy Press.
5. National Research Council. (2001a). *Knowing and learning mathematics for teaching: Proceedings of a workshop*. Washington, DC: National Academy Press.
6. National Research Council. (2001b). *Testing teacher candidates: The role of licensure tests in improving teacher quality*. Washington, DC: The National Academies Press.
7. National Research Council. (2008). *Assessing accomplished teaching: Advanced-level certification programs*. Washington, DC: The National Academies Press.
8. National Research Council. (2010). *Preparing teachers: Building evidence for sound policy*. Washington, DC: The National Academies Press.
9. National Research Council. (2014). *Exploring opportunities for STEM teacher leadership: Summary of a convocation*. Washington, DC: The National Academies Press.

Technology in Education

1. National Research Council. (2006). *Learning to think spatially: GIS as a support system in the K-12 curriculum*. Washington, DC: The National Academies Press. doi:10.17226/11019.

2. National Research Council. (2011). *Learning science through computer games and simulations*. Washington, DC: The National Academies Press. doi:10.17226/13078.
3. National Academy of Engineering. (2013). *Educating engineers: Preparing 21st century leaders in the context of new modes of learning: Summary of a forum*. Washington, DC: The National Academies Press. doi:10.17226/18254.
4. National Academies of Sciences, Engineering, and Medicine. (2016). *A vision for the future of center-based multidisciplinary engineering research: Proceedings of a symposium*. Washington, DC: The National Academies Press. doi:10.17226/23645.
5. National Academies of Sciences, Engineering, and Medicine. (2016). *Envisioning the future of health professional education: Workshop summary*. Washington, DC: The National Academies Press. doi:10.17226/21796.
6. National Academies of Sciences, Engineering, and Medicine. (2016a). *Achieving science with cubesats: Thinking inside the box*. Washington, DC: The National Academies Press. doi:10.17226/23503.
7. National Academies of Sciences, Engineering, and Medicine. (2016b). *Future directions for NSF advanced computing infrastructure to support U.S. science and engineering in 2017-2020*. Washington, DC: The National Academies Press. doi:10.17226/21886.
8. National Academies of Sciences, Engineering, and Medicine. (2016c). *Quality in the undergraduate experience: What is it? How is it measured? Who decides? Summary of a workshop*. Washington, DC: The National Academies Press. doi:10.17226/23514.
9. National Academy of Engineering and National Research Council. (2006). *Tech tally: Approaches to assessing technological literacy*. Washington, DC: The National Academies Press.
10. National Research Council. (2001). *Investigating the influence of standards: A framework for research in mathematics, science, and technology education*. Washington, DC: National Academy Press.
11. National Research Council. (2002a). *Enhancing undergraduate learning with information technology: A workshop summary*. Washington, DC: The National Academies Press.
12. National Research Council. (2002b). *Improving learning with information technology: Report of a workshop*. Washington, DC: The National Academies Press.
13. National Research Council. (2002c). *Preparing for the revolution: Information technology and the future of the research university*. Washington, DC: The National Academies Press.

14. National Research Council. (2003). *Planning for two transformations in education and learning technology: Report of a workshop*. Washington, DC: The National Academies Press.

15. National Research Council. (2006). *ICT fluency and high schools: A workshop summary*. Washington, DC: The National Academies Press.

16. National Research Council. (2011a). *Promising practices in undergraduate science, technology, engineering, and mathematics education: Summary of two workshops*. Washington, DC: The National Academies Press.

17. National Research Council. (2011b). *Successful K-12 STEM education: Identifying effective approaches in science, technology, engineering, and mathematics*. Washington, DC: The National Academies Press.

18. National Research Council. (2012). *Infusing real world experiences into engineering education*. Washington, DC: The National Academies Press. doi:10.17226/18184.

Appendix C

Study Populations in Research on Learning

Often, groups of learners are categorized according to shared attributes, such as age, ethnicity, socioeconomic status, achievement profile, or, in some cases, a learning disability. Generalizing across groups of people is important for understanding trends, such as the effects of poverty on learning and development. Generalizing is also important for building evidence-based theories of learning and teaching. If every individual is treated as completely different from every other person, it would be an intractably complex task to make assertions about the types of teaching interventions that are most effective for the majority of learners or for teaching a class of students, or even for running a school. And yet, overgeneralizing can dangerously blind one to people's complexities, nuances, and variability.

Although race, culture, and ethnicity are frequently used demographic variables in medical, sociological, psychological, and genetic research (Lillie-Blanton and Laveist, 1996), attempting to fit individuals within a single descriptor of race or culture and then generalizing the results of the research to a broader population is highly problematic for a number of reasons. First, all individuals function within culturally plural societies, so the identification of any singular cultural groups is likely to be inaccurate. Moreover, whereas a particular cultural group may share a set of values, the development of any one person is influenced by particular values as he experiences them within one or more of the microsystems that he inhabits (e.g., the home, school, workplace, or peer group). Thus, researchers should be very cautious about drawing conclusions about individuals based solely on the cultural group with which they are identified or affiliated. Likewise, because culture is not a single construct, the influence of culture on learning will vary by individual and learning context (formal and informal educational settings).

Second, the means by which race is determined for research purposes is rarely described, but it most often occurs through the limited methods of observation of physical characteristics, self-identification, or a review of medical records (Dirette, 2014; Kaplan and Bennett, 2003; Williams, 1994). Often, the racial description categories in research studies are too broad to capture all of the possible descriptors accurately, or they simply do not fit an individual's self-identification. For example, in the United States, a child who has one European American parent and one African American parent is often treated as African American (an example is President Barack Obama) and may identify as African American. But a growing trend is for mixed-race/ethnicity individuals to identify as biracial or multiracial. Moreover, some researchers argue that race is a product of the ways that people think about human differences (Appiah, 1992; Goldberg, 1993), while others note that because race plays a prominent role in human social practices, race is a social, not biological, construct (Appiah, 1996; Omi and Winant, 1994; Outlaw, 1995; Root, 1998; Zack, 1993).

Conceiving of race or ethnicity as a "box" to be checked on a form may bias instructors' perspectives with respect to categories of students. At the same time, cultural practices are resources that every student and teacher brings to a learning situation. There is evidence that learning and identification with school are facilitated when teachers recognize and support the perspectives and practices of their students.

Forcing mixed-race individuals to select a single identity on surveys and questionnaires may also have negative consequences for survey respondents. Townsend and colleagues (2009) asked mixed-race participants to fill out two versions of a demographic questionnaire. In one version, only one racial background could be specified; in the second, respondents could select multiple races. Mixed-race respondents compelled to choose a single race scored lower on subsequent motivation and self-esteem questions than did mixed-race respondents who were allowed to select multiple races on the questionnaire. In short, the denial of multiracial identities had negative consequences for respondents' self-perception, in the context of the questionnaire, which in turn may influence how they learn (see Chapter 3 for the role of motivation, identity, emotion, and culture on learning).

The use of race as a demographic variable in research is also highly problematic from a scientific perspective. The Human Genome Project has shown that race is neither a genetic nor a biological construct (Collins, 2004). Genetic research scholars have concluded that racial categories do not accurately reflect genetic diversity and that the use of race in genetics research should be phased out (Yudell et al., 2016). An example that demonstrates that genetic differences are not fixed by race is a comparison of the full genomes of American scientists James Watson and Craig Ventner (both of European ancestry) with that of Korean scientist Seong-Jin Kim. The genetic sequences of Watson and Ventner shared fewer variations than either shared with that of Kim (Levy et al., 2007; Ahn et al., 2009).

The distinction between race and culture is not clear-cut. For instance, in the United States, racial categories reflect historical factors such as racism, inequality of opportunity, and social stratification. Although the United States is rapidly becoming a majority minority population—a population in which the majority of persons identify as being of one or more racial/ethnic minority groups—the status of these groups is highly dependent on the race construct as it has developed in the mainstream culture. Some behaviors and practices that may be conceptualized as "cultural" have developed within a context of adapting to social positioning (e.g., race, social class, ethnicity, and gender) and in response to social stratification mechanisms (e.g., racism, discrimination, and prejudice) as well as segregation. Under these circumstances, what appear to be cultural practices may emerge as a direct response to macro-level societal factors, such as discrimination (García Coll et al., 1996).

Although scholars strive to be unbiased and objective, doing so can lead to blindness to the cultural nature of one's own constructions of reality. It is important to realize that the dominant Western scientific-cultural model is one perspective on reality and carries with it its own biases and assumptions. The perspectival nature of "scientific" views of reality is illustrated through the history of shifting dominant paradigms in any field of scientific inquiry. But practitioners typically apply this abundant evidence of cultural embeddedness only to their predecessors, not to themselves. The lack of awareness many social and educational scientists have of their own cultural perspectives has a number of counterproductive consequences.

For example, researchers may design studies that reflect the assumption that cognition and learning are universal processes, and they may further assume that therefore any study population will serve as well as any other. In an important review paper challenging this assumption, Henrich and colleagues (2010a) argued that the overwhelming choice of research subjects—namely Western, highly educated, industrialized, rich, and democratic (WEIRD) samples—for studies of perception and cognition has yielded findings that not only fail to generalize to the world at large but also are especially atypical and unrepresentative (see also Sears, 1986; Hartmann et al., 2013).

Second, this narrow research study population base (usually college students in the West) can bias how research questions are framed and limit the resulting conclusions. For example, there is a considerable body of research on effects of diversity in groups where the natural comparison or baseline has been a homogeneous (nondiverse) group. But as Apfelbaum and colleagues (2014) pointed out, this research typically leads to conclusions about the effects of diversity but remains blind to the possibility that homogeneity has independent effects of its own on the baseline group's processes of learning and cognition.

A third negative consequence of a researcher's embeddedness in her own culture is that the proper focus of her research, the study materials developed, and the methods employed will tend to be guided by her own (cultural) intuitions and consequently are likely (inadvertently) to favor people from the same cultural group (Medin et al., 2010). For example, in developmental research it is common for researchers to interview children one at a time and to ask children questions to which the researchers assume they themselves know the answer. This may not be at all unusual in Western, middle class communities, but in many cultures, isolating a child from his peers and using known-answer questions may be very peculiar, to say the least. The methods as presented may be the same in the two cultures, but the methods as received could be dramatically different.

For efficiency and efficacy, this committee has taken a middle ground with respect to the literature we have examined. Although some of the literature cited in this report refers to groups of people or cultures, such as East Asian, Mayan, or Western (referring to North American and European), we recognize that it is useful to analyze and understand the relevant determinants, processes, and outcomes of learning and the relationships among these factors. But we also recognize that the responsible use of research in educational contexts includes taking the time to integrate the findings to understand what they mean for individual learners: learners who are whole, unique persons, who each live in particular contexts.

Appendix D

Committee and Staff Biographies

Cora Bagley Marrett (*Chair*) is an emeritus professor at the University of Wisconsin–Madison, where she served on the faculty for more than 30 years, including 5 years in the concurrent position of senior vice president for academic affairs for the University of Wisconsin System. Her academic career includes appointments at the University of Massachusetts Amherst, where she was provost and vice chancellor for academic affairs; the University of North Carolina at Chapel Hill; and Western Michigan University. On leave from the University of Wisconsin–Madison, she held administrative positions at the National Science Foundation, including the first assistant director for social, behavioral and economic sciences, assistant director for education and human resources, acting deputy director for the foundation in 2009, permanent deputy director in 2011, and two periods as acting director. Other national service includes appointment by President Carter to the Presidential Commission on the Accident at Three Mile Island. She received an Excellence in Teaching Award and Distinguished Alumna Award from the University of Wisconsin–Madison and is a fellow of the American Association for the Advancement of Science, the American Academy of Arts and Sciences, and Sigma Xi, as well as a residential fellow (inaugural class) and national associate of the National Academy of Sciences. She holds a B.A. from Virginia Union University, and an M.A. and a Ph.D. from the University of Wisconsin–Madison in sociology.

Patricia J. Bauer is the Asa Griggs Candler professor of psychology at Emory University. Her research focuses on the development of memory, particularly the determinants of remembering and forgetting, links between cognitive and neural developments and age-related changes in memory, and the elaboration of the semantic knowledge base through learning and productive processes. Previously, she was a professor in the Department of Psychology and Neuroscience at Duke University and was on the faculty of the Institute of Child Development at the University of Minnesota. She earned her Ph.D. in psychology from Miami University.

Cynthia Beall (NAS) is distinguished university professor and the Sarah Idell Pyle professor of anthropology at Case Western Reserve University. She is a physical anthropologist whose research focuses on human adaptation to high-altitude hypoxia, particularly the different patterns of adaptation exhibited by Andean, Tibetan, and East African highlanders. Her current research deals with the genetics and physiology of adaptive traits and evidence for natural selection. She is a member of the National Academy of Sciences (NAS), the American Philosophical Society, and the American Academy of Arts and Sciences; she also was a Guggenheim fellow and is a current member of the board of the American Association for the Advancement of Science. In addition to active participation in the nomination processes for NAS members and NAS governance, she has chaired and been a member of the Board on International Scientific Organizations, was a delegate to the 28th ICSU General Assembly, and was chair, vice-chair, and a member of the U.S. National Committee of the International Union of Biological Sciences, was a member of the Division of Behavioral and Social Sciences and Education Advisory Board and is a current member of the Advisory Board for the NAS Koshland public engagement program. She earned her M.A. and Ph.D. in anthropology from Pennsylvania State University.

Margaret E. Beier is an associate professor of psychology at Rice University. Her research interests focus on learning and intellectual development throughout the life span; she investigates the individual determinants of learning, particularly as related to age and to cognitive (intellectual abilities and working memory capacity) and noncognitive (personality, interests, motivation, and self-regulation) predictors of knowledge and skill acquisition. Her work examines the effectiveness of various educational interventions and the interaction of individual factors and these interventions on learning and noncognitive outcomes such as self-efficacy, self-concept, and interests. She has published book chapters and articles in peer-reviewed psychology journals. Her awards for teaching and research include the Rice Center for Teaching Excellence Fellowship and the George R. Brown Award for Superior Teaching from Rice University. She is a member of the American Educational Research Association, a fellow of the Association for Psychological Science, and a Division 14 fellow of the American Psychological Association (Society for Industrial and Organizational Psychologists). She is on the editorial board of *Human Performance*, the *Journal of Business and Psychology* and *Work, Aging, and Retirement*. Her M.S. and Ph.D. in psychology are from the Georgia Institute of Technology.

Sujeeta Bhatt (*Study Director*) is a senior program officer with the National Academies of Sciences, Engineering, and Medicine and currently directs two studies: How People Learn II: Science and Practice of Learning, and the Social and Behavioral Sciences for National Security: A Decadal Survey. She was formerly a research scientist at the Defense Intelligence Agency (DIA), detailed to the Federal Bureau of Investigation's High-Value Detainee Interrogation Group (HIG). Prior to that, she was an assistant professor in radiology at the Georgetown University Medical Center, on detail to DIA/HIG. Her work at DIA and HIG focused on the management of research on the psychological and neuroscience bases for credibility assessment, biometrics, insider threat, and intelligence interviewing and interrogation methods and on developing research-to-practice modules to promote the use of evidence-based practice in interviews/interrogations. She received an Intelligence Community Postdoctoral Fellowship Award and an American Psychological Association Science Fellowship. For her work in deception detection and interrogation, she has been invited to speak to audiences ranging from universities to U.S. government entities and has trained law enforcement agents across local, state and federal levels. She holds a Ph.D. in behavioral neuroscience from American University.

David B. Daniel is a professor of psychology at James Madison University. His work forges reciprocal links between cognitive-developmental psychology and teaching practices/pedagogy. An Association for Physiological Science fellow, he has received the Transforming Education through Neuroscience Award and was recognized as one of the top 1 percent of educational researchers influencing public debate in the United States. He was the founding managing editor of the journal *Mind, Brain and Education* and has received many teaching awards throughout his career. His scholarship and related activities focus on translating findings from the Science of Learning, the Scholarship of Teaching and Learning, and other relevant literatures to useable knowledge, particularly for educational practice, policy, and student learning. He received an M.A. and a Ph.D. in life-span developmental psychology from West Virginia University.

Robert L. Goldstone is distinguished professor in the Department of Psychological and Brain Sciences and Cognitive Science Program at Indiana University, where he has been a faculty member since 1991. He directed the Cognitive Science Program during 2006–2011. His research interests include concept learning and representation, perceptual learning, educational applications of cognitive science, decision making, collective behavior, and computational modeling of human cognition. His interests in education focus on learning and transfer in mathematics and science, computational models of learning, and the design of innovative learning technologies. He was awarded two APA Young Investigator Awards, the 1996 Chase Memorial Award for Outstanding Young Researcher in Cognitive Science, a 1997 James McKeen Cattell Sabbatical Award, an APA Distinguished Scientific Award for Early Career Contribution to Psychology, and a 2004 Troland research award from the National Academy of Sciences. He has been executive editor of *Cognitive Science*, associate editor of *Psychonomic Bulletin & Review*, and associate editor of *Cognitive Psychology* and *Topics in Cognitive Science*. He is an elected fellow of the American Academy of Arts and Sciences, the Society of Experimental Psychologists, the Association for Psychological Science, and the Cognitive Science Society. He received a B.A. from Oberlin College in cognitive science, an M.A. in psychology from the University of Illinois, and a Ph.D. in psychology from the University of Michigan.

Arthur C. Graesser is a distinguished university professor of interdisciplinary research in the Department of Psychology and the Institute of Intelligent Systems at the University of Memphis and an honorary research fellow in the Department of Education at Oxford University. His primary research interests are in cognitive science, discourse processing, computational linguistics, and the learning sciences. He has developed automated tutoring systems with conversational agents and automated text analysis systems. He was editor of the journal *Discourse Processes* and *Journal of Educational Psychology* and president of the Society for Empirical Studies of Literature, Art, and Media; the Society for Text and Discourse; the International Society for Artificial Intelligence in Education; and the Federation of Associations in the Behavioral and Brain Sciences Foundation. He has chaired or been a member of expert panels for the Programme for International Student Assessment and the Programme for the International Assessment of Adult Competencies, and he consults for the Educational Testing Service. He received lifetime research achievement awards from the American Psychological Association, the Society for Text and Discourse, the McGraw-Hill Research Foundation, as well as the first University of Memphis Presidential Award for Lifetime Achievement in Research.

Mary Helen Immordino-Yang is professor of education, psychology and neuroscience at the University of Southern California, at the Rossier School of Education and the Brain and Creativity Institute. She studies the psychological and neurobiological bases of social emotion, self-awareness and reflective thought across cultures, their connections to social, emotional and academic development, and implications of these connections for pedagogy and teacher professional development. Her interdisciplinary approach combines human development psychology with social neuroscience and field studies in schools. She is associate editor for *Mind, Brain, and Education*, and the American Educational Research Association's *AERA Open*, serves on the editorial boards of the *Journal of Experimental Psychology: General and Culture and Brain*, and is currently serving as president of the International Mind, Brain, and Education Society. She serves on advisory boards for multiple schools, school districts, and scientific research institutes and commissions in the United States and internationally, including as a distinguished scientist on the Aspen Institute's National Commission on Social, Emotional and Academic Development. She has received the *Proceedings of the National Academy of Sciences* Cozarrelli Prize and early career awards from the AERA, the American Association for the Advancement of Science, the Federation of Associations of Behavioral & Brain Sciences, and the Association for Psychological Science, and commendations from the Army and Los Angeles County. Her Ed.M. in cognitive development and Ed.D. in human development and psychology are from Harvard University.

Ruth Kanfer is professor of psychology at the School of Psychology, Georgia Institute of Technology. Her research, which focuses on the influence of motivation, personality, and emotion in workplace behavior, job performance, and worker well-being, has examined the impact of these people factors and situational constraints as they affect skill training, job search, teamwork, job performance, and the development of workplace competencies. Recent projects have focused on adult development and workforce gaining, job search–employment relations, motivation in and of teams, and person determinants of cross-cultural effectiveness. She is director of the Work Science Center and codirector of the Kanfer-Ackerman laboratory, which conducts longitudinal and large-scale laboratory and field collaborative projects on topics such as workforce aging, work adjustment, cognitive fatigue, skill acquisition, adult development and career trajectories, and self-regulated learning. She has served on the editorial boards of the *Academy of Management Learning and Education*; *Applied Psychology: An International Review*; *Human Performance*; *Journal of Applied Psychology*; and the *Journal of Occupational and Organizational Psychology*. She received the 2007 Distinguished Scientific Contributions Award and the 2006 William R. Owens Scholarly Achievement Award from the Society for Industrial and Organizational Psychology. She earned her Ph.D. in psychology from Arizona State University.

Jeffrey D. Karpicke is the James V. Bradley professor of psychological sciences at Purdue University. His research sits at the interface between cognitive science and education, with a specific emphasis on the importance of retrieval processes for learning. A primary goal of his research is to identify effective cognitive strategies that promote long-term learning, comprehension, and knowledge application. His research program examines learning strategies in children, metacognition and self-regulated learning, and educational technology. He received the Early Investigator Award from the Society of Experimental Psychologists in 2017, the Janet Taylor Spence Award for Transformative Early Career Contributions from the Association for Psychological Science in 2015, the Outstanding Young Investigator Award from the Psychonomic Society in 2013, a National Science Foundation CAREER Award in 2012, and the Presidential Early Career Award for Scientists and Engineers in 2012. He earned his Ph.D. from Washington University in St. Louis.

Barbara M. Means is executive director of Learning Sciences Research at Digital Promise. Previously the founder and director of the Center for Technology in Learning at SRI International, she is an educational psychologist whose research focuses on ways technology can support students' learning of advanced skills and the revitalization of classrooms and schools. Her 2014 book, *Learning Online: What Research Tells Us About Whether, When, and How*, describes the state of the art in online learning from kindergarten through higher education and adult learning and provides a critical appraisal of the research base for practices in each of these domains. Her recent work includes evaluating the implementation and impacts of newly developed adaptive learning courseware developed with funding from the Bill & Melinda Gates Foundation. Previously, she helped the Office of Educational Technology, U.S. Department of Education, develop a framework for describing new research approaches and forms of evidence made possible when students learn online. She has been an author or editor for eight books on topics in education, learning technology, and education reform. She earned her bachelor's degree in psychology from Stanford University and her Ph.D. in educational psychology from the University of California, Berkeley.

Douglas L. Medin (NAS) is the Louis W. Menk professor of psychology and holds a joint appointment in Psychology and Education and Social Policy at Northwestern University. Dr. Medin taught at Rockefeller University, the University of Illinois, and the University of Michigan. From his earlier research on concepts and categorization, recent research has extended to cross-cultural studies of biological categorization and reasoning, cultural and cognitive dimensions of moral reasoning and decision making, and culturally based and community-based science education. The latter work involves a partnership of the American Indian Center of Chicago, the Menominee tribe of Wisconsin, and Northwestern University. He has conducted research on cognition and learning among both indigenous and majority culture populations in Guatemala, Brazil, Mexico, and the United States. He received an American Psychological Association (APA) Presidential Citation, the APA distinguished Scientific Contribution Award, and the Association for Physiological Science William James Lifetime Achievement Award and is a member of the National Academy of Sciences, the American Academy of Arts and Sciences, and the National Academy of Education. He received a James McKeen Cattell Sabbatical Fellowship Award and has served as editor for *The Psychology of Learning and Motivation* and *Cognitive Psychology.* He earned his M.A. and Ph.D. in psychology from the University of South Dakota.

Linda Nathan is the executive director of the Center for Artistry and Scholarship, which fosters and mobilizes creative, arts-immersed schools, where students are making and doing, teachers are asking how and why, and schools are engaged in their community. In this role, she oversees key programs including the Perrone-Sizer Institute for Creative Leadership in partnership with the University of Massachusetts, Boston. She also works closely with the leadership of Conservatory Lab Charter School to support its development as a national model of project-based learning and arts-immersed education. Dr. Nathan was the founding Headmaster of Boston Arts Academy, Boston's first public high school for the visual and performing arts. As an experienced leader in education, Dr. Nathan actively mentors teachers and principals, and consults nationally and internationally on issues of educational reform, leadership and teaching with a commitment to equity, and the critical role of arts and creativity in schools. Dr. Nathan also facilitates workshops and conversations about issues of race, equity, and culturally relevant pedagogy for school leaders, teachers, parents, and students across the nation. She is the author of two books: *Hardest Questions Aren't on the Test* (2009, Beacon Press) and *When Grit Isn't Enough* (2017, Beacon Press). Dr. Nathan is also an adjunct lecturer at the Harvard Graduate School of Education where she has taught for 17 years. She earned master's degrees in education administration from Antioch University and in performing arts from Emerson College and received an Ed.D. from Harvard University.

Annemarie Sullivan Palincsar is the Jean and Charles Walgreen Jr. chair of reading and literacy, Arthur F. Thurnau professor, and a teacher educator at the University of Michigan. Her primary research interest is in supporting students' sense-making and knowledge building especially in the context of project-based learning. A particular interest is children who struggle with challenging academic work. With her research group and in collaboration with computer scientist Elliot Soloway, she designed and studied the use of a cyber-learning environment in which students collaborate as they read texts, view video, use simulations, write, and draw, while engaging in scientific inquiry. She participated in studies investigating the value of educative supports for science teaching in the upper elementary grades and in design-based research to investigate the process and outcomes of teaching English learners the use of functional grammar analysis as an aid to interpreting and learning from narrative and informational text. She has served on expert panels and committees to prepare evidence-based reports on teacher preparation and learning, including the OERI/RAND Reading Study Group and the International Reading Association's Literacy Research Panel. She served on the National Advisory Board to Children's Television Workshop, was co-editor of *Cognition and Instruction*, and is a member of the National Academy of Education. Her Ph.D. is from the University of Illinois at Urbana–Champaign.

Daniel L. Schwartz is the Nomellini & Olivier professor of educational technology and director of the AAA Laboratory at Stanford University, where he has taught since 2000. He is also the I. James Quillen dean of the graduate school of education, Stanford University. Previously, he was an associate and assistant professor at Vanderbilt University. He studies student understanding and representation and the ways that technology can facilitate learning. His research—at the intersection of cognitive science, computer science, and education—examines learning and instruction in laboratory, classroom, and informal settings. Informed by his 8 years as a middle school teacher in Los Angeles and Alaska, a theme throughout his research is how people's facility for spatial thinking can inform and influence processes of learning, instruction, assessment, and problem solving. In particular, new media enables exploitation of spatial representations and interactivity in fundamentally new ways that complement the verbal approaches dominant in traditional educational research and practice. He has published on learning, assessment, technology, and the relation between perceptual-motor systems, physical environments, and higher-order cognition. His recognitions include Stanford Graduate School Advisor of the Year, Teacher of the Year, AERA Article of the Year, Research Article of the Year (Association for Educational Computing and Technology), and Outstanding Young Teacher in Los Angeles Unified School District (Alumni of the School of Education, University of Southern California). His Ph.D. in human cognition and learning is from Columbia University.

Heidi Schweingruber directs the Board on Science Education (BOSE) at the National Academies of Sciences, Engineering, and Medicine. In this role, she oversees the BOSE portfolio and collaborates with the board to develop new projects. She has worked on multiple National Academies projects on science, technology, engineering, and mathematics education, including co-directing the study that resulted in the report *A Framework for K-12 Science Education*, which provided the blueprint for new national standards for K-12 science education. She co-authored two award-winning books for practitioners that translate findings of National Research Council reports for a broader audience: *Ready, Set, Science!: Putting Research to Work in K-8 Science Classrooms* (2008) and *Surrounded by Science* (2010). Prior to joining the National Academies, she was a senior research associate at the Institute of Education Sciences in the U.S. Department of Education and the director of research for the Rice University School Mathematics Project, an outreach program in K–12 mathematics education. She holds a Ph.D. in psychology (developmental) and anthropology, and a certificate in culture and cognition from the University of Michigan.

Zewelanji N. Serpell is an associate professor and director of graduate studies in the psychology department at Virginia Commonwealth University. Her research focuses on developing and evaluating school-based programs for underperforming students. Her work harnesses advances in cognitive science to develop and test interventions that target students' executive functioning. For example, she has a project exploring whether cognitive activities associated with playing chess enhance executive functions and whether improvements transfer to academic outcomes for African American elementary school students. She also studies ways to optimize learning experiences using computer-based programs with African American students from middle school to college. She served as a AAAS Science and Technology Congressional Fellow sponsored by the American Educational Research Association. She is also a fellow of the APA Minority Fellowship Program and was a postdoctoral research fellow of the National Science Foundation's Quality Education from Minorities Network and of the National Center for Research on Early Childhood Education (University of Virginia, Curry School of Education). Previously she held academic positions at Virginia State University and James Madison University (JMU). At JMU, she was associate director of the Attention and Learning Disabilities Center and the Alvin and Nancy Baird professor in psychology. In addition to her published research, she coedited two books on school mental health. She earned her M.S. and Ph.D. in developmental psychology from Howard University.

Barbara A. Wanchisen directs the Board on Behavioral, Cognitive, and Sensory Sciences at the National Academies of Sciences, Engineering, and Medicine. Previously, she was the executive director of the Federation of Behavioral, Psychological, & Cognitive Sciences, a nonprofit advocacy organization. Before that, she was a professor in the Department of Psychology and director of the college-wide honors program at Baldwin-Wallace University. She is a member of the Psychonomic Society, the Association for Behavior Analysis International, and the American Psychological Association, where she is a fellow of Division 25 (Behavior Analysis). She was on the editorial boards of the *Journal of the Experimental Analysis of Behavior* and *The Behavior Analyst* and a guest reviewer for a number of other journals. She received her B.A. in English and philosophy from Bloomsburg University of Pennsylvania, an M.A. in English from Villanova University, and her doctorate in experimental psychology from Temple University.

Tina Winters is an associate program officer with the Board on Behavioral, Cognitive, and Sensory Sciences (BBCSS). During her time at BBCSS, she has worked on a wide variety of projects under BBCSS's portfolio, including overseeing projects related to Alzheimer's disease, behavior and sun exposure, and healthy aging. She has worked on many National Academies reports, including *Enhancing the Effectiveness of Team Science, Measuring Human Capabilities: An Agenda for Basic Research on the Assessment of Individual and Group Performance Potential for Military Accession,*

The Context of Military Environments: An Agenda for Basic Research on Social and Organizational Factors Relevant to Small Units, Review of Disability and Rehabilitation Research: NIDRR Grantmaking Processes and Products, Using Science as Evidence in Public Policy, Strengthening Peer Review in Federal Agencies That Support Education Research, Advancing Scientific Research in Education (which she co-edited), and *Knowing What Students Know: The Science and Design of Educational Assessment.*

Renée L. Wilson-Gaines is a senior program assistant with the Board on Behavioral, Cognitive, and Sensory Sciences. She joined the National Academies staff in 2009 and currently supports the following projects: How People Learn II, Substance Abuse and Mental Health Services Administration, and Measuring Human Capabilities. Previously, she supported studies on the Context of Military Environments, Mine Safety: Essential Components of Self-Escape, Sociocultural Data to Accomplish Department of Defense Missions, The Role of Human Factors in Home Health Care, Field Evaluation in the Intelligence and Counterintelligence Context, and A Database for a Changing Economy: Review of the Occupational Information Network.